THE ORPHANS OF DAVENPORT

THE ORPHANS
OF DAVENPORT

Eugenics,
the Great Depression,
and the
War over Children's Intelligence

MARILYN BROOKWOOD

LIVERIGHT PUBLISHING CORPORATION

A Division of W. W. Norton & Company

Independent Publishers Since 1923

For information about permission to reproduce selections from this book, write to
Permissions, Liveright Publishing Corporation, a division of W. W. Norton & Company, Inc.,
500 Fifth Avenue, New York, NY 10110

For information about special discounts for bulk purchases, please contact
W. W. Norton Special Sales at specialsales@wwnorton.com or 800-233-4830

Manufacturing by LSC Communications, Harrisonburg
Production manager: Beth Steidle

Library of Congress Cataloging-in-Publication Data

Names: Brookwood, Marilyn, author.
Title: The orphans of Davenport : eugenics, the Great Depression, and the war over
children's intelligence / Marilyn Brookwood.
Description: First edition. | New York, NY : Liveright Publishing Corporation, [2021] |
Includes bibliographical references and index.
Identifiers: LCCN 2021005096 | ISBN 9781631494680 (hardcover) |
ISBN 9781631494697 (epub)
Subjects: LCSH: Eugenics—United States—History—20th century. |
Children of parents with mental disabilities—Intelligence levels—Iowa—Davenport—
History—20th century. | Children of parents with mental disabilities—
Institutional care—Iowa—Davenport—History—20th century. | Nature and nurture—
United States—History—20th century. | Child development—United States—
History—20th century. | Child psychology—United States—20th century.
Classification: LCC HQ755.5.U5 B76 2021 | DDC 305.2310973/0904—dc23
LC record available at https://lccn.loc.gov/2021005096

Liveright Publishing Corporation, 500 Fifth Avenue, New York, N.Y. 10110
www.wwnorton.com

W. W. Norton & Company Ltd., 15 Carlisle Street, London W1D 3BS

1 2 3 4 5 6 7 8 9 0

The Orphans of Davenport *is dedicated to the women with intellectual challenges living at the Woodward State Hospital for Epileptics and Home for the Feebleminded and the Glenwood Institution for Feebleminded Children, who without thought for themselves gave caring attention to Davenport's orphans and radically changed the lives of so many, even today.*

CONTENTS

PART I
Origins

PART II
Backlash

Contents

PART III
Revival

AUTHOR'S NOTE

America's eugenics era began at the start of the twentieth century and persisted into the early 1940s. During that period, intelligence tests were used to assess schoolchildren, as well as children and adults committed to institutions, immigrants arriving at Ellis Island, patients confined in mental hospitals, prisoners, those considered to be intellectually challenged, and army recruits. Intelligence test results, known as IQ scores, were reported on a scale in which the average range was between 90 and 109. A score from 110 to 119 was labeled superior, from 120 to 139, very superior, and a score of 140 and above was considered in the genius range. At the lower gradient, scores from 80 to 89 indicated low average or dull intelligence, and scores from 70 to 79 indicated borderline ability. But the IQ designations expressed something more particular for those in the lower IQ ranges when they slid from neutral descriptions to labels that stigmatized persons with those test scores. Those who scored from 50 to 69 were called "morons," from 20 to 49, "imbeciles," and those with scores below 20 were known as "idiots." The umbrella term, feebleminded, identified those with scores of 70 or lower. From highest to lowest, the terminology was standard in medicine, psychology, education, and the law. These identifiers only began to be erased from professional usage in the 1960s, although by then they had entered the vernacular as repugnant slang. They are used in *The Orphans of Davenport* as they were used during the time the events in the narrative occurred.

THE ORPHANS OF DAVENPORT

Prologue

———◆◆◆———

NATURE OR NURTURE?

T he young woman who presented herself for indigent maternity care at Iowa City's University Hospital on May 7, 1934, appeared confused and gave the nurses two first names and four last names; because she would not or could not say which were really hers, hospital officials chose for her, and in Iowa's public records she is Viola Hoffman.[1] Hoffman could provide so little information about herself that her file did not include how far she had gone in school or even her age.[2] As a matter of routine, the hospital asked women like Hoffman for permission to test their IQs. Because of her unfortunate mental state, it is hard to know whether Hoffman understood what an IQ test was or that if she had a poor result she might be institutionalized and sterilized. Although she consented to the test, she may have realized that with her low social status she was in no position to refuse. This is how it happened that one day for about an hour, Hoffman sat in a sparsely furnished hospital office with a psychologist who asked her question after question, many containing concepts that in her condition she might have had difficulty grasping. For example, she was asked to consider contrasting ideas, the difference between laziness and idleness, between poverty and misery, character and reputation, and evolution and revolution. If she correctly answered three out of four of these, Hoffman's IQ would have been assessed in the average range. In another part of the test, she had to mentally compute arithmetic problems. In yet another, designed to test attention and memory, she had to repeat a series of seven digits forward and then backward and then do the same with another series and then another.[3] Hoffman's test result of 66 indicated that her IQ was well below the average range of 90–109, and her diagnosis, "moronism," became part of her official state of Iowa file. During this period, the terms *moron*, *imbecile*, and *idiot* were official identifiers for persons whose IQ test scores numerically fit categories of low intelligence.

Intelligence tests were first published in America between 1910 and 1916 and soon became tools in a mainstream public policy crusade called eugenics. Eugenicists believed that all human traits were biologically determined and inherited and that problematic traits, such as alcoholism, criminality, a tendency toward poverty, epilepsy, insanity, and promiscuity, among others, resulted from a person's low intelligence. Those who exhibited such traits could be institutionalized and sterilized, decisions often supported by IQ test score evidence. Designed to rid communities of the unfit, state governments and the educated class believed that the policies promoted a modern ideal— the creation of a society of the able—to be achieved by improving the racial stock. A pioneer in the testing field, Lewis Terman, of Stanford University, called IQ tests "a beacon of light for the eugenics movement."[4] In addition, eugenicists promoted "selective breeding," which encouraged the socially stable and well educated to have larger families.

In the service of eugenic goals, medical doctors diagnosed those who might have problematic conditions such as epilepsy or alcoholism, and court officials had responsibility for diagnoses of criminality and sexual perversions, including prostitution. Claiming that IQ tests were scientific, mental test psychologists became America's acknowledged experts in the evaluation of the intelligence of persons accused of crimes, recruits in the United States Army, those confined to institutions, and hospital patients like Hoffman.

By the end of the 1920s, nearly all states had passed laws permitting the involuntary sterilization of those with low intelligence, most of them poor, most of them women.[5] For some, sterilization may have been a choice freely made, but for others—particularly women of low social status—the power distance between those designated for the procedure and medical or court officials made refusal difficult.

Before her baby's birth, doctors informed Hoffman that her delivery would be by cesarean section. Although the reasons for this are not included in her case history, when she learned of that decision she asked to be sterilized. Because she was now considered "feebleminded," a state guardian was appointed to sign her sterilization consent. (Iowa was one of the few states that required consent.) It is impossible to know whether sterilization was coercively suggested to Hoffman or whether she directly requested it. Either way, for her doctor it would have been a routine procedure. From the perspective of most ordinary people, "human ability and success were determined by genetics and not environment" and accounted for "the superiority of middle-class and upper-class whites."[6] Therefore, Hoffman's sterilization would have been viewed as beneficial to society and to Hoffman herself: it would free her from the burden of raising a child whose dysgenic traits and unfortunate heredity would lead to a hopeless life. Better to prune the withering branch of the genetic tree.

In July, after Hoffman delivered a normal baby boy, whom she named Wendell, her mental status deteriorated further. Although she took care of her newborn son, she was unaware that she was his mother. Her hallucinations increased and she stopped keeping herself clean. Six weeks later doctors diagnosed her as "insane" and committed her to Clarinda, an Iowa state hospital for the mentally ill. Not considered by authorities who evaluated her were the traumatic events that occurred during her pregnancy when her husband—who had already been married three times—divorced and abandoned her.[7] Hoffman's appearance of mental illness may have been related to antepartum depression, that is, depression that occurs during pregnancy. Along with postpartum depression, both conditions are recognized today as treatable with psychotherapeutic and medical interventions.

With his mother institutionalized, Wendell spent his first year in a Des Moines juvenile center. In the summer of 1935, when her son was 1 year old, Iowa declared Viola Hoffman cured of mental illness and released her to the care of a sister in Chicago. The state would have permitted Hoffman to resume custody of her son, but instead she chose to relinquish her parental rights.

During the Great Depression, a divorced mother with a history of mental illness would have faced nearly insurmountable economic and social barriers to
finding work and successfully caring for herself and a young child. Officials
therefore transferred Wendell, now a ward of the state, 170 miles east, to the
nursery at the Davenport Home, Iowa's principal state-run orphanage.

———

The first orphans arrived at the Iowa Soldiers' Orphans' Home in Davenport one mild Indian summer morning in mid-November, 1865, aboard
the Mississippi River steamboat Keithburg. To cheers from the town's residents, 130 children whose fathers had died fighting in the Civil War walked
down the gangway to begin their new lives. "It was a blessed idea . . . to bring
the little ones of the brave soldiers of Iowa who fell victims to bloody war
in defense of their country," one community leader told the *Quad City Times.*
Townsfolk from the Orphans' Aid Society served the children breakfast and
then in horse-drawn carriages bought them to a refurbished army camp, once
Camp Kinsman, where some of their fathers may have trained for the war.
"The children seemed delighted with the pleasant spot," one town member
told the newspaper. Entering the Davenport Home's cottages—former army
barracks in which they would live—each child found their bed covered with
a colorful patchwork quilt hand embroidered by a local citizen.[8]

Within a few years, the Davenport Home accepted not only war orphans
but any normal dependent child "older than two years, and mentally and physically sound."[9] Recognizing the need to modernize, by 1901 the state had transformed the Soldiers' Orphans' Home by replacing its wood-framed buildings
with modern brick structures and constructing several new ones. Its superintendent boasted that its location was "one of the most beautiful and healthful in the
vicinity, with grounds made attractive by shade trees, flowers, and shrubbery."[10]

In that first decade of the twentieth century, Iowa took great pride in
Davenport's care of its residents, advertising that its school, the only regular
public school in Iowa connected to an institution, had a music teacher who
taught singing and musical sight reading and that children were "supplied
with everything in the line of recreational amusements [including] balls, bats,
footballs, . . . swings . . . croquet, and other customary playthings."[11] During

that same period, the institution began to encourage children's adoptions, and by the 1920s, the Davenport Home had become Iowa's central adoption facility, a residence where infants and toddlers lived until a family embraced them. Davenport children who were not adopted remained until they were 21.

But by the summer of 1935, when Wendell Hoffman arrived at the Davenport Home, Great Depression hardships had transformed it into an institution crammed with infants and older babies, many, like him, born in the University Hospital's indigent ward. The catalog of reasons that babies and children entered Davenport reads like a biblical description for the punishment of the innocent: some had been given up when Depression-battered families lost their farms or jobs and could not feed the children they already had. Others were the children of mothers left penniless when their husbands deserted them. Many of their mothers were prostitutes unable to sustain themselves and a child. Then there were infants removed by the courts because of parental neglect, alcoholism, mental or physical illness or abuse. Some mothers, like Viola Hoffman, were of low intelligence and were also mentally ill.

Increased numbers of babies and toddlers meant that Davenport's overburdened nurses were only able to deliver utilitarian care, propping bottles beside babies' mouths and efficiently changing diapers with little time left to show affection. Ordinary caring attention that babies received in families was unknown. The most fortunate, babies between 2 and 6 months who appeared normal and were healthy, soon were adopted into the comfortable homes of financially secure middle-class parents, while their Davenport cribs quickly filled with more babies. Adopted, too, although less frequently, were older babies, toddlers, and even nursery school–aged children.

Because of a recent mandate to test the IQ of every Davenport Home resident, Wendell was tested when he arrived at the institution, and it was found that his IQ score was in the range of most normal children his age. However, not the pediatrician who examined him, not the nurses who diapered and fed him, and certainly not the psychologist who administered the IQ test expected his mental ability to remain average for long. As the child of a low-intelligence, mentally ill mother, eventually those same traits would emerge in Wendell. His earliest Davenport records indicate that he was an "inactive, lethargic child" who rocked back and forth in his crib.[12] Young children's perseverative rocking, a form of self-soothing, is understood today as symptomatic of severe neglect and childhood depression.

When Wendall was about 2 years old, his IQ was tested again. During the year he had lived at Davenport, his test score had declined and he had become feebleminded, an outcome that made him ineligible for adoption. Because Davenport was designated for the care of normal children, Wendell would now be transferred to an institution for children like him, where he would probably live for the rest of his life.

Harold Skeels, the psychologist responsible for Wendell's IQ assessment, was a professor at the Iowa Child Welfare Research Station, a quasi-independent research group at the University of Iowa, in Iowa City. He was assisted by his colleague, Marie Skodak. Both Skeels and Skodak were especially compassionate clinicians with a keen interest in children's family histories and circumstances.

Just at the time that Wendell's test confirmed his lost intelligence, Skeels was beginning an unorthodox study prompted partly by Davenport's extreme overcrowding. Eleven "retarded" children would be sent from the orphanage to become residents in a home for the feebleminded where they would live with adult women identified as "morons." The outplaced children would be tracked against a control group who remained at Davenport. The results were startling, even to the researchers who designed the study. After one to two years of consistent, attentive care from the women, the orphans' intelligence improved; all but two attained IQ scores in the normal range. Meanwhile, the intelligence of a control group living in Davenport's usual conditions declined to "retarded levels."[13]

Wendell had become one of the experimental eleven. The infant whose life had seemed hopeless, whose mother had been sterilized to prevent any further offspring from entering the world, would eventually experience an IQ increase of 17 points—among the smallest gains of Skeels's experimental children—but something never dreamed of when he languished at Davenport. Wendell would find a loving family, a new name, and a new life; later, he would attend college and graduate school and become a university administrator. He was only one of the children whose progress would amaze the researchers at the Iowa station and help to change the history of psychology.

Because none of the children in either group suffered from any organic brain disorder, Harold Skeels realized that the members of one group could have changed places with those in the other and led completely different lives, simply as a result of the strikingly different environments in which they developed. Skeels's study, together with several others conducted by the station's psychologists, provided evidence essential to the modern understanding of early development and inequality: heredity and environment act together. Decades later, when neuroscientists began to penetrate the workings of the brain and its development, their work would be confirmed.

Hamilton Cravens, renowned scholar of social science, later described the Iowa station as a "singularity"—there wasn't another research group like it in the nation, possibly in the world.[14] It had an all-embracing mission to investigate the requirements for raising normal children, which until then had been a process governed by homespun advice, recycled hearsay, unchallenged custom, and assumption. Never intending a revolution, the Iowa psychologists' investigations defied universally held beliefs and theories and ushered the way to the modern field of child development.

From the 1930s into the early 1940s, Cravens noted, the station became "the only secure dissenting fiefdom in the realm." Its research, he said, had "national significance and meaning."[15] But no one, not even the Iowans themselves, would have predicted that the study of institutionalized children from society's lowest social and economic strata would launch the unknown Iowa group into a revolution. Their discoveries that the interaction of heredity and experience determines much of children's development, including their intelligence, were assailed by their profession's leaders, most of whom were eugenicists convinced that environment played no role. Soon, those relentless attacks and the public's response to the positive implications of the Iowans' work became a frontline drama followed in newspapers and magazines throughout the nation.

But how did the Iowa psychologists lay the groundwork for their discoveries? Compared with prestigious universities like Stanford, Harvard, and Princeton that had renowned faculties and were located in culturally rich areas of the nation, during the 1930s the University of Iowa was a backwater—only 5 percent of the state's roads were paved and 90 percent

of its homes lacked electricity. Nevertheless, in that decade two convention-
ally trained young psychologists, Harold Skeels and Marie Skodak, joined the
station. They worked along with Beth Wellman, at the station since 1925,
who found that preschool increased young children's intelligence test scores,
and George Stoddard, the station's director, who was certain that intelligence
was influenced by environment. Within this harmonious group the Iowa psychologists' research flourished.

Their success resulted from Stoddard's impressive intellect and leadership, daring station investigators who pursued inexplicable or accidental
findings, and the station's uncommon freedom from university bureaucracy.
Moreover, Iowa's isolation allowed its radical studies to move forward, at
least for a time, with little attention from psychology's mainstream. Critical, too, were large grants received from the Laura Spelman Memorial of the
Rockefeller Foundation, funds that promoted the study of children's development. Taken together, the Iowa work developed in a milieu of uncommon
intellectual freedom, invaluable in any academic field, but at the time rare
in psychology.

The Iowans' investigations unfolded in the face of the Midwest's 1930s
extreme misfortunes, when simultaneously national history and events of
nature changed the lives of many, including those who lived and worked at
the Davenport Home. The Great Depression ruined Iowa's economy. Dust
Bowl winds lifted its topsoil—said to be the finest in the nation—into
loamy clouds that blocked the sun as they blew thousands of miles east and
south. Historic heat, and a drought recorded as the most severe in 1,000
years, followed numbing ice storms that ravaged farms and killed livestock. With no social safety net in place, poverty-stricken, hopeless parents
unable to feed and shelter their children gave them up to the state, and the
orphanage at Davenport, already crowded with the children of the socially
marginal, now overflowed. Eugenic mandates also filled other institutions
with inferior deviates who had been segregated into state facilities in order
to "dry up the streams that feed the torrent of defective and degenerate
protoplasm."[16]

Against this setting, Iowa's researchers turned away from the customary paths of most psychologists who studied the intelligence of racial and

class groups. A typical report of that time was "Racial Differences in the Intelligence of School Children."[17] Instead, when the Iowa group noticed that children's IQ test scores fluctuated with environment, they sought to know more. Also, at Iowa, the case study method of exploring individual children's histories and experience became a research tool,[18] along with what today would be called field studies of children in real-world environments such as preschool. At the time rarely used, these techniques allowed the Iowa psychologists to observe changes in children's intelligence that should not, according to current understanding, have occurred. Finding unconventional results, the Iowans then detoured from accepted explanations and methods. And the psychologists worked collegially, challenging one another's ideas, yet maintaining an investigatory fellowship that supported their risky research paths.

Another factor that favored the Iowans' discoveries was their work in institutions, not only at Davenport but in many Iowa facilities. At the time, few psychologists had familiarity with children's institutional lives, but the Iowa psychologists had great empathy for children who lived in such materially harsh and emotionally bleak circumstances. Davenport's overcrowding also played a role when it forced moves of children to less congested facilities where they had exposure to differing environments. And the people of Iowa who adopted children from the home played a part, as most seemed unconcerned with the eugenic doctrine that heredity was fate. Middle-class, educated Iowans with professional standing regularly arrived at Davenport to adopt children born into families with the lowest social and economic status and, according to multiple accounts, never inquired about the children's heredity or family history. This permitted Skeels and Skodak to initiate studies of adoptees that revealed radical intelligence shifts or that contradicted hereditarian assumptions. And of signal importance was that Stoddard, the station's director, was an original thinker who earlier had studied with a colleague of the French psychologist, Alfred Binet, someone certain that environment shaped development. In Iowa's orphans, Stoddard found obvious confirmation of Binet's concepts.

The highly productive Iowans discovered environment's profound effect on children's development and intelligence in not one, but four populations: in middle-class, and separately, in orphanage children, exposed to preschool; in children born to parents from the lowest levels of society and adopted before 6 months of age into middle-class homes; and most exotically, in children identified as "feebleminded" who were placed in the care of institutionalized women labeled "morons." Here, in preliminary form, were the contours of the modern understanding that environment and heredity work together in children's mental development. Never intending a revolution, the Iowa station's research findings would ignite the overthrow of long accepted racist and classist views of human development. Their contributions were fundamental to psychology's most important discovery of the twentieth century.

But it would be a revolution delayed. Psychology's scholars, who held fast to ideas that human traits were strictly inherited, that environment played no role, relentlessly attacked the station's discoveries. They misrepresented the work, accused the Iowans of incompetence and dishonesty, and condemned their studies as "dark and devious"[19] and based on fantasy. Lewis Terman, who led the onslaught, attacked the Iowans personally, branding Skeels's study "absurd" and casting the Iowans' belief in early stimulation as "authoritarian," even comparing the Iowans to Stalin.[20] And the authority of these critics prevailed. Almost no one stepped forward in the Iowans' defense, and the few who did lacked the professional stature to convince the rest. The next generation of psychologists would pursue professionally safe, less controversial areas—for example, theories of how animals and people learn.

A well-worn joke among scholars asks, "Why are academic debates so bitter?" The usual cranky reply is, "Because the stakes are so small." But in the conflict between the Iowa station and its critics, the stakes were anything but small. At issue was not just scholarly prestige, but children's fates. Convinced that young lives were blighted by the belief that intelligence was fixed at birth, their arguments for early intervention were driven by empathy and moral concern. The hereditarians, for their part, infuriated by the Iowans' assault on widely accepted doctrine, accused them of peddling intellectual snake oil or, in the words of one critic, "a gold brick."[21]

Far more than an intellectual debate, stark political and ethical consequences followed psychology's denial of the Iowans' discoveries. Potential reforms in education, child psychology, medical training in child development, protections of the social safety net, judicial decisions, and parents' encouragement of their children all lost ground to the persistence of hereditarian ideology. Not until the 1960s would investigators again consider the Iowans' discoveries and venture into research about environment's essential role in cognitive development. And when they did, psychology finally entered its modern age.

PART I

Origins

Chapter One

---•◆•---

HOW IT ALL BEGAN

M arie Skodak expected that her first weeks at Ohio State University in the fall of 1927 would be filled with promise, but instead they were joyless. Not exactly poor, but without a lot of money, her Hungarian immigrant parents had sacrificed to send her to college, and she felt pressure to succeed.[1] It didn't help that she also felt out of place, especially around her well-to-do roommate, a society girl with elegant clothes and refined ways. Then there was Skodak's disappointment in the university itself, which seemed to lack academic rigor. Could her required English course truly be at the college level? The assignments seemed remarkably easy. Skodak had been an honors student in her Ohio high school, taking home prizes and medals and routinely scoring in the 99th percentile. When she expressed disappointment to her English instructor, it was eventually realized that an administrator's error had placed her in a remedial course. And now weeks had been lost.[2]

In another surprise, Skodak's planned major in chemistry and metallurgy turned out to be far more difficult than she expected, requiring complex math that, to her, was nearly incomprehensible. She had been so certain of her academic plan that she never considered any other. Though bewildered and questioning her own judgment, she became increasingly aware of the background of radio news and newspaper headlines. Always they throbbed with ominous reports of the Midwest's economic distress: area dust storms and the Dust Bowl's effects, crops worth less than they cost to grow, plummeting farm values. The region's precipitous decline followed its World War I industrial and agricultural prosperity, when banks had encouraged farmers to borrow and even overborrow to purchase additional land and machinery. But when prices returned to their prewar levels after the war, the Midwest suffered a "decade of farm tragedy,"[3] and even if farmers sold their land, the profits would not cover their debts to the banks. With economies in other areas of the nation booming and the New York Stock Exchange soaring, America's heartland faced severe financial trouble.[4]

Skodak's anxieties came to a head one day that fall when a letter arrived in her dormitory mailbox that brought terrible news: her father wrote that their home—the family's financial security—was now worthless. The Midwest's economic collapse had arrived in her Lake Erie town, industrial Lorain, Ohio.[5] For years her parents had carefully saved for her education; now, their financial calculations were useless. Skodak had some small reserves—she could afford one more term—but had no idea how she would pay for her degree.

On Ohio State's campus life went on as usual. Autumn days grew shorter and colder; grounds' crews raked fallen leaves into containers for open-air burning. Pulling their jackets tight against the chill, young women and men walked the trim paths to lecture halls, searched card catalogs at the library, and queued for dining hall meals. But for Skodak and most of her classmates, the ground had shifted. Futures they counted on, their families' well-being, their plans for their degrees, careers, even for where they would live—everything was about to change. It would be two more years before New York's stock market crashed and economic catastrophe struck the rest of America, but the Midwest's early start only deepened its economic pain. In 1932, when the nation's unemployment rate climbed to 25 percent, Ohio's rate reached nearly 40 percent.

Skodak understood that she had to make quick, dramatic adjustments. She had not liked her expensive, fancy dorm anyway, so she found a tiny room in a small red brick "approved" house run by a watchful elderly woman who made certain to lock the front door at curfew. Together with a much older graduate student with an even more limited budget than her own, and whose wardrobe was even less impressive, Skodak cooked frugal meals on a one-burner stove over a gas grate in an improvised basement kitchen. Over dinners of day-old bread, milk, an egg, and some spices, the two settled the world's problems. They would remain friends for more than sixty years.[6]

Harsh times had taught her, she would say later, that "solutions to problems were in one's own hands, that one could not rely on other people."[7] But she was more prepared for hardship than most. When she had been only three years old, she watched her bitter, homesick mother return to her family in Hungary. Feeling abandoned, she spent lonely days with a nanny while her father sold steamship tickets and insurance. When many months later her mother returned, she found a gloomy, dispirited little girl. The experience of her mother's absence—later she called it traumatic—taught Skodak resilience and independence. "I just went my own way," she said. "I watched what adults did, then taught myself."[8] Even before she entered kindergarten, Skodak could crochet and sew, and using a saw, hammer, and screw driver—all adult sized—she built a small boat that floated. She also taught herself to read in Hungarian and to cook breakfast.[9]

On her first days in kindergarten, Marie Skodak displayed her independence. Assuming she could not speak any English, her teacher assigned Skodak to the blue table set aside for less advanced children. When Skodak noticed that the books and games at the red table were more intriguing, she moved there. Gently, the teacher coaxed her to move back, but she was not prepared for Skodak's passionate response, "I stay here!" When she returned to her classroom the next day, under her small arm was a book she brought from home. Seating herself at the red table she proceeded to read a story aloud—in fluent Hungarian. The teacher didn't understand a word, but she got the message. "I probably had more than the normal load of self-assurance," Skodak remembered, "and if I was regarded as overbearing, that would not be a surprise."[10]

At Ohio State, Marie Skodak quickly understood that she had to rethink her future. Could she even stay in college? Should she give up her education and find work at home to help her financially hobbled family regain its bearings? Looking around she saw thousands of students, most of whom also faced dismal financial woes, or soon would. At the same time, she assured herself that she was probably as capable as they were, and "if they could figure out a way to the future it must be possible."[11]

To cover expenses, Skodak landed a position as a waitress at the Ohio State Faculty Club, a job that helped her support herself and also pulled back the curtain on professorial civility. She discovered that scholars who lectured about lofty ideas all morning arrived down-to-earth hungry at lunch time, and when their meals didn't get to their tables quickly enough, some turned irritable. Her salary of 35 cents an hour (today, about $5) along with what were, for her, much needed discounted meals, encouraged her to take their irritation in stride.

As the newest hire, she was assigned to two sections of the dining room: one reserved for the military (ROTC), from whom the attractive Skodak kept her distance, and the other for the faculty members with the least prestige and known as the most difficult patrons, the psychologists. Unbothered by the psychologists' foibles, as she served meals and cleared plates, she overheard fascinating conversations.[12] Until then, the word *psychology* was unknown to her. In the early decades of the twentieth century, the discipline was separating from its intellectual parent, philosophy,[13] but its direction was unclear and American students found their way to it more by serendipity than design. Psychology had also affiliated with the field of education, and that, too, brought students into its fold.

Though somewhat unsophisticated when she entered Ohio State, through various part-time jobs Skodak learned much about the world of intellectuals. Serving meals, cleaning faculty homes, and babysitting for faculty children, she glimpsed the lives of academics—a reality, she said, with characteristic irony, "that dusted away reverence and awe of the professionally eminent."[14]

Skodak had planned to study chemistry and metallurgy at Ohio State because she and her father, an adventurous dreamer, hoped one day to prospect for silver in South America. But the collapsing economy ended that hope and she needed to explore other academic possibilities. In search of a new direction, Skodak met with deans from several programs—history, literature, education (she quickly rejected home economics)—to research what their programs could offer. After much study she decided on an education major with the aim to work in a public school, perhaps teaching history, at the time a conventional choice for intellectually talented women. The pragmatic Skodak assumed that even during the Depression, teachers would have jobs, but beyond an economically secure career, the details of her plan were unformed.

As she continued to serve lunch and dinner to psychologists, Skodak's curiosity about their discipline increased. Lingering over their water glasses and coffee cups, she eavesdropped on debates over theories of human behavior. She especially admired the few psychologists who were women, appreciating their success and finding them "different, more casual in dress and behavior."[15] Her mealtime snooping so absorbed her that she worried she might spill coffee down the patrons' backs.

It happened that the study of psychology was required for her education curriculum, and she enrolled in an introductory course with child psychologist Sophie Rogers, the first female full professor in Ohio State's Department of Medicine. Skodak was impressed that, "without belligerence or unpleasantness," Rogers had made it in a man's world.[16] Rogers's class was formative for Skodak when it convinced her to become a psychologist who treated children in need of support. Because the field of psychology would be unfamiliar to her parents, who wanted so much for her to succeed, Skodak struggled with how to explain what psychology was and what its professional application might be. She expected that in the midst of an economic catastrophe, they might be skeptical about her pursuit of a career in an almost unmapped area. But what neither they nor she could have forecast was her newfound passion for the study of human behavior.

With tremendous energy Skodak overloaded her program, attended two summer sessions, and enrolled in nearly every course the psychology department offered. Most of that work was at the graduate level, and as the youngest student in the department, she often felt out of place. Always in need of money, she continued waitressing and paid for her overextended schedule with a nonexistent social life. Determined to get the highest grades, that isolation did not seem a sacrifice and, she said, never troubled her.

As Skodak grew familiar with the psychology curriculum, she focused on the area of school psychology, a certification that required dual psychology and education degrees. Typical for such a new field, requirements were flexible, and her department mentors, psychologists Henry H. Goddard and Francis Maxfield, helped her knit together coursework to prepare her. Each had deep knowledge in areas that focused on students with intellectual and physical challenges. Skodak recalled that Goddard showed "a kindliness and warmth toward children, parents, and teachers that contributed to [his] skill as a clinician . . . his Quaker background seemed to give [him] an approach that was both objective and empathic."[17] Skodak did not mention that Goddard, a eugenicist, believed that intelligence was strictly determined by heredity; his viewpoint was so commonplace among American psychologists, and indeed the entire educated class, that it didn't merit a second thought.

———

By 1931, Skodak had earned a BS in education and an MA in psychology, along with a teaching certificate. She took practicums at a school for the mentally ill, earned a minor in social work, was elected to three academic honor societies, and was Phi Beta Kappa. She had achieved her objective, an outstanding academic record with impeccable credentials. With an honors degree from a prestigious psychology program and recommendations from two of the profession's leaders, Skodak's future should have been obvious, her job search straightforward. At any other time, she would have received multiple offers from schools everywhere. But in the depths of the Great Depression, school personnel were being paid in scrip. School boards considered the position of a school psychologist a frill and in cost-saving moves, their jobs were the first to be sacrificed. The few who had those positions were unlikely to leave their posts.

With family connections in Hungary, Skodak decided that her college graduation in 1931 might be the moment to escape from America's downturn. Awarded grants for travel and room and board, she set off for a university in Budapest. It didn't take long for her to find that Europe was experiencing its own period of economic hardship, made worse by a winter so severe that her university shut down for want of coal. She found her courses—when they even met—unstimulating. She was also deeply shaken by local reports of a young man in Germany "active in organizing the discontented." His name was Adolf Hitler. With the Depression unrelieved and US schools still underfunded, Skodak put off her school psychologist plan and from Hungary applied for the PhD program at Ohio State. Unsurprisingly, she won the university's most prestigious psychology graduate assistantship and would be mentored by her undergraduate adviser, Henry Goddard.[18]

———

The authority of an illustrious academic in the intellectual development of a novice scholar cannot be overstated, and Skodak had every reason to rely on Henry Goddard's counsel. A giant among American psychologists, his prominence first emerged when he became a leader in mental testing of the retarded. As head of the Vineland Training School for Feeble-Minded Girls and Boys, Goddard understood what anyone who worked with low-intelligence children knew: the "feebleminded" label that defined their status obscured that their mental abilities differed markedly from one to another. In search of a method to accurately measure those levels, in 1908 Goddard toured Europe's psychology laboratories hoping to discover a test for this purpose. Tucked away in his suitcase when he returned to America was a copy of an assessment used in France, given to him by a Belgian psychologist he met during his travels: the Binet-Simon test of intelligence.[19] At the request of the French government, Alfred Binet had created the test to evaluate the ability of schoolchildren who required learning support.

After a skeptical reading, Goddard was not certain the test could help him,[20] and for about a year it remained neglected in his files. But with the encouragement of an assistant, he finally experimented with the test and quickly understood that Binet's method yielded a way to closely evaluate ability. The test did more than answer Goddard's needs; following his and others' revisions, it also became the foundational instrument used in the United States for intelligence testing.

Binet, who compared a child's mind to a field that required cultivation,[21] was considered the most powerful thinker of his time in the examination of children's intelligence. As noted by historian of psychology and Goddard biographer Leila Zenderland, Binet's test provided what ought to have been intuitive in the diagnosis of retardation, but wasn't, a means to "sharply distinguish the body from the mind."[22] That is, at a time when most low-intellect children were assessed by medical doctors, Binet advised psychologists to be wary, that lacking a proper evaluation tool, physicians regularly drew "conjectures [about] the mental from the physical."[23] Pointing to Helen Keller, Goddard explained that children's difficulties of the senses, like blindness or deafness, might mislead physicians about their intelligence. Binet also understood that a doctor who treated children with physical disabilities such as palsy might draw incorrect conclusions about the child's intelligence. He advised physicians that only children's test responses revealed their intellects.

In testing children, Binet rejected rote knowledge that might have been learned in school as an indicator of intelligence. Rather, he suggested, there was no one entity of something called intelligence but rather "a hierarchy among diverse intelligences,"[24] qualities he identified as comprehension, judgment, reasoning, and invention. He emphasized that of those, he considered only one, judgment, to be fundamental. By judgment Binet meant the quality of the child's logic.[25]

To gauge a child's mental ability, Binet established the chronological age when most French children accurately answered each of his test's questions. For example, he asked children of different ages, "What is the difference between a fly and a butterfly?" When a 5-year-old child did not know, Binet recognized that children's judgment may be limited by their experience, and he would inquire about the child's environment. Some children, he found, had never seen a butterfly. Although all of the children Binet evaluated lived in Paris, some had never seen the Seine.[26] Binet was one of the few psychologists of his time to recognize the possible role of environment in development, a factor he discovered by considering children on a case-by-case basis.

In another test of judgment, Binet showed children who were between 7 and 11 years of age five boxes that looked identical but were of different weights. He asked the children to arrange the boxes from lightest to heaviest.[27] When, inevitably, there were incorrect answers, Binet responded with sensitivity for the child's injured pride. He advised other testers that "one must never point out . . . the errors."[28] Here, Binet distinguished between the educator's desire to teach by correcting students and the psychologist's goal to evaluate children's reasoning.

For each examination question, Binet located the age when almost all children responded accurately, what he called that question's "mental age." The child's score was a ratio of his or her chronological age and the averaged mental ages of the questions answered. Binet's scoring method seemed awkward to Goddard. For example, if a 10-year-old child scored a 10 in mental age on the Binet test, the ratio was 1. To make the numbers easier to handle, Goddard multiplied the ratio by 100, and the child's test score was described as 100. If a 10-year-old child's mental age was 8, the score was 80.

There were striking differences in the ways Binet and Goddard understood intelligence in children. Binet never doubted that in a dynamic process a child's environment influenced their mental development; he saw his test as an indicator of a child's functioning at that moment and that with support the score could change. Goddard, by contrast, believed that mental ability was an inherited quantity, fixed and unchanging. Despite this difference, each grasped the importance of assessing the abilities of intellectually challenged children, Binet because he developed and tested his method in classrooms and witnessed teachers' struggles to understand their students' learning needs, and Goddard because he hoped to classify the intelligence of the children at the school he headed. In the field of psychology these contrasting views of intelligence tests would become momentous.

Both scholars worked apart from traditional academic milieus. Binet's strong views and abrasive personality kept him from appointment to standard academic positions, while Goddard made his contribution in an institutional population. Most significantly, they both understood that medical doctors who diagnosed low-intellect children had little understanding of how to accomplish their task. Binet, especially, warned against "intuition and subjectivism" and observed that doctors "permit themselves to be guided by a subjective impression which they do not seem to think necessary to analyze."[29]

In America, Goddard became the Binet test's ardent proponent, and by 1912 the test had found approval from the nation's educators, and even more, from physicians, now better able to assess the intelligence of the disabled children and adults they treated. That year, Goddard published his own study, one that would become foundational in the literature about the inheritance of intelligence and character: *The Kallikak Family*. Goddard's book told the history of an aristocratic Revolutionary War—era family he called the Kallikaks (a pseudonym, based on the Greek words for "good" and "bad") in which Goddard compared two genealogical family lines that he attributed to one man. One line was the product of an illegitimate child fathered with an "imbecile" tavern maid. Goddard claimed that the descendants of this pair, whom a Goddard assistant discovered living in the Pine Barrens of New Jersey, represented multiple generations who were eugenically undesirable, including degenerates, alcoholics, prostitutes, and many who were feebleminded. The same scion later married a righteous Quaker woman, and the ensuing generations of their offspring flourished and maintained the family's aristocratic tradition.[30] Goddard argued that these dissimilar outcomes revealed that heredity determined intelligence and character, which were then passed from generation to generation as single traits. From the turn of the century to the 1930s, when Skodak began her doctoral studies with Goddard, much of the educated class agreed.

———

Marie Skodak returned from Europe in the spring of 1932 and looked ahead to beginning PhD studies at Ohio State that fall. For the intervening months, she accepted a position in which she would test the intelligence of children at what was—despite its forbidding name, the New York State Custodial Asylum for Un-Teachable Idiots—the most progressive institution in the nation for children of low intelligence. It was located in Rome, New York.

The Rome school was founded in 1827 as a home for the poor and insane, but by 1893 it segregated intellectually limited women, ages 15 to 45, to prevent their bearing children. In 1905, an unconventional physician, Charles Bernstein, once an orphan cared for by a harsh relative, became Rome's superintendent. Although at first he held severe views of the inmates, Bernstein soon transformed the school into one of the nation's first institutions to provide education and training for those with low intelligence.[31] A humanist, Bernstein established that the feebleminded were capable of more, sometimes far more, than the asylum's name implied. They were entitled, he insisted, to opportunities equivalent to those available to all other citizens, and he arranged employment for residents in reforestation and on farms and in many other work areas. At the Rome school the residents "virtually ran the institution, producing most of the food, helping to care for other inmates, and producing the inmate newsletter."[32]

According to a colleague, Bernstein believed that the motto for the majority of institutions ought to be "Abandon hope all ye who enter here."[33] Instead, Bernstein created groups of small homes called colonies where residents lived, worked, and led relatively normal lives. During his administration, from 1905 to 1942, a period when eugenic thinking dominated the nation, Bernstein was "one of the few institutional superintendents to challenge eugenic orthodoxies . . . such as involuntary sterilization and permanent incarceration."[34] Bernstein's contribution became widely recognized, and in 1908 leaders of institutions for the intellectually challenged elected him president of the American Association for Mental Deficiency (AAMD). The model he created in which low-intelligence adolescents and adults could live and work was copied nationally.

Marie Skodak had arrived at the Rome school confident that the limitations of cognitive inadequacy in those considered mentally deficient were inevitable, that no amount of education or training could alter their effects. But one day that summer she witnessed the arrival of elderly parents who brought their "severely handicapped forty-year-old son to the school in a basket."[35] For the first time, Skodak confronted the suffering of a family for whom no effort had been made to intervene in a needy child's development. This disturbing experience would stay with her for the rest of her life. It is plausible that it led Skodak to reconsider her view of inevitable outcomes for the mentally deficient, yet it would be some years before her ideas actually shifted.

There is no record that when Skodak began her studies at Ohio State that fall she and her mentor, Henry Goddard, discussed her Rome experience. There is evidence, however, that around this time Goddard's own ideas about intelligence were evolving. He had recently begun to recognize the potential for change in those who were classified as "morons,"—those with IQs between 50 and 69—a term he himself had originated.[36]

This was also a time when some in the United States were reconsidering hard-edged eugenic prescriptions for the control of human reproduction, and it is likely that Skodak's graduate coursework exposed her to a complexity of views. On the side of strict eugenic control, she probably read *The Science of Human Improvement by Better Breeding*, the 1910 work of Charles Benedict Davenport, head of Cold Spring Harbor's Eugenics Record Office. She might also have found a more moderate view in *Heredity and Environment in the Development of Men*, a classic textbook by Edwin Grant Conklin, of Princeton University. Nevertheless, as she began graduate training in the early 1930s, it was Goddard's eugenic ideas that most influenced her.

———

In 1933, with no relief in sight from the effects of the Depression, in downtown Columbus men sold apples on the street, and Marie Skodak completed her first year of doctoral studies. To keep the university running and faculty employed, salaries at Ohio State were reduced by 30 percent. Skodak's own stipend for the next year would be drastically cut by 50 percent. Anxious about her finances, she studied the psychology department's postings of summer jobs, but nothing paid very much. Then she spotted a notice of a position in Iowa.

The first thing Skodak checked was the salary. She no longer waited tables in the Faculty Club, but when she had, she made about $14 a month (in current dollars, about $300). The advertised job—a position invented by Harold Skeels—would pay $50 a month for three months (today, about $1,000 a month) and provide room and board. To Skodak—in fact, to most people at the time—this was a royal sum. The position required IQ testing of low-intelligence children and adults in several Iowa institutions, one of which was the Iowa Soldiers' Orphans' Home at Davenport. The notice was signed by Harold M. Skeels, PhD, Director of Graduate Training at the Iowa Child Welfare Research Station at the University of Iowa in Iowa City. An expert in testing children's intelligence, Skeels had recently been asked by the state's Board of Control for Institutions to assess the abilities of residents in Iowa's institutional facilities.

Skodak raced to her typewriter. In a letter to Skeels, she reviewed her experience, which in every detail matched the job he described. She told of her Ohio State training in testing intelligence in young children and of her experience testing institutionalized children at the Rome school. But what Skodak could not have known was that to a child who lived at the Davenport Home, the Rome school would have been paradise. Rome was a well-managed and well-funded residential setting where highly trained responsive staff treated residents kindly and provided educational stimulation and real-world experiences. While some of Iowa's institutions provided caring environments for the state's low-intellect children, the full-to-bursting, destitute Davenport Home crowded over 700 normal-intelligence residents into a facility designed for about 400, with many children housed in small "cottages" that once served as Civil War barracks. Untrained, overwhelmed cottage matrons were too busy to supply the children with attention or affection or even to satisfy their ordinary needs for clean clothing or adequate hygiene, everyday care that most families provide.[37]

Skeels offered her the position, but also warned of what lay ahead. As he would discover, Skodak was not easily discouraged, but once in Iowa she would find that Iowa station researchers joked darkly about the Davenport Home: that it was barely in Iowa (they were right, it was on the banks of the Mississippi River, about a mile from Illinois); no soldiers' orphans lived there (right again, most children were there because their parents could not support them or had abandoned them, or the children were sent by the courts because of their parents' mental or social incompetence); and as Skeels had warned, it was anything but a "home" (again, exactly right).

─────────

S kodak had limited experience traveling in the United States. She had been to Hungary, and from there visited Germany and Austria, but "anything west of Toledo," she admitted, "was a mystery." In 1933's record-breaking heat, Skodak's bus from Columbus, Ohio, to Iowa City, with stops in Indianapolis and Peoria, traveled 550 miles of Iowa's primitive roads. In the entire state only 139 miles of nearly 8,000 miles were asphalt covered with an additional 3,000 miles considered paved, but those surfaces were gravel.[38] During her journey, which probably took about 20 hours, passengers had no choice but to close their windows to keep out the road dust.

As her bus crossed the Mississippi River into Iowa, Skodak anticipated

a pastoral landscape of picturesque farmhouses surrounded by rolling fields
of rich dark soil, rows of thriving corn and golden wheat, and herds of graz-
ing livestock, all set against the bluest of blue skies. But the parched landscape that unfolded outside the bus windows was almost a photonegative of
what Skodak envisioned: dry corn stalks rustling like stiff paper; Iowa's famed
wheat desiccated from drought and fierce heat; occasional shabby farmhouses,
their paint peeling from dust storms.

At the time of Skodak's June 1933 trip, the front page of an Iowa newspaper warned, "Agriculture Reports Forecast Crop Failure Over Most of
United States." The paper told that "drouth, pestilence, dust storms, and
burning heat waves have besieged crops in the center of the agricultural belt
since planting time."[39] Only a year earlier, Iowa's National Guard held farmers
in an outdoor barbed wire prison because they had dragged a judge from his
courtroom and placed a noose around his neck. Furious and desperate when
the judge sided with banks that foreclosed on their farms, the farmers wanted
retribution.[40] From her bus Skodak saw what happened in a rural state when
nature turned dangerous and the economy failed. To her, those first views of
Iowa seemed forbidding, almost threatening.[41]

Waiting at the University of Iowa Student Union when she arrived were
Harold Skeels, along with research station graduate student Orlo Crissey, who
would coordinate her summer work and that of two other young psychology
students, Emalyn Weiss, from the University of Pennsylvania, and Marjorie
Page, from the University of Minnesota. Crissey teased that the women were
the "brain testers." But the institutionalized children they met the next day
decided they should have a different name, and that summer they became
known as the "brain sisters."[42]

No matter what they were called, their assignment was daunting. In six
institutions across the state in which Iowa housed hundreds of low-intelligence
children and thousands of dependent adults, from 7:30 in the morning to late
afternoon, the women administered and graded IQ tests, and to ensure accu-
racy, regraded the tests of one another. They had no secretarial assistance and
maintained testing records themselves. They worked without breaks until
lunch and then dinner, and while institutional meals were filling, with a lot of
potatoes and corn and chicken on Sundays, not much more could be said for

them. At the end of each day, Skodak and her colleagues accompanied child residents outdoors for games or stories, and when darkness drove them inside, the women finished grading and recording the day's results.[43]

Seeking some relief, there were occasional stays with station graduate students in Iowa City who offered congeniality and sleeping accommodations on the floor. Happy to receive Iowa's warm hospitality, Skodak and her colleagues forgot, almost, about comfort. And then there was the dust. With nighttime temperatures much warmer than usual, air conditioning was an open window. Many, probably including Skodak, slept with damp cloths over their faces. Each morning she found that anything left out at night would be etched in the fine beige-yellow dust that permeated her clothing and got into her eyes and mouth.

As the end of summer approached, Marie Skodak found that despite harsh conditions and endless workdays, it would not be easy to say good-bye to the children. She and her two colleagues had "learned so much . . . we were aware of their loneliness, and worried about our brief friendships with them."[44] She understood why society thought of them as "institutional children"—throwaway children really—why adults, even most psychologists, expected so little from them. Deprived of adults' interest or affection, they had a job no child would want: they had to raise themselves. With unmet health needs, meager educations, and detached relationships, their eagerness to spend time with a kind adult often emerged when the psychologists asked to test their intelligence. In that setting, one in which many children grow restless, their yearning for adult attention made them too eager to cooperate. To convince themselves, some children whose parents had left them at the Davenport Home told others that soon their families would return to take them home.[45] Skodak feared that when she left at the end of the summer, they would think that she, too, had deserted them.

Working alongside Harold Skeels, Skodak found that he also cared deeply about the fates of these cast-off children, and the two psychologists grew to respect and trust one another.[46] When she shared with him her fears about leaving, he reminded her that the results she gathered would contribute to the research station's mission to transform the study of child development into a science that would help these and other children like them. Packing up, Sko-

dak thought about the farm families she had met that summer who had suffered crushing threats to their survival. Compared with those concerns, the
fine dust that drifted everywhere didn't seem a problem, and she returned to
Ohio State with some regret.

―――

As the new academic year began, Skodak found that long-simmering rivalries within the Ohio State psychology department might imperil her
future. The struggle concerned whether the experimental psychology faculty would prevent candidates who were in the field of clinical psychology,
like Skodak, from earning PhDs. Experimental psychologists believed then,
as some still do, that psychologists who worked in the clinic were not rigorous, scientific thinkers. Consultation with needy groups and individuals, they
reasoned, was more an art than a science, and its academic preparation did
not meet the standards of scholarly pursuit and was not worthy of the PhD.
The conflict between the two factions was almost a war.

A rumor that the experimentalists would relentlessly fail clinical candidates when they took their qualifying exams was made real when the department published a devastating exam failure rate. Even Skodak's illustrious
mentor, Henry Goddard, would be unable to protect her. Adding to her distress, the university's increased hardships meant even deeper cuts in graduate students' stipends. The self-confidence Skodak felt when she declared she
would sit at the red table had carried her far, but now her stellar future might
be slipping away. Her situation was grim.

Anxious about money and struggling with possibly fatal departmental
politics, Skodak was surprised to hear again from Harold Skeels. On official
state of Iowa stationery, he wrote that in addition to his position as a research
psychologist at the Iowa station, he had been appointed Iowa's first state psychologist and invited her to return to Iowa as his assistant.[47] She didn't know
that he had already set up a salary line with her name on it, although her
acceptance was a gamble he probably thought he would lose: working for the
state of Iowa on a project connected to the little-known research station was
no competition for the professional advantages of Ohio State's distinguished
psychology department.

Rebuffed, discouraged, and remembering the warmth of the Iowa station and Iowa's people, Skodak decided to flee a situation that many seeking a prestigious degree might have endured. She considered Skeels's job offer "her salvation" and immediately resigned her assistantship, left Henry Goddard's mentorship, and settled in for another bus ride from Columbus to Iowa City. Her salary would be $100 per month (today, about $1,900), plus room and board at the institutions, and a car, necessary to visit institutions around the state. Marie Skodak was on her way.

Chapter Two

———•••———

STARTING OVER

Trading her life as an Ohio State doctoral scholar to become the state of Iowa's assistant psychologist in January 1934 propelled the high-energy Marie Skodak on a completely new path. Alongside Harold Skeels, Skodak tested the intelligence of children in the overcrowded, under-staffed Davenport Home and traveled the state to test children in other institutions as well. Absorbed in her work, Iowa's winter ice storms and then its fierce summer heat and dust seemed small inconveniences—she was too fascinated by her work to let anything stop her.

To prepare for each test session, Skodak read a child's record, often including a report from the indigent care ward of University Hospital in Iowa City about the child's mother and the mother's and (if known) the father's family. Typically, the hospital psychologist had tested the mother's intelligence, and those scores were included in her child's file. To Skodak and Skeels, and to most people of that period, children's IQ scores were like crystal balls—they predicted the child's future mental ability. If Skodak knew before her arrival that some Iowa station psychologists questioned those forecasts, she did not mention that in her later writing about this time.

Skodak had returned to Iowa to work with Skeels, but in addition to his Davenport assignment, he was a faculty member and researcher at the

Iowa station. This connected her to the station's professors and graduate students who now became her social and intellectual base. At the station she met experts in children's language development, learning, social development, nutrition, and parent education, among other specialties. She never expected, however, that station members would challenge an idea she had no reason to question: that heredity determined children's intelligence. Skodak's certainty about heredity's role was shared by her own family, the academics and her fellow students at Ohio State, and by most ordinary people. The aphorisms "like begets like" and "blood will tell" summed it up—those who came from genetically inferior parents would also be genetically inferior.

To her surprise, Skodak's new Iowa station associates viewed her not only as a talented psychologist who assisted Harold Skeels and who held conventional hereditarian beliefs about child development, but as an unofficial emissary from one of eugenics' leaders, her former mentor Henry Goddard. When asked by some station members to defend Goddard's theories that intelligence was fixed, that "intellectual deficiencies" ran in families, Skodak was caught short. Behind those questions, she discovered, was a competing idea, that perhaps environment and stimulation played a role in the development of children's intelligence. Station research had begun to suggest an idea Skodak had never considered, that like physical growth, a child's cognitive capacities could be influenced by their environment.[1]

———

Despite Iowa's grim Depression conditions, dangerous weather, and raging Dust Bowl windstorms, during the 1930s more graduate students arrived to study at the Iowa Child Welfare Research Station than at any other psychology program in the nation.[2] This suggests that since the station's founding in 1917, word of its child development explorations had reached a new audience. That was precisely what the station's founder, a Des Moines matron and mother with no formal academic training, had hoped.

Born in 1858, Cora Bussey Hillis was in her early 20s when her mother died and she assumed the care of her disabled younger sister, who could not walk and was shut out of participation in many activities. Although doctors had little hope for her sister's recovery, Hillis searched for therapies to support her return to health and eventually helped her attend college and enjoy a productive life.[3] From this lesson, Hillis, the daughter of a Civil War brigadier general and now married and with her own family, became deeply interested in child welfare and development. When she tragically lost three of her five young children to accident and illness, Hillis recognized that, as with her sister, not even doctors had the necessary information to keep young children healthy and safe. From that terrible awareness, Hillis defined her life's mission: the establishment of a center that would "give the normal child the same scientific study by research methods that we [in Iowa] give to crops and cattle."[4]

To support her goal, Hillis began a search for scientific theories of child development. She was amazed not by what she found, but that there was nothing *to* find: "I waded through oceans of stale theory written by bachelor professors or elderly teachers. I discovered there was no well-defined science of child rearing, there were no standards. All the knowledge was theoretical with no research basis."[5] Hillis became convinced that what was needed was the replication of a model already ubiquitous in Iowa—the United States' agricultural scientific laboratories, called stations, where research about crops and livestock helped propel the nation to agricultural dominance. To strengthen her trees and shrubs, Hillis knew she could get direction from the local station about how to "make them luxuriant." If she needed to protect her chicks from the cold, the experimental station could tell her how to do that as well.

From the last decade of the nineteenth century into the second decade of the twentieth, Hillis pursued her mission to advance research about children's healthy development. In 1901, she sought state funds to establish a vital statistics registry for the study of infant mortality. When that money went instead to rural farm projects, the strong-willed Hillis established Iowa's first hospital-based children's ward, served on President Theodore Roosevelt's Country Life Commission, and eventually became a leader in the National Congress of Mothers.

As she gained expertise and contacts, Hillis's mission became widely known, but when asked about her idea's origins she would say, "Oh, it's in the air." She feared that if it were known that the concept came from a woman, what she called "humble origins," it would not be seriously considered. But Hillis was an innovator—she had an idea that no one before had considered—one she believed was "God's work."[6] In an effort to enlist advocates, she approached the University of Iowa, where four of its presidents barely heard her out before turning her down. One suggested that she apply herself to raising money for the campus carillon. Hillis also attempted to find support from the state's legislature, but in nearly twenty years just six legislators agreed to speak with her.

To generate a lobbying force, Hillis gave talks on "Corn Culture vs. Child Culture" at the Farmers' Institute. She organized a conference that brought together university leaders with representatives of the leading Iowa women's organizations. Later, she convened a meeting of over thirty state organizations, including officials from Iowa's eleven congressional districts. Eventually, Hillis developed contacts with newspaper reporters, won endorsements from superintendents of all of Iowa's public schools, the state's labor unions, its Federation of Women's Clubs, parent teacher associations, medical societies, Sunday schools, and from the Women's Christian Temperance Union.[7]

In 1915, her plan moved toward fulfillment when Carl E. Seashore, a psychologist and the dean of the University of Iowa's Graduate College, agreed that child development required rigorous, scientific study. He predicted that the establishment of a research station would support "experiments on children under the most favorable conditions. . . . This," he said, "is the psychological moment."[8] About that time, Hillis persuasively argued before the legislature that in just nine years Iowa spent $18 million maintaining inmates in institutions. If four children per county per year avoided delinquency or other "defects," the money saved would easily recover the costs for the station.[9] Her blueprint included the study of the orphans at the Davenport Home, although that did not get underway until Harold Skeels began his work a decade later.

By 1917, just as Hillis's proposal had reached the brink of approval from the Iowa legislature, the United States entered World War I. Anticipating that the state's funds would now go to the war effort, at the last minute her campaign was rescued when local newspapers headlined that "only forty-one of two hundred and fifty Iowa young men were sound enough to go to war."[10]

Hillis immediately took to those same newspapers to suggest that the rejected recruits had been brought up by mothers who relied on "inherited tradition and the leadings of instinct" because they lacked scientific information about how to raise fit children. Then Hillis placed a cartoon in the *Des Moines Register* advertising that Iowa spent more money on goats and hogs than on its own offspring. In response to that pressure, Hillis's bill finally was passed. Importantly, but without a lot of fuss, Hillis, Seashore, University of Iowa president William H. Jessup, Iowa's state legislators, and Iowa's governor, along with 500,000 women's group supporters, had taken a stand on the side of environment's influence on development. Now chartered by the state, the Iowa Child Welfare Research Station finally opened for business.

Under its director, Harvard-trained Bird Baldwin, the Iowa station hired nurses, doctors, nutritionists, teachers, and psychologists who began studies of children's height, weight, strength, health, and eventually, intelligence. These were some of the first such studies in the nation—they reflected Baldwin's understanding that children developed in an environment of "interactions and contingencies of . . . interrelated factors that went into making the normal child,"[11] and they established his national reputation. But it was Baldwin's own groundbreaking 1920s investigation of public school achievement in two rural communities, anonymized as "Homeland" and "Cedar Creek," that foretold the station's future.

To a casual observer, the one-room schoolhouses in each small town would have seemed indistinguishable. But Baldwin explored further, examining variables of cultural and religious backgrounds, parents' educational attainment and employment, parental attitudes toward education, the amount of time children spent in school, and, notable for the time, contrasting backgrounds of individual children. He discovered that the mean IQ test score of children in one community was nearly one standard deviation higher than in the other and that those in the higher-scoring group were more than twice as likely to attend college.[12] With this investigation Baldwin launched Iowa station research into unexplored territory, one of the first indications that its work would reconsider long-accepted ideas about fixed intelligence. According to historian of social science Hamilton Cravens, Baldwin's work suggested that in the "ideology of the Iowa Station in the late 1920s . . . there was no controversy about how development worked: nature and nurture interacted."[13]

Refining that lens, Baldwin also embedded the case study method into the station's research. Although used by Binet and by Jean Piaget, a Swiss psychologist who studied children's development, in the 1920s and 1930s, case studies were rarely incorporated into American psychologists' reports. With the use of this method, however, Baldwin conveyed that empathic exploration of an individual child's life circumstances might help psychologists avoid errors in interpreting the child's intelligence status. It was an unconventional approach, a kind of fieldwork, and would surface in station psychologists' later studies.

Baldwin's accounts are especially remarkable for his refusal to apply eugenic assumptions in interpreting children's behaviors and abilities. For example, in his book, Baldwin narrates a case study interview with a girl whose mother had died and left ten young children to be cared for by their blacksmith father. When the father's job was no longer needed in the community and the family was left destitute, the conduct of the girl and her siblings changed. The school then labeled two of the siblings "morons" and suspected the girl, now 14, should also be so labeled. Baldwin wrote:

> She was extremely dirty, poorly dressed and unattractive in her manner, a lonely figure among the other pupils who, with the teacher, shared the belief that the family was "no account." Her reactions to the psychologist were armed with the hostility with which all of her family intrenched [sic] themselves against strangers. Her attitude gradually changed under sympathetic questioning, and the interview established that she was not mentally deficient, but bewildered and resentful about a situation for which she was not responsible.[14]

In addition to the case study approach, Baldwin's commitment to quantitative research methods set him apart from his peers. Moreover, he was also ahead of his colleagues in recognizing the importance of current biological studies that suggested that environment shaped development.

In a 1924 paper published in the *American Naturalist*, at the time a descriptive and theoretical journal with popular as well as scientific appeal, Thomas Hunt Morgan, a biologist and geneticist then at Columbia University, had proposed that environment influenced genetic outcomes in animals and humans.[15] Morgan had made this suggestion in other papers as well, and it is likely that Baldwin recognized the idea's significance for psychology. Although the science that supported Morgan's discoveries was not obscure, the Iowa station was the only research group to draw on those findings. At the time, graduate study in psychology rarely included biology, the scientific method, or statistics.

In 1928, Baldwin sharply criticized psychology's decadal compilation of its latest findings published in the *Yearbook of the National Society for the Study of Education, Nature and Nurture*, edited by Lewis Terman. Baldwin wrote, "Education [and psychology] have not grasped the fundamental concepts of scientific research. . . . That maturation is influenced, accelerated, retarded, and modified by environmental factors is accepted by most of the leading biologists of today."[16] Tragically, that year, after an accidental nick from a barber's razor, Baldwin died of erysipelas. Another University of Iowa psychologist, 31-year-old George Stoddard, was named Baldwin's successor.

Born in Carbondale, Pennsylvania—he called it "a little anthracite town"—Stoddard's older sister encouraged him, he said, with "ambition honeyed over with love."[17] As an undergraduate at Pennsylvania State University, Stoddard began in engineering, then tried mathematics, but was uninterested until he discovered education, at the time a close cousin to the fledgling discipline of psychology. "Now I was hungry," he said, "for the intellectual life that chemical engineering had denied me."[18] Stoddard then made the unusual choice among American psychologists to take some of his graduate training in Europe. Speaking almost no French, in 1922 he presented himself at the Sorbonne and was accepted for study under a group of psychologists that included Theodore Simon, the research partner of the recently deceased Alfred Binet. Simon's area of expertise—mental testing—informed his lectures. In addition, Simon allowed Stoddard free run of Binet's former laboratory, including access to all of his papers. For a year Stoddard steeped himself in journals and research that revealed Binet's core ideas about the development of children's thinking, his idea that "any abstract psychological variable—including intelligence—was neither unitary nor simple of measurement," but had to include both its complexity and diverse forms of expression.[19] That year Stoddard earned a master's degree with honors.

When he returned to the United States in 1923, at the suggestion of a Penn State dean Stoddard entered the University of Iowa to earn a PhD in psychology. From the window of the train taking him to Iowa City, Stoddard looked out upon "acres of rich dark . . . farmland—corn, wheat, oats, alfalfa, soybeans" and wondered where in the world there could be enough people to consume those oceans of produce. His Iowa mentor would be G. M. Ruch, a demanding perfectionist in tests and measurements who had been a star pupil of Lewis Terman.

Terman and Stoddard had not met, but because of his connection to Ruch, Terman later offered Stoddard a "richly endowed fellowship at Stanford . . . mine for the asking."[20] Stoddard turned him down. In 1916 Terman had authored a widely accepted revision of Binet's test which lifted him, and all of mental test psychology, to professional dominance. Accepting Terman's offer would have assured Stoddard a prestigious career and secure future. However, neither Stoddard nor Ruch, both test measurement specialists, endorsed Terman's revision of Binet. They believed that Terman had misinterpreted or even misappropriated Binet's understanding of the dynamic nature of intelligence as related to children's judgment and experience. Binet, who never felt confident that he could define intelligence, had created an individualized assessment to identify areas in which children's learning needed support and remediation. His test did not produce a score, but rather an evaluation. On the other hand, Terman's revision of Binet's test contrasted sharply with Binet's. It was typically administered to groups of schoolchildren, with results called the intelligence quotient (IQ) computed numerically—a score used to rank students into appropriate school placements. Terman's test was also used to evaluate the intelligence of individuals in hospitals, institutions, and prisons.

To define a child's intellectual level, Terman placed their IQ score on a gradient that ranged from "idiot" to "genius." For example, a score between 50 and 69 positioned the child at the "moron" level; an average score was between 90 and 109; and a score between 120 and 139 rated the child as "very superior."[21] Ruch labeled Terman's approach to intelligence testing "web spin-ning"; that is, he suggested it offered a mistaken—even impossible—precision about an individual's intellectual ability, a precision Binet had rejected. (While the terms *idiot*, *imbecile*, and *genius* had been around for centuries, and *moron* was suggested by Goddard, Binet never attached them to definitive score ranges.) "Binet's brilliant hypotheses about the [complex] nature of intelli-gence," Stoddard said, "were lost on Terman. . . . The Stanford group [of Ter-man supporters] was highly successful . . . without so much as a nod to Binet's theories."[22] But Terman's many admirers may not have recognized the sharp contrasts between his and Binet's approaches.

Stoddard may also have rejected Terman's invitation because he found Iowa's intellectual and artistic milieu appealing—he prized its creativity in theater, writing, and its art programs as well as in psychology—and in 1927 he accepted Iowa's offer to become an assistant professor in the psychology department. Stoddard had already published a book on achievement tests and looked ahead to a conventional teaching and research career. But when Bald-win died a year later, he accepted the university's offer to become director of the Iowa station. Unusually curious, a reader of Freud, Bertrand Russell, and William James, as well as Thomas Hunt Morgan and other biologists and geneticists, as station director Stoddard would have the freedom to explore Binet's vision of environment's role in development, obvious to the French, but to most Americans unknown or unacceptable.

Stoddard had been station director for about six years when Marie Sko-dak arrived in Iowa in 1934. Recalling her first impression of him, she noted that Stoddard had assembled a committed staff of unusually curious, per-ceptive, self-directed psychologists, for whom he was the "guiding spirit." With meticulous questions he demanded they search for explanations, always asking how they knew something, what evidence they had, how certain they were.[23] Stoddard's demands for exacting revisions of graduate students' research, often due the next day, made them fear showing him their drafts. But if those around him found him intimidating, they were also in awe of his quick grasp of station discoveries that soon would lead to radical investiga-tions of a question in which American psychologists had shown little interest: did environment influence the development of intelligence in young children?

Psychology's inattention to young children may have reflected the certainty that heredity determined intelligence and that even as children got older, intelligence seldom changed. This belief in fixed IQ, labeled "IQ constancy," had the support of almost all psychologists, including Lewis Terman, and was rarely questioned. If the IQ score at age 4 remained the IQ score at age 40, then experience played almost no role, so why investigate it? But Stoddard considered constancy "the diet upon which most American psychologists had been raised" and thought it open to challenge. [24]

After Iowa's first doubts about constancy had appeared in Bird Baldwin's 1928 study of farm children, research from station psychologist Beth Wellman, published in 1932, questioned it further. Wellman, born in Iowa in 1895, arrived at the Iowa station in 1920 to study psychology. She brought with her a degree in elementary education and traditional ideas about children's intelligence. During her doctoral studies, she also worked as Baldwin's secretary, a period when Baldwin became widowed. Eventually, he and Wellman became engaged. After she earned her PhD in 1925, Wellman did postdoctoral work at Yale and Columbia, where each offered her a faculty appointment. But in 1928, Wellman returned to Iowa to marry Baldwin, who died just weeks before their wedding. Wellman became the guardian of Baldwin's three young children.

In 1932, Wellman published findings that middle-class children who attended the University of Iowa's laboratory preschool and upper school—many from the homes of university faculty—gained in intelligence. To test the children, Wellman had used Terman's well-regarded 1916 Stanford-Binet and a similar test for preschool children, the 1928 Kuhlman-Binet. Wellman tested children from ages 2 to 14 (5-year-old Arthur Schlesinger Jr. was one) and found that some children's IQ scores showed remarkable increases. Wellman found children with below-average preschool test results who, over time, had risen to the superior range, and some with average scores had advanced to the very superior range.[25] A few children Wellman studied made even greater gains. One, for example, advanced from an IQ of 89, in the low average range at age 3, to an IQ of 149 at age 10 and down to 132 at age 13. Over ten years, another child moved from an IQ of 98 to an IQ of 153.

Wellman discovered that gains in preschool children were related to the amount of time they spent in school and that children limited to half-day sessions did not gain as much as those who attended for a full day. She also found that preschool children's IQ scores plateaued or declined during summer vacations. But Wellman's bombshell finding was that children who entered preschool with lower IQs made greater gains than children who entered with higher IQs.[26] Wellman explained this counterintuitive finding by suggesting that while heredity did not determine intelligence, it might place limits on the individual's response to experience. She also thought it plausible that children who received much home stimulation might gain less from additional stimulation in school, and children with less early stimulation might experience greater benefits.

Wellman and her station colleagues did not know what to make of her peculiar results. How definitive were they? Was the reliability of the tests she had used as well established as they had thought? One thing the Iowa psychologists *were* sure about was that some earlier investigations of preschool children—none done at Iowa—had produced what another psychologist, Northwestern University's Paul Witty, labeled "the IQ dogma" of constant, fixed intelligence. While Witty questioned Wellman's discoveries, he suggested that if Iowa's results were uncertain, results from other investigators might be, too. After all, everyone used the same tests. Witty also suggested possible bias in those who reported the constant IQ. As an example, Witty looked to a study from Lewis Terman's graduate student, Barbara Burks, who dismissed declines of intelligence due to lack of stimulation because such decreases "occur only once or twice in a thousand times in American communities."[27] Marie Skodak recalled that Wellman's discovery of IQ score changes "rocked conventional beliefs, not only for education and psychology, but for much of society."[28] These unexpected results would set the table at the Iowa station for its next decade of research.

―――――

As a graduate student, Wellman had briefly assisted Lewis Terman at Stanford with one of his studies, and for a while she had been influenced by his racial and nationalistic bias toward an innately determined intellectual meritocracy. Now, her unanticipated results triggered disagreements at the station that were not, Marie Skodak said, "congenial" for the research team, yet everyone agreed her findings demanded further investigation. Because she was the first of the Iowa psychologists to challenge the orthodox view, the brilliant, shy, conscientious Wellman became a lightning rod for criticism from her profession, the most severe from Terman and his associates.[29] Eventually, under Stoddard's leadership, Wellman's studies and those of her colleagues Harold Skeels and Marie Skodak extended the station's evidence that environment might influence developmental outcomes.

Skeels, a young station psychologist with a special interest in early development, was skeptical of Wellman's conclusions. Born in 1901 into a family with traditional views—his father was a well-known evangelical preacher and his mother was the church organist—Skeels's early education was in a rural Iowa one-room schoolhouse, then in a high school for about 200 students, where he won debate contests and was first in his class. Not obviously ambitious, after graduating from high school Skeels taught agricultural methods to 4-H groups. As an undergraduate he studied animal husbandry and agricultural education at Iowa State, in Ames. His college training provided a platform for him to become a livestock manager, where he could apply his knowledge of the genetic basis of trait inheritance. After earning his degree, he worked in a dairy as an analyst of the butterfat content in milk produced by various breeds of cattle, a factor that assisted farmers in selective breeding.[30]

Skeels left almost no paper trail about his life events, so it isn't clear what led to his turn from an area of expertise that assured his future in Iowa's agriculture economy to a career in the little-known profession of psychology. But in a move more radical than his background predicted, in 1928 he began doctoral studies at the Iowa station. It is plausible that the station's outreach to farm families through radio broadcasts and pamphlets, a mission written into its charter, made the field highly visible. Awarded the PhD in 1932, Skeels had developed expertise in tests of the intelligence of young children and so had a special interest in Wellman's discoveries.

As station psychologists questioned, debated, and analyzed their findings in meetings Stoddard called *soirées*, he nurtured their curiosity and intellectual camaraderie. In her plain-spoken way, Skodak later explained to historian of child development Milton Senn that she and her colleagues were not sharing breakthroughs, but simply talking.[31] And to Lewis Terman's biographer, Henry L. Minton, she related:

> There was an air of freedom at Iowa, you could pursue an area
> of research that made sense and people would support you. . . .
> If you needed subjects or facilities, somehow they were made
> available. There was something there that was more important
> than your own personal pleasure or personal comfort.[32]

"[Stoddard] was the intellectual light of the time," another station member remembered. And Skodak was clear about Stoddard's leadership: "Under him, the station had its finest hour."[33]

Psychologists studied child development at Stanford, Columbia, Berkeley, Minnesota, Chicago, and other schools, but none matched what became one of the most stimulating and productive research milieus in the history of psychology. At the Iowa station, an ensemble of scholars made landmark contributions that created new knowledge about children's intellectual development and that became known as "the Iowa point of view."[34] In little more than a decade, station researchers published over seventy studies. Of its core investigators—Bird Baldwin, George Stoddard, Harold Skeels, Marie Skodak, and Beth Wellman—Wellman was the most prolific and the most dauntless. Despite personal tragedy that overnight made her the guardian of three young children, then a diagnosis of ultimately fatal breast cancer, from 1932 to 1949 she published twenty-five investigations in research journals and countless articles in the popular press. Taken together, the station's body of work signaled Iowa's arrival at the gateway of modern cognitive science, although for decades that would not be recognized.

———

Bird Baldwin's audacious thinking about the role of environment in children's development, followed by George Stoddard's research leadership and very likely Wellman' investigations, attracted the interest of a young intellectual, polymath psychologist—Beardsley Ruml, director of the Laura Spelman Rockefeller Memorial Foundation, with its mission to support research in child development. An Iowan himself, two years after he graduated from Dartmouth College Ruml had earned a PhD in psychology and education at the University of Chicago. He was 23 years old.

Ruml and his associate director of the Memorial, economist and social scientist Lawrence K. Frank, combed the nation for research that had the potential to improve the welfare of mothers and children. Together, they steadied a foundation whose goals were out of focus when they quickly assessed what had been holding it back, the inadequacy of current social science research. Ruml wrote a paradigm-altering memorandum to the Rockefeller board, a paper still referenced in the field, in which he insisted that research in social science needed to reform its approach; one commentator said that at the time social science research "was like a physician who practiced in the absence of medical science."[35]

Stoddard's outlier ideas appealed to Ruml, and at the station he found rich soil for the Memorial's investment. Iowa was awarded about $1 million (today, about $14 million) to pursue its research, far more than any other institution and a sum that put the unknown station on the map. Stoddard's intellectual independence supported the Spelman Memorial's hope for innovations in the field. That the station had remarkable self-determination can be attributed partly to Stoddard's gifts as an administrator and visionary and to a university that harnessed his talents. Concurrently he served as director of the Iowa station, head of the University of Iowa's Graduate School, and head of the psychology department, a fusion his colleagues referred to as "The Holy Trinity." At other university research sites for child development, such as Berkeley and the University of Minnesota, turf competition interfered in access to the Memorial's grants. Although those centers were awarded some resources, Ruml and the Memorial, concerned that those rivalries would get in the way of productive collaboration, found the infighting discouraging.[36] The Spelman Memorial had supported Baldwin's 1928 study of farm children and made possible many of the studies that would be completed in the 1930s by Wellman and Skeels. (Skodak began her work later in the decade, after most of that money had been disbursed.) Yet, at the station there was no ideological "party line" that suggested IQ constancy was incorrect, only endless discussions and each researcher had to find their own way.

keels's ideas about constancy first began to change in 1934 as he tested the intelligence of residents at the Institution for Feebleminded Children, in Glenwood, on Iowa's western border. In the mix of about 1,000 children and adolescents with below-average IQ test scores, Skeels was surprised to find that some inmates were intellectually average. Investigating, he discovered that they were delinquents from upper-class homes who had, for example, set fires or even raped other children. According to Stoddard, they had been placed at Glenwood because judges did not want to commit them to Iowa's homes for delinquents or send them to jail. At Glenwood, a well-resourced institution with enough staff, they did not continue their offending behaviors.

However, because their intelligence tested in the normal range, as the state psychologist it fell to Skeels to transfer them to Davenport, an institution for normal-intelligence children. What happened next disturbed him. After the children had lived in Davenport's emotionally and materially impoverished environment for a year or two, their IQ test scores declined. Bewildered, Skeels demanded of Stoddard, "How could this happen?"[37] At Davenport Skeels found additional evidence of IQ variability in the scores of siblings from destitute families who arrived there when courts ruled that their parents were not competent to keep them. He discovered that those children's IQs tracked with the length of time they had been exposed to parents' deficient care: the oldest children had the lowest intelligence. A study of 407 children from 132 families confirmed those observations.[38] Yet another example of IQs that changed with environment occurred when judges sent children of alcoholic parents to live in Davenport for six months while their parents got sober. If parents missed their sobriety deadlines, the court granted them another six months, and then six more. During these extensions, both Skeels and Skodak noticed that the children's IQ scores drifted downward.[39]

Because they were consulted about adoptions, Skeels and Skodak also noticed changes in IQ scores if the adoption of a Davenport child were delayed. If the delay went on long enough, the score could become so low that the child would become unadoptable and would be transferred to a home for the "retarded."[40] Such delays happened for all kinds of reasons. A family that had surrendered a child might not have signed an adoption release and might even have left the state, halting the process until bureaucratic issues were resolved. Delays happened, too, because of illness, such as otitis media, an ear infection today treated with antibiotics, that could sweep through institutions, sicken children for long periods, and even kill.[41] Across the road from the Davenport Home is the orphans' cemetery of the Oakdale Memorial Gardens, where child-sized headstones mark hundreds of graves of those who died in Iowa's care.[42]

Chapter Three

———— ◆◆◆ ————

TRANSPARENT WAIFS, PITIFUL CREATURES

U ntil the Depression pulled the lid down on its economy, the small city of Davenport had flourished. Geography provided it with a dream-come-true location for the nation's first Mississippi River rail crossing, the Rock Island Railroad Bridge to Illinois, completed in 1856. (A conflict between rail interests and riverboat owners about whether to build the bridge went to court with Abraham Lincoln as attorney for the railroads against Jefferson Davis for the riverboat owners.[1]) In the next two decades, as Iowa's agricultural bounty rolled west to the Pacific coast, east to Chicago, and then on to New York, the city was transformed into a railway shipping hub and its population shot up by nearly 600 percent. In the two decades before the Depression, the city's population rose another 50 percent.[2] But now, near the Rock Island Bridge and close to the Iowa Soldier's Orphans' Home, men, women, and children filled a shantytown. Inside the orphanage, things were a little better, but according to Harold Skeels, "standards of diet, sanitation . . . general care . . . and philosophy" were close to criminal.[3]

The Davenport Home had always sheltered infants, children, and teenagers, many of whom remained until they were 21. Older residents labored at jobs that sustained the orphanage, and that included work on its farm. Before and after their schoolday, residents

> *dug turnips, milked cows, and shoveled manure. They snapped*
> *beans, shelled peas, ironed uniforms or unloaded coal. They*
> *washed pots and pans in the kitchen, drove trucks to the field,*
> *worked alongside and were supervised by prisoners from the*
> *county jail. . . . They scrubbed hospital floors on hands and*
> *knees, washed dishes, and worked in the fields.*[4]

To make room for more residents, during the Depression teenagers were often "placed out" to work as unpaid labor for local families. One former resident recalled that the superintendent sent her to work so that she would have more to eat. He did not realize that each day before school, "this little, skinny sixteen-year-old girl had to get up at dawn to start the fire in the cook stove, then go down to the barn and milk [eight] cows and then come back and eat her own breakfast outside, summer or winter."[5] In exchange for their labor, the state expected the teenagers would receive training for adult employment, but that did not always happen. Working residents, older children and teenagers, had to attend school, but farming and work schedules had priority. When discipline seemed required, in the "typical practice in the era, children were whipped with a leather strap for low grades, misbehaviors, and running away."[6]

At the worst of the Depression, from 1933 to 1935, wave upon wave of children arrived at Davenport, nearly doubling the institution's census to about 800.[7] New Deal social programs had not yet arrived, and although Marie Skodak and Harold Skeels described orphanage conditions as "Dickensian," overworked staff appreciated having jobs at all. Recognizing Iowa's crisis, in 1935 the state planning commission advised "better care in institutions by having more adults in contact with children, shorter hours, better provisions for education and recreation."[8] No staff increases were considered. Davenport's deficiencies, Skeels and Skodak explained, resulted from the effects on the institution of the Great Depression and the Dust Bowl, but also from the state's "prevailing simplicity of life" which, as was common knowledge, had long kept the finances of its agencies and all public institutions tightly controlled.[9]

Public and private charity funds were penniless, and no social safety nets existed to aid impoverished families. "The usual community support systems," Skodak could see, "were . . . exhausted," and at Davenport she watched as "disintegrated families . . . unable to feed and shelter their children, released them—five or six or more"—to the orphanage.[10] Bereft, heartbroken parents assured their children that they would soon return for them, but few were able to. An adult who, as a child, had briefly lived at Davenport reported that when children were "dropped off," some at first treated the experience as an exciting adventure, as if they had arrived at summer camp. But as they began to fear that their parents had abandoned them, they resembled "lost souls" and became sad, angry, and hostile to the adults charged with their care.[11]

Some of Davenport's children had not been abandoned but had been removed from abusive families by the state, an increasingly common outcome as Depression hardships grew more extreme. Also, maltreated children who were found living on the streets or in shantytowns were brought to Davenport. Others were placed there because of parental alcohol or drug abuse or because their parents were found to have low intelligence or were mentally ill, syphilitic, tubercular, or unwell in some other way.[12] When resources at other state and private social service programs became exhausted, Davenport became the option of last resort.[13] No other shelter existed for neglected children, and some expressed joy at their new institutional lives. "I didn't know that you were supposed to eat three times a day," a child, now an adult, who was one of nine abandoned siblings told an interviewer for a Davenport oral history project. Another, who said that before Davenport he "probably got one meal every three days or two days" felt that the institution saved him. "All of a sudden," he said, "you've got clean clothes, a bed, clean bedding . . . and kids to play with. I think I must have been born to live in an institution. I fell right in."[14]

———

For Marie Skodak, Davenport's condition that winter and spring of 1934 was not a surprise—she had worked there the previous summer— although since then the institution had further deteriorated. However, her new responsibilities included an uncommon assignment: in every kind of weather, over terrible roads, in her 1930s car with its uncertain heater, she conveyed newborn infants from the University Hospital in Iowa City to the Davenport Home's nursery, a distance of about 65 miles. As she navigated this rough passage, a days-old baby tucked into a wicker basket beside her, Skodak had little hope for the child's future. She was conveying her helpless charge to a destitute, overcrowded orphanage in which the state would provide inadequate nutrition, poor health care, no stimulation, and affectionless attention. Often the child of a prostitute and believed to have inherited low intelligence, the baby would be treated by Davenport's staff like the dependent, institutional inmate they assumed the infant was fated to become.

To feed her hungry, fussy passenger, Skodak carried the infant into the only travelers' rest stops available, roadside bars. Warming the baby's bottle on a coal stove in a saloon lit by kerosene lanterns—electrification did not arrive in rural Iowa for another decade—the bar's rural Iowa patrons of mostly farmers and other workers gathered around, relishing the presence of such uncommon visitors and learning that Skodak and the newborn were headed to the Davenport Home. During her work at the Iowa station Skodak made many of these trips and remembered there would always be someone who would ask, "Is that baby available for adoption?"[15]

After she tucked the tiny infant back into their nursery basket, Skodak drove the last miles to the Soldiers' Orphans' Home, not only a residence for abandoned children, but also the state of Iowa's central adoption facility. Taking the baby from the car, perhaps as she walked the path to Davenport's baby nursery she even sang a lullaby to the infant, whom she knew might only rarely again experience such gentle, unhurried attention. She might even have cuddled the baby a little longer, describing the mature ash trees to her right and the distant rolling hills, a scene of an infant in a woman's arms that any onlooker would have thought unremarkable. But Skodak knew better: unless Davenport babies were adopted, they rarely again experienced such ordinary care.

The Davenport Home served as the hub for Iowa's adoptions, and even during the Depression hundreds of couples applied to adopt children. The brief application asked the characteristics of the child they would like—its sex, coloring, age, religion—and couples provided records of their occupational and financial status. They also provided three references, usually from a local clergyman, a banker, and a community leader. From Skodak's many detailed reports about the process, it is clear that parents did not request information about a child's family history or its intelligence.[16]

The state hoped to place infants into loving homes, and its agents and field workers—politically connected, well-meaning young women who might have graduated from high school—conscientiously reviewed applications, interviewed references, and made detailed pre-adoption home inspections. The numbers of requests to adopt infants far exceeded the supply, and the agents knew they could be selective. Occasionally, agents had to screen out couples who might be seeking a child whom they could eventually put to work.

Yet with Davenport's meager resources and its constant need to make room for more infants, its own adoption process ignored the agents' pre-adoptive reports and went forward as rapidly as possible—placing children almost at random. The process also disregarded Skeels and Skodak's efforts to match children with families.[17] Without any consideration for the infant's birth family history, babies who were usually 10 to 16 weeks old were randomly placed. One psychologist at Iowa, Boyd McCandless, later a leader in child development research, remembered, "The mother might be retarded, might be schizophrenic, might be whatever . . . as long as the baby was found by a pediatrician to be healthy, he was placed in any 'respectable' home," most of them middle and upper middle class.[18]

Private adoption agencies often refused to accept for adoption a child whose parents had limited intelligence or other problematic traits. In one of many such cases, when the Christian Home Orphanage in Council Bluffs, Iowa, refused a child because the mother's IQ score was 69, the court sent him to Davenport.[19] Such agencies, where babies of the well-to-do were available for other well-to-do families to adopt, looked askance at Davenport's placements of very young infants. Fearing a baby might have inherited "bad blood,"[20] those agencies routinely kept infants for observation for about a year.

At Davenport, adopting couples generally requested infants, but occasionally toddlers or even 3-, 4-, and 5-year-old children were adopted with no effort made to keep siblings together. A former resident remembered, "I happened to see my younger sister (who was about three years old) . . . dressed in a little red snowsuit with white shoes and I saw her get into a car and I knew that she was gone."[21]

Davenport's adoptions were administered by its superintendent, Roscoe Zerwekh, who had led the Home since 1927. The state's specialized institutions that housed feebleminded residents or those with psychiatric illnesses or health infirmities such as epilepsy were generally headed by medical doctors. But orphanage superintendent positions were typically filled by untrained political appointees. Although Superintendent Zerwekh directly managed all adoptions, he lacked experience in the assessment of children's IQs or knowledge of psychology or sociology or any aspect of childcare. Moreover, he had no experience in institutional administration, had limited understanding of nutrition or child health and development, and was isolated by Davenport's distance from any large city and therefore from new ideas about institutional management or about children's well-being. Zerwekh maintained the official records of Davenport's residents in a dairy farmer's ledger that he referred to as the "Herd Book."

Davenport was an institution designated for the care of children with normal intelligence. The state considered those who had lower than normal intelligence unadoptable and required their transfer to specialized facilities. But because Superintendent Zerwekh lacked the training to assess children's intelligence, many were not transferred and had accumulated in Davenport's wards.

In 1933, the superintendent's deficient administration was exposed when a family that had adopted a baby boy discovered the intelligence of their now 6-year-old was below normal. When local school officials informed them that their son could not be educated, the family feared he would be unable to manage the valuable farm they planned to pass on to him. Claiming that Davenport had "misrepresented" the child and that they had been "shortchanged," they threatened legal action and challenged Iowa's policy that adoptions were "irrevocable."[22] The couple received a settlement, the first of its kind, in which Iowa broke its own rule and terminated the adoption, thus returning the boy to the state's care.[23]

Harold Skeels knew nothing of this unfolding catastrophe when he arrived at Davenport one day that summer to renew his acquaintance with

Superintendent Zerwekh. Although both the orphanage and the Iowa station focused on the lives of children, at the time the two institutions had no official connection. However, years earlier, while earning his PhD at the station, Skeels's research had included the study of young children's intelligence and he had done some of that research at Davenport. Skeels now supervised the station's graduate training and planned to propose to the superintendent that Davenport might be a site where students could practice the administration of intelligence tests. He reasoned that this would be helpful to the institution because it would supply information about its residents, but Skeels may also have hoped to establish a foothold at Davenport for the station's research. As Skodak reported, Skeels had talents that promoted the station's work with Iowa's political boards and state appointees like Zerwekh. He had "skill in opening doors for research [that] made the studies possible."[24] During this visit, Skeels also planned to suggest that Zerwekh house some of the station's cash-strapped students on Davenport's campus.

Skeels had great compassion for the loneliness of Davenport children, and when he arrived that day he walked over to their playground to visit them. What he did not know was that Superintendent Zerwekh's medical staff had allowed children who were ill—the institution was in the midst of a chicken pox epidemic—to play outdoors, and during his visit Skeels fell ill with the same malady. Embarrassed, apologetic, and fearful of being perceived as an inadequate manager, Zerwekh took great pains to make the university professor comfortable and each day chatted with him nervously. This is how Skeels learned that as a result of an adoption that Zerwekh himself had arranged, Iowa's Board of Control faced a potentially momentous lawsuit. Defending the decision that had permitted the adoption of a retarded child, the superintendent asked Skeels, "Was there anybody who could have predicted this?"[25]

Skeels realized that Zerwekh did not seem aware that for over twenty years mental tests had saturated the nation's understanding of children's abilities. In 1920 Lewis Terman had advocated "a mental test for every child," and by 1924 2 million children had taken IQ tests.[26] By 1933, psychology journals had published hundreds of analyses of young children's intelligence test results, including a few from the Iowa station. Also, the teaching staff at Davenport's on-site elementary school must have had knowledge of intelligence testing—it was almost a national craze. And the Iowa station itself published dozens of informational pamphlets and also broadcast radio programs about child development and intelligence, although Zerwekh, who had no children, did not seem familiar with those reports. Skeels also knew that the intelligence test results of the mothers of many Davenport residents were at that very moment filed in the institutional records not far from where he and Zerwekh sat talking.

While the intelligence of babies was not measurable with the kinds of tests used on even very young children, Davenport's nursing staff, as well as a pediatrician who regularly visited, probably gauged babies' motor responses as indicators of their development. Yet when Skeels informed the superintendent that measures existed to estimate the intelligence of infants and very young children, Zerwekh was incredulous. Skeels might as well have told him that men had walked on the moon. Hoping the superintendent would appreciate that mental tests might improve Davenport's adoption process, Skeels became his tutor.

Zerwickh quickly understood that the use of what he called "these funny tests" could prevent the adoption of low-intelligence children and so keep the state out of court by preventing the adoption of low-intelligence children, and he immediately suggested that the Board of Control hire Skeels to test the intelligence of every Davenport resident. The board agreed and went even further, naming Skeels as the state's first psychologist. Superintendent Zerwekh may have hoped that this *deus ex machina* would restore the board's confidence in his leadership. That did not happen, and in February 1934, due to "ill health," he resigned. H. A. Mitchell replaced him, and during his tenure, and in collaboration with Harold Skeels, the modernization of Iowa's adoption and orphanage services got underway.

Like Zerwekh, Mitchell lacked professional preparation for his position. But he did run an informal child development laboratory in his own home— he was the father of five—and he proved sensitive to the realities of children's lives. Shortly after he arrived, in April 1934, Mitchell reminded the Board of Control that "an institution can provide the necessities of life, care for and educate a child, but it cannot give it the individual attention to which it is rightfully entitled."[27]

Although the lawsuit that alarmed the board had concluded, officials feared that this genie would not go back into its bottle, so it was no surprise that during the spring of 1934, the board asked Skeels to reform Davenport's adoption procedures. Thus, in under a year, the young Iowa station professor and researcher became Iowa's first state psychologist, initiated the first working partnership between the Iowa Child Welfare Research Station and the Davenport Home, and became the liaison from those institutions to Iowa's Board of Control. Skeels's professional adroitness would be instrumental in the Iowa station's research into institutional populations and would pave the way for radical studies of children's intelligence related to their family histories, their mothers' intelligence, their fathers' occupations, and their adoptions into middle-class homes.

Working with the Board of Control, Skeels amended Iowa's casual adoptions into a formal two-stage procedure. In the first stage, a team consisting of Superintendent Mitchell, a pediatrician, a Davenport nurse, Iowa's state adoption agent, and Skeels himself assessed whether a child matching the adopting family's request was healthy and appeared to be in the normal range of intelligence. Skeels excluded formal intelligence tests for babies who were under 6 months because he lacked confidence that those measures could be reliable. Rather, he depended on his own experience in noting children's attainment of developmental milestones. Although he did not cite a source for these, at the time few formal milestone evaluations were available. In 1935, Arnold Gesell, head of Yale University's Clinic of Child Development and the most widely known pediatrician of that time, would write that from birth infants have "a mental make-up [and] behavioral equipment" and that "the reactions of the infant assume visible and ascertainable patterns." By 24 weeks, Gesell reported, the infant's hands become "unfisted," and its fingers "curl over every object they touch."[28] While neither Skeels nor Skodak referenced Gesell, it is reasonable that they were familiar with his ideas about normal infant development. Skodak, trained by Henry Goddard in the evaluation of infants, also contributed to the assessments. The standardization of certain milestones as landmarks of babies' sensorimotor developmental status, while commonplace today, did not formally become part of the evaluation of young children until the 1950s, when Gesell published his recommendations for the use of milestones in assessment.

Once Davenport's team approved the adoption, a state agent, and sometimes Skeels himself, brought the child to the parents' home, where they were "joyfully and uncritically welcomed."[29] The adoption's second stage arrived about a year later, when Skeels or Skodak would visit the family to assess the now 15- to 18-month-old child's intelligence. Using a test developed for young children—the Kuhlman-Binet—they would measure coordination, imitation, word recognition, and other developmental landmarks. If the child tested in the range of average intelligence, the adoption would be approved. Should the test reveal that the child was not in the average range, they would be removed and placed in an institution for the feebleminded, probably to live there for the rest of their life. There would be no appeal.[30] No reports address how the state might have responded if the family asked to keep a child found to have low intelligence, but Marie Skodak's summary of Iowa's policy offers a clue: the state aimed to short circuit the adoption "early in the . . . relationship to prevent . . . [the] disastrous consequences of placing a retarded child with a normal family."[31] Many parents, as well as Skeels and Skodak, who were hereditarians, may have agreed.

In June 1933, at the University Hospital in Iowa City, a baby known as CD had been born to a prostitute. CD weighed 6.5 pounds, and in every way appeared to be a robust, healthy infant. Soon after CD's birth, her mother's intelligence was assessed at 56, in the range of morons, and her mental age was found to be 9 years, scores that became part of CD's Iowa records.[32] Given her illegitimacy and her mother's low intelligence, CD matched the profile of a baby assumed to have inherited poor character, inadequate mental ability, and a tendency toward social undesirability.

Almost no information about CD's father could be found, except that he may have attended high school. Although CD's mother told hospital officials that she completed eighth grade when she was 16, this may not have been true. Parents' accounts of their family histories and educational accomplishments could be unreliable, and in Iowa, as in other states, school policy promoted students "regardless of attainments."[33] But it may also have been the case that when low-intellect parents felt intimidated by the power distance between themselves and officials, they sometimes falsified their family backgrounds or exaggerated their educational performance.

Such dissembling might have been motivated by fear. It is likely they knew that Iowa's Board of Eugenics, established in 1929, sometimes institutionalized those who seemed deviant or had trouble caring for themselves or their children, and once detained, some were sterilized. Although the board claimed it limited sterilization to inmates it considered "a menace to society,"[34] others might have feared this possibility. Then again, as Iowa historian of eugenics Amy Vogel suggested, when they faced a hearing before the board, "patients may have been persuaded to believe in their own deviancy, backwardness or incompetence and [saw] no viable alternative to sterilization."[35]

Until the 1940s, compared with other states, such as Virginia and California, Iowa sterilized very few citizens—in 1933 only 94.[36] However, institutions did not always report the operations, or camouflaged them as other medical procedures—appendectomies, for example. In the late 1940s, advocacy for sterilization in Iowa increased, and in 1963 the state performed nearly 2,000. More than two-thirds of those surgeries were performed on girls and women.[37]

For three months, CD's mother and other family members attempted to care for her, but in September 1933, the state ruled the family inadequate, severed her mother's parental rights, and brought CD to the Davenport nursery. Skodak recalled that when the state discovered a family wasn't able to care for its children it did not hesitate to remove them.[38]

At Davenport, CD was placed in a nursery crib that had muslin sheets wrapped around its sides. Wrapping cribs in this fashion—a practice ubiquitous in institutions into the 1950s—was intended to shield infants from drafts that might carry airborne diseases such as whooping cough or diphtheria or that caused diarrhea.[39] Whether the sheets were effective is not clear, as studies of the practice are almost entirely absent from the literature, but institutional infant mortality in the United States of 30 to 90 percent may have incentivized their use.[40] Most childcare staff of that time did not consider that the well-intentioned safeguard isolated babies from their surroundings. Today, neuroscience studies suggest that prolonged limitation of young children's visual stimulation—Davenport's babies remained in the cribs until they were about 6 months old—may have harmful consequences for later social awareness, including the ability to read facial expressions.[41] There are no reports of sheets placed around babies' cribs in family settings.

A baby of CD's age who lived in a family would be frequently held, helped to sit, and have colorful toys to reach for. They would have affectionate engagement with parents or caregivers who spoke to them in the distinctive, high-pitched, repetitive "language," called "motherese" or "parentese," that adults use to mirror "baby talk" back to infants. Although babies do not understand the words spoken to them, they recognize caretakers' attentiveness and answer with their own noises and body movements. Reflecting babies' sounds and motions back to them encourages a social exchange—a "conversation" that cues the infant to the adult's responsiveness. Today this "serve and return" interaction, defined in the last decade by Harvard's Center on the Developing Child,[42] has been found to support the growth of neural networks considered essential to cognitive development. Of course, had she lived in a family, CD's needs would have been met with much affection as well. It is now known that caressing babies stimulates the production of growth hormones, essential for physical, mental, and emotional development.[43]

Cocooned in her crib, CD would have seen light stream each day through the nursery's large windows, and in the evening the moon's glow may have washed over her. Light to shadows to darkness and then light again would have been everything she learned about the world. Really, she might as well have been blind. CD was scarcely touched, never held, rarely spoken to; no one approached her crib warm with love. If the bottle propped beside her mouth slipped away, or if she became cold, or wet, or ill, or cried from loneliness or fear, an overburdened nurse responsible for too many babies would rarely respond.[44] Even if she did not know it, CD may have lost all hope of being mothered.[45]

Most babies arrived at Davenport when they were only days old, but some, like CD, began life in inadequate homes and had endured every sort of neglect. Neil J. Van Steenberg, a 1930s researcher sent to Iowa by the Carnegie Foundation in New York, characterized some of the birth parents of Davenport orphans as having "abandoned any attempts to attain normal social status,"[46] a description that might well have fit CD's family. But despite her mother's background and low intelligence, nothing in CD's record indicated that at her admission to the Davenport Home she was not a normal baby. This suggests she had achieved some of the milestones typical for 3-

month-old infants: she probably made eye contact, visually followed objects, and responded to voices. Had such age benchmarks not been met, Davenport's nurses and its psychologist would have suspected possible developmental anomalies.

In January of 1934, when CD was 7 months old, Davenport transferred her to the nursery for older babies up to 2 years of age. That month another baby, 11-month-old BD, entered Davenport and was also placed in that nursery. The child of a mother with deficient intelligence who was an inmate in an institution for the insane, BD had experienced extreme early deprivation, and when she arrived at Davenport, she was checked for possible contamination from her mother's syphilis and gonorrhea.

Typically, Iowa sterilized institutionalized women who had this array of social, cognitive, and medical histories, and it is unclear why BD's mother had escaped the procedure. BD's father, said to have been an "inebriate," had run off from the same institution. Despite her parents' diagnoses, BD was born after a full-term pregnancy, had no birth injuries, and showed no evidence of her mother's sexually transmitted illnesses.[47]

BD's history told of a mother who had been slow to sit, to walk, and to talk. An uncle had died in a state hospital of "paralysis of the insane." An aunt had died of epilepsy, at the time considered a brain condition related to feeblemindedness or mental illness. When she was an infant, BD's mother's family attempted to care for her, but by the time she was 11 months old, the courts removed her and brought her to Davenport, where, on entry, she was assessed as retarded. A baby of about 1 year should sit without help, crawl, use the "pincer" grasp necessary to pick up small objects and food, and attempt some words, such as "da" and "ma."[48] BD may have appeared retarded because she was unable to accomplish these tasks.

BD and CD's nursery had four or five cribs in each of several small rooms, one of which was the matron's home. No sheets wrapped those cribs, and for 2 hours a day the babies played alongside one another on the floor—in CD's case, her first close contact with anyone in three months—half of her lifetime. A few toys were available, but if one rolled out of reach or broke, no one retrieved or fixed it.[49] The matron's responsibilities included dressing and feeding the children, washing and mending their clothes, caring for them when they were ill, maintaining the nursery equipment, and all other house-keeping and hygiene duties, such as toilet training, chores Skodak and Skeels called "endless."[50]

At the developmental stage when most babies grasp the sides of their cribs or furniture and pull themselves up, adults encourage them to practice standing and take their first steps. At Davenport, if these milestone achievements happened at all, it was by accident and they went unnoticed. Talking, object naming, self-feeding, or learning to walk came much later than for children who lived in families. But the toddlers' slow development did not surprise Davenport's matrons and administrators. It was what they expected from infants of degenerate heredity.

When they were 2 years old, CD and BD would graduate to small, Civil War–era cottages—once barracks—that housed thirty to thirty-five children up to 6 years of age. The caregivers for each cottage were a single matron and a few resentful teenage residents. Now referred to as inmates, the children were dressed each day from random clothing piled on the floor. They went nowhere, owned nothing, and if they learned something on their own, they had no one to tell. Adult attention and affection were unknown. Davenport's institutional regimentation meant they walked to meals and everywhere else, even to use bathroom facilities, in two straight lines.[51] Noise was not tolerated and the matrons discouraged talking or questions. Treating institutionalized children harshly was thought to prepare them for the harsh lives they could expect after they left Davenport's shelter. When they were alone, the children amused themselves with a game they invented, dressing and undressing one another.[52] Skodak recalled that life at Davenport deprived these children of even ordinary interactions with adults, that the institution's emotionally bleak environment and excessively strict routines were nothing like the experience of children who lived in ordinary families. When Davenport children did receive special attention, it was as physical punishment for some perceived transgression—stepping out of line, not finishing a meal, losing something, not being mindful of a rule. Their overburdened caretakers, saddled in the congested institution with the care of too many children, were short-tempered, poorly super-vised (or not supervised at all), and greatly underpaid. When Skeels and

Skodak visited, the children's neediness was easy to observe in their joyful responses to a gentle pat on the head, or to being picked up and talked to a little.[53]

———

In the spring of 1934, Marie Skodak joined Harold Skeels and some Iowa station graduate students in assessing the intelligence of Davenport's nearly 800 residents, and on July 14 Skeels tested BD and CD. When BD had entered Davenport at 11 months, her intake record described her as "retarded." Now, 6 months later, her IQ test score was 35 on the Kuhlman-Binet test, but Skeels had no baseline score and no way to measure her lost intelligence, if any. He recognized, however, that he would have to commit her to an institution for persons with very low intelligence, where he knew she would spend the rest of her life.[54]

However, as Skeels studied CD's record, he found that her case was quite different. When she had arrived at the Davenport nursery, CD appeared to be a normal 3-month-old. Until she was 6 months, she had lived in an environment barren of ordinary human contact and also experienced restricted visual stimulation. Now, Skeels found, her IQ test score was 46. With his traditional training, Skeels never doubted that both girls' low intelligence reflected their poor heredity. While he considered Davenport's treatment of its young children indefensible, he also had to know that CD's decline was extreme, although he made no comment about this in her file. In each child's official record, Skeels wrote the same diagnosis:

> *Mental deficiency of imbecile level, which will probably continue with an increase in age. Prognosis poor. [They] will be unable to make [their] way outside of the care and protection offered by an institution for feebleminded children. Relatives are not in a position to give the continuous care [they] will need.*[55]

Skeels planned to commit the toddlers, fragile, wretched, defective infants, to a children's ward in one of Iowa's institutions for the retarded.[56] But despite urgent efforts, he failed to find places for BD and CD—

institutions were overcrowded and the girls' compromised development was too troubling. Skeels began to fear they might be "unplaceable."[57]

That summer a Midwest heat wave broke every record in Iowa's sixty-two years of weather reporting. In seven days in August, "crop yields declined as fast as the mercury shot up" to 115°F,[58] some areas suffered dust storms and the crop-killing chinch bugs they brought, and seventy-two Iowans died of the heat.[59] With conditions deteriorating, Skeels feared that Davenport's crowding would soon become even more extreme. Adding to his burdens, he also needed to find places for older low-intelligence children who should have been transferred from Davenport months and years earlier, a backlog that contributed to the orphanage's severe overcrowding. An overwhelmed staff continually pressed Skeels for the relief such transfers would bring, reminding him that with fewer children care would improve. Skodak remembered that Skeels made use of every possibility to lessen the crowding.[60]

Late in the summer, Skeels finally received an invitation for BD's and CD's placement from the Woodward State Hospital for the Epileptic and School for the Feebleminded, located 200 miles west, in Boone County. The institution proposed to place each girl on a ward of older girls and women institutionalized due to their "moron" level of mental ability. To send very young children whose fate was sealed by their extremely low intelligence to live with residents institutionalized because their IQ scores were also very low was unheard of. In fact, the proposal, which came not from an administrator but from Woodward's institutional workers, led to one of the most unorthodox arrangements for children's care in the history of psychology. If Skeels agreed, BD and CD would live at Woodward with residents whose chronological ages ranged from 16 to 52 and who had mental ages of 5 to 9 years. The women had been committed to the institution in compliance with Iowa's eugenic policies, and Skeels knew that some, of course, had children of their own.[61]

Immediately, plans were made for the 13- and 16-month-old children, severely underdeveloped and almost skeletal in their frailty, and for whom there seemed no hope,[62] who were not deaf but did not turn to the sound of voices, did not visually follow objects or people, who could not sit or crawl, and who had extremely low intelligence, to live with the Woodward Home's low-intelligence women.

"At the time," Skodak and Skeels wrote, "neither the Board, nor the institutional staffs, nor the field workers . . . included a single person who had any formal training."[63] None of the Woodward staff were experienced in child development; some had not graduated from high school. The psychologists also indicated that although Woodward had a children's ward, it cared for severely disabled hospital patients who required continual medical attention.[64] While the psychologists appreciated BD's and CD's handicaps, they knew that the girls' impairments did not reach the level of extreme physical disability. And if Woodward's superintendent, a seasoned physician, played any role in these events, neither Skeels nor Skodak mentioned him. In fact, he was ill and died about six weeks after the girls arrived. Relieved to have secured a placement for the girls, Skeels quickly agreed to Woodward's offer, since as he saw it, he had done his job and the arrangement was completed.[65] Yet his acceptance may be understood as a decision of last resort.

On September 8, when temperatures had fallen into the 70s, Iowa station graduate students gathered up the little girls along with some random orphanage clothing and set out for Woodward, a town so remote that even today its county's website warns visitors of its poor roads and inadequate electrical and telephone service. Only a week after BD and CD arrived, Iowa's scorching summer gave way to what a Woodward area farmer called "unprecedented frosts," and soon to an early and severe winter. In his diary entry for Thanksgiving, 1934, the tough, stoic Elmer Powers, who like most of his neighbors had lost his entire year's harvest, wrote, "Of the many Thanksgivings I remember, this one is outstanding in the few things we have to be thankful for."[66]

Chapter Four

FROM A DOG YOU
DO NOT GET A CAT

—*French proverb*

One of Lewis Terman's favorite books as a child was *The World's Wonders*, a collection of adventurers' travels in Africa and the Arctic.[1] Growing up in an Indiana farm family and attending a one-room school, he easily memorized his textbooks and had a drive to go far in life. Born in 1877, and one of nine surviving children, Terman believed that his early interest in learning and his outstanding school record stemmed not from environmental stimulation but from his own, genetically determined maturation. With financial support from his parents, he entered a small teacher training college, the first in his family to take the step to higher education. He then went on to the University of Indiana, where, although he was uninterested in the traditional sciences, he discovered psychology and said he hoped to contribute to that world.[2]

With a loan from his family, in 1903 Terman entered graduate school for doctoral studies at what he called "the American Mecca for aspiring psychologists," Clark University, in Worcester, Massachusetts.[3] Clark's founder, G. Stanley Hall, became his mentor. Considered one of psychology's towering figures, Hall founded the American Psychological Association (APA) and established the Child Study Movement, a turn-of-the-century effort to discover everything that could be learned about children, including their physical characteristics, memory, and attention span, among many other traits. At Clark, Terman experienced intellectual stimulation unlike any he had imagined: a university with a range of erudite scholars, a library so well endowed it could not spend all of its funds, and Hall, who attacked intellectual questions, Terman recalled, with "erudition and fertility of imagination that always amazed us."[4]

When Terman informed Hall that mental testing would be his dissertation's subject, Hall warned "of the danger of being misled by the quasi-exactness of quantitative methods."[5] Terman selected a new adviser and continued his proposed research. For his 1906 dissertation, *Genius and Stupidity*, he created an intelligence test to evaluate "bright" and "stupid" boys. Although he later recognized that the study of statistics would have aided him, no statistics courses were offered at Clark. (In his research career, Terman relied for statistical analysis upon his students and colleagues—among them Arthur Otis, Truman Kelley, and Quinn McNemar.[6])

Following his first year at Clark, Terman suffered a serious pulmonary hemorrhage diagnosed as tuberculosis and was advised to seek a warmer climate. When he graduated in 1906, he accepted an appointment as a psychology professor at an obscure California teacher training college. In 1910, Terman's fellow Clark graduate, Edward Huey, turned down a job at Stanford University in Palo Alto, California, recommending Terman in his stead. Stanford first appointed Terman to head its School of Education, but when an opening to lead the psychology department soon arose, the university appointed him to that post. Around that time, Huey gave Terman a copy of Alfred Binet's recently published intelligence test, in wide use in French schools to discover students in need of remediation, and encouraged his friend to rework the test for American students. As one scholar observed, "Terman never received better advice in his life."[7]

Terman's support for eugenic principles was unwavering, and like Henry Goddard, he saw great value in applying Binet's test in educational settings, where it could be used to classify those with low intelligence. As he revised the Binet, in 1913 Terman convened a meeting of educators who had used the test—ten papers were presented—to examine its value in school applications, such as testing students' intelligence and assigning their class levels based on their IQ scores. (Binet, who died in 1911, made no claim that his test measured intelligence, which he had never been able to define, and which he thought of as "a complex phenomenon" that was not inherited.[8]) In the meeting's summary, Terman described the Binet's ability—not mentioned by other attendees—to validate the institutionalization of those with low IQ scores. He wrote:

> The segregation of the feeble-minded, which is sure to follow the further use of intelligence tests, will besides aiding in the elimination of degeneracy, remove a demoralizing and retrograding influence from the lives of many normal children . . . those who are compelled to associate with the feeble-minded either in the home or in the school.[9]

In interpreting Binet test results, Terman employed the term *mental age*, borrowed from Wilhelm Stern, a German psychologist of the era, and also used Stern's term *intelligence quotient* (IQ). Binet had considered intelligence too complex for numerical measurement and preferred the more circumspect *mental level*.[10] Terman had no such qualms. Like Goddard, Terman multiplied Stern's ratios by 100, avoiding the need for decimals, so a normal IQ became 100 rather than 1. He claimed that the IQ number indicated an innate, unmodifiable entity, "an amount of quantifiable brain stuff."[11] By 1919, Terman's Stanford-Binet Revised had become a multiple-choice test of discrete facts—for example, definitions of vocabulary words and answers to mentally computed arithmetic problems—questions Terman claimed could be used to test every sort of child, from the intellectually challenged to those he identified as "wonder children."[12]

Terman wrote reverentially of Alfred Binet as a "creative thinker" and "unpretentious scholar," and although his test conflicted with Binet's philosophy, he used Binet's name in its title and dedicated his book about the test to him. The late Steve McNutt, of the University of Iowa, characterized Terman's dedication as "an inspired move towards co-opting Binet's . . . reputation."[13] Further, Binet's research partner, Theodore Simon, branded Terman's use of numerical scales for the measurement of intelligence a "betrayal" of Binet's work.[14] Reductive as it was, the simplicity of capturing the measurement of intelligence in a single number made the IQ test an irresistible tool for any profession or institution concerned with mental capacities. By 1924, and for decades after, Terman's Stanford-Binet became the most utilized IQ test in the nation, recognized by psychologists and by the public as a reliable and authentic measure of intelligence. A clash between Binet's few American followers and Terman's ubiquitous American supporters would become inevitable.

———

When published in 1916, Terman's monograph, *The Measurement of Intelligence*, along with his 1919 monograph, *The Intelligence of School Children*, captured the imagination of American psychologists and launched his career. He predicted that the Stanford-Binet test would reveal "significant racial differences in general intelligence . . . which cannot be wiped out by any scheme of mental culture."[15] His aim for his test was the identification of low-intelligence children and adults who would be involuntarily institutionalized and sterilized, measures he advocated for the improvement of society. "The struggle of civilization," Terman wrote in 1922, "will be, not to advance, but to hold its own against a relatively increasing spawn of inferior mentality."[16] He labeled those who disagreed "dogmatic deniers of biology's influence."[17]

With publication of the Stanford-Binet, Terman joined America's small, informal mental test circle. Some of his fellow members were Henry Goddard, who in addition to his use of the test at the Vineland School also applied it to assess immigrants' intelligence when they debarked at Ellis Island, and Robert M. Yerkes, of Harvard University, who had written his own intelligence test although it was little used. Goddard had demonstrated the test's value for understanding differing levels of ability in low-intellect children and adults. Yerkes brought to the group his eminence as president of the American Psychological Association and leadership of the Eugenics Section of the American Breeders' Association's Committee on the Inheritance of Mental Traits, a prestigious eugenics group that advocated institutional segregation and sterilization for persons with low intelligence.

World War I had just begun when, led by Yerkes, the psychologists proposed to the United States Army that mental tests could assist the assignment of recruits to their proper duties. As one psychologist argued, the tests could be used to prevent a low-intelligence recruit "from giving away the whole unit to the enemy." The army agreed, and in just six weeks the psychologists devised the army test.[18] During America's participation in World War I, from April 1917 to November 1918, the army tested the intelligence of 1,726,966 recruits, a rate of about 3,200 per day. Harvard paleontologist, biologist, and historian of science Stephen Jay Gould reported that to achieve this result, Yerkes hired about 200 examiners who faced hostility "from the brass at several camps . . . and were rarely able to carry out more than a caricature of their own . . . procedure."[19]

In groups of up to 200, with some seated on the floor, literate recruits took the Army Alpha test, and immigrants with limited English facility and African Americans took the Army Beta. In the second group, instructions were given with the use of hand signals, and test questions were asked in the form of pictographs or with pantomime, which the tests' authors called "gesture language."[20] The possibility that unfamiliarity with English or inadequate educational backgrounds might influence recruits' test performance was not considered.

In 1921, when Yerkes published the report of the tests' results, they stunned the nation. The average white American soldier, Yerkes found, had the mental age of a 13-year-old, and the average African American soldier had the mental age of a 10-year-old.[21] Until the Emancipation Proclamation in 1863, a subjugated African American who was discovered to know how to read or write faced certain death. Many of the young men who took the army test were the grandchildren of those formerly enslaved persons. If they had any education—few schools had been established in areas where those populations had settled—they were likely taught by inadequately trained teachers in impoverished, segregated classrooms stocked with cast-off books and supplies. Commonly, African Americans seeking to study independently were not permitted to use public libraries.[22] (In 1868, an African American Iowa businessman won the first school desegregation suit in the nation. By 1920, Blacks made up about half a percent of Iowa's population.[23])

A credulous public expressed horror at the army test's findings. On April 1, 1921, the *Baltimore Sun* headlined "VAST ARMY OF ADULTS MENTALLY DEFICIENT"; on November 24, 1921, a *Seattle Star* headline blasted "THIRD OF ARMY WAS ILLITERATE"; and on December 7, 1923, Davenport's *Daily Times* reported that "the mental tests of the army, though laughed at and ridiculed at the time . . . are nevertheless being accepted now. . . . They eliminated the feeble minded from our army."

Among the reasons the test results received abundant press coverage was an aggressive campaign waged by Yerkes himself. In one effort, he urged the dean of the University of Chicago "to properly inform interested individuals . . . concerning psychological service in the Army."[24] Yerkes's efforts were richly rewarded. "Wartime publicity," he said, "accomplished what decades of academic research and teaching could not have equaled."[25]

Yerkes's report also included a chart of the gradient of recruits' mean intelligence scores listed by their nationalities.[26] Those who had the highest IQ scores had come from English-speaking nations like Scotland and Canada. The gradient of IQs for more recent immigrants, those from the Mediterranean "races," were far lower. Lower still were scores among African Americans. Some of the test subjects had never been to school, and the day they took the army test was the first time they held a pencil.[27]

In the coming years, Yerkes and his colleagues enjoyed increasing status as the army tests reshaped the field of mental test psychology from a vocation that owned almost no intellectual acreage into a recognized profession of landholders with a claim to precious turf.[28] The scholar who gained the most was Lewis Terman. His 1916 test and his work on the army test, as one historian observed, made mental testing the most prestigious area of psychology.[29] In 1923, Terman rode this new prominence to his election as president of the American Psychological Association. At his installation, he dazzled the membership as he reminded them that psychology

> transformed the "science of trivialities" into the "science of human engineering." The psychologist of the pre-test era was . . . just a harmless crank, but now psychology has . . . classified nearly two million soldiers; has grad[ed] several million school children; is used everywhere in our institutions for the feeble-minded, delinquent, criminal and insane; . . . is appealed to . . . in the reshaping of national policy on immigration.[30]

While IQ tests were administered in courts, hospitals, prisons, and some institutions, their primary application became the classification of elementary and high school students by levels of ability. Terman, however, intended far more. "What Terman wanted," his biographer Henry Minton observed, "was to achieve a meritocratic society in which each individual was functioning and contributing according to their native potential. Those who were the most intellectually gifted would provide the leadership necessary for social progress."[31] To this end, according to Harvard psychologist and Terman friend Edwin Boring, as Terman's mental test continued to grow in stature, it came to be understood as "the operational definition of intelligence. . . . That he profited from the sale of the tests," Boring wrote, "is incidental."[32] And for psychologists trained in test administration, IQ tests became a full-employment guarantee. Most significantly, as APA president, Terman came to be the standard-bearer for the mental test movement. Predictably, psychology's newfound status and financial incentives encouraged students to enroll in graduate programs, and from 1928 to 1938, the number of students earning PhDs in psychology increased 133 percent.[33]

In 1921, Terman helped found the Psychological Corporation, which became a leading marketer of test materials, later taken over by Harcourt Brace Publishers. Soon after, with World Book Publishers, he launched a lucrative book series, and in 1925 he published the first volume of a multi-year study about the achievement of highly gifted children, *Genetic Studies of Genius*, its title inspired by the first eugenics study, Sir Francis Galton's 1869 effort, *Hereditary Genius*. Terman's study went on to become a much-admired longitudinal report about the life paths of middle- and upper-middle-class children—many the children of Stanford faculty—who had IQ test scores of at least 140.[34]

Once the considerable financial rewards from Terman's test and many projects washed over the members of his profession, they became difficult to relinquish. Further, the now prominent Terman grew his small Stanford department into the best-endowed graduate psychology program in the nation.[35] In 1924, Terman's vision that eugenicists and mental testers would join forces in support of America's tightened immigration laws proved accurate when the army test score results were endorsed as scientific evidence of immigrants' low intelligence. That year saw the passage of restrictive immigration legislation known as the Johnson-Reed Act, which, during the 1930s, barred entry into the United States of Jews fleeing Germany.[36]

Mental testing and eugenic ideology remained inseparable during America's interwar period when, as Terman had predicted, low IQ test scores provided evidence for the institutionalization and sterilization of the unfit. Rarely mentioned was that the tests' findings were applied largely to those with low economic or social status and to the disabled. Thus, intelligence tests proved useful in reinforcing a caste system in which many who lacked the means, connections, or skin color to become well educated and well employed might pay a steep price. But the tests' influence went even further: they became a kind of Rorschach indicator for two opposing views of society. For some, IQ results provided proof of biological determinism in human abilities and limitations, while for others the scores exposed society's failure to provide education and opportunities that promoted social equality. In 1928, twelve years after he published his test, Lewis Terman was elected to the National Academy of Sciences, the highest scientific honor the nation bestows.

This was a time, Marie Skodak noted, when eugenics influenced attitudes about everything.[37] Indeed, America's acceptance of eugenics, with its fantastical ideology of improving society through the segregation and sterilization of those with low intelligence, provided the context in which the Iowa station's work would eventually be judged. Invented in 1869 by a genius, by about 1940 the adult fairy story of eugenics had become ubiquitous in psychology, public policy, politics, and ordinary American life. But how did that happen?

———

A s British aristocrat Francis Galton (1822–1911) walked London's streets during the second half of the nineteenth century, the well-traveled, independently wealthy polymath and scientist-inventor grew concerned. Around him he saw thousands of his rural countrymen, who previously worked in their homes or in small shops, crowding into London in response to the Industrial Revolution's need for factory labor. Galton's unease was not out of concern for the workers' low wages, poor health, and unsafe working conditions or for the extensive use of child labor required for families' survival, but the workers' "degeneration . . . into a distinct sub-species."[38] Repelled by their rough manners and squalid living conditions, Galton observed that even those who appeared successful in industrial work paid with a life of fewer opportunities and premature aging, leading him to conclude that "modern industrial civilization deteriorates the breed." Hence, he claimed, "little distinguishes the lower classes of civilized man from that of barbarians."[39]

Galton's contributions to science and mathematics reveal a prodigious scope of innovation. For example, based on his attention to the intricate ridges of fingertips, he invented a system for fingerprint recognition; and from his study of the relationship between air pressure and temperature, he created the first maps for weather forecasting. Both innovations remain in use today. And Galton's facility in numerical reasoning resulted in transformative concepts for statistical analysis, the index of correlation and the law of regression. Further, to analyze factors that marked factory workers as starkly different from his own associates, Galton applied his analytical talents to human heredity and intelligence.[40]

Galton made deductions about the laboring class that reflected the radical theory of his cousin, Charles Darwin (1809–1882), who in 1859 had authored *On the Origin of Species*. Darwin had observed that in natural settings, survival is enhanced when those with certain traits outcompete rivals for resources and mating partners. Galton advanced ideas for the improvement of the human stock by transposing Darwin's thesis to humans' competition for superiority. Coining the term *eugenics* (from the Greek for "good birth"), he called this "the science which deals with all the influences that improve the inborn qualities of a race . . . that develop them to the utmost advantage."[41] Galton did not use the term *dominance*, although that is what his ideas implied.

Galton's defining work, *Hereditary Genius, An Inquiry into Its Laws and Consequences* (1869), opened with the author's aim "to show . . . that a man's natural abilities are derived by inheritance, under exactly the same limitations as are the form and physical features of the whole organic world."[42] To support this idea, he recounted biographical histories of judges, military commanders, men of science, poets, and senior classics professors at Cambridge University, among others, whom he regarded as "eminent." He then traced the careers of those figures' descendants and attributed their many successes to qualities they inherited from their forebears. From this analysis, Galton concluded that increases in the numbers of children from the talented class—that is, people like him—would result in a better society.

In 1873, Galton offered his "scheme for [society's] improvement whose seeds would be planted almost without knowing it, and would slowly . . . grow, until [they] had transformed the nation."[43] He linked individuals' perceived superiority to their inherited intellectual ability, but his investigation preceded intelligence tests by about thirty years. Later Galton wrote:

> What nature does blindly, slowly and ruthlessly, man may do
> providently, quickly and kindly. . . . It becomes his duty to work
> in that direction, just as it is his duty to be charitable to those
> in misfortune. The improvement of our stock seems one of the
> highest objects that can be . . . attempted.[44]

Galton, who had no children, encouraged the fittest to increase their numbers in order to raise the "miserably low standard of the human race" and tip society toward "the best stock,"[45] an idea of the time called "positive eugenics." Although this thinking characterized Britain's eugenics philosophy, close to the end of his life Galton also advocated "negative eugenics . . . the prevention of conception in the unfit."[46]

Unexpected support for Galton's eugenic theories would arrive in 1900 when nearly forgotten botany investigations from 1866 resurfaced and demonstrated in what way traits might be inherited. In an experiment that no one had tried in the 10,000-year history of agriculture, a modest Augustinian friar from Brno, Moravia (today in the Czech Republic), had used simple garden plants to investigate patterns of trait inheritance. The monk, Gregor Mendel (1822–1884), crossed purebred purple and white garden pea plants and found that their colors were transmitted as single units of heredity and not, as Darwin and others had suggested, in the blending of traits from each parent.[47] In his experiments, Mendel repeatedly crossed purebred plants having one characteristic with purebred plants having another. He discovered that one "dominant" trait could mask a "recessive," producing a hybrid. While in the hybrid generation the recessive trait might seem to vanish, it would reappear in later offspring. Mendel established stable ratios for the appearance of dominant and recessive traits, something that could only happen if traits were inherited separately, one of science's most significant discoveries.

Unit trait inheritance supported Darwin's theory of natural selection: those individuals survived who inherited traits that made them more robust and attractive to potential mates. A member of a religious order, Mendel knew of the rancor within the church concerning Darwin's theories. According to Mario Livio, an astrophysicist who studies the history of scientific discoveries, Mendel recognized that Darwin would appreciate the significance of his discovery, but "probably did not think it prudent to express any explicit support for Darwin's ideas."[48] Subsequently, Mendel's studies faded from view.

But when the work was rediscovered in 1900, the concept of unit trait inheritance transformed eugenics "almost with the power of a revelation,"[49] as adherents understood that traits could be classified as dominant or recessive Mendelian unit characters. From that point, Mendelism became foundational to eugenicists' explanations for each human quirk or attribute—recklessness, perhaps, or being a gossip, even thalassophilia, or "love of the sea," a male trait said to be common in sea captains. Scientists also invoked Mendel's discoveries to warn of lurking genetic dangers. For example, historian Daniel Kevles writes that eugenicists "blithely extended Mendel's discoveries to account for social phenomena, such as alcoholism, prostitution, criminality, shiftlessness, and even poverty."[50] In a 1908 analysis, A. F. Tredgold, a British authority on mental deficiency, calculated:

> *In 90 percent of patients suffering from mental defect, the condition is the result of a morbid state of the ancestors . . . which so impairs the vital powers of the embryo that full and perfect development cannot take place . . . mental deficiency is the result not of chance, but of law . . . the ancestors usually being insane, epileptic, or sufferers from some other marked mental abnormality.*[51]

Extending this scrutiny, British eugenicists feared that the numbers of births from those with undesirable heredity, which they claimed was predominant in the lower classes, would surpass births from the middle and upper classes, a phenomenon labeled the "differential birth rate." The birth rate problem was "associated almost exclusively with the working class . . . and the excessive fecundity of the poor. Social problems were primarily manifestations of individual inadequacies," which could be controlled if only the number of those with good heredity increased.[52]

Eugenicists predicted that the growth of dysgenic traits like feeblemindedness in future generations would doom society. Under Galton's advocacy for positive eugenics, the British entreated those in the upper classes to have more children, an effort that met with no success. Britain's attempt to apply coercive negative eugenic methods such as compulsory sterilization never got through Parliament. Although Galton's efforts to transform society went unfulfilled, his remarkable mathematical and scientific discoveries brought recognition, and in 1909 he was knighted by King Edward VII. By the time of his death two years later, his eugenic ideas had taken root in the United States.

Like their British counterparts, early twentieth-century American eugenicists feared that traits of low intelligence and moral degeneracy would be passed from parent to offspring and overwhelm the population. Among those who spread this alarm was Samuel J. Holmes, a zoologist at the University of California at Berkeley, who, in 1921, explained:

> We are losing the elements of our population that have achieved success financially, socially, or in the field of intellectual achievement . . . none of these classes is reproducing itself . . . [which] constitutes a very serious menace to our present social welfare. . . . The elements of the population that are of subnormal mentality exhibit at present the highest degree of fecundity.[53]

To control this risk, American eugenicists encouraged marriage and reproduction of those with family histories of good intelligence and good health and without signs of problematic traits such as mental illness or alcoholism.[54] Organizations sponsored contests for sermons that preached positive eugenic messages, as well as contests for "Fittest Families" and "Better Babies."[55] Around this time some states began to require a medical examination before marriage. But America's eugenic direction soon took a darker path than its British sister's when it became a mainstream, classist, widely agreed upon, scientifically erroneous master plan for social improvement that promoted coercive sterilization and the institutionalization of the unfit. According to Lewis Terman, such policies were needed to prevent a "biological cataclysm,"[56] and eventually they became legal in every state.

A remarkable document of early twentieth-century American eugenic thought comes from Yale University's psychologist and developmental pediatrician Arnold Gesell (1880–1961), whose reputation rests today on his insights into normal maturational patterns in young children's development. Although not much recalled as a eugenicist, in October 1913, while head of Yale's child development clinic and also a medical student at Yale, Gesell published *The Village of a Thousand Souls, Illustrated with Photographs and Diagrams*, a study of Alma, the small Wisconsin town in which he grew up and where his family continued to live. Gesell's earlier background as a young socialist—in New York City he lived and worked in an immigrant settlement house—left no question of his concern about "saving the individual from corrupting and oppressive environments."[57] Yet, lacking in empirical evidence and partially based on his mother's observations of her neighbors, his article contained descriptions, photographs, and graphics that might have seemed a cruel rebuke to families he had known since childhood.

Gesell wrote that in Alma there were "37 families . . . in which feeblemindedness appears in one, two, three or four individuals" and explained that "about 80 percent of all cases of feeblemindedness are due to an undefined neuropathic heredity."[58] Further, from his hand-drawn map, readers learned the locations of the town's thirteen saloons as well as the homes of "36 families in which there is alcoholism." He tied alcoholism to feeblemindedness in which "alcohol operates as a contributing, if not as an initiating cause in the production of defects and deficiency of the nervous system."[59] Gesell informed readers that including those who were epileptic, 10 percent of the village's families contained members who were insane. He went on to report on the eccentrics, of whom he said there were 34 in the village: "[some] give the world sparkle and spice. . . . Another kind . . . undoubtedly constitute potential or incipient insanities." An additional group, "the mediocre," included half of the town's 110 normal families. "Mediocrity and mental health often go together," he wrote, associating mediocrity with "those homely virtues of 'sturdy commonplaceness,' the ballast of civilized life: sympathy, neighborliness, self-sacrifice, industry, respect for law, love of children, and a moderate fund of common sense."[60]

But why would Gesell, a talented academic and psychologist soon to become a physician, and surely aware of science's demands for empirical verification, publish so subjective an analysis? According to Ben Harris, professor of the history of psychology at the University of New Hampshire, at the time Gesell wrote his article, he was attempting to establish himself as an authority in the area of children's health, and Harris suggests that Gesell may have been seeking to become more widely known. Harris also reports that Gesell's ideas about eugenics fluctuated and that similar inconsistencies characterized many eugenicists' thinking.[61] An appreciation for environment may be found, for example, in a 1910 paper by outspoken eugenicist H. J. Laski, who wrote, "Man cannot be separated from his environment and . . . we should render it as healthy as we can."[62] And eugenics' progenitor, Francis Galton, told a 1905 group at the London School of Economics that while his goal was to improve man's inborn qualities, he also wanted to "develop them to the utmost advantage."[63] Further, during the period in which Gesell wrote his article, he was studying with eugenicist Henry H. Goddard, who later became Marie Skodak's Ohio State mentor.[64] While Gesell and Goddard became lifelong friends, following his article's publication Gesell did not again write in support of eugenics.

Though Gesell's article never referenced immigration, it appeared during an interval of time, from 1880 to 1920, when 20 million immigrants had entered the United States. Their arrival generated fears—some called it a race panic—about the unregulated reproduction of those from "inferior" nations and classes and recast Americans' attention to immigration from a local to a national movement. About this time, what had been small groups of eugenicists coalesced into what historian of eugenics Jonathan Spiro termed an "interlocking directorate" of much larger societies dedicated to immigration restriction and control of reproduction. These included the American Eugenics Society, the Eugenics Research Association, the Race Betterment Foundation, the Immigration Restriction League, and the Galton Society.[65] Members of the Galton Society, the most exclusive and extreme of the groups, led other eugenics organizations, notably the larger, less selective American Eugenics Society. The Galton Society also became home to two of America's trailblazing eugenicists, Charles B. Davenport (1866–1944) and Madison Grant (1865–1937).

Trained at Harvard University, Davenport made his life's mission "the science of human improvement through better breeding."[66] One of his Harvard students, Herbert Spencer Jennings, later a Johns Hopkins University biologist, wrote in 1895 that Davenport "is too strongly set in one way . . .

to attach enough importance to facts that go against his theory." Davenport's conclusions, Jennings observed, "are just about as far from correct as you can get."[67]

A naturalist who yearned to establish a zoological research center, Davenport had explored possible sites where he might organize a program for the study of animal evolution, including at Cold Spring Harbor, on Long Island. In 1902, he proposed such a laboratory to the newly established Carnegie Institution, in Washington DC, and two years later, Carnegie funded a Station for the Experimental Study of Evolution and named Davenport as director. There, Davenport continued his earlier work in quantitative methods in biology, the use of exact statistical measurement as also employed in physics and chemistry. According to a Davenport biographer, American geneticist Carlton MacDowell (1887–1973), his work had "unquestionable importance."[68]

Yet, MacDowell also reported that Davenport's research program was poorly defined, lacked a methodical approach, and had limited focus, which caused him to jump from investigation to investigation. Despite these failings, with support from the Rockefellers and other wealthy families, each summer Davenport's station attracted outstanding American geneticists to its labs.[69]

During his first years at the experimental station, Davenport expressed doubt about Mendelian genetics; but by 1909, he accepted that Mendel's findings had far-reaching implications for eugenic investigations of human populations. To mount a more comprehensive research attack, he hunted for money to expand, and in 1910, with financial support of over half a million dollars (today about $14 million) from Mary Williamson Harriman, the wealthy widow of a railroad baron, Davenport created a second Cold Spring Harbor enterprise, the Eugenics Record Office (ERO). It would research trait inheritance, preach eugenic gospel, and become consequential in national policy.

To assist him, Davenport hired an unknown Iowan, Harry H. Laughlin (1880–1943), an expert in breeding thoroughbred horses and an instructor at the First District State Normal School in Kirksville, Missouri, as ERO superintendent. Together, they would investigate the laws of human heredity, especially those that defined social behaviors. To advance their agenda, in 1912, shortly after Davenport was elected to the National Academy of Sciences, he published *Heredity in Relation to Eugenics*, in which he argued that "poverty means . . . mental inferiority,"[70] and warned of the threat posed by certain inherited traits:

> *Imbecility and "criminalistics" . . . can be traced back to the darkness of remote generations in a way that forces us to conclude that these traits have come to us directly from our animal ancestry and have never been got rid of. . . . If we are to build up in America a society worthy of the species man then we must take such steps as will prevent the increase or even the perpetuation of animalistic strains.*[71]

At the ERO, Davenport and Laughlin launched ambitious research in which they collected data about individual traits found in members of families. Their methodology took the form of a detailed questionnaire, the Record of Family Traits, distributed by the ERO's trained fieldworkers or that families requested. Working nationwide, fieldworkers especially interviewed inmates in asylums and institutions, patients in hospitals, and residents in poor houses about themselves, their close relatives, and their relatives as far back as they could remember. Their reports included subjective descriptions that could not be verified and that workers labeled "community reactions" (actually, local gossip).

These conscientious workers painstakingly recorded information into the ERO's *Trait Book*, its catalog of every human behavioral feature—physical and mental. Chess-playing, as one example, "is number 4598, where 4 signifies a mental trait; 5, general mental ability; 9, special game-playing ability; and 8, the specific game, chess."[72] Altogether, the ERO systematized five trait categories: physical traits, including height, weight, eye color, hair color, and deformities; deficiencies, such as color blindness and diabetes; mental traits related to intelligence and insanity; personality characteristics, such as rebelliousness, irritability, and radicalness; and social traits, such as criminality, scholarship, alcoholism, and traitorousness. All these data, including hundreds of subcategories, were entered on thousands, eventually about a million, 3-by-5 index cards.[73]

To promote awareness of biodeterminism, Laughlin established *The*

Eugenical News, a monthly newspaper for "the dissemination of eugenical truths."[74] From 1916 to 1939, the newspaper published articles on the menace of the feebleminded, differential fertility, the evils of race crossing, among many other eugenic concerns.[75] Headlines in one edition included "Eugenical Ideas in Tennessee," "Quality, Not Quantity of Population," and "Prenuptial Examinations in Belgium, Luxemburg, Germany."[76] Under Davenport and Laughlin, the ERO became the beating heart of American eugenics, "a clearinghouse for eugenics information and propaganda, a platform from which popular eugenic campaigns could be launched, and a home for several eugenical publications. . . . [It] was the only major eugenics institution with a building, research facilities, and a paid staff."[77]

So that Laughlin's academic credentials would measure up to the authority of his position, in 1916 Davenport arranged for him to attend Princeton University, where in two years he earned his master's and doctorate degrees.[78] In 1920 and again in 1922, Laughlin testified before the US House of Representatives Committee on Immigration and Naturalization about the dangers of immigrants flooding the United States. Specifically, he spoke against the immigration of Italians and Jews, who from 1900 to 1920 comprised 9 percent of those entering the United States. The committee named Laughlin its Expert Eugenics Agent, and he played a key role in the 1924 passage of the Johnson-Reed Immigration Restriction Act, the law that limited immigration from any country to 2 percent of that nation's population.[79] The Head of the Carnegie Institution called Laughlin's influence "monumental."[80]

With ERO enthusiasm for perfecting the human race charting the way, through the 1920s the educated public absorbed a blizzard of eugenics-focused radio coverage, newspaper and magazine articles, public lectures, conferences, YMCA programs, museum installations, and even community celebrations, such as church picnics that featured eugenicist speakers. Eventually, there would be hundreds of college courses—including at Harvard, Columbia, and Princeton—in which eugenic science was taught to thousands of students. At state fairs, families submitted to physical and psychiatric exams, as well as intelligence tests, as they participated in highly popular Better Baby and Fitter Family competitions.[81]

The ERO's message accelerated further in 1922 when Albert E. Wiggam,

America's foremost journalist-promoter of eugenics, published his treatise, *The New Decalogue of Science.* A hyperbolic sermon in support of eugenic sterilization, Wiggam's book broadcast his devotion to eugenics' creed, a crusade for "the highest truth man will ever know," along with eugenics' "Ten Commandments of Science."[82] Also in 1922, the *New York Times* reported Lewis Terman's belief that the intelligence of the white race was declining. Terman advised, "If the seed of unusual success is not in the original germ cell, there is no chance for the developed man or woman to become intellectually 'unusual.'" He said his fears reflected statistics showing that the intellectually superior were slower to reproduce and therefore had fewer children than the "socially incompetent."[83]

Meanwhile, despite secretly suffering from epilepsy,[84] a condition thought related to mental illness and reason to institutionalize and sterilize those afflicted, Laughlin committed himself to the extension of laws for involuntary sterilization of the degenerate. His strident 1922 tract, *Eugenical Sterilization in the United States,* included a model sterilization law, and as he intended, many states used his suggested text to win passage of sterilization legislation. But the Eugenics Record Office did not lift the heavy burden of saving the nation from the menace of inherited degeneracy alone. It received significant assistance from the talented and well-connected New York City aristocrat Madison Grant (1865–1937).

One of America's most celebrated eugenics leaders, Grant was an environmentalist without portfolio. Despite his lack of scientific training, the Columbia Law School graduate headed the Bronx Zoo and New York Aquarium, served as a trustee of the American Bison Society and the American Museum of Natural History, and created the Bronx River Parkway and Glacier National Park.[85] But in a feat every bit as remarkable, his ideas managed to shift eugenics' focus from "a skirmish against individuals who were socially unfit to a war against groups who were racially unfit."[86] Historian of eugenics Mark Haller, of Temple University, described Grant as "the nation's most influential racist."[87]

The Passing of the Great Race, or the Racial Basis of European History, Grant's milestone eugenics treatise published in 1916 by Charles Scribner's Sons, went to four editions and seven printings. Here Grant explicated a biologically determined racial caste system in which blond, blue-eyed "Nordics" were ascendant.[88] In close to 500 pages, he described nonexistent pathways that racial groups traveled as they crossed Europe; humanity's progress related to race; race-based summaries of European civilizations; and—scattershot—excoriations of degenerate races. Through this lens, for example, Grant interpreted the racial qualities that made Rome a dominant civilization: "its love of organization, of law and military efficiency, as well as its ideals of family life, loyalty, and truth, obviously point to a Nordic rather than to a Mediterranean origin."[89] He also assailed ideas that drove the French Enlightenment and American Revolution:

> There exits to-day a widespread and fatuous belief in the power of environment, as well as of education and opportunity to alter heredity, which arises from the dogma of the brotherhood of man, derived in its turn from the loose thinkers of the French Revolution and their American mimics.[90]

Grant's book found favorable academic reception and popular success. One supporter, John C. Merriam, a member of the National Research Council's Committee on Scientific Problems of Human Migration, passed the book on to several colleagues. In 1920, Merriam, a paleontologist, had become president of the Carnegie Institution in Washington, DC, the institution that provided significant financial support to the ERO. Another supporter was Robert M. Yerkes, coauthor of the intelligence tests given to World War I army recruits.[91] Adolf Hitler wrote Grant to say that the book was his bible,[92] while later, Nazi war criminals cited Grant in their Nuremburg trial defenses.[93] And ERO head Charles Davenport asked Grant: "Can we build a wall high enough around this country, so as to keep out these cheaper races?"[94]

Although America's eugenic cause—some called it a mania—appeared to be thriving, voices skeptical of its doctrine were emerging. In 1913, two physicians reported to the National Academy of Medicine that after examining 1,000 incarcerated young recidivists, they could find "no proof of the existence of hereditary criminal traits."[95] Further, in the pages of the *New Republic*, in 1922, journalist and public intellectual Walter Lippmann, who had advised President Woodrow Wilson and later won two Pulitzer Prizes, challenged Lewis Terman's insistence that IQ tests measured

> *innate, hereditary, predetermined intelligence. . . . This dogma could not but lead to an intellectual caste system in which the task of education had given way to the doctrine of predestination and infant damnation. . . . The claim that we have learned how to measure hereditary intelligence has no scientific foundation. We cannot measure intelligence when we have never defined it . . . we cannot speak of its hereditary basis after it has been fused with a thousand . . . environmental influences.*[96]

————

In 1926, attorney Clarence Darrow (1857–1938), who had defended a Tennessee teacher's challenge of a law against teaching evolution, published a biting essay, *The Eugenics Cult*, in which he attacked "semi-cultured citizens [who] read eugenist books . . . then shudder with horror at the . . . rising tide of undesirables." Darrow summed up arguments that "inevitably, the superior stocks will be submerged. . . . The only wonder is that with the persistent and senseless breeding of the unfit this hasn't happened long ago." Darrow also raised a skeptical eyebrow at Albert Wiggam's declaration that with eugenics "we already have enough science at hand to bring the world into an earthly paradise" and at another eugenicist's claim that it would take "less than four generations [to] eliminate nine-tenths of the crime, insanity, and sickness . . . in our land." Darrow asked, "Amazingly simple, isn't it?"[97] According to British statistician R. C. Punnett, inventor of the Punnett square for computing the appearance of dominant and recessive traits, it would take "250 generations—roughly 8000 years—of selective breeding before feeblemindedness could be eliminated from the United States."[98]

However, the most knowledgeable, if least heeded, of eugenics' critics were geneticists and biologists. In 1909, biologist Thomas Hunt Morgan questioned the Mendelian concept of "an adult character somehow residing in a particle within a cell."[99] Although Morgan and Charles Davenport were close friends, by 1924 Morgan noted the false logic of eugenic claims of unit trait inheritance when he recognized that trait expression is influenced by environmental conditions.[100] At about that time, because of its "reckless statements and unreliability," Morgan resigned from the American Breeders Association, a eugenics organization that supported Davenport's work.[101]

By the mid-1920s, nearly all geneticists "felt compelled to speak up" and reject eugenic theories. According to historian Garland Allen, they recognized that "the arguments of eugenicists were totally out of touch with advances in the field."[102] However, in the 1930s, when young Rockefeller Institute cell biologist Alfred Mirsky asked Morgan why he had not challenged Davenport's eugenic ideas, Morgan replied, "It would hurt too many old friends."[103] Another scientific voice opposed to eugenics was that of anthropologist Franz Boas (1858–1942), of Columbia University. Boas, who in 1887 had immigrated to the United States from Germany, termed eugenics "racism disguised as science."[104]

Before geneticist Herbert Spencer Jennings (1868–1947) ever got to Harvard or even attended college, he had been hired to teach zoology at Texas A&M. A born scientist, Jennings eventually earned an undergraduate degree at Harvard, where he studied under Charles Davenport. In 1924, as a Johns Hopkins geneticist, Jennings wrote a paper in which he described the "linear arrangement of genes in the chromosomes,"[105] noting "the double serial arrangement, like a pair of strings of beads."[106] Here Jennings anticipated by three decades DNA's double helix, captured in 1952 in an image by crystallographer Rosalind Franklin and described by Francis Crick and James Watson in their 1953 Nobel Prize–winning work. But Jennings's paper was notable for another reason: it rebuked the United States for passage of the 1924 Immigration Restriction Act because Congress had used the work of Mendel to claim that immigrants had inferior traits that were genetically based. Jennings wrote:

> *Mendelism has become grotesquely inadequate and misleading. . . . There is indeed no such thing as a "unit character" and it would be a step in advance if that expression should dis-*

appear. . . . Nothing can be more certain . . . than that hun-
dreds of genes are required to make a mind—even a feeble
mind. . . . Development, it turns out is a continual process of
adjustment to environment. . . . All characteristics are heredi-
tary, and all are environmental.[107]

———

In 1927, sterilization received the nation's highest judicial endorsement and became the law of the land when the Supreme Court decided the case of marginalized Virginia citizen Carrie Buck. Placed at age 3 with a foster family after her mother's incarceration for drug use and sexual promiscuity, when she was a teenager Carrie's foster parents removed her from school, where she had been an average student with no behavior problems and made her their servant.[108] After she was raped and became pregnant by a foster family relative, the family advised the state that she was feebleminded and epileptic and should be institutionalized and sterilized. A credulous state agent agreed.

In a plan to win Supreme Court approval for the state's newly crafted sterilization law, Virginia officials colluded to challenge Carrie's sterilization and assigned complicit legal counsel to defend her. When the case reached the Supreme Court, false testimony and a deposition by ERO leader Harry Laughlin sealed her fate. Laughlin, who never met Carrie, included in his deposition the invented claim that her baby was feebleminded. He also quoted from his own well-regarded book on sterilization, which promoted "the right of the state to limit human reproduction in the interests of race betterment." Laughlin's deposition painted Carrie's family as a "shiftless, ignorant, and worthless class of anti-social whites of the south" whose "feeblemindedness is caused by the inheritance of degenerate qualities"; he said that Carrie was the "potential parent of social inadequate or defective offspring."[109]

With a single dissent from a Catholic justice who objected on religious grounds, the Supreme Court supported Virginia's claim, and in a five-paragraph decision, Justice Oliver Wendell Holmes upheld the state's right to forcibly sterilize Carrie. Regarded as one of the most infamous verdicts in American jurisprudence, Holmes wrote, "Three generations of imbeciles are enough."[110] On June 4, 1927, a social worker returned Carrie to the Virginia State Colony for Epileptics and Feebleminded, where the Supreme Court's verdict was accomplished.

Following the court's decision, every state legalized involuntary steriliza-tion, although some rarely used the statute. The decision still stands, and some state laws remain in place. From about 1920 until today, a total of 65,000 to 70,000 Americans have been sterilized, most of them low-status women.[111] Reports about Carrie's later life tell of her love of crossword puzzles, her avid reading of newspapers. Her daughter, who died at age 8, was also of normal intelligence. Borrowing Thomas Chatterton William's phrase, Carrie Buck's was a "crime of being."[112]

———

In 1929 in Germany, Otto Kankeleit credited Harry Laughlin's work when he demanded sterilization of "inferior" women.[113] In the 1930s, German National Socialism's sterilizations, institutionalizations, and murders of the mentally ill, the disabled, gypsies, homosexuals, and Jews continued to find support from Davenport, Laughlin, and many civic leaders and mainstream citizens in the United States.[114]

After Hitler's 1933 ascendance, Laughlin mobilized the ERO, the *Eugeni-cal News*, and the Eugenics Research Association to support the Nazi cause. In 1934, when New York State asked for Laughlin's opinion about whether to admit into the United States persecuted Jews who arrived at Ellis Island, he advised they make "no exceptional admission for Jews who are refugees from . . . Germany." New York agreed.[115] In 1934, Charles Davenport retired and assumed the role of eugenics' "elder statesman."[116]

At the same time that Laughlin was supporting Germany's attempts to establish sterilization laws, some extreme eugenic ideas had surfaced in Iowa when a state committee that represented a White House Conference on Child Health and Protection met in Des Moines. An item on the meeting's agenda focused on the plight of Iowa's low-intelligence children. The committee noted that "public sentiment does not as yet permit the elimination of these unfortunates even when their mere existence is obviously of no value to any-one, including the unfortunates themselves."[117]

In 1935, California banker Charles M. Goethe, a member of the Human Betterment Foundation and with Lewis Terman a member of the American Eugenics Society and the Eugenics Research Association, had just returned from Germany when he told fellow eugenics activist financier Ezra S. Gosney, "Your work has played a powerful part in shaping the opinions [about sterilization] of the . . . intellectuals who are behind Hitler. . . . You have . . . jolted into action a great government of 60,000,000 people."[118] Goethe referenced Gosney's 1932 report, written with another eugenicist, Paul Popenoe, about the benefits of sterilization to 6,000 persons, which they claimed led to a reduction in sex crimes. In 1933, the report was published in Germany, where the "example of California illustrated the 'beneficial effects' of sterilization laws."[119]

Also, in 1935, Laughlin requested expanded Carnegie Institution support for the ERO. In the words of journalist-historian Edwin Black, this triggered an exhaustive site review in which Carnegie concluded that "the Eugenics Record Office was a worthless endeavor from top to bottom, yielding no real data, and that eugenics . . . was a social propaganda campaign."[120] Laughlin's work, however, was so admired in Germany that in 1936 the University of Heidelberg awarded him an honorary degree. As Nazi attacks on Jews accelerated, Laughlin defended German programs—including the Nuremberg Laws legalizing discrimination against Jews, which he called sound science.[121]

While Carnegie officials never disavowed Laughlin's anti-Semitism, after a failed attempt to salvage ERO research they gave up on his leadership, and on New Year's Eve, 1939, they closed the ERO's doors. The records it had collected, over 1 million index cards and tens of thousands of questionnaires, amounted to a catalog of subjective, often hearsay judgments of supposed family traits, such as, "holding a grudge," "sense of humor," and thousands of others, "worthless for genetic study."[122]

The 1920s acceleration of scientific studies led most American geneticists and biologists to turn away from eugenics,[123] which they had come to view as a pseudoscience mania. However, America's mental test psychologists were inattentive to biology's investigations of the mechanisms of development and behavior and remained uninformed or uninterested in cellular-level discoveries of the role of environment in development.[124] Lewis Terman's writings

betrayed little awareness of recent discoveries in biology. In a personal communication, Terman biographer Henry Minton confirmed that "hereditarian
psychologists were not aware of the 1920s–1930s work on developmental
biology."[125] Minton also noted that he had found "no discussions relevant to
this work in any of their correspondence or publications."[126]

Psychologists' continued belief in Mendelian unit trait inheritance, along
with their insistence that heredity acted without the influence of environment, would persist until about the 1950s, when some began to consider
other possibilities. In this context, the brutal 1930s attacks by mental test
psychologists on the findings of the Iowa Child Welfare Research Station
should not have been a surprise. They were led by Lewis Terman, who would
give no quarter.

Chapter Five

A CLINICAL SURPRISE

As the winter storms of 1935 gave way to prematurely springlike weather, Marie Skodak and Harold Skeels began their travels to every corner of Iowa to visit the families of children who, during the previous year, had been conditionally adopted from the Davenport Home. Separately and sometimes together, they would test the children to certify that their intelligence was in the normal range—the last hurdle before Iowa made the adoptions official.[1]

Most of the children were between 15 and 18 months old and of course were unaware of the reasons for these strangers' visits. Yet for them and for their parents, the psychologists' tests were potentially life changing: by state policy, those children who did not have intelligence in the average range would be removed and committed to an institution for the feebleminded. As one parent remarked to Skodak, "We were taking an examination in parenthood. Our success was shown by the results in our child."[2] A mandated requirement of the adoption process, the visits fulfilled a eugenic prescription so embedded in government policy and popular thought that Skeels and Skodak were never asked to explain its reasoning: when those who had low intelligence remained segregated in institutions (where some would also be involuntarily sterilized), society reaped the benefit.

Families were not usually asked to travel to Davenport for the evaluations. For some it would have been an arduous journey, and for others perhaps impossible because of farmers' planting and harvesting schedules or Depression-limited finances. Also, the psychologists anticipated that testing children in the family's living room or, as often happened, at the kitchen table would ease the children's anxieties about the psychologists' presence and elicit the children's best performance. Over the next months, Skeels and Skodak made their way to families who lived on farms or in Iowa's small rural towns and occasionally to the homes of more prosperous families—a school superintendent, a local newspaper editor, or a town doctor.

Before each visit, the psychologists closely read the children's birth family histories, which to Skodak resembled those of the Kallikaks' children, whose parents Henry Goddard described as "social incompetents," dependent on the state for their care. Skodak knew that some of the children's parents were alcoholics and persons who might be in jail, that many had dropped out of school, and most had not attained the respectable educational levels common in Iowa. Further, nearly all had abandoned society's accepted social and behavioral norms. She wondered how children born into such deficient families could "measure up to the demands of cultured, educated [adoptive] parents." Skodak knew that children from families in which "violations of social and legal codes was the rule," would not have been accepted as potential adoptees by most private adoption agencies. Those officials would have felt that the danger the children would turn out like their birth parents was too great.[3]

The psychologists' concern was heightened because the children had been adopted so early—they had been between 2 and 6 months—that no IQ test could have been given to them. Rather, they had been assessed by several specialists, including Skeels, and appeared to have normal development. But now Skeels and Skodak wondered how to respond if children were not in the normal range of intelligence: "What would we say to these prospective parents? How would we explain this and what would we offer to do?"[4] Neither doubted that it would be necessary to remove some intellectually challenged toddlers from the only secure family attachments they had known.

Factors in the toddlers' birth family histories that concerned Skodak and Skeels told their own sad tale: at a time when Iowa was the fourth wealthiest state in the nation and one of nine states with the highest high school gradua- tion rates,[5] 46 percent of the toddlers' birth mothers had left school at eighth grade. Sixty-five of the children were illegitimate, and many of their moth- ers were prostitutes. Only 10 percent of the birth mothers had IQs above 100, the mean intelligence test score, and 38 percent had IQs below 80, in the range of low and very low intelligence. In addition, 72 percent of the fathers were known to the mothers, which allowed reasonable estimates of their work status, at the time considered a proxy for male intelligence.[6] Just 13 percent of the birth fathers were professionals, while 46 percent had jobs at the lowest employment levels; many were not self-supporting, and some were chronic paupers or criminals.[7]

There were no IQ test scores for the adopting mothers,[8] but their edu- cational attainments were consistently higher than those of the birth moth- ers. All had completed eighth grade and most had finished eleventh grade. While almost none of the birth parents graduated from high school, over half of the adopting parents had done so. In a period when high school was con- sidered much the way college attendance is today, as training for life, these stark differences between the birth and adoptive parents' education levels concerned Skeels and Skodak. They also had misgivings about differences in the occupational levels of the birth fathers versus the adoptive fathers. Taken together, the psychologists understood that the adopting fathers had higher attainment and higher occupational status than the birth fathers and therefore better heredity.

Furthermore, Davenport's random placement of babies was out of step with that era's accepted adoption practice. Most private and public adoption agencies relied on a process known as *selective placement* (many still do), in which a child's background or observed traits are matched to similar quali- ties in an adopting family. In studies that compare the effects of heredity and environment on adopted children's development, selective placement becomes a significant confounding factor as adoptive parents' backgrounds, education, interests, and temperaments, to name but a few possibilities, may affect the stimulative experiences they provide. At Davenport, however, apart from health concerns, the adoption process lacked any social or fitness filters. When he became Iowa's psychologist in 1934, Skeels had hoped to revise that practice but had not yet succeeded.

In several detailed interviews and memoirs, Marie Skodak described making possibly life-altering visits to unpretentious homes, only 10 percent of which had electricity. Iowa's citizens' naivete about bureaucratic process, and their matter-of-fact acceptance of the state's adoption procedures impressed her.[9] Eager to be approved, potential adoptive parents who had been informed at the start that their child could be removed may never have expected it would happen: all the parents consented to surrendering their child if the child did not test in the normal range. Yet the parents-to-be would have made that agreement before the child had come to live with them and the bonds of a loving family unit had formed. Of course, some parents, perhaps even many, may have agreed with Iowa's policy.

With "deep foreboding," the psychologists steeled themselves for heart-breaking scenes when they presented terrible news: this child's IQ was lower than the state required and she or he would have to be returned to Davenport.[10] To prepare, Skodak and Skeels arrived at their visits equipped with a mental script: almost as if the toddlers were off-the-shelf commodities, they would offer to exchange the child for one who was more promising.[11] Hoping for good results, the Iowans entered modest farmhouses where furniture and floors sparkled and child and parents had dressed in their Sunday best. In some homes, Skodak remembered, "You could hardly get through the toys, and the baby was dressed up fit to kill and the house was shining. The father had stayed home from work. It was a big day."[12]

In rural Iowa, farm responsibilities, great distances between homesteads, unpredictable weather, and often impassable roads isolated neighbor from neighbor. Conversations after church and casual encounters with friends on weekly trips into town did not always include gossipy exchanges from a family's informal treasury of child-rearing. Rarer still was advice on the private, even intimate, subject of adoption. And no Dr. Spock or other manual of how to raise a child even existed. Sensing the parents' eagerness for a dialogue, the psychologists invited just that. They listened to mothers and fathers report how extraordinary their child was, and many craved advice. "When should you start to read to a child?" they asked. "Is it all right to take a child with you to the local bar?" Inevitably, questions about adoption arose. "Should you tell a child that he or she was adopted? If you do, how do you explain?" Skeels and Skodak's skill in establishing trusting exchanges with concerned parents created a warm rapport with the families. At the time the psychologists could not have realized that these relationships would become central to their later research.

To put the children at ease, Skeels and Skodak typically began their sessions by singing songs and playing games. Now and again a child might scan the room in search of a reassuring smile from parents who, from their vantage point in the doorway—they leaned forward so intently that Skodak feared they would tumble right into the room—tried to catch the child's eye. Sometimes the tests had to be interrupted when a toddler insisted on taking the psychologist to visit a pet pony or when a parent brought in a plate filled with warm cookies.

———

In their first visits the psychologists found it puzzling that infants from inadequate backgrounds who had seemed normal when adopted had not declined to the levels of their birth families. Not only had the children retained the appearance of normality, they were consistently scoring in the average or above-average range on the IQ tests. As they tested more children the psychologists' puzzlement became incredulity: despite their poor heredity, every child had at least normal intelligence, with the scores of some even higher. After many months, when all of the first year's tests had been completed, Skeels and Skodak could not believe their results: the mean IQ of the children's test scores was 116, considered in the superior range. As Skeels later told an interviewer, "These were the IQ scores of the children of university professors."[13]

As they continued testing, the results almost never varied: after four years, during which they tested 600 children, they had to remove only two.

Such outcomes challenged the fundamental theory of America's psychology establishment that intelligence was hereditary, and they challenged eugenic certainties that mental ability reflected family history, nationality, class, and race and could not be modified by experience. They challenged what Skeels, Skodak, and every American psychologist had been taught. The Iowans' results seemed unthinkable. Heretical. Or wrong.

The prospective adoptees' higher-than-anticipated test results raised questions. Were the test scores the product of examiner bias? Did they reflect the inadequacy of tests of young children? The psychologists also wondered, "Were the scores temporarily inflated from some environmental cause analogous to coaching?"[14] Because they had been afraid that their scoring would be too permissive, Skeels and Skodak had overcompensated by scoring rigidly. Bewildered, they now considered whether they had made test assessment errors and questioned one another as they checked and rechecked the children's performances. Although they had been overly careful, they understood that slight inflections in an examiner's tone or body language might inadvertently cue a child's response. Yet they found no reason to doubt their methods. Because they had largely worked separately, they could compare the mean scores of the children each had tested. Skeels's mean test score was 116. Skodak's was less than a point lower.

The psychologists also questioned whether the test they used, normed for infants and toddlers, was suitable for these children who had briefly been institutionalized and whose family histories differed radically from those of most adopted children.[15] They had no comparative investigations against which to check their results because other than in Iowa, very young children with problematic heredity had rarely been adopted by middle-class parents and subsequently studied.

Skeels also wondered whether a factor not much considered in psychology, the parent-child relationship, might have affected the children's development, especially, he hypothesized, in homes "where parents went to great effort to bring all this about . . . and may [have taken] greater cognizance of the need for play equipment [and] books . . . than true parents. . . . They may be more willing to answer [children's] questions and encourage the quest for knowledge. . . ."[16] Although Skeels had not referenced Binet, his thinking borrowed from Binet's observations that environmental stimulation influenced intellectual development. Further, because Binet recognized that intelligence was difficult to measure, any test performance might be only an estimate. The Iowa psychologists proceeded nonetheless because despite the risk of possibly arbitrary results, the tests were the only tool available to discriminate lower from higher mental ability. In subsequent decades, other test instruments with wider applications have been developed, but the tests remain controversial because structural differences in children's experience have been found to influence test outcomes and because, even now, no definitive definition of intelligence exists.

When the adopted children's test results suggested that heredity might not tell development's entire story, Skeels and Skodak faced a revelation and a mystery: if heredity was not determinative, what was? The two psychologists recognized that unraveling why the children's intelligence did not fit any known pattern could become the subject of a remarkable investigation, one Davenport's superintendent, Roscoe Zerwekh, had, by sheer chance, made possible. Beth Wellman, another Iowa station psychologist, later confirmed that Skeels and Skodak's results occurred only because the superintendent "followed his own unique policy of placement of children in foster homes, without any regard to the teachings of best social service practice."[17]

Skeels now recognized that "the limits within which modifiability is possible are much greater than we had . . . assumed."[18] Because Marie Skodak had tested most of the children, their unexpected outcomes became her research investigation. "The work," she said, "accumulated under [my] own hands,"[19] and she would not consider turning it over to anyone else. To complete an extended study of Davenport children adopted early in their lives into middle-class families, in 1936 Skodak entered the Iowa Child Welfare Station's PhD program, where an investigation of these adopted children's intelligence became her dissertation research topic.

———

Just as Skeels and Skodak had begun their first adoption visits, the Board of Control asked the state psychologist to take on yet another assignment— to test the intelligence of each child resident and some of the adults in Iowa's several institutions. Numbering about 5,000, many of the children had very low intelligence, but some were deaf or blind or suffered from serious medical conditions—polio, for example, or cerebral palsy or epilepsy. The board asked for the tests to help institutions plan for the residents' futures. Skeels, Skodak, and the many graduate students enrolled for advanced degrees at the Iowa station would organize and carry out the work.

This is how it came about that on the balmy first day of spring in 1935, with the temperature nearly 70°F, Harold Skeels and Marie Skodak drove along a gravel road through farmland already furrowed for planting to the site of one of those institutions, the Woodward State Hospital for Epileptics and School for the Feebleminded.

Newly opened in 1917 and set on 1,200 acres, the modern institution appeared nothing like the imposing Civil War–era Davenport Home. Rather, Woodward's low-key semi colonial architecture resembled an early twentieth-century modest resort hotel. Originally intended only as a home for persons with epilepsy, in 1921 it opened its doors to low-intelligence adults and some medically impaired child residents. As the psychologists arrived that day, off in the distance they saw Woodward's greenhouses and cattle barns, a hog house, and a hay loft, all, like the main building, constructed by laborers from a local prison.

A report from Woodward's superintendent, M. N. Voldeng, told of the school's educational mission:

> *The problem before the educational department is the necessity of bringing out potential mentality by means of concrete stimulation. The child's happiness and well-being are best served by meaningful experience. At the same time, attention is given to developing interest in the enjoyment of music, games, handicrafts, and the other subjects taught.*[20]

For approximately 300 medically and intellectually disabled child residents and for several hundred older persons with low intelligence, Woodward created a school program designed to meet their special needs. Students who might chronologically be in their 20s, but whose mental ages were under 3 years and who were called "high-grade idiots" and "younger imbeciles," attended the school's lowest-level classes. A kindergarten play group engaged those with mental ages of 3 to 6 years. More advanced "older imbeciles" were taught hand-work, music, and games and received speech training. Residents considered more advanced still, called "morons," and some children and adults who had epilepsy, received academic training in reading, writing, spelling, citizenship, and physical education.

In a vocational education program, those with epilepsy, who were often more able, learned weaving, rug making, sewing, and other fabric arts as well as woodworking and agricultural skills. Residents also participated in a choir and were taught to play musical instruments. In a 1,000-seat assembly hall the school held weekly concerts attended by the residents' families and by some of the town's 900 citizens.[21]

Because Skeels regularly tested children in the state's institutions, he knew many of Iowa's dependent children by sight. But as the psychologists began their rounds in Woodward's wards of low-intelligence women that day, they were surprised to find two "outstanding" young children, clearly favorites of the women inmates and of Woodward's staff. The girls were lively, appealing, and acted just as most toddlers do.[22] "With life in their eyes and colorful ribbons braided into their hair," the girls played happily with the ward's adult women.[23] Since there did not seem to be anything wrong with them, Marie Skodak was not quite sure why they were even there.

Inquiring, the psychologists were dumbfounded to learn that here were BD and CD, the two forlorn Davenport toddlers who whined and rocked endlessly in their cribs and who, eight months earlier, Skeels found had intelligence at the level of "imbeciles." There is no indication that after the transfer either psychologist had given the girls any thought, and neither referred to the transfer when they had arrived at Woodward. For Skeels and Skodak, the information that the little girls were the two hopeless cases sent from Davenport was unnerving.[24] How could once frail children with limited intelligence have been so transformed when their genetic histories had not changed?[25]

Amazed by their transformations, the following day Skeels and Skodak administered a version of the IQ test they had used at Davenport, but adapted to assess slightly older children. On their first tests, *added together* the girls' scores had totaled 81, barely in the low normal range of intelligence. Now they found that two children who previously had almost no ability to express or respond to language could recognize about a dozen words and had some ability to construct short sentences.[26] They could follow brief commands, such as "Bring me the shoe," draw something that looked like a circle, thread a large bead onto a string, and put a spoon into a cup and stir it. The test results revealed that CD, now 22 months old, had advanced from an IQ score of 46 to 77, a considerable increase, though still below the average for her age. BD's score, which had been 35, was now 87, nearly in the range of most 26-month-old children.

Incredulous, the two psychologists realized that in testing the girls they were also assessing themselves. Had their original evaluations been incorrect? Were the behaviors they observed at Davenport a mistaken indication of the children's true intelligence? They discarded those possibilities because each had evaluated hundreds of young children and trusted their assessment skills. They considered whether they made errors when they administered the intelligence tests or in scoring the girls' responses, but again, each was well schooled in the evaluation of young children. They asked each other whether some developmental fluctuation had occurred and whether the girls' gains might indicate a rare genetic blueprint. But BD and CD were genetically unrelated and that explanation could not have been correct.

Crucially, at Woodward the girls lived in separate wards, yet their intelligence had changed simultaneously and nearly identically. The factors responsible had to be something they shared with each other, but not with anyone else. Months earlier the psychologists expected that BD's and CD's extremely low IQs would mean they would be unable to care for themselves or manage in a wider world. Now one of the girls demonstrated close to ordinary intelligence, with the other not far behind.

With BD's IQ in the range of normal children, it would have been reasonable, and doubtless better for her, if Skeels had immediately returned her to Davenport to be adopted into a loving home so that she could experience the benefits of life in a family. Although that was his first impulse, Skeels's Iowa station research training pushed him to dig deeper.[27] He recognized that if such dramatic change had occurred in only a single child, he might have thought it represented "some accident in the earlier testing."[28] But, he said, "there were two."[29]

Two instances of such unprecedented changes increased the odds that the girls' situations were not idiosyncratic, but perhaps responses to some external factor. Thus, Skeels made the decision to keep BD at Woodward with CD in order to collect more data about an unheard-of developmental outcome, which, if seen before, had never been reported. Although Skeels and Skodak thought the girls' intelligence changes might be precarious and that soon, or eventually, they would revert to their earlier status, Skeels felt compelled to discover what had happened. Although he does not report George Stoddard's response to the girls' changed development, the Iowa director's confidence that intelligence was not fixed had to have influenced Skeels's decision to investigate. Later, Stoddard said, "It is strange that persons have ever expected IQs to remain constant or to be unrelated to . . . environmental effects." The true surprise, Stoddard thought, was that anyone was surprised.[30]

Advising no one at Woodward that he planned a formal study, for about a year Skeels observed BD and CD in the context of Woodward's ordinary activities. The 18- to 52-year-old women had mental ages from 5 to 9 years. Many, Skeels knew, had their own children and had been institutionalized to keep them from bearing any more. Some may also have been involuntarily sterilized. Yet, as a reporter later wrote, here were "two babies . . . unfit for adoption into normal society [who] had literally been adopted [and thrived in] the society of the abnormal."[31]

Skeels discovered that the women easily managed the mothering tasks of bathing, feeding, and diapering the girls. They competently taught them to walk, talk, and feed themselves and trained them in toileting. Yet, following no prescribed plan other than what they had learned in their own lives, they accomplished far more. On the wards of a state institution, the women created their own version of nearly ordinary family life, one that enfolded BD and CD in its warmth. In each case, an inmate who, Skeels said, was brighter than the others "adopted" and mothered one of the toddlers, while the other women played the roles of adoring aunts.[32]

Because the residents had the intelligence of children, the wards were stocked with dolls and dollhouses, dress-up clothes, and toys that young children enjoyed. And as the women taught and played with them, Skeels realized that although their language use was simple, they talked to the girls nonstop. "This goes here," one might say, or "Pretty chair." They also taught the girls nursery rhymes and children's songs and sang along with them. Some of the women's families sent them spending money, and they had Woodward's staff purchase dresses and hair ribbons for the girls.[33]

Placed in the center of the women's lives, the children and their caregivers spent nearly all of their time in shared activities. The women lavished affection on the toddlers; their delight in caring for them was contagious, and Skeels observed that the wards' attendants became involved in the girls' care—sometimes

> borrowing them to take them in cars and on busses to town and into stores where they bought them books that added new experiences to the ward's environment. . . . All of the waking hours of all of the people in the wards revolve[d] around the two little girls. . . . Here was a 'home' setting, rich in wholesome and interesting experiences and geared to a preschool level of development.[34]

As in any caring home, the women provided consistent, good-hearted positive attention, a factor that psychologists today understand promotes healthy development. In fact, it has been suggested that in many species, evolution has programmed young members to "expect" and respond to such care.[35] And unlike Davenport's institutional staff, the women's self-assigned "responsibilities" never overburdened them, none of their "work assignments" changed, none went on "vacation" or vanished from the children's lives because she quit her "job." Rather, during the time that they cared for the girls, the women unofficially exchanged their lives as forcibly institutionalized inmates and state dependents for those of reliable and loving nurturers.

With no hypothesis or experimental research design, and exerting no influence on how the women and the children interacted, Skeels observed that the women provided each child with a one-to-one emotional connection and stimulative experiences, especially in the use of play and language. Their constant chatter enlivened the girls' attention, their unwavering approval made the toddlers feel special, and, of course, the girls were very young when these ingredients for normal child development became embedded in their lives, exactly as in the lives of children everywhere who are raised in ordinary families.[36]

As Harold Skeels patiently watched, he never observed behaviors toward the girls other than good care and healthy encouragement. After about six months, when he next tested the girls' intelligence, he found even more growth, especially in CD, who was now 33 months. Her IQ score had risen 23 points, from 77 to 100. BD, now 36 months, had a score that had risen only 1 point, to 88. When CD was 40 months old in September, 1936, her score had declined to 95, and BD's score at 43 months had advanced to 93.

Although their intelligence scores were somewhat unstable, they had remained in the average range, and Skeels became convinced that neither girl showed signs of soon returning to her intellectual level of two years earlier. In a caring, stimulative environment, both girls had become normal. No changes like these in young children's intelligence had ever been reported in psychology.

There was no epiphany, no crystalizing moment, when Harold Skeels could explain how everyday care from the women transformed BD and CD; but as their IQ scores advanced, he began to fear that the girls intelligence would outpace the women's and they might lose what they had gained.[37] He recognized, too, that the girls' new status had radical consequences: both had become adoptable, and he made plans to return them to Davenport for that purpose. But before he did, with the knowledge of Woodward's staff, he altered the girls' records to indicate that at Woodward they had not been residents—that would have officially labeled them as "retarded" and unadoptable—but that due to Davenport's overcrowding they had lived there as "house guests."

Two years after they had left Davenport, in the fall of 1936, the girls returned. In mid-December, CD was adopted, and on Christmas Eve, 1936, BD arrived in her adoptive home. Her adoptive mother had herself been an orphan and was raised in an institution, the Home for the Friendless. As Harold Skeels observed when he first saw them at Woodward, and as their adoptive families, who did not know their histories, must have appreciated, here were two children who seemed to have a sense of security and an expectation they would be treasured and cared about.[38] They were thriving. But why?

————

Harold Skeels was not by nature an iconoclast, not an academic who pursued research that challenged prevailing ideas, nor someone who would chase opportunities to promote his own renown. If anything, he was the opposite. As a college undergraduate he wrote for a student magazine, the *Iowa Agriculturalist*, was president of the literary society, joined the Cadet Officers Association, had roles in several student productions, and took photos for the college yearbook, *The Bomb*. In his one undergraduate psychology course he did outstanding work. His conventional interests profile a student preparing for a career consistent with a rural Iowa background. Nothing predicted his joining the Iowa Child Welfare Station's psychology PhD program, and even there, Skeels remained a traditional thinker whose college training in livestock genetics informed his ideas of human development.

Yet in 1932, his station colleague Beth Wellman had found that preschool changed children's intelligence. Then, in 1935 Skeels and Skodak found unanticipated intelligence outcomes in adopted children that hinted that established ideas about intelligence might need revision. Now, in 1936, Skeels found baffling changes in BD and CD. Collectively, these results suggested a silhouette about children's intelligence that Skeels and others at the station believed should be further examined. With a radical plan for an investigation, Skeels approached the chairman of Iowa's Board of Control, Harold E. Felton. A political appointee, the owner of a grain and feed business, and the father of five, Felton later would be elected to Iowa's legislature. With no idea of what to expect, Skeels posed a strange question to the chairman. Would Felton allow Skeels to shift some young toddlers of low intelligence to live in a state home with women of low intelligence so as to "make them normal"?[39] Skeels and the chairman both knew that Davenport's conditions foreshadowed hopeless futures that included low-intelligence, mental illness, and even death.[40] But Skeels also hoped his plan would be approved because, he said later, "here was a goldmine for formal research, a situation that could not have been set up by choice."[41] Skeels held his breath as the chairman looked at him queerly. But then Felton said, "Sounds crazy, but tell me more."[42]

Skeels reviewed BD and CD's troubled birth family histories and then told of the girls' remarkable IQ gains, which, strange as it sounded, might have resulted from the women's affectionate attention. Although the chairman remained unconvinced, Davenport's overcrowding provided a strong incentive and he gave the psychologist what he came for: permission to place eleven low-intelligence children with low-intelligence women on the chance that they could become normal. Immediately, Skeels began to search Davenport's records for children who might enter his peculiar experiment.

PART II

Backlash

Chapter Six

A REVELATION
AND A MYSTERY

During the fall of 1936, Harold Skeels identified eleven Davenport residents who were between 1 and 2 years old, had no birth defects that might impair their development, and whose low intelligence made them unadoptable. Some had average or superior IQ test scores when they entered the orphanage but now were below average. Others arrived with lower than average development and had declined further. In mid-October, Skeels began to transfer them, two and three at a time, from the Davenport Home, which hugged the Mississippi's shore, 300 miles west to the Institution for Feeble-Minded Children, in Glenwood, on Iowa's border with Nebraska. He had no idea what lay ahead.

Typically, residents at the Glenwood Home had been born into ordinary Iowa families. When it became clear that they had limited intelligence, their parents were advised that life would be "better . . . for the rest of the family if this child [were] cared for someplace else."[1] Many agreed and placed their children at Glenwood, where they usually remained for the rest of their lives. But unlike the Davenport Home, Glenwood was led by a physician, Harold Dye, someone experienced in the care of those with low intelligence. Dye oversaw a program described as a "veritable beehive of activities,"[2] with school classes geared to residents' abilities; daily religious services; trips to local attractions; dances; and even movie showings. Skeels and Dye had worked together years earlier when Skeels had tested the intelligence of some Glenwood residents, so it was natural for them to collaborate on the Davenport children's entry into Glenwood's adult wards.

Set on a hill overlooking the Missouri River valley, in clear weather Glenwood's turreted administration building, resembling a minor castle, could be seen from miles away. On its carefully landscaped thousand-acre campus, the institution was a self-contained village that included a hospital, fire station, several playgrounds, a chapel, and a 160-acre farm where some residents worked. Others cared for the grounds and cultivated its apple orchards and gardens.[3] Glenwood housed more than twice as many residents as the Woodward Home, in all about 1,800, including 623 children.

Unlike Woodward, where only two wards housed women with mental ages from 5 to 9 years, Glenwood had seven wards that were home to women whose mental ages ranged from 5 to 12 years, making it suitable for the number of Davenport children Skeels would transfer. As the children arrived, staff members, along with low-intelligence women whom the courts had ruled were too intellectually limited to live freely, marry, and have their own children, helped settle them into their new home. Although the women's chronological ages ranged from 16 to 52, everyone referred to them as "girls." Residents with mental ages from 5 to 8 years comprised the lowest-level wards; women whose mental ages were from 7 to 10 years lived in the next level. The highest-functioning women, with mental ages between 9 and 12 years, lived together in two wards. There is no evidence that Skeels sought to have children placed with women of certain mental age groups; in fact, he wrote that the placements were "largely a matter of chance."[4]

Several times during their Glenwood stays, Skeels tested each child's intelligence and found some relation between their progress and the intelligence of the women with whom they lived. While he suspected that placements with brighter women, or with women who were more caring, might promote higher intelligence, he held that information back, perhaps because his Glenwood investigation included many other variables. For example, at

Woodward BD and CD experienced almost pseudo-adoptions, but at Glenwood a few Davenport children did not become the special charge of one woman, nor receive added attention from a staff member. Instead, they became "everyone's" boy or girl.

————

Had Harold Skeels's contemporaries known of his Glenwood experiment, they would not have taken it seriously. Almost no mental test psychologists doubted the principle that IQs were constant, that children's intelligence remained stable from birth to adulthood. However, at the time of Skeels's experiment, there were at least three significant problems with existing investigations of constancy. First, psychology's leaders denied that intelligence in young children could change, and therefore studies of that theory were considered a waste of resources and were seldom done. Second, almost no investigators tested whether IQ constancy held when the subjects' environments were altered.[5] And third, most psychologists neglected biology's evidence that environment influenced development.[6] Hence, studies that appeared to confirm constancy might only reflect the stability of the child's environment. Skeels recognized that BD's and CD's shift from Davenport to Woodward defied the constancy interpretation. If he were right, his findings could profoundly call into question psychology's understanding of intelligence. The outcomes in the children he transferred to Glenwood could be pivotal to discovering new knowledge about this process.

Lewis Terman, recognized as the leader of mental test psychology, rejected out of hand the study of children younger than 4 years and scorned suggestions that early stimulation influenced later outcomes. Terman never addressed his reasons for this position, and psychologists who differed may have chosen to avoid an argument with someone known for sarcastic, even vitriolic attacks on those who disagreed with his ideas.[7] However, in 1922, public intellectual Walter Lippmann suggested in the *New Republic* that "the earlier the [environmental] influence the more potent," and that "the effects of superior and inferior environments persist," and he stressed that Terman had conjectured about a period of child development that neither he nor anyone else had studied.[8]

.

In reply, Terman sneered,

> And just to think that we have been allowing all sorts of myste-
> rious, uncontrolled, chance influences in the nursery to mould
> [sic] children's IQ's this way and that. . . . It is high time that
> we were investigating the IQ effects of different kinds of baby-
> talk, different versions of Mother Goose.[9]

Although Terman had little interest in the study of young orphanage children, he was quite interested in promoting the use of intelligence tests, and in
1918 he studied 68 children in a California orphanage, the Home of Benevo-
lence, research with no defined hypothesis. Here he asserted, "Several clinical
studies which have been made of children in orphanages, have revealed a large
amount of mental inferiority and even of feeble-mindedness." His remarks are
of special interest because he provided no references and 74 percent of the
children who entered the home were there because of a parent's death.

Curiously, Terman tacitly recognized the possible role of environment
when he suggested that a good orphanage should stabilize or raise its residents' intelligence because "the well conducted orphanage offers a cultural
environment as good as that of the middle grade home, if not better."[10] Terman's study found that the median intelligence for the 68 children was 92.3.
Presuming their good intelligence was hereditary, he did not examine intelligence shifts experienced by the children during their orphanage stays. His
paper stated no conclusions, but its interest lies in his suggestion that a control
group could be used in future studies, one of the first occasions in psychology
that a control group was proposed.[11] It is also worth noting that although Terman claimed in this research that environment *was* a variable, he concluded
that there was "no support to the environment hypothesis."[12]

During the 1920s, the decade before Harold Skeels and Marie Skodak
started their work at Davenport, intelligence tests had begun to reshape
American's ideas about the evaluation of children's ability. Where parents,
teachers, and psychologists previously trusted subjective estimates, most now
believed that IQ test instruments yielded reliable, scientific appraisals, and
nearly all of the nation's schools used them to evaluate students. That shift

from impressionistic assessment to mental test results could not help but unite the fields of education and psychology.

Terman published his IQ test in 1916 and in 1921 leading educators, educational psychologists, and mental test psychologists gathered to discuss the test at the decadal meeting of the National Society for the Study of Education (NSSE). The NSSE investigated many aspects of education and the psychology of learning and for each meeting published and presented for discussion a *Yearbook* collection of the latest research in the area under discussion.

Along with many positive reviews of mental tests, the IQ test critiques of several psychologists took a more critical position. For example, Edward L. Thorndike, of Columbia University, advised that "only the baser parts of education can be counted and weighed, that the finer consequences for the spirit of man will be lost in proportion as we try to measure them."[13] Stephen S. Colvin, of Brown University, suggested that "the testing movement might grow out of all bounds; that it may be misunderstood . . . and [be] even harmfully applied in practice." He suggested those with "the greatest potential . . . will never become highly intelligent in an environment that affords scant opportunity to learn."[14] And a harsh warning came from another Columbia scholar, Marion Trabue. "The tests at present . . . are so inadequate and crude," Trabue said, "that one who uses a single test score as the sole basis for a vital decision . . . is guilty of . . . unscientific practice and possibly of a great injury to the child."[15]

Those 1921 reports became a prelude to a 1922 skirmish when Columbia University psychologist William Bagley attacked Lewis Terman's declaration that intelligence tests revealed ability that was hereditary and fixed from birth. "No theory in the whole history of science," Bagley wrote, "has been based on . . . assumptions so questionable."[16] Bagley then challenged Terman's nativist bias that low intelligence was "very common among Spanish-Indian and Mexican families . . . and also among negroes."[17] He also charged that Terman's suggestion that schools provide "new types of secondary education which would be better suited to inferior intellects"[18] subverted democracy.

Terman's riposte accused Bagley of preferring "to believe in 'miracles' rather than search for the order . . . which would make prediction [of intelligence] possible." Terman then asked, "Does Dr. Bagley really believe that native differences in intellectual endowment are mythical? . . . [If so] his vision is blurred by moist tears of sentiment."[19] In a response to Terman, Bagley asserted that his criticism was "mild . . . compared with . . . appalling fallacies [of mental tests] pointed out by recognized authorities."[20]

Following Bagley's criticism, investigations about possible environmental influences in the intelligence of young children modestly increased, with one of the most salient from Helen Thompson Woolley at the University of Chicago. In 1925, Woolley compared the IQ scores of children admitted to nursery school with a matched group of children on a waiting list and found that those who attended the program made significant gains. She noted, "Young children seem to be more rapidly and spectacularly affected by changes of environment than . . . older children."[21] But Woolley's later work did not include studies of very young children, and for health reasons she left the field prematurely.

By 1927, preparations were underway for the 1928 NSSE review of mental tests (the scheduled meetings were only roughly decadal), and Lewis Terman, selected to plan and chair the meeting, chose as its theme "Nature and Nurture." As chair, he would also edit the meeting's *Yearbook*. Although his NSSE leadership role required that he balance invitations and *Yearbook* articles representing all viewpoints, the *Yearbook* was slanted toward the hereditarian view, with four of thirty-eight articles, about 10 percent, from a single scholar, Terman's prize graduate student Barbara Burks. No other psychologist on either side contributed more than one.

The contentiousness of the 1921 debate led psychologists to anticipate that this meeting would be a call to arms. But concerned that his past responses to critics might work against him, Terman preemptively advised all invitees, "We should avoid everything that would savor of appeal to emotional bias. In making this suggestion I am not unconscious of the fact that I myself have 'sinned' in this respect."[22] Nevertheless, two outstanding psychologists rebuffed Terman's invitations. The first, William Bagley, was no surprise. Bagley advised Terman to invite someone "who has not made the question so much of a personal issue."[23] Pressured by a Terman ally, Bagley agreed to attend but he would present no research.

The second refusal came from one of Terman's own, Carl C. Brigham, of Princeton University. Following World War I, Brigham and his colleague, Robert M. Yerkes, had analyzed IQ test data collected from army recruits. Along with Terman, Brigham and Yerkes were members of the American Eugenics Society (AES), the largest and best-funded eugenics organization in the nation.[24] In the foreword to Brigham's army report, *A Study of American Intelligence*, Yerkes advised that "none of us . . . can afford to ignore the menace of race deterioration or the evident relations of immigration to national progress and welfare."[25]

Brigham's study asserted that the gradient of recruits' intellectual superiority to inferiority measured by their test scores tracked with their national backgrounds and "race." His conclusions fell into the envelope of nearly identical "facts" published in 1917 by his mentor, eugenicist Madison Grant.[26] Heredity, Brigham wrote, explained why the highest intelligence scores were found in recruits from Nordic backgrounds. He claimed that the lowest scores were from eastern and southern European recruits, followed by African Americans.[27] But Brigham went even further when he claimed to have calculated "the proportion of Nordic, Alpine and Mediterranean blood in immigrants from each of the European countries."[28] Brigham also found that immigrant recruits who had lived in the United States for over sixteen years had test results "almost as high as native born" recruits, but reasoned, "we are measuring *native or inborn intelligence* and any increase . . . due to any other factor may be regarded as an error."[29]

Yet Brigham declined Terman's invitation to join an NSSE panel on nature and nurture, sending a telegram that said he "positively cannot undertake criticism." In an explanatory letter, he wrote, "My own opinions on the subject have undergone radical alterations and I have not yet reached any solution which is satisfactory."[30] By 1929, Brigham told eugenicist Charles Davenport, "The more I work in this field the more I am convinced that psychologists have sinned greatly in sliding easily from the name of the test to the . . . trait measured."[31] Then, in an astonishing 1930 paper, *The Intelligence of Immigrant Groups*, Brigham recanted his 1923 findings about national and racial groups and in a self-scorching confession said, "One of the most pretentious of these comparative racial studies—the writer's own—was without foundation."[32]

What led Brigham, who earlier assured Yerkes, "I am not afraid to say anything that is true, no matter how ugly the facts,"[33] to fundamentally revise his view of what the facts of hereditary intelligence actually were? Brigham's reconsideration reflected his recent discovery that the Mendelian argument that human traits were inherited as single units was insufficient to explain behavioral outcomes. According to eugenics scholar Garland Allen, of Washington University in St. Louis, during the 1920s American geneticists— Thomas Hunt Morgan and Herbert S. Jennings were two—"had advanced arguments against the scientific credibility of eugenics."[34] Then, in 1927, biologist Raymond Pearl, of Johns Hopkins University, once a fervent adherent, also disavowed eugenics, portraying it as "a mingled mess of ill-grounded and uncritical sociology, economics, anthropology and politics, full of emotional appeals to class and race prejudices, solemnly put forth as science, and unfortunately accepted as such by the general public."[35] Brigham paid attention to these defections, and they moved him.

In that dynamic context, Brigham told Terman that recent discoveries— he labeled them "very much more important than any investigation included in the *Yearbook*"[36]—suggested that the army intelligence test erred in presuming that intelligence was a unitary inherited function. Here he referenced the recently published work of Truman L. Kelley, of Stanford University, later of Harvard, who posited that verbal, quantitative, and spatial abilities were probably separate from one another,[37] that mental ability was not a single characteristic but an assembly of skills. Brigham also recognized that accurate test results had to compare "only individuals having equal opportunities" to acquire the language used on the test.[38] By 1934, his analysis had turned even more damning: "The [mental] test movement . . . accompanied one of the most glorious fallacies in the history of science . . . that the tests measured native intelligence without regard to training or schooling. I hope nobody believes that now. . . . The 'native intelligence' hypothesis is dead."[39] Brigham did not reject ability testing per se. His was a moral argument—he opposed the tests because he recognized their potential to injure individuals who had not had the opportunity to learn the information or skills being tested.

While 1920s geneticists and biologists had abandoned eugenics en masse, unlike Brigham, few mental test psychologists followed, and into the late 1930s desertions from the Terman camp were rare. Later, Brigham assumed a leadership position at the College Board, where he advanced another test, "a metamorphosis from the Army . . . test," the Scholastic Aptitude Test.[40]

———

Although Lewis Terman weighted the NSSE 1928 *Yearbook* to favor hereditarian views—it came to be known as the Terman *Yearbook*—he also included challenges to that dogma. For example, Barbara Burks's fair-minded analysis of every research paper in the area of nature versus nurture from the 1869 work of Sir Francis Galton to papers published in 1927—a total of 279—was often skeptical of data that supported claims of an association between intelligence and heredity. Burks also criticized the findings of her mentor, Lewis Terman, whose 1918 paper showed that environment had negligible influence on orphanage children.[41]

Following the 1928 NSSE meeting, two new reports suggested that environment counted. The first, a modest 1930 examination of young orphanage children, came from Helen E. Barrett and Helen L. Koch, at the University of Chicago, and showed that the mean intelligence score for children who attended nursery school rose significantly compared with a matched group that was not in school: after six to nine months, the mean IQ score of the schooled children rose from 91.71 to 112.57. The mean IQ of children in the control group rose from 92.59 to 97.71.[42]

Subsequently, in 1932, Mandel Sherman, a psychologist at the University of Chicago, and Cora B. Key, from the Washington Child Research Center, published an ambitious field investigation of a deprived population. In *The Intelligence of Isolated Mountain Children*, the researchers compared residents of four Blue Ridge Mountain hollows, each separated from the next by a high mountain ridge. The hollows' populations descended from immigrants who, as newer immigrants arrived, moved deeper and deeper into the mountains.[43] Nearly all of the hollows' adults, including the parents of the study's subjects, were illiterate, and almost none were employed.

Sherman and Key identified factors that influenced the children's intelligence test scores: the distance of their hollows from the main road; the amount of time they spent in school; and, notably, the ages when they were tested. They found significantly lower IQ scores in older children, suggesting that the longer children lived in deprived environments, the greater their losses. As a contrast, the authors studied a nearby town located on a paved road that had a developed economy, better schools, and significantly higher school attendance. The town's children had average intelligence test scores, while the hollows' children's mean intelligence scores were well below average.[44]

While these reports had not yet come to the attention of the public, they were well known at the Iowa station and provided intellectual context and research support for what the Iowans had begun to suspect: deprived environments and limited education impeded the development of children's intelligence. Then, in 1933, Frank N. Freeman, also at the University of Chicago, directly challenged the core claim of IQ tests, that intelligence was constant and did not change. In the proceedings of an important child development conference, Freeman wrote that the concept of unmodifiable IQ had little science behind it and had arisen from "hasty and uncritical interpretations" of intelligence tests and from psychology's "uncritical" acceptance of Mendelian development.[45]

While the several 1930s accounts that supported the role of environment came from researchers at Chicago, those psychologists were not members of a cohesive enterprise sharing an intellectual quest. By contrast, under Stoddard's leadership and with financial resources provided by the Spellman grants, the Iowa station's psychologists—Baldwin, Stoddard, Skeels, Wellman, and, after 1936, Skodak—developed an integrated vision that made the decade from 1928 to 1939 a critical investigatory period during which they pursued clues no matter how unreasonable they seemed at the time.[46]

This highly productive phase of the station's work had begun in 1928 with Bird Baldwin's report that outcomes of children's educational experiences varied, depending on school environments. Then followed Wellman's 1932 discovery that preschool children's intelligence test scores advanced with the amount of time spent in school, a report that challenged traditional beliefs among educators and the public. In 1934, Wellman published follow-up studies of her nursery school research. That same year she and Stoddard published their monograph *Child Psychology*, in which they wrote, "Perhaps there are few environments for younger children . . . as stimulating . . . as a modern nursery school." At the time that concept had little to support it, but it would not be long before Skeels's Woodward and Glenwood studies would drive those nascent ideas further.

————

The Davenport orphans—three boys and eight girls—who arrived at Glenwood during the fall of 1936 entered a shining world that replaced Davenport's bleak, unstimulating wards and overwhelmed inattentive matrons with sociable inmates, attendants, and staff delighted to have them. Each day they awoke to new experiences—ordinary in the lives of children raised in families, but unknown to these children. They learned how to use play materials like paint, crayons, and glue. They sang nursery rhymes, listened to stories, played games, tossed balls, ran races. And importantly, with the women's help they became toilet trained.

Children who owned no personal belongings, who had been dressed in threadbare institutional clothing overdue for washing, received colorful outfits made just for them by ward residents—and also received clothing warm enough for outdoor play during Iowa's harsh winters. The women also used their small allowances to purchase gifts of toys and picture books for the children. Each morning the women and children sang in chapel. As soon as the very youngest of the transferred children could walk, they began preschool, and those who were older attended the more formal kindergarten. Their new lives included excursions to parks and other sites, learning to dance at school dances, and with rapt attention following the twists and turns of movie plots.

For indoor play the residence had a spacious living room, and its outdoor areas had slides, sandboxes, and swings, equipment so foreign that it might have been dropped directly from outer space. The Glenwood matron responsible for planning activities singled out individual children for private hours alone with her, the first occasions in their lives when they had the complete attention of a caring adult. Further, interactions with teachers, matrons, staff, and adult inmates brought language stimulation and social development through "invitations" for reciprocal conversations and emotional responsiveness. All of these adults took pleasure in the children's accomplishments, and the women competed to show them off. They became stars in the women's lives and in their own.[47]

But who were these children exposed to this treasury of experience? Each child Skeels transferred had a history of severe early neglect, abuse, and deprivation that for many seemed even more extreme than the experiences of BD and CD. Skeels wondered whether Glenwood's environment could possibly replicate the intelligence changes that the Woodward experience had provided for the two girls. Would the intelligence of even one child revive? If the children thrived, how much gain would be possible? What timing of new experiences might be optimal? If a child's intelligence increased, would it remain stable in the future? Would the differences between Glenwood's wards and Woodward's influence outcomes? And, Skeels wondered, what if nothing changed?

One of the first children transferred, case 7, began life with virtually everything against her. Illegitimate, she was born to a 22-year-old mother who reported that she had completed eighth grade, and who had syphilis and gonorrhea. Despite being two months premature, case 7 had received no incubator care.[48] When she was admitted to Davenport at 9 months, she had no teeth due to nutritional deprivation; she suffered from an acute ear infection and other health concerns and could not sit up or achieve expected infant milestones. Worse still, like BD's and CD's initial assessments, her 32 IQ was at the "imbecile" level. By the time she was transferred to Glenwood at 18 months, her intelligence score was 65 but her development matched that of a 10-month-old baby.[49]

At Glenwood, case 7 lived with women who had the highest mental ages, between 9 and 12 years. Because of her frailty, a ward attendant took individual care of her, especially at night, and the women residents lavished attention on her. Three months after she arrived, she began kindergarten, quickly moving from half to full day. Four months later her teacher reported, "She is alert, independent, amusing. Tries almost all of the group activities." In three more months, case 7's IQ score tested at 104, the middle of the normal range. During one year at Glenwood, when illnesses and hospitalizations of institutional children were commonplace, case 7 remained robustly healthy. The next month, when she was 2½, she was adopted. From October 1936, when Skeels began his study, to October 1937, when case 7 arrived to live with her new family, her IQ had risen 39 points. At the study's conclusion, three years later, case 7's intelligence was 115, in the superior range.

Another child, case 4, was illegitimate and may have been born prematurely (hospital records are unclear). Her 19-year-old mother, who had an IQ score of 55, lived in a small home with her parents and her nine siblings. The identity of the baby's father was not known. Admitted to Davenport at 3 weeks, case 4 had symptoms of syphilis and was briefly hospitalized, but based on milestone evaluation, aside from health concerns she appeared to be a normal infant. After she had lived at Davenport for a little over a year, her IQ score tested at 73, below the average range. When case 4 was 15 months old, Skeels transferred her to Glenwood, where she lived with women who had high mental ages. At first she could only tolerate the half-day kindergarten program, but gradually she gained stamina, and her teacher wrote, "A very promising child. Seems to have average intelligence for her age. Takes simple directions, enters into practically all games and rhythms and tries whether she can do them or not. Good disposition." At about 2 years of age, when her IQ test score was 100, case 4 was adopted. Over the course of Skeels's study, her IQ test score had risen 27 points. Her adoptive mother had also been adopted and perhaps had special insight into her daughter's needs. Skeels tested the child's intelligence again when she was about 4½. It was 116, in the superior range.[50]

Yet another child, case 9, was one of two children in the experimental group who did not achieve average-range intelligence. Skeels recorded the sad early life of an infant brought to the emergency room after sucking on the torn nipple of a baby bottle that her parents had mended with tire cement. Both alcoholics, the parents were imprisoned for neglect. At the hospital their baby required treatment for syphilis, and when she was well, Davenport admitted her. At 8 months, her IQ score was 61, in the range of morons. At 10 months, she did not speak, but had begun to stand alone. At 1 year, Skeels moved her to Glenwood, where she lived on a ward with the brightest women. Although one woman took a special interest in her, Skeels reported that she did not receive the individualized care enjoyed by some of the other children.

When case 9 was almost 3 years old, she began to put two-word sentences together, something children of average intelligence do at age 2 or earlier. She attended half-day kindergarten and her IQ test score rose to 80, in the low average range. But unlike most of the experimental group children, at that point this child's progress halted. Because Skeels's study ended, case 9 had to be returned to Davenport, where she received almost no attention or stimulation and her IQ score began to decline.

When she was 5 years old, problems with case 9's vision became obvious, and with proper ophthalmic testing, the first such examination in her record, it was discovered that she was blind in her right eye and had only moderate vision in her left. Lenses did not correct this. At age 6, with an IQ score of 71, she remained in preschool. A few months later her IQ had fallen to 63, then 61. Skeels suspected that the syphilis she had contracted from her mother during her birth had not been adequately treated and might have progressed. It is also possible that the tire cement chemicals caused neurological damage that impaired her intellectual development. Despite her visual limitations, at one point case 9 experienced a 19-point IQ test score increase. Nonetheless, Skeels returned her to Glenwood as a long-term resident.[51]

Case 10 in Skeels's study experienced more IQ test score instability than any other of Skeels's subjects. When he arrived at Davenport at 8 months of age, he seemed a normal baby but by age 2 his IQ score was 72. Skeels then moved him to Glenwood, where during his first two years he lived with the lowest-functioning women. Skeels reported that he wasn't a child whom adults found engaging and no one took much interest in him. But when case 10 was about 2½ and began kindergarten, his IQ quickly rose 16 points to 88, in the low-average range. When he was 3 years old, his teacher described him as a "sweet looking child with a somewhat different disposition. Affectionate." About then, case 10 was transferred to a ward with the brightest women, one of whom showed great interest in him, and where an attendant also provided much attention. His teacher reported, "He has many more friends," and an "improving disposition, likes to be the leader, but likes to show off. Affectionate."

Early in his childhood, case 10 had suffered repeated ear infections and at age 4, after a brief hospitalization for treatment, his IQ score declined to 79. At this point the study ended and case 10 was returned to Davenport, where he entered its new, highly stimulative preschool program, part of another Skeels investigation. When his IQ was tested five months later, it had jumped to 96, a solidly average score. When he turned 5 he was adopted, but for unspecified reasons, two months later he was returned to Davenport. Two weeks after that another family adopted him, and this adoption succeeded. When this boy was about 6 years old, Skeels again tested his intelligence, and now found his IQ was 92. Although during his Glenwood stay case 10's IQ had gained 7 points, during his post-Glenwood period his score advanced 13 points.[52]

Almost all of Skeels's Glenwood children had entered Davenport during infancy. One child, however, had a significantly different chronology. Case 13, whose mother Skeels described as feebleminded and psychotic, and whose father was employed, entered Davenport at just over 2 years of age. She weighed under 18 pounds and could not sit or stand. Her medical examination revealed "arrested" hydrocephalus (an accumulation of fluid in the skull) that may have been responsible for her inadequate physical and mental development. After three months she learned to hold her own baby bottle, but Skeels described her as "just another hopeless case."

Because of this child's multiple developmental and medical issues, Skeels did not at first transfer her to Glenwood's experimental group, but when she reached about 3 years, had an IQ of 36, remained too weak to walk, and was not toilet trained, he decided to place her in Glenwood's hospital ward. After 6 months she could walk and became toilet trained, and Skeels moved her to a ward with the lowest-level women. There, a staff member took a special interest in her, taking her on short trips and visits to town. After about a year, her IQ tested at 70. By age 6 it reached 74, and at age 7 it rose to 81, just into the normal range. Skeels then transferred case 13 back to Davenport, and she was adopted. During four years at Glenwood, her IQ had advanced 45 points. After the study, when case 13 had turned 10, Skeels tested her again and found that her IQ score had now reached 94.[53]

———

Among the Davenport children moved to Glenwood was case 11, Viola Hoffman's son, Wendell. When he entered Davenport at 1 year of age, Wendell had normal intelligence; but by the time he turned 2, his intelligence test score had declined to 75, and Skeels included him in the group placed at Glenwood. There, Wendell lived on a ward with the lowest-functioning women—their mental ages were from 5 to 8 years. Although he remained on that ward for eighteen months and began kindergarten, no one woman took a special interest in him. Still, the kindergarten teacher found him "the most promising of the children from Davenport . . . says many words, dislikes being scolded and is repentant." Yet after more than a year, Wendell's intelligence score, now 78, had barely moved. Perhaps for this reason, officials transferred Wendell to a ward where he lived with women whose mental ages were higher, from 7 to 10 years. Here everyone made a fuss over him, and a woman named Mary "adopted" him. Wendell bonded with her, and as an adult he still remembered her "colorful dresses different from Davenport's drabness, her long red hair and that she loved to sing."[54] (Because as an adult Wendell spoke publicly about his life, the author was able to interview him.)

Wendell's Glenwood teacher found him "alert," reporting that he "thoroughly enjoys [the] entire school program." After about eight more months, Wendell's intelligence rose further, to 82. Although his IQ test score rose modestly, Wendell's teacher tells of his profound awakening: "Remarkable development in energy, stability, and personality . . . has a very good memory and enjoys stories, converses freely and asks intelligent questions. Prognosis appears more promising for the first time." She noted as well, "Wendell was changed to a ward of brighter girls."[55]

Around the time that Wendell turned 4, his stay at Glenwood became even livelier when in the evenings he left his ward to explore the grand institution's back rooms. He reminisced:

> There was a lot to explore, and no one interfered with my meandering. I met a misshapen child—they called him 'Monster'—he hadn't come from the Davenport Home. His face was distorted and he was ugly, but he wasn't stupid. He knew his way through hallways and into rooms where no one ever went. Together we explored the place. And there was a boy who couldn't talk, they called him 'Grunt.' The staff thought he was deaf, but he wasn't. I met him one night coming through a broken wall. Somehow, we could communicate.[56]

(Although Skeels did not describe this phenomenon, institutional staff throughout America regularly bestowed offensive nicknames on institutionalized children.[57])

As Wendell continued his evening rambles, he met another, much older resident, Mayo Buckner. Buckner had lived at Glenwood since 1898, when his mother dropped him off, telling the director that her 8-year-old son—who, she said, "could sing before he could talk," and on key—had many odd mannerisms. She also said that he had a fine memory. Her family doctor agreed that Mayo needed special care, but at the time IQ tests were unknown in the United States and admissions decisions were made "by the eye." When admitted to Glenwood, Mayo was assessed as "a medium-grade imbecile."[58]

Buckner probably benefited from lessons in instrumentation provided by Glenwood's music program. Eventually, he taught himself to score music for a twenty-five-piece orchestra and participated in the town of Glenwood's community music events. In the 1950s, a new superintendent tested Buckner's IQ and found that although he had been raised in the limited environment of an institution, his intelligence test score was 120, in the very superior range. It's fair to wonder what Buckner's life might have been if he had grown up in an understanding family and received musical training. Asked as an adult how he saw himself, Buckner replied, "I always thought I was normal."[59] In his 60s Buckner was given the opportunity to leave Glenwood, but, aware that he lacked the skills to build an independent life, he chose to remain.

Wendell attempted to play music with Buckner, by then a sweet-natured man of 47, who, farmer style, dressed in bib overalls and played the violin, flute, and six other instruments by ear. Pretending to hold a stick, Wendell would move his fingers up and down as he saw Buckner do. "I thought he was playing a narrow tree branch," Wendell remembered, "and asked him to teach me how to make music come out of one of those."[60]

On evenings when Wendell heard the whistle of a railroad train, he ran to a window or sat outside on a favorite tree stump to catch sight of the cars as they passed close by. "Maybe it was going to Omaha, or Chicago," he remembered, "and in beautiful dining cars, with white linen on the tables, I saw families eating together on their way somewhere." Wistfully he recalled, "I wished that I were sitting there in one of those golden-lit cars."[61]

In 1939, when Wendell was about 4½ years old, he was adopted by Gen-evieve and Louis Branca, who knew little of his early history, his previously low-ered IQ, or his remarkable recovery in Skeels's study. Now named Louis after his adoptive father, the Brancas settled their son into their comfortable St. Paul home. But although Louis had received better care at Glenwood than at Dav-enport, the effects of institutional life lingered, and he hoarded food, toys, and personal possessions, a sign he later interpreted as a lack of trust: "I was very quiet and independent. I knew there were different kinds of orphans . . . [and that some] were . . . [like me] motherless and abandoned."[62] Leaving an institu-tion to live in a real home reminded Louis of the children's story that tells of a jaguar released from a cage, who first scans his environment trying to grasp that it is free. "When I let an insight like that in," he said, "it goes right to the bone."[63]

That fall Louis began parochial school, and the Brancas hired a tutor to catch him up to the academic levels and behaviors of most middle-class chil-dren his age. The next year, when he turned 6, he and his parents traveled to Davenport so that Skeels could test his intelligence to certify his adoption. Louis feared that if he didn't do well he would be returned to Davenport, but in fact, his score had risen to 92, in the range of most children. During the course of Skeels's study, Louis's IQ score rose 7 points. Following the study, it rose 10 points more. Louis and another child whose test scores also rose 7 points made the smallest gains of the thirteen children. However, Louis's relatively small score changes belie the blossoming of his imaginative alertness and rich interior life, possibly unleashed because of Glenwood's environmen-tal stimulation. As Skeels had hoped, the Glenwood experience had trans-formed the lives of Louis and most of the other children in his experiment. These results also call attention to a long-standing question: just what does an IQ test measure? How may individuals' intelligence be affected by circum-stance, relationships, exposure to stimulation, and, as in Louis's case, to the opportunity to make use of one's gifts?

———

As Harold Skeels concluded his Glenwood study, in Davenport's records he identified a statistical group—he called this his contrast group—twelve once normally intelligent children, four girls and eight boys, close in age to the children in the Glenwood experimental group, who had either continued to live as usual at Davenport or, because of severe intelligence declines, had been committed to Glenwood as permanent residents. The children in both the experimental and contrast groups had received periodic IQ tests. Most of the contrast group children entered Davenport with normal IQ scores and should have been adopted. They were not placed due to improper state procedures, especially poor family histories, or suspicion of untreated syphilis.

To the extent possible, Skeels matched the contrast children's histories with those of his experimental group. Each group contained eight children who had normal births, while three experimental children were born prematurely and one contrast child was premature. In the experimental group, one child appeared to have been cured of syphilis. In the contrast group, there were two who appeared cured. From Skeels's records, here are some of the contrast children's histories.

Case 15, an illegitimate girl, arrived at Davenport when she was 4 days old. Her mother was a psychiatric hospital resident with an IQ of 62. Her father had spent time in jail for forgery. When case 15 was a little over a year, her intelligence tested at 92. However, after she had lived at Davenport for an additional seven months, her IQ test score had fallen to 54 and she had to be committed to Glenwood as a permanent resident. Repeated IQ tests showed that her intelligence continued in that range, and at age 17 Glenwood ordered her sterilization.[64]

Case 17, a boy whose mother had an IQ of 47, arrived at Davenport when he was 10 days old. On his first IQ test, at 9 months, his score was 105. Five months later it was 96. Two years after that, it had fallen to 58, and when he was 4 years old, Skeels committed him to Woodward's ward for low-intelligence children. It was noted that he was very small for his age, that when excited he stuttered badly, and although he wore glasses, he still had visual difficulties. Although case 17's IQ scores remained in the retarded range, when he was about 16 another type of intelligence test, the Wechsler Adult Intelligence Scale, became available.

Until Wechsler's test, intelligence had been assessed largely through a child's verbal abilities. Wechsler transformed mental testing by adding a measurement of *nonverbal* intelligence, identified as "performance." Performance abilities are revealed in the context of actions and through spatial intelligence, that is, visualizing and manipulating objects in space. Children and adults with limited expressive and/or receptive language may have good and sometimes superior ability on nonverbal tasks, known as nonverbal abstract reasoning. For example, Wechsler's performance test asks subjects to arrange a series of pictures into a logical story; arrange blocks to match visual patterns; and to discover important details missing from pictures. Although case 17's Wechsler verbal score was 46, his performance score was 74. With support from a vocational agency, he left Woodward for a work placement in which he could use his relative nonverbal strengths.[65]

Skeels's report of case 20, a 3-month-old baby given by his biological parents to a passing Syrian-American peddler, reveals ethnic bias that altered the boy's life. Those parents, a mother crippled by polio who had an IQ score of 36 and a father known in the community as feebleminded, believed that their solution relieved them of the burden of caring for their infant. The peddler, a US citizen who had fought in World War I, and his wife, had lost two babies prematurely and delightedly accepted the child. For about six months case 20 lived with his new family while the couple made heroic efforts, supported by the American Legion and local residents, to legally adopt him. The Davenport superintendent reported, however, that local social service agencies objected to the couple's adoption of a "fair skinned, white haired, 'whitsh' boy." He added, "It was because it was alleged that they were of Mohammed religion. [The father] declares that he . . . became an American citizen and that he attends the Lutheran Church."[66]

To dissuade the peddler from the adoption, authorities told him that the boy's family had a history of insanity and feeblemindedness. But the peddler said they loved him and that "only God knew what he would grow to be." The superintendent continued, "There can be no doubt of the love and affection the couple show toward this baby . . . and the little thing did seem to respond to them. There is a beautiful mother love there . . . and the man seemed equally as affected. . . . The whole objection seems to be because of their racial and religious tendencies."[67]

Rejecting the couple's pleas, the state did not approve the adoption and kept the boy at Davenport, where his once normal intelligence declined from a high of 91 to 71. When he was 16, he ran away to search for his birth mother,

only to discover that she had died months earlier. Once out of the institution, however, he committed some petty crimes. In returning him to Iowa, a
probation officer wrote of the importance of being kind to him because "he
has been so deprived affectionally all of his lifetime and . . . he has wanted so
much, and been without a home so long, it will be a little difficult for him."[68]

Another contrast child, case 19, represented to Skeels the proof of principle that his ideas about environment's influence were correct.[69] The illegitimate son of a divorced mother, case 19 entered Davenport as a healthy,
normal, 9-day-old. Like many Davenport children, he then suffered recurrent
otitis media, a middle ear infection that, in a time before antibiotics, resisted
treatment. When case 19 was a year old, he was adopted but returned for
health reasons. At 15 months, his IQ test scored at 87. Seven months later, it
had declined to 80. His otitis became chronic, and when he was 2 years old,
he had an operation for mastoiditis. Following the surgery, a visiting pediatrician tested the boy and found a slight hearing loss. Because of his diagnosis,
case 19 received more attention from teachers and staff than did other children,[70] but over four years his intelligence declined from 87 to 67, a dramatic
change, but comparable to the losses of about half the contrast children. At
age 5, he entered Davenport's kindergarten, where Helen Dawe, an Iowa station graduate student studying early language development, found him a more
active learner than other children and encouraged him with individualized
support and special attention.

Marie Skodak reported that case 19's slight hearing loss did not affect
his everyday experience. But it did bring something life changing: it qualified him for admission to a special Iowa boarding school, the Iowa School for
the Deaf. "He heard so much better than anyone else, [this] was humorous,"
she said. But the boy's slight impairment allowed Skeels to rescue him from
Davenport's "barren affectionless detached childhoods" and place him in an
institutional environment that saved him.[71] At his new school, a dormitory
matron found him especially engaging and informally became his mothering
figure, bringing him home each weekend to her family. A year later, when he
was 9, his revived IQ tested at 89. At that time the school also administered
the Stanford Test of Achievement, a measure of school learning. He scored at
grade level 10.6, typical of the average American 15-year-old.

Perhaps as important as attention from caring adults, in his new school case 19's classmates came from normal homes, had caring parents, and became friendly companions. During summer vacations, the boy returned to Davenport but kept his distance from the other children and spent his days with the office staff, who took him on trips to town and provided positive attention. Marie Skodak and Harold Skeels maintained that case 19 had an intellectual revival as significant as any child in the experimental group. "The good fortune of his intellectual recovery," Skeels said, "can be traced to his affliction."[72]

When Skeels brought his Glenwood experiment to a close in the fall of 1938, he found that BD's and CD's recoveries had been replicated in the Glenwood children. The intelligence of nine of the eleven children had risen to the normal range, and they had been adopted. Two children who had experienced especially damaging early lives gained in IQ test scores, but not enough to permit their adoptions. However, the results in his contrast group couldn't have been clearer: once normally intelligent young children at Davenport who were deprived of reasonable levels of stimulation and attention suffered dramatic intelligence declines that severely limited their lives; four would spend the rest of their lives in institutions. As audacious as the idea had once seemed, a stimulative environment saved one group while its absence doomed the other. Remarkably, the mean IQ score gain for the experimental group, 27.5, almost exactly equaled the 26.2 loss in the other.[73]

Chapter Seven

ORPHAN STUDIES
OUT IN PUBLIC

The Intelligence gains that Harold Skeels found in BD and CD at Woodward and also in the children placed at the Glenwood Home, along with the losses he discovered in the Davenport contrast children, led him to reconsider the earlier work of his station colleague Beth Wellman. In 1925, Wellman had begun collecting IQ test data on children from middle-class homes who attended the University of Iowa's laboratory preschool. Twice each year, when the children returned to school in the fall and again before they left for summer vacation, Wellman had tested their IQs.

In 1930, when she analyzed data on 600 children, she found that during the summer period the children's IQ test scores did not change, but that during the school year their IQ test scores rose—about 10 points over two years of schooling. Her data also showed that children who attended preschool for a full day had higher IQ test scores than those who attended for a half day. Because intelligence was thought to be unaffected by environment or education, and almost no other research had shown that it could change, Wellman mistrusted her findings. She wondered if these results might be random errors that occurred because she had tested children after intervals of several months, when typically children's IQs were tested at intervals of several years. To evaluate that hypothesis, she rechecked her data, and what she found amazed her: the children's IQ score changes were not random—they were systematically related to the amount of time the children spent in school, something neither Wellman nor most American psychologists believed possible.[1]

In 1932, Wellman published a report that considered the effect of preschool attendance on IQ scores of those 600 children and a more extensive report on nine years of data (including records collected earlier by others) on 3,000 children who were from 2 to 14 years of age.[2] In this second study, she found that during a twelve-year period, many children's IQ scores continued to increase. Wellman's studies became some of the first in the field of mental test psychology to suggest that environmental stimulation influenced the development of intelligence. Although not every station psychologist accepted her findings—Skeels's and Skodak's traditional training led them to have doubts—from that point forward the station psychologists became engaged in a different conversation, one not based on subjective impressions or untested speculation, but on the discovery of new evidence. Only George Stoddard, with his firsthand knowledge of Alfred Binet's theories, unreservedly accepted Wellman's reports. He encouraged the psychologists to explore the possibility that IQs could change and ensured they had the resources to support that work.

After Wellman had published her early data, in 1933 she and Skeels initiated a study to investigate the effects of preschool on the Davenport orphans' development. At the time, no preschool existed at Davenport, and to establish one Skeels skillfully brought together resources from the Iowa station, the Iowa Board of Control for State Institutions, and the Davenport Home. Ruth Updegraff, a station member with expertise in nursery education, and another psychologist, Harold M. Williams, also joined the study.

Because the orphanage lacked a suitable space to house a preschool, the undertaking required ground-up construction financed by the Iowa station at a cost of $7,280 (in current dollars, about $136,000) and built with Iowa state workers' labor. Soon, a picture-postcard cottage in a style suited to the English countryside took shape in an attractive area at the edge of the orphanage property. To spare children reminders of their institutional lives,[3] Skeels arranged for the preschool to look out over the Iowa hills.

While Davenport's children had been rescued from destitution and abuse, at the Home they faced other hazards: indifference and neglect. Thirty to thirty-five children lived crowded into each of eighteen small cottages, little changed since they lodged wounded Civil War soldiers. In each, a single caregiver, untrained in child development, was responsible for every aspect of the children's lives as well as all cottage maintenance. Overwhelmed, they applied firm, often stifling, discipline. At the sound of a matron's whistle, children walked in lines to meals and ate silently from battered tin plates. Small children spent their daytime hours seated on chairs placed against the walls of a room 15 feet square.[4] Further, the institutional environment isolated children from everyday experience—even related to what they wore—as matrons dressed them each day in random, shabby clothing that always needed washing. Clothing for outdoor play in cold or damp weather was inadequate or nonexistent.[5] Personal hygiene in adult bathrooms not adapted for children made cleanliness, especially toilet training, difficult. Questions took too much of the matron's time and went unanswered. Personal attention came only with punishment.[6] To receive approval meant to accept things as they were.

Learning that objects had names, mastering language, expressing curiosity, hearing a favorite story, playing games, singing, and affectionate interactions with adults, all routine in ordinary children's lives, were unknown to these children. They had no idea what distances meant, they had never seen a town, they knew nothing about stores, banks, restaurants, or traffic lights. If they learned anything it was that there was nothing to learn. Of course, such conditions were not unique to Davenport. They defined the lives of children in most of America's state institutions.[7]

Considering Iowa's Great Depression hardships, it might have been out of the question for a university, a state agency, and a state institution to join in a three-year investigation that required construction of a school, the commitment of four psychologists, and the hiring of one half-time and two full-time preschool teachers, all to study children no one previously thought worth the trouble. But a new Davenport superintendent, Syl McCauley, recognized that Davenport had neglected its young residents' development. It's plausible,

too, that Stoddard's ideas impressed McCauley and contributed to his support. Responding to a suggestion from Skeels, the superintendent proposed
building a preschool and conducting a trial to study its effect.[8] Embracing
this opportunity, Skeels and Wellman planned to investigate whether preschool experience would affect children's cognitive and social development.
Although Stoddard felt confident that the findings would be positive, in 1934
when the study began, only a few scattered investigations about preschool had
been published, and his hope awaited confirmation.

———

The Iowans' research design for what would be their *Study of Environmental Stimulation: An Orphanage Preschool Project* would strike today's
cognitive psychologists as primitive. But for their time, its radical research
structure was uncommon in psychology. There would be an experimental
and a control group, each with twenty-one subjects matched for chronological
age, mental age, intelligence, sex, nutritional status, and length of orphanage
residence. Moreover, the psychologists arranged an immersion-style experience in which the experimental group would attend preschool for a full day,
five days a week; and based on Wellman's findings that children did not gain
in intelligence during summer vacations, they would attend school twelve
months each year. To minimize exposure to orphanage conditions, the children were awakened at 5:30 a.m. for breakfast and arrived at the school by
7:00 a.m., although after a year the schedule was adjusted to somewhat later
hours. To tighten the immersion protocol, instead of having children return
to Davenport's dining hall for lunch, the noon meal was brought to the school.
At 5:00 p.m. the children left for dinner in Davenport's dining hall, followed
by an early bedtime. The control group children would follow their usual
orphanage schedule as if no study were in progress. The intelligence, language
achievement, social maturity, and motor achievement in both groups would
be regularly evaluated.[9]

The ages of the children to be studied spanned from 18 months to 5½
years, with the placement of children into the experimental or control group
decided by the psychologists and Davenport's superintendent. The median

chronological age for the preschool group was 39 months, and for the control group, 41.9 months. Each group had a median IQ score of 80. No child with an IQ under 60 was included. The preschool children had lived at Davenport for a mean of 21.8 months, and the control group children for 18.4 months.[10]

As they readied the preschool for the children's arrival, the Iowa station psychologists believed that they had anticipated every aspect of what children in the experimental group would require, including furnishing its two classrooms in ways that young children would find stimulating and appealing. Based on Wellman's laboratory preschool experience, they provided high-quality supplies, books, toys, and equipment that any preschooler in the nation might envy. But according to historian of child institutions Bernadine Barr, in 1934, life for children in institutions was "an unknown world [that] had never been subject to systematic investigation."[11] Further, the psychologists found that institutional considerations limited their preparations, and they were unable to introduce the children into the school gradually, as they would have preferred.

———

On a mild October morning in 1934, twenty-one Davenport children were awakened well before dawn, dressed by their matrons, given early breakfasts, and, as the sun began to rise, were walked to a corner of Davenport's property they had never before seen. Excited, they pushed open the gate of a picket fence and found themselves in a play yard just outside the small stone cottage that was their new preschool. In the cottage's open doorway three smiling teachers greeted these young students who had rarely been welcomed anywhere. Neither the children nor the teachers could have predicted what happened next.

As the first children entered the schoolroom, those behind pushed forward, and in seconds an agitated mass of twenty-one children exploded toward open shelves, cupboards, bins on the floor, all stocked with painted toys, colored papers, building blocks, crayon boxes, children's books, dolls of all sizes, brightly hued metal trucks, toy cars and trains, each a strange object never before seen or even imagined. In the classroom, too, were child-height tables, small personal lockers with the children's names, and off to one side a bathroom with child-sized fixtures. Perhaps most perplexing were the three soft-spoken teachers offering to gently guide the children into this universe of new experiences.

Freed from Davenport's institutional bondage but inexperienced in childhood's universal language of play, the children erupted, pulling open drawers, reaching onto shelves, grabbing objects, and with no thought about what would happen, throwing and breaking toys, ripping books and paper, then feverishly searching for more objects. If one child held something that another wanted, they tore it from the other's hands. They rejected all instructions and fought teachers' efforts to calm them. One of the teachers wrote:

> The first weeks of school the equipment mortality rate was extremely high . . . their favorite thing was to throw [toys] over the railing down the cellar entrance because they made such a good crash. . . . The children weren't used to playing . . . they carried the toys clutched in their arms to have something to say "Mine" about.[12]

Overwhelmed by their desire for possessions, the children removed papers from wastebaskets, especially if they were brightly colored, and clutched those, too. They urgently clung to these riches, distrusting assurances they would be there the next day. Reassuring words would cause a child to nearly detonate,

> to lose control of himself completely . . . throw himself on the floor, scream and kick his heels on . . . anything in reach (including another child or adult), take off his shoes . . . throw or break anything he got hold of. If not stopped, a child would overturn every object in the room.[13]

Skeels observed that while liberated for much of each day from the rough discipline of their cottage matrons, even after several weeks the children showed *a strange mixture of defiance, wish for affection, desire for attention . . . [yet] there was little desire for the teacher's approval . . . a promise or consequence . . . seemed not so much to be disbelieved as to be ignored . . . Strangers and visitors were objects . . . the children's reaction would probably have been the same to wax figures . . . yet the young child's need for affection, understanding and security loomed large . . . for all too little of these . . . had been the lot of most of these children.*[14]

As the preschool's first year unfolded, the teachers also had to remedy a further mark of institutional deprivation—Davenport's failure to provide reasonable hygiene and toilet training. Even after seven decades, the adult-sized bathroom fixtures in the children's cottages had not been replaced: small children used pots, and boys were required to sit while urinating.

Skeels also found that the children did not recognize that in toilet training, as in all other aspects of the program, teachers wanted to help them, and their kind interventions were met with resistance and sometimes attack. Worse still, children who had almost never been comforted didn't recognize that adults might understand or care about them, and because they lacked experience listening to another person, "they didn't acquire ideas,"[15] not even the idea of listening.

It became obvious that Davenport's strict institutional control had left the children unmotivated and disconnected—nothing seemed to anchor or calm them. The psychologists even wondered if children who had done everything in regimented groups and were guided by fear of punishment "had any consciousness of themselves as individuals with distinctive likes, powers, and accomplishments."[16] Instead of the playful explorations that Skeels and his colleagues anticipated, the children's responses to the preschool environment unleashed suspicion, moodiness and blindness about the consequences of their actions. Just as troubling, their ignorance of the world left a void where curiosity about the world around them might have been.

With meager vocabularies and poor enunciation, even basic communication seemed out of the question. The children did not have conversations, they mumbled, and small events caused them to yell. They had almost no experience of verbal exchange with another child or an adult. Communication came only in situations when the child felt extreme discomfort. "The favorite last resort," Skeels said, "was crying."[17] From time to time a child who somehow had adjusted to the preschool would be adopted. When that child left, another orphanage child, similar in age, sex, and IQ score, would be added, requiring the teachers to stabilize the group anew. Under these extreme conditions, the nursery school staff of one half-time and two full-time teachers for twenty-one children was inadequate, but to the overburdened cottage matrons, even that number seemed indulgent, and to preserve institutional comity it could not be altered.

Through the teachers' tremendous consistency, limited goals, and almost heroic patience, very gradually the children were able to establish new behaviors based on hard-won but tentative, trust. As an example, to promote the children's sense that they could exercise some control over themselves, teachers focused on skills that the children had learned to enjoy: washing up, combing their hair, and toileting. Step by small step, and with much backsliding, the staff extended these successes to other activities. The teachers found, too, that one activity engaged every child—music—and they used singing to scaffold efforts in other areas.

By the second year of the study, from 1935 to 1936, the children's responses became more organized, and some routines became possible. Children came to trust that materials would be available later and to respect the use of books. Rather than aimlessly turn pages, they learned to focus on a book's pictures. Eventually, some asked questions about stories, such as *The Tale of Peter Rabbit* and *Millions of Cats* and even shared a book with another child. Although at first the children had little interest in dramatic play, they began to engage in the world of pretending typical of most preschool children, acting out the roles of doctors and nurses or scenes from their cottage lives. Temper tantrums calmed, and during rest time children began to rest.

During that year, anything that triggered interest—a character in a book, leaves fallen from trees, insects flying into the classroom, a thunder and lightning storm, stones on the ground, a robin's nest or a cocoon found in the yard—initiated a discussion. These exchanges signaled to the children that their interests mattered. Based on their increasing curiosity, teachers orga-

nized excursions to the airport, fire station, grocery store, even the orphanage laundry, and one day to a farm to see a thousand newly hatched chicks.
Constructive and dramatic play invariably followed each excursion:

> Older children were taken to the office to see the mail truck
> arrive and having watched the sorting process, brought the
> teachers' letters back . . . to deliver them . . . [and] since the
> trip, some . . . watch for the mail truck each day and eagerly
> report its arrival.[18]

The children asked more questions, and with the answers came the message that what they said was important. The second year saw reasonable progress and they began to trust their teachers. In the third year, with the gains
of the second year established, teachers concentrated on a specific disability
common among the orphans: infantile speech and language. Teachers took
every opportunity to repeat words correctly, to read stories and also articles
from magazines, and they focused for much of the day on communication.

Even before the study concluded in the fall of 1937, George Stoddard
wrote, "Untrained observers could see the differences . . . which were accu-
mulating."[19] The Davenport preschool children had learned self-control,
were kinder to other children, spoke with greater clarity, asked questions,
and seemed more mature, qualities that led to adoptions for nearly half of
the group. As the study continued, the improved development in those who
remained at Davenport became evidence that the children needed more
attention from adults, and the orphanage administration reduced the numbers in each cottage by one-third.[20]

But had preschool attendance influenced the children's cognitive development? And what had happened in the development of the control group
children who continued to live in Davenport's deprived environment? "When
we began," Wellman recalled, "our expectation was that the preschool children would probably increase considerably in IQ while the non-preschool
children would probably maintain about the same IQ. That was not what we
found."[21] The researchers had tested the intelligence of both the experimental
and control group children at six-month intervals. In those who had lived at

Davenport the longest, over 400 days, the differences between the preschool children and the control group children were stark. Unexpectedly, the preschool children made only small IQ gains, though none lost intelligence, but *every* control group child—even those who began with IQ test scores of 90, had scores that declined to between 70 and 79, making them unadoptable.[22] This drove home to the Iowans that Davenport's orphanage environment relentlessly undermined children's development. It is plausible, even likely, that had there been no study, such declines would have been the fate of many of the preschool children as well. Because Davenport was not a home for those with low intelligence, almost all of those children would eventually have spent the rest of their lives as inmates at Woodward or Glenwood.

In his report of these findings, Skeels noted the very different outcomes of the two groups. Fourteen preschool group children who began the study with IQ test scores between 60 and 69 gained a mean of 12.0 points. Control group children with those same IQ test scores gained 4.4 points. Two preschool children who began the study with IQ scores of 100 or more lost 4.5 points, while two control group children with those initial IQ test scores lost 28.5 points.[23] The study's most striking finding was that environmental stimulation favored the preschool children because it prevented the declines suffered by those in the control group. The researchers discovered, too, that stimulation protected the children in another way: although the preschool children spent a few hours each day and two days per week in the same environment as the control group, their intelligence did not decline. From the Iowans' nearly 200-page analysis of the children's intelligence, language use, vocabulary, social competence, and motor achievement, it is clear that in every area except motor development, where the groups were equal, the preschool children had higher attainment than the control group. But Skeels also found that language achievement in both groups was well below that of children growing up in families.[24] Convinced that they had proved their hypothesis, Beth Wellman summarized the study's conclusions: "Intellectual development," she said, "is directly and seriously affected by educational experiences inside and outside of preschool."[25]

O verlapping the period of the preschool study, from 1935 to 1937 Marie Skodak had been researching the effects of adoption on Davenport infants placed into middle-class families. As Wellman noted dryly, Skodak's findings resulted from Davenport's unique adoption practices in which no attention was paid to the infant's family history. "Probably nowhere in the country," she said, "[could] that condition be duplicated."[26] As Skodak discovered that the children were thriving, she recognized what earlier she had not fully accepted: their home environments had to be the factor that accounted for their good intelligence; their heredity seemed hardly to count.

Driving every numbered Iowa highway and most of the unnumbered ones, Skodak's research took her to established farms and small towns, where she found Davenport children in homes that provided stability and financial security and supported their educations. They were flourishing. From the children's records Skodak knew that when their families had given them up or the courts had removed them, it was because social inadequacy, extreme financial instability, mental and physical illness, incest, abandonment, and criminality marked the homes of their birth.[27] To see firsthand the circumstances of the children's birth families, Skodak also traveled to distressed backwaters, shabby schools, and ramshackle homes lacking indoor plumbing and adequate heating. She now understood that the adoptive families provided enriched lives that the children would not have known if they had spent their early years in these impoverished circumstances or in the Davenport orphanage. Skodak also recognized that Davenport's very early placements of babies, which earlier she had scorned, might have handed her the rare opportunity to answer a question about the effect of the *timing* of adoptions on development. Was it possible, she wondered, that the age at which a child entered a secure, stimulative environment influenced their development?

To examine that question, Skodak tracked sixteen children whose birth parents had especially low intelligence and who were adopted at 2.8 months. Almost none of the mothers graduated from high school, and many had not completed grammar school. Their IQ test scores ranged from 54 to 74. In school, both parents had been passed from grade to grade because they appeared physically mature. The fathers' occupations fell into the unskilled and slightly skilled categories. Almost all of these families relied on government assistance and were well known to state and local penal institutions, mental institutions, and local charities.[28] But in the adopted group, 40 percent of the adopting fathers and mothers had educations beyond high school, and half of the adoptive fathers' occupations were at the professional level.

Skodak found that these adopted Davenport orphans had a mean IQ of 111.5.[29] When Skodak divided the children into the half whose adoptive fathers had the two highest occupational levels and the half in the midrange, she found another factor that influenced the children's outcomes: the IQ mean of the first group was 5 IQ points higher than the mean of the other. In 1938, Skodak published these findings as *The Mental Development of Adopted Children Whose True Mothers are Feeble-Minded.*

In 1939, Skodak extended this study in her PhD dissertation, *Children in Foster Homes: A Study of Mental Development.* Here she reported on two groups of Davenport children: 154 adopted at about 2.8 months and 65 adopted when they were between 2 and about 5 years of age. She found that every early-adopted child had good to superior intelligence and that the occupational levels of the adopting fathers also appeared to influence the children's IQ scores. Children adopted when they were older made gains too, but their IQ test scores were not as high. In what might have been the first such discovery, Skodak suggested that the earlier children received environmental stimulation from responsive families, the higher their intelligence. She also confirmed the effect on the older children's intelligence of the father's professional level. Further, she confirmed what Wellman had found in nursery school children: those who began at the lowest intelligence levels gained the most.[30]

Sensitive to the life stories of those she studied, in her 1939 paper Skodak included brief reports of the birth parents of the under-6-month-old babies. One read, "This girl [the mother] was herself an illegitimate child. Her two sisters have had illegitimate children." Another read, "The girl's father is poor, hardworking, but unable to get ahead. An additional child would be more than this already too large family can bear." And, again, "When the husband died Mrs. K. became very promiscuous. The father of this child could be any one of a number of men who frequent a certain low-grade tavern."[31] But more than sensitivity prompted Skodak to detail these histories: she wanted to clear the air. In that period, and perhaps later, if the child of a prostitute seemed bright, it might be whispered that they inherited their intelligence from one of their mother's well-to-do clients. Skodak warned, "The popular belief that the fathers of illegitimate children are markedly superior to the mothers cannot be substantiated on the basis of any available evidence."[32]

Because Skodak presented striking new knowledge about child development, her work drew challenges. One came from George Speer, a psychologist at a Springfield, Illinois, adoption agency. Determined to prove her wrong, Speer methodically reviewed his department's child placement records of birth mothers who had a mean IQ score of 50 and found the error was his. Exactly as had Skodak, Speer discovered that children adopted early into middle-class homes developed intelligence in the average range, and many had superior IQ test scores. Speer also found that the longer children lived in deprived conditions, the lower their intelligence.[33]

Skodak's discoveries also aroused the skepticism of Frederick H. Osborn, a New York aristocrat and eugenicist who was a research associate at the American Museum of Natural History and a student of anthropology. According to George Stoddard, Osborn recommended that the Carnegie Foundation in New York dispatch a researcher to Iowa to investigate Skodak's claims about the children's natural parents. That was why Neil J. Van Steenberg, a geneticist, psychologist, and statistician, spent a year in Iowa seeking verification of Skodak's work. He discovered that her reports of the birth families *were* inaccurate—the families of the children she studied were even more benighted than she had described. Van Steenberg informed Skeels:

> *I have found upon examination that . . . her report does not even come near a true description of the lower levels of social strata from which these people, the true mothers and true fathers, were drawn. I was astonished that living conditions in a rural and rather prosperous state like Iowa could reach such a low level.*[34]

He expressed amazement "at the filth, squalor, and pitiable living conditions" and recommended that Skodak's descriptions "should be revised downward." If Skodak's portrayal of her subjects' birth families had been more accurate, he speculated, she would not have been believed.[35] Van Steenberg's report was never published.

Marie Skodak was awarded the PhD from the Iowa station in 1939. She attempted to find an academic position, but perhaps because she had almost no earlier publications, or because her dissertation topic challenged psychology's mainstream thinking, or because she was a woman, her search was unproductive. Instead, the pragmatic Skodak accepted a clinical position at Michigan's Flint Child Guidance Clinic, whose director, Orlo Crissey, was a friend from the Iowa station.

———

From 1934 through 1937, a period that included the years of Skodak's research, several other important investigations were afoot at the Iowa station, but the station's publications were limited. In 1934, Wellman published a study showing that children who left the University of Iowa's preschool to attend other nursery programs took their IQ gains with them. She also showed that in their new environments, their test scores failed to increase. After comparisons with those who did not transfer, Wellman suggested that the transfer programs may have lacked the stimulation of the university's preschool.[36] Her investigation included precise statistical analyses, but skeptics—that is, most mainstream psychologists—belittled her findings. After all, what advantage could one preschool program have over another?

In 1936, Harold Skeels published two interim reports that described the investigation he and Skodak had begun about the intelligence of young children from poor-hereditary backgrounds who were adopted into middle-class homes. Skeels confessed surprise at finding that the children's IQ scores were higher, sometimes much higher, than expected. Neither of these reports, he wrote, reflected "any preconceived ideas as to the effect of environment on the growth of intelligence."[37] In fact, neither report had begun as a study at all. Skeels was just doing his job.

Also during this period, Skeels and Wellman's preschool study was in progress, and in 1936, Skeels wrote a preliminary report about its positive findings, but warned, "The study's conclusions are not clear at this time."[38] He also published a study that found that sixty-five Davenport infants adopted early into the homes of high-achieving fathers had mental test levels "higher than would be expected for children from . . . their true parents." He found a zero correlation between the children and their birth mothers' IQ test scores. Yet, here too, Skeels labeled his results "tentative."[39]

The closest Skeels came to publishing unambiguous findings were the results of a 1937 investigation based on a hunch and completed with station graduate student Eva A. Fillmore. Skeels had noticed that in sibling groups removed by the state from inadequate parents, older children had lower intelligence test scores than their younger sisters and brothers. He wondered whether the scores reflected that older children had lived for longer periods in deprived, unstimulating home environments. When Skeels and Fillmore analyzed IQ test scores of 407 children who ranged in age from 1 to 14 years, Skeels's conjecture proved accurate. The mean IQ test scores of the older children from these families was significantly lower than the mean of their younger siblings.[40]

———

Then, just days before New Year's Eve, 1937, Wellman and Skeels ended several years of low-keyed station reports when they announced their radical discoveries at an important scientific meeting, captured in an explosive *Washington Star* headline, "Report on Test Variations Blasts Old Theories on I.Q." The *Star*'s readers learned that "Beth Wellman . . . at the University of Iowa . . . had 'torn to shreds' ideas of I.Q. constancy," that she found breathtaking shifts in children's IQ test scores, and just as amazing, that the effects of preschool stimulation persisted into the college years. Wellman, the *Star* reported, "made mincemeat" of psychology's dogma that IQ could not change.[41] At the same meeting, Harold Skeels showed that children of low-intelligence parents placed into very good homes had at least normal intelligence and frequently much higher. "There was no relationship whatsoever" the newspaper reported, "between the intelligence of the children and . . . their birth parents."[42]

Wellman and Skeels had brought the Iowa station's dispatches about IQ test variability to hundreds of psychologists and to journalists at the 101st annual meeting of the American Association for the Advancement of Science (AAAS), the nation's premier scientific society. The newspaper's showcase article would be frequently quoted and widely reprinted under the headline "The Wandering I.Q."[43]

Wellman told the AAAS members that in 160 students who took two different college entrance examinations, those with more years of preschool had higher test scores. These effects of environment on intelligence, Wellman said, "are not exceptional examples."[44] Intelligence, she argued, is not a *thing*; it is a *functional process* that requires human interaction and that changes, depending on environment and experience.

In her talk, Wellman challenged what she called the "mystical" theories of Lewis Terman,[45] who was not present. "The facts," she said, "demand an entire revision of previous concepts of intelligence. . . . Any theory of intelligence which does not allow for . . . extreme flexibility during childhood . . . must be considered incomplete and . . . misleading."[46] Reports of Wellman's and Skeels's remarks appeared in newspapers from Rochester, New York, to Helena, Montana, to Knoxville, Tennessee, and when the *Star*'s article was circulated, Wellman's news covered the nation.

For the Iowa psychologists, the *Washington Star*'s report launched a year in which they took their discoveries, recently published in academic journals, to the public. On April 16, the *New York Herald Tribune* and the *Miami Herald* wrote that the psychologists had "produced results so revolutionary that they have caused discussions in psychological gatherings throughout the country."[47] On June 28, George Stoddard addressed 1,600 delegates gathered for the annual meeting of the National Education Association (NEA) in New York. Across the nation, newspapers reported his claim that intelligence could change with environment. Journalists from the two national wire services, *Associated Press* and *United Press*, put Stoddard's words on their tickers, and the next day they turned up everywhere.[48] In the *Minneapolis Star Tribune*, readers discovered: "Right Environment Can Improve I.Q." The *Daily Capital Journal*, in Salem, Oregon, carried the news that "offspring of feeble-minded parents may become normally bright . . . in good homes." And the *Brooklyn*

Daily Eagle's readers learned that "illegitimate children of worthless or feeble-minded parents stand more than an even chance."

Two weeks later, on July 11, *Time* magazine, the nation's leading news weekly, carried just two sentences about Stoddard's NEA talk, and like Wellman's reports, they sent tremors through the public. Later it would be learned that they unsettled academic psychology as well. Under the headline "Bold Talk," *Time* described

> *a remarkable report on experiments that proved intelligence is affected by environment. . . . 1) illegitimate children of feeble-minded mothers and laboring fathers, after being placed in good homes, turned out to be bright children; 2) apparently normal youngsters, kept in an overcrowded orphanage, "deteriorated."*[49]

At the NEA meeting, Stoddard said that when adopted into good homes, babies from "poor stock" developed superior IQs. He also reported that intelligence rose in intellectually challenged young children when mentally limited women provided stimulation and affection. It sounded inconceivable, and the news media wanted to know more.

That summer, the *New York Times* asked Wellman for an article about her studies, and on July 17, the *Times* published her report that stimulation raised children's IQs. On September 10, the *Times* wrote that Wellman shocked those gathered for the American Psychological Association's annual meeting with a "Bombshell"—her explanation that environmental stimulation, or its opposite, neglect, could change IQ test scores in either direction up to 40 points. The *Times* wrote, "The IQ . . . has been reported by most psychologists . . . as something so nearly fixed by birth that it changes only slightly from babyhood to old age," but that Wellman had shown environmental stimulation could radically influence IQ results, even causing normal children to lose intelligence.[50]

Iowa's news storm continued on November 7, when *Time* covered Stoddard's address to New York's Educational Records Bureau, publisher of the admissions tests used by nearly all independent schools. In a full-page report under the headline "I.Q. Control," readers learned,

Strange and heretical to those orthodox [psychological beliefs] are reports that have come . . . from a little group of psychologists at Iowa's State University. Last week . . . they laid astounding proofs supporting Iowa's heresy: that an individual's IQ can be changed.[51]

"Changes in intelligence occur mostly in young children," Stoddard said. "To improve a child's intelligence, give him security, encourage [his] . . . experiencing, inquiring, relating, symbolizing."[52] To hundreds of educators and *Time*'s millions of readers, what the magazine called Iowa's "heresy" might have suggested that the nature-nurture controversy had finally ended. Intelligence depended, it appeared, on both nature and nurture: In the space of five months, Iowa's revelations had traveled from academic colloquiums to conversations around kitchen tables.

———

Months after *Time*'s article, in mid-April 1939, eugenicist author Albert E. Wiggam left his Central Park West apartment in New York City and set out for Iowa City, where he would interview the Iowa psychologists. Over two previous decades, Wiggam had written two best sellers and hundreds of articles advocating eugenic policies of sterilization and institutionalization, policies that he said would improve humankind. In *The Fruit of the Family Tree*, he illustrated "good" genetics with a genealogical chart (including photos) of one prominent family that, he claimed, included Winston Churchill, General Ulysses S. Grant, Mrs. Theodore Roosevelt, and Grover Cleveland.[53] Wiggam opined, "Heredity is the preponderant factor in the relative character of men, and almost the whole factor in mental capacity."[54] He wrote:

We cannot have a progressive civilization . . . until the more richly endowed are given both the opportunity and encouragement to reproduce their kin in greater numbers than those of less natural endowments. . . . Without an eugenical policy . . . civilization is self-destructive. It sets going forces that often silently and slowly wreck the race that built it.[55]

GENERAL VIEW OF GROUNDS AND BUILDINGS.

The Davenport Soldiers' Orphans' Home, 1901. Engraving. *(University of Iowa Libraries.)*

French experimental psychologist Alfred Binet testing a
child's intelligence, ca. 1905. *(AF Fotografie / Alamy Stock Photo.)*

Meeting of the National Congress of Mothers, Des Moines, 1900. The Congress was an element of Cora Bussey Hillis's campaign to establish the Iowa station. *(State Historical Society of Iowa, Des Moines, Iowa.)*

Wanted: A Child Welfare Bureau. Cartoon by Iowa artist Ding Darling, 1915. *("Ding" Darling Wildlife Society owns the copyright of "Ding" Darling cartoons.)*

Bird Baldwin, first Iowa station director, ca. 1920. *(State Historical Society of Iowa, Iowa City, Iowa,)*

Beth Wellman (second adult from left), with University of Iowa
laboratory school staff and preschool children, ca. 1930.
*(F. W. Kent Photographs Collection, RG 30.0001.001,
University of Iowa Archives.)*

Bird Baldwin
and laboratory
preschool staff.
*(F. W. Kent
Photographs
Collection, RG
30.0001.001,
University of Iowa
Archives.)*

Harold Skeels
at Iowa State
College, 1927.
*(Iowa State
University Special
Collections
and University
Archives.)*

Marie Skodak
at The Ohio
State University,
1933. *(Ohio
State University
Libraries.)*

The Girls' Cottage at the
Glenwood Institution for
Feebleminded Children housed
adult low-intelligence women
who were called "girls." The
Davenport orphans lived with
the women in their wards.
(Photo by Marilyn Brookwood.)

George Stoddard, second
director of the Iowa station,
ca. 1935. *(Staff and Faculty
Vertical File Collection
(folder: Stoddard, George),
RG 01.0015.003, University of
Iowa Archives.)*

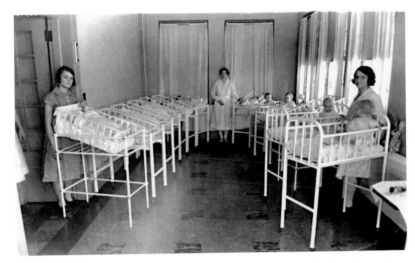

The Nursing cottage,
Davenport Home, ca. 1930.
(Davenport Public Library.)

Typical wicker basket Marie
Skodak would have used to
transport infants to the Davenport
Home. *(F. W. Kent Photographs
Collection, RG 30.0001.001,
University of Iowa Archives.)*

Chapter III

THE NURSERY SCHOOL

THE SETTING OF THE NURSERY SCHOOL

The building, situated within the group of buildings constituting the orphanage but just at the edge of one corner of the group, occupies a choice spot on the grounds. On two sides there is full view of the rolling country separating the institution from the edge of the city. The site itself is somewhat higher than that of the other buildings so that a terrace and rock-wall provide an attractive approach.

In outward appearance the school approximates an English cottage. Its dark red brick, stone, and weathered timbers fit well into the background of trees. The play yard, enclosed by stained, irregularly cut pickets, is on two sides of the building and its wide expanse, which

Davenport Home preschool,
1934.
*(University of Iowa
Libraries.)*

Charles B. Davenport, American biologist and director of the Cold Spring Harbor Laboratory and the Eugenics Record Office, 1914. *(Courtesy of Cold Spring Harbor Laboratory Archives.)*

...wan Henry A. Wallace, who served as ...cretary of Agriculture (1933–1940) under ...anklin Delano Roosevelt, and as FDR's Vice ...esident from 1941 to January 1945.

Eugenics Record Office workers, Cold Spring Harbor, New York, ca. 1920. *(Courtesy of Cold Spring Harbor Laboratory Archives.)*

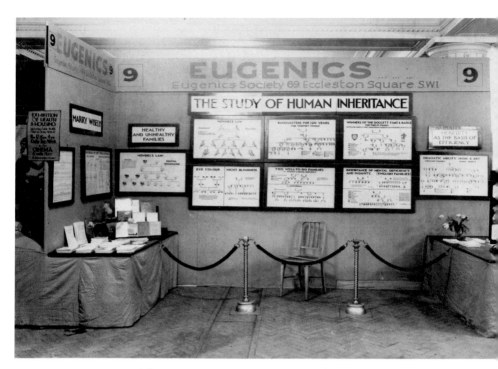

Eugenics Society exhibit on human inheritance, used at meetings and state fairs, 1920s–1930s.

Eugenicist Henry H. Goddard in his Ohio State University office, ca. 1930. *(Drs. Nicholas and Dorothy Cummings Center for the History of Psychology, The University of Akron.)*

Lewis M. Terman,
Stanford University, 1923.
(*National Library of Medicine.*)

Carrie Buck with
her mother, 1924.

Journalist Walter Lippmann, who challenged Lewis Terman's eugenic ideas, ca. 1920. *(Getty / Bettmann.)*

Herbert Spencer Jennings, Johns Hopkins geneticist who rejected eugenics, ca. 1925. *(From* History of the University of Michigan, *1906, by Burke Aaron Hinsdale, p. 353.)*

Nazi eugenic policies portrayed by Iowa cartoonist
Ding Darling, 1933. (*"Ding" Darling Wildlife Society owns the
copyright of "Ding" Darling cartoons.*)

Depression-era Iowa hut, ca. 1938. *(Library of Congress, Prints & Photographs Division, FSA/OWI Collection.)*

Potatoes, cabbage, and pie: Christmas dinner near Smithland, Iowa, 1936. *(Library of Congress, Prints & Photographs Division, FSA/OWI Collection.)*

"This Farmer is not on Government Relief." Sign posted at a Rock Island, Illinois, farm, 1 mile from Davenport, Iowa, 1940. *(Library of Congress, Prints & Photographic Division, FSA/ OWI Collection.)*

Cell biologist Alfred Mirsky (right) with developmental biologist Eric Davidson, Rockefeller Institute, 1963. *(Getty / Art Rickerby.)*

Children at Vasliu Orphanage, Romania, ca. 1990. *(Getty / Bernard Bisson.)*

Developmental neuroscientist Charles Nelson, who studied the Romanian orphans.

Neuroendocrinologist Bruce McEwen, one of the scientists who pioneered the study of how stress impacts the brain. *(The Rockefeller University.)*

Jack Shonkoff, director of Harvard's Center on the Developing Child, which relates developmental science to governmental policies that impact children and families.

Louis Branca, during army training for his pilot's license, ca. 1952.
(Courtesy of Cass Dalglish, Lou Branca's widow and literary executor of his memoir Little Boy Blue—Case Number Eleven.*)*

Louis Branca in 2012, holding Kennedy Foundation's International Award, sent to him in 1970 by Harold Skeels. *(Photo courtesy of Marilyn Brookwood.)*

A disciple of the eugenicist Madison Grant, Wiggam approached his mission the way a cleric approaches the preparation of a sermon, as an act of holy persuasion. On his return from Iowa, he would join with religious leaders from the Congregationalist, Catholic, and Jewish faiths, as well as representatives from the World Council of Churches, for a conference about eugenics.

The idea for Wiggam's Iowa visit came from his editors at the *Ladies Home Journal*, who suggested he write about the station's discoveries now filling the pages of the nation's press. In the small world of 1930s New York City publications, the editors may have known that a competitor, *Parents* magazine, would soon publish Beth Wellman's article "Can an I.Q. Change?" Wiggam would have been an obvious choice to write an opposing piece and could perhaps generate a controversy that would benefit both magazines.

Before accepting the assignment, Wiggam alerted Lewis Terman, with whom he had a decades-long association, that he intended to consider the assignment. Terman argued that the Iowa work was fraudulent and that Wiggam should not dignify it with any report. Tempted to let the project go, Wiggam also consulted with Barbara Burks, Terman's student, who told him that Iowa's ideas were wrong but were "exactly what everyone wants to believe."[56] Still, Wiggam decided to meet with the station psychologists and on April 21, 1939, Skeels, Wellman, and Stoddard, along with a stenographer, sat down with him. Marie Skodak had left Iowa to work in Flint and did not participate.

For the Iowans this was exactly the right moment for such a conversation. They had recently published all but one of their seminal papers, and two weeks later, in Chicago, Skeels would offer the last, his report on the remarkable changes in the Woodward and Glenwood children. Meeting with Wiggam allowed the Iowans to offer their evidence to an influential skeptic, although considering his background and his connection to Terman, they had no idea what to expect. But Wiggam arrived well prepared and questioned them with unfeigned curiosity. Discovery by discovery he had the psychologists review their findings, a discussion that generated a transcript of seventeen single-spaced pages.

Skeels stepped up to take the lead, answering Wiggam's first inquiry about how the Iowa group understood the importance of intelligence test scores. Skeels explained that in cases in which a child's environment does not change, IQ tests are accurate measures of ability. Wiggam wondered whether functional ability would change with stimulation, and Skeels explained that it would. He added, "Psychologists are . . . much to blame [for assuming] that intelligence was fixed at birth and little could be done . . . that it is a measure of innate capacity, which it is not." What seemed like consistency in IQ test scores, Skeels stressed, "may have come from the constancy of other factors."[57]

Citing example after example of remarkable intelligence changes that Wiggam might previously have dismissed, Skeels told of adopted children from inadequate backgrounds whose intelligence had reached levels that were appropriate to the levels of the homes into which they had been placed. He also reported on intellectually challenged Davenport orphans sent to live with low-intelligence women who gained a mean of 27 IQ points, while a matched group of once normal children who remained at the institution lost 26 points. "Nobody . . . is arguing that there are not hereditary differences . . . there are ceilings," Skeels said, but he emphasized that the possibility for intelligence gains "are wider than we knew."[58] He illustrated with a study of 407 Davenport children in groups of their siblings in which about a third of the mothers had been institutionalized because of mental illness or low intelligence and all of the fathers worked in the lowest occupational categories. Forty-five children from 1 to 7 years, who had lived in their families for the shortest period of time, had a mean IQ test result of 92.6. The mean for twenty-six of their siblings, from 12 to 13 years, was 78.9. Skeels's message could not have been clearer: long exposure to deprivation lowers intelligence.

Turning to Wellman, Wiggam wondered whether she agreed with Binet, who fought the idea of IQ constancy. Although she did not mention Lewis Terman, Wellman explained that some American psychologists had promoted the idea that because IQ test scores measured innate ability they could not change with environment. Wellman said that the children who showed such constant IQs lived in environments that were constant, and explained, "To get . . . shifts you have to subject children to marked differences in environmental conditions." His curiosity energized, Wiggam responded, "Tell me more on the human side of this," and wondered about children "where the whole environmental stimulus is very poor."[59]

Wellman challenged, "What do you mean by poor environment? . . . Even a home of low socio-economic status may have a mother [who] is very alert to the needs of the child and who has the relationships that are good for mental development." Echoing observations that Stoddard, Skeels, and Skodak had made, she emphasized that what young children need from adults was not just mental stimulation, but "the right kind of personal bond between them—a sense of security, mental security, emotional security. This is the background on which the more strictly intellectual sorts of things have to be built."[60]

Continuing to probe the issue of heritability, Wiggam wondered why Wellman's studies showed that children who came from the homes of college professors had not gained even higher IQs. She clarified, "A child who comes [to school] with a 140 IQ may already have a very good environment. The home may have done much that the preschool could do. My objection is to the labeling of the child either superior or inferior—if he is inferior . . . teachers [may] not have a philosophy of hope that you can do something for the child."[61]

As he often did, George Stoddard reframed the conversation, describing Sherman and Key's investigation of children who lived in mountain hollows, and the studies of Otto Kleinberg, who in 1935 found that African Americans who had migrated North and attended better schools had higher intelligence than those who remained in the South. Questioning the theory of IQ constancy, Stoddard pointed out that in every area of animal development, science had found that external environments changed outcomes, yet eugenicists insisted that "nothing external could change the rate of mental growth."[62] Because so much is unknown, he said, the Iowans could not account for each environmental effect. But Stoddard emphasized that the station's research showed that significant intelligence test score changes were not rare and that they demonstrated biology's ability to improve intelligence based on continuing stimulation. He expressed incredulity that anyone still believed that IQ could be constant. Echoing the 1928 thinking of his Iowa predecessor, Bird Baldwin, that environment changed development in almost all living creatures, Stoddard advanced an argument that most psychologists would not accept for decades:[63]

Back of all change, either for the worse or for the better, there is organic change within the individual. We feel that if physiologists and neurologists could get far enough along in their work they would be able to examine cases and find out what is happening when mental growth shows: constancy; acceleration; or deceleration. . . . The mental growth and behavior of the organism is in part dependent upon what happens to it. . . . The nervous system of the organism is in constant organic change. We think a child who is growing at a faster rate does not have the same . . . mechanism he had previously.[64]

Although what Wiggam heard that day may have shaken his eugenic certainties, he made no effort to stir the pot for controversial effect. Soon after, he wrote Terman that although he was reluctant to accept the Iowan's positions, he felt "humble compared to those who create new knowledge" and he had a responsibility to the public to report current science. He continued, "If I waited for what is called 'science' . . . [to be] confirmed I would have very little to report." Wiggam said that he and his editors felt a duty "to be responsible agents."[65]

Furious, Lewis Terman responded with an implicit threat:

I can assure you now most emphatically that if your report to the Ladies Home Journal has to be satisfactory to the Iowa people, it will be a d———poor job of reporting. I have never run across any scientist or any group of scientists as unduly impervious to unanswerable criticism.[66]

Eight months later, in March 1940, the *Ladies Home Journal* published Albert Wiggam's article, "Are Dummies Born or Made?" In it, Wiggam wrote sympathetically of the Iowa station's discoveries that showed unexpected intellectual development, and he encouraged parents to make every effort to develop their children's abilities. In his closing sentences, Wiggam had advice for adopting parents and offered a revelation:

> *Those excellent people who have adopted children or plan to adopt them, [should have] a greater faith in the influence of a good home in determining human destiny. On this last point, I speak with profound personal feeling, because I myself was an adopted child.*[67]

Neither Wiggam's article nor his correspondence contained an explicit rejection of eugenic beliefs. Following its publication, he suggested to Terman that the editors had altered text in his article that was critical of the Iowans, and he threatened to sue. However, Wiggam never again took up the eugenic cause. Subsequently, he wrote a syndicated personal advice column, "Let's Explore Your Mind," in which he quoted psychologists' answers to questions about relationships, children, and family life. To one question, "Does the fact that you struggle to secure a good environment indicate that you have good heredity?" Wiggam responded: "Yes, environment acts either to develop or suppress your heredity. It is the people with good heredity who make good environments."[68]

———

With Iowa's arsenal of fresh ideas gaining public traction, but mainstream psychology's opposition seeming to harden, in the fall of 1953 an endorsement of IQ flexibility arrived from an unexpected source. Writing in the *Scientific Monthly*, a journal of the hard sciences and occasionally of psychology, Frederick H. Osborn, who recently had arranged for the Carnegie Foundation's study of Skodak's Iowa reports, published an essay that wondered, "Is a Science of Man Possible?"

Osborn reviewed psychology's previous answers—he labeled them subjective observations—and charged that some biologists and psychologists had inadequate training and that much research about IQ testing had been poorly conducted. Osborn left little doubt that he had Lewis Terman and the mental test movement in his crosshairs when he described, but did not name, Iowa's recent work:

> We know now that a stimulating environment in the home, in pre-school, in College and in later life tend to raise the I.Q. . . . In a stimulating environment, able individuals show a capacity for response which takes them . . . out of the class of those of average ability.[69]

While Osborn's paper also advocated eugenically driven ideas, he wrote that if hereditary factors in intelligence were somewhat limited, then educational systems "should not be permitted to become a class affair" and that the characteristics attributed to race do not represent genetic inheritance but are the result of social factors.[70] The Iowa psychologists could not have hoped for better support, but Osborn did not directly cite their papers. (The inconsistent use of citation was a shortcoming of scientific writing during this era.) And while Osborn cannily wondered what Hitler would have thought about race if he had this new knowledge, he had not surrendered his eugenicist beliefs. He continued to support Hitler's sterilizations and almost all American eugenic polices, and throughout a long life he enthusiastically promoted eugenic causes and publications.

Lewis Terman, however, appeared rattled by Osborn's article. In a November, 2, 1939, letter to Florence Goodenough, he briefly referred to Osborn's paper, mentioning that Osborn would soon address the decade's most important gathering of psychology's researchers—the NSSE meeting set for February 1940. It seemed that George Stoddard, the meeting's chair, had invited Osborn to give an opening address. Faced with potential opposition to his eugenic positions from two highly regarded hereditarian supporters, Wiggam and Osborn, Lewis Terman found the stakes for the February meeting had now been raised.

Chapter Eight

THE WAY THE LAND LIES

The Iowa station's 1938 surge of publications intensified discussions among psychologists and educators about the development of intelligence and through press coverage excited the public. The new thinking had even made an impact on eugenicists like Albert Wiggam and Frederick Osborn. This made it inevitable that the forces of orthodoxy would mount a fierce backlash. Since the early 1930s, Lewis Terman and others had occasionally critiqued Iowa's work, but their retaliation began in earnest in January 1939, with a jeering review by Benjamin R. Simpson, of Case Western Reserve University, titled "The Wandering IQ: Is It Time for It to Settle Down?"

Here, Simpson targeted Beth Wellman, labeling her a "psychological spiritualist" and an incompetent "under the influence of wishful thinking." Her research, he said, was "dark and devious . . . and her work shoddy."[1] He also pummeled Skeels for his report on the improved intelligence of Davenport orphans adopted into middle-class homes. Suspicious of the findings that environment could stimulate children's intelligence, Simpson wrote that if Iowa's work were accurate, "such improvement would . . . receive front page presentation in the newspapers of the nation."[2]

As if he were lecturing a hapless student, citing no evidence Simpson advised the Iowans that "the level of learning and the absolute amount of learning are lowest in early infancy and highest as adulthood is approached or reached. . . . It is the rate of physical maturation that is rapid in infancy, not the rate of . . . learning."[3] He also labeled Skeels's preschool report "deceitful," suggesting, with no evidence, that the IQ scores of nursery school students had improved because their teachers had trained them to take IQ tests. Simpson concluded that the Iowans' errors stemmed not from their "quackery," but from their "statistical incompetence."[4]

In 1936, Simpson had published an article assailing another environmentalist researcher, John B. Watson, of Johns Hopkins, but that paper did not discuss the station's work, little of which was yet in print, and it went uncited by anyone except Simpson himself. By 1939, his timing had improved. The level of interest in Iowa's new work meant that Simpson's assault attracted attention—notably from Lewis Terman, who until then knew nothing about him. Now, Terman sent him a letter praising his analysis as "a little masterpiece" and decrying the Iowa studies as "the most appalling mess I have ever worked over."[5]

Terman's comment is of interest because no published or archival evidence exists that Terman analyzed, or even read, the Iowans' reports of the children's orphanage experience. Terman asked Simpson for copies of his paper to send to all of the members of the American Psychological Association and to America's leading pediatricians. Terman, who edited a widely read and lucrative book series, *Measurement and Adjustment* ("adjustment" referred to adjusting school curricula according to IQ score ranges), also offered Simpson a higher royalty than most of his series' authors for a volume that would expose the Iowans as charlatans.[6]

Although Simpson had been withering about Wellman's statistical work, in a discussion with Terman he confessed his own technical insecurity in the analysis of complex statistics.[7] Further, reports from two sources, one of them Terman's former student, Mae Seagoe, and the other, Terman himself, suggest that Terman, too, lacked statistical expertise. In her biography of Terman, Seagoe described his unfamiliarity with statistics and said he relied on his former student Quinn McNemar and others to interpret and review his data.[8] Later, Terman told Raymond Cattell, a psychologist at Duke University who sought his help with a statistical problem, "I am not myself competent" to discuss a statistical analysis, and directed Cattell to McNemar.[9] When Terman later labeled the Iowans' reports statistical atrocities, that judgment might not have reflected his own analysis.

Additional concerns for the Iowans soon arrived. In April, Florence Goodenough, whose place in Terman's circle could not have been more secure, wrote to her friend, psychologist Leta Hollingworth, at Columbia University, that her patience with the "Iowan people" had reached its endpoint. Her letter does not disguise her biliousness toward the Iowans, and especially her contempt for Wellman—once her friend—whom she described with false charity:

> *I am really quite concerned about Beth Wellman. . . . Terman thinks she has deliberately attempted to . . . deceive the reader. . . . I am entirely convinced of her sincerity. She has deceived herself . . . like a religious fanatic who hears the wings of angels in every rustle of the dishtowels on the family clothes line.*[10]

Goodenough was dismissing Wellman unfairly, but her sense of "where the land lies" was accurate. The Iowans were still fighting a tough enemy, and an onrush of even more severe criticism was about to strike them.

———

If Harold Skeels had the traits of a visionary—audacity, say, or reckless self-confidence—those might have served him well as he stepped to the podium that Saturday afternoon, May 6, 1939, in Chicago. But the matter-of-fact psychologist could not even have been labeled an ambitious scholar seeking to promote remarkable findings in order to lift his reputation. Instead, by chance Skeels had pushed open a door that no one else had noticed and confronted evidence about development that challenged everything he thought he knew. If it took daring not to look away, he never said.

Skeels had come to this sixty-third annual meeting of the American Association for Mental Deficiency to set before his professional colleagues a most remarkable discovery: intellectually challenged young children labeled "imbeciles" who had been cared for by women with low intellect, labeled "morons," had become normal. A few years earlier, Skeels himself would have dismissed such a report as ridiculous. But what he had seen at Glenwood, others had, too—the children's teachers, institutional staff, the women, and Harold Dye, Glenwood's superintendent. A physician, but not an academic, Dye coauthored Skeels's report, suggesting the two shared its observations and conclusions about what had begun as a "clinical surprise."[11] But as Skodak described, Skeels had concerns that the children's intelligence gains might be precarious. Even after he documented the children's gained intelligence, he worried that the gains would not persist. He feared the intellectual advances he witnessed might be as fleeting as the blooming of a flower, some transient phase doomed to end when the child's heredity came to resemble their parents' low intelligence.[12] The Iowans had produced other controversial studies of changes in children's IQ test scores, but Skeels's carefully documented case histories of two children at Woodward and eleven at Glenwood were the most challenging to the orthodoxy and so the most suspect.

Skeels's revelations resulted from the interlock of terrible and fortuitous events. Had the Great Depression, the Dust Bowl, and extreme weather not overwhelmed Iowa's families and filled the Davenport home with abandoned children; had the state not been sued by adoptive parents and so never hired Skeels to test Davenport children's intelligence; had Woodward not inexplicably placed BD and CD in wards with low-intelligence women, allowing Skeels to find their IQ scores dramatically altered; had Skeels not cultivated connections with state officials who permitted Iowa's research to go forward; had Director George Stoddard not encouraged the Iowans to dig for explanations; had state eugenics boards not mandated the institutionalization of women with low intelligence in the first place; if even some of this had not happened, probably the Iowans would not have chanced upon their radical discoveries. Like researchers who worked alone or who dismissed data that did not fit the conventional model as faulty test standardization, the Iowans might not have searched for explanations. More likely, they would have looked no further because, really, no one thought there was anything to find.

———

Early in 1939, before Skeels's report about the Woodward and Glenwood children had been presented or published, details of his discoveries had begun to circulate in psychology departments around the nation, and many skeptical colleagues singled Skeels out for mockery.[13] Who could blame them? His findings were Iowa's most sensational. It's likely that in the hotel corridors and meeting rooms of the Chicago conference, mental test psychologists had already casually ridiculed Skeels's investigation and Skeels himself, describing his paper, "A Study of the Effects of Differential Stimulation on Mentally Retarded Children," as the "Moron Nursemaid Study."

Conference attendees almost certainly included Florence Goodenough and Benjamin Simpson, two scholars who had openly expressed their disdain for Iowa's work, and John Anderson, director of Minnesota's Institute for Child Development, another of Iowa's harsh critics. Lewis Terman's former student, now his Stanford colleague, Quinn McNemar, may have been there as well. Skeels's paper was one of the final presentations of the four-day meeting; no doubt over those days Skeels, Skodak, and Harold Dye overheard sneering remarks about the work Skeels would present. Yet he might have hoped that by sharing the evidence that had changed his mind, he might change the minds of others.

Unseasonably warm weather arrived in the Midwest that first week of May, and by Saturday afternoon, temperatures in Chicago had climbed to 88°F. In the stuffy hotel ballroom, electric fans attempted to cool an audience of several hundred that included some reporters, one from *Time* magazine. Over the fans' low hum, Skeels laid down the core issue that he and Dye considered: if intelligence were static, then no environmental shifts would alter it; but if it changed under differing conditions, as Wellman suggested, its definition required revision. So far, Skeels's argument seemed reasonable. But in the next moments he turned to a quotation from Alfred Binet that told of surprise "at the prejudice against [intelligence] . . . modifiability."[14]

In drafting his paper, Skeels might easily have omitted Binet's ideas, limiting his remarks to a more typical report of unexpected findings. Such a paper, though still provocative, might have been less confrontational of mainstream beliefs. What, then, motivated the reserved Skeels to excerpt the words of the eloquent French psychologist? Skeels was a clear, if workmanlike, writer, so one might wonder whether he reached for Binet to inject into his remarks some of the Frenchman's eloquence. Yet the specific Binet passage that Skeels quoted directly challenged many in his audience:

> Some recent philosophers appear to have given their moral sup-
> port to the deplorable verdict that the intelligence of an individ-
> ual is a fixed quantity, a quantity which cannot be augmented.
> We must protest and act against this brutal pessimism. We shall
> endeavor to show that it has no foundation whatsoever.[15]

Binet, and now Skeels, may have been implicitly censuring Henry Goddard, who in 1910 had begun to use Binet's test to demonstrate that feeble-mindedness was inherited.[16] Thus, Skeels, who had been reluctant to fully embrace environmentalist thinking, now announced that like the children in his report, he, too, had been changed. But the elephant in the room was not Henry Goddard. Everyone in attendance that day knew that in 1916, five years after Binet's death, then novice psychologist Lewis Terman had recast Binet's test into his own. Skeels, in short, was challenging Lewis Terman and the entire intelligence measurement paradigm he represented—and doing it with the words of the very scholar on whose shoulders Terman had attained giant stature.

In his summary, Skeels captured what he believed had fundamentally changed the Davenport orphans:

> A close bond of love and affection between a given child and one
> or two adults assuming a parental role appears to be a dynamic
> factor of great importance . . . the nine children favored with
> such a relationship made the greater gains, an average of 33.8
> points. . . . The four children who had more general contact
> made average gains of 14 points.[17]

Thus, Skeels became one of the first psychologists to suggest that a one-to-one attachment may be a critical factor in the development of intelligence. He argued that because young children's intelligence was unstable, it required *persistent* stimulation; that the developmental clock was ticking, and when the youngest children received such stimulation, they made the greatest gains; that inadequate stimulation of the children in his contrast group left once normally intelligent youngsters intellectually challenged. In under an hour, the little-known Iowa psychologist had challenged centuries of traditional belief, along with decades of eugenic assumptions dressed up as science.

After delivering such a provocative paper, a psychologist might expect questions or comments from colleagues seeking to clarify an idea or indicating disagreement, and Skeels would have scanned the audience in search of raised hands. Instead, Skeels's audience sat in "stony silence," not even offering the polite applause that routinely followed conference presentations.[18] That silence, however, lasted only a moment: as historian of the Iowa station Hamilton Cravens observed, after Skeels gave his report, harsh criticism rained down on him, and he found he had "walked into a hurricane."[19] It is not known whether Goodenough and Simpson were in the hall, but if they were, it's plausible that they led the assault.

As Skodak later recalled, for Skeels the events at the Chicago meeting were some of the most painful in the controversy over the station's work. In a 1970 obituary for Skeels, she wrote, "As the one responsible for the most dramatic of these studies . . . Harold Skeels was particularly singled out for attack . . . among the most corrosive . . . at the American Association on Mental Deficiency in Chicago in 1939."[20] Although he did not cite the Chicago meeting, scholar of early development Joseph McVicker Hunt, of the University of Illinois, remembered that the Iowans were subjected to "polemics of a rare height of violence."[21] And almost thirty years later, in a newspaper profile, Harold Skeels himself evoked his memory of the attack as a physical trauma. "They cut me ear to ear," he said simply.[22]

Yet for journalists, and therefore for the public, Skeels's Chicago report quickly became another lightning bolt that environment could alter development. A *New York Times* headline read, "Put among Morons, Dull Babies Improve," the story highlighting the "value of affection."[23] The *Atlanta Consti-*

tution reported that "stimulation and affection . . . bring the desired result."[24] And in what must have seemed like wizardry, *Time* described that when "fee-bleminded love [was] lavished upon deficient babies [their] intelligence quotients . . . rose sharply."[25] More than anything else, the magazine wrote, for mental growth "children need adult affection and stimulation, no matter from whom it comes."[26] In the following months, articles telling of Skeels's report appeared across the nation—for example, in the *Arizona Republic*, the *San Bernardino County Sentinel*, the *Missoulian*, and the *Akron Beacon*. These many accounts did not mention that Skeels's discoveries had been greeted by his profession with nothing but contempt.

Perhaps alarmed that he was losing the public debate, a few months before Skeels spoke in Chicago, Terman told wealthy Pasadena eugenicist Eugene S. Gosney, whose book touting the success of California's sterilization laws had just been translated into German,[27] "I am amazed at the propaganda from the Child Research Institute at Iowa . . . [their] preposterous contributions are not backed up by data at all convincing."[28] As Skeels's report received even more press coverage in the coming months, Terman increased his complaints about the Iowan's public profile, describing the steady flow of news reports about the work as a "deluge."[29]

———

After the publication of groundbreaking studies, many researchers follow up with work that further extends their conclusions. During the years 1939 to 1942, Beth Wellman produced seven articles about environment and children's intelligence, some of which were published in the popular press, such as *Parents* magazine. A more theoretical paper, "The IQ: A Problem in Social Construction," written with George Stoddard, appeared in a progressive journal of ideas, *The Social Frontier*. Here, the two suggested that children who enter first grade with higher IQ scores gained in nursery school continue to have an advantage in learning to read, understanding arithmetic, and in other school areas.[30] Wellman also made public presentations. Also, during that period, Marie Skodak published her dissertation, and George Stoddard wrote six articles about the influence of environment, among them, "The IQ: Its Ups and Downs," published in a widely read education journal, *School and Society*. Stoddard, who continued to promote the idea of establishing universal kindergarten in the United States, frequently addressed national groups on the Iowa station's work, and he began his next book, *The Meaning of Intelligence*, to be published in 1943.

But in a radical downshift for someone who, in the previous seven years, had directed eight important investigations and published eleven research reports, after Chicago Skeels's investigations nearly halted. In the next three years, he published only one study, a 1942 follow-up of the post-adoption gains of the Woodward and Glenwood children. Unlike Stoddard, who never let an opportunity to advocate for Iowa's vision go by, and Wellman, who had been hurt by severe criticism but who did not curtail her work or its defense, Skeels retreated, speaking mostly to sympathetic audiences at small events located close to home. The Chicago attack so unsettled him that he now asked himself if his critics might be correct, that his extraordinary discoveries represented inauthentic growth.[31] Skodak recognized that while Skeels had always stayed clear of the spotlight, self-doubt now made him even more retiring.[32] He might even have believed that his challenge of those considered the finest minds in psychology may have ended his career.

In this light it is of interest to wonder what prompted Skeels, who must have known that some responses to his research would be critical, to write a paper that disputed his profession and to announce those views at a major conference. One explanation may have been the self-assurance the Iowans felt after the previous year of positive press and public response. Another might have been that Skeels believed that his work's potential to improve children's lives was worth the risk of mainstream criticism. Perhaps, too, he thought that if his evidence was powerful enough to change his own view, it might change that of others. And, after all, could anyone have forecast an attack that a later academic observer would label "violent"?[33] The record is silent as to whether Skeels considered any of these contingencies. Nor is there any surviving commentary from him about what led to his retreat, although that choice might have reflected a premonition that further attacks lay ahead.

―――――

A fter Skeels's report had generated much favorable press coverage, it would have been naive not to anticipate further retaliation from Terman, whose principal target now became Iowa's defender-in-chief, George Stoddard. Yet, the table for future attacks had been set some time before, in 1937, when Stoddard had been named to lead the February 1940 meeting of the National Society for the Study of Education. Along with that honor came the editorship of NSSE's important *Yearbook*, which would publish state-of-the-art research on environment versus heredity. The title Stoddard gave that *Yearbook* was *Intelligence: Its Nature and Nurture*, and it would include research that psychologists would then present at the meeting. Two previous NSSE *Yearbooks*, in 1921 and 1928, had addressed the same issue, with *Yearbook* contributors debating their work at those meetings. The 1928 volume, titled *Nature and Nurture: Their Influence upon Intelligence*, had been so powerfully shaped by its editor that it was known as "the Terman *Yearbook*." It left little doubt that the effect of children's environment or education on their intelligence was negligible.

But by 1937, views were shifting, and the NSSE recognized that Iowa's recent discoveries challenged accepted doctrine. Now, a scholar from a little-known university—looking back, Stoddard called himself a "fringe psychologist"[34]—would appoint the committee that would set the agenda for the gathering and would also shape the contents of NSSE's milestone compendium.

As the NSSE meeting's chair, Stoddard organized a planning committee, inviting participation from advocates on all sides of the controversy. For the environmentalist position there were two voices, his own and Beth Wellman's. Three members supported the hereditarian argument: Stanford's Lewis Terman, Minnesota's Florence Goodenough, and Leta Hollingworth, of Columbia University. The last three committee positions went to outstanding scholars who were not aligned with either side: Frank N. Freeman, dean of education at the University of California, Berkeley; Leonard Carmichael, president of Tufts University; and Harold E. Jones, director of Berkeley's Institute of Child Welfare. Of these, Freeman more often accepted the environmentalists' point of view, but not always.

The committee's early decisions went smoothly enough and their invitations to scholars from a range of specialties were accepted. For example, the committee invited Franz Boas, of Columbia University, an anthropologist and environmentalist who planned to explain, "In so far as intellect is dependent upon structure, it is heritable; in so far as . . . it is expressed in behavior, it is variable. The same individual in different situations . . . will show differences in intelligence."[35] Another was Frederick Osborn, the eugenicist who had recently critiqued the orthodoxy of fixed IQ. Osborn would remind the meeting that the 1928 *Yearbook* "was of major importance to the advance of eugenics," but that current work in psychology recognized "organic and social factors" in intelligence, although some "fail to recognize . . . that neither factor can be said to be more important than the other."[36] Also invited was E. W. Burgess, head of the sociology department at the University of Chicago, who planned to assert that studies of nature and nurture "without doubt . . . give support to a program of eugenics."[37]

Papers for the *Yearbook* on every side of the controversy poured in—they would fill two volumes. Among the star contributors were Arnold Gesell from Yale, Jane Loevinger from Berkeley, and Donald B. Lindsley from Brown University. But the rancor of the IQ debate seeped into the *Yearbook*'s editing process. Following about a year of planning, and shortly after the positive press coverage generated by Skeels's Chicago paper, in early June Terman wrote to Benjamin Simpson that a recent committee meeting had been "a continuous headache" and that Stoddard had attempted to rule out contributions from researchers who supported the "nature" position.[38] Goodenough later made the same assertion to Guy Whipple, NSSE's executive secretary. No evidence exists to support those claims, and Stoddard emphatically denied them.[39] If, in fact, Stoddard had wanted to exclude "nature" proponents, he would hardly have invited them to outnumber him and Wellman on the committee.

But at that same committee session, Terman revealed that he would withhold from the *Yearbook* a paper written by his colleague, Stanford psychometrician Quinn McNemar, one the committee had already approved for *Yearbook* publication. To Stoddard's surprise, Terman revealed that he and McNemar had circulated the paper among their Stanford colleagues and submitted it for publication to the American Psychological Association's *Psychological Bulletin*, where it had been accepted, making it unavailable for *Yearbook* publication. For someone of Terman's stature to withhold an important, even essential paper from a publication whose raison d'être was to present the most cutting-edge research in the field was a slap in Stoddard's face.

Terman's obstruction blindsided Stoddard and Wellman. Having read McNemar's paper, they knew it represented the most significant criticism of the Iowa work to date. Published in the *Yearbook*, it would have delivered a matchless opportunity at the February conference for the Iowans to engage in head-on-debate with their chief critic, whom all knew to be a proxy for Terman. Now that possibility had been abruptly confounded. Never one to be outflanked, Stoddard quickly arranged for an Iowa rejoinder to McNemar to appear in the same *Psychological Bulletin* issue.

As Stoddard might have expected, further hostilities soon broke out. On July 4, in San Francisco, before hundreds of delegates to a meeting of the National Education Association, Terman launched a broadside against the Iowa group. With Stoddard sitting a few feet away, Terman used sarcasm, mockery, and misrepresentation to malign Beth Wellman's discoveries:

> If the Iowa claims can be substantiated we have here the most
> important scientific discovery in the last thousand years. Well-
> nigh unlimited control over the IQ. . . . Either the educational
> program provided by other investigators are less stimulating
> than those provided at Iowa or the Iowa effects are in some
> way spurious.[40]

But Terman was not finished. On July 7, Stoddard drove 40 miles from Berkeley, where he was teaching in a summer program, across a bridge spanning San Francisco Bay, and as the sun began to set, continued south to Stanford, in Palo Alto. At Terman's invitation, the two would appear at a national meeting of educators and psychologists. Following Terman's recent attack, Stoddard may have anticipated another onslaught, and as he entered the university auditorium and scanned the event's program, he found a mute signal that he was right: his name had been omitted from the list of the evening's participants.

Alerted by reports of Terman's earlier attack on Stoddard, newspaper reporters who typically might not have turned out on a Friday evening to cover a university conference on "Educational Frontiers" decided to attend. They would not be disappointed. Seated side by side on the stage, Stoddard found that as the featured speaker Terman had double Stoddard's allotted presentation time. Addressing an audience of 1,200, many of whom had heard the Stanford psychologist's criticism of the Iowa work at the NEA meeting, Terman lost no time before pouring scorn on Stoddard and his colleagues, what one newspaper called an "unrestrained . . . denunciation" of the Iowa station's discoveries.[41] Insinuating that the Iowa work had deceived the public, Terman attacked "a deluge of monographs, magazine articles, newspaper stories and radio addresses . . . alleged . . . proof that feebleminded children can become normal."[42]

Especially singling out Skeels's study of the Woodward and Glenwood children, Terman misstated the children's ages and distorted the reasons for placing them with the women. As if the children's orphanage environment had not been a factor in the experiment, he omitted Skeels's account of Davenport's institutional neglect. He questioned, rightly, as had Skeels, that an IQ test could accurately measure the intelligence of children under 18 months, but ignored that nursing and pediatric specialists had confirmed the children's intellectual development. He did not acknowledge the Iowans' alerts about the tentative nature of their earlier findings; he failed to note that the children's IQ gains emerged slowly; and he cast aside the information that from age 2, the children's IQ test score changes had been regularly verified, a process that continued until they reached 3 or 4, and after their adoptions, confirmed again.

In a remarkable falsehood, Terman told the audience that other than the Iowa studies there were no reports of IQ changes in children in which psychologists or investigators had confidence. He did not share with his audience what might have been the most significant outcome of Skeels's research: eleven children who otherwise would have been committed as inmates to state institutions instead would grow up in caring, adoptive families. As if his misrepresentations did not go far enough, Terman then further targeted Skeels, sniping that the Iowa psychologist had brought his study to "its most absurd limits . . . and found . . . a more stimulating environment than the

orphanage . . . in an institution for the feebleminded! [where] . . . the cure
was carried out by moron nursemaids."[43]

According to newspaper accounts, Stoddard heatedly defended the Iowa
work, but none elaborated on what that meant. The *Los Angeles Times* wrote
that Stoddard was confident and quick on his feet, that he "flatly said he could
not agree with Dr. Terman [and began] a discussion so technical the chair of
the meeting deflected [it] to other channels."[44] Journalists hoping for a battle
royale may have been disappointed when Stoddard chose not to respond in
kind to Terman's tactics. However, Stoddard, whose Iowa mentor had studied
under Terman, likely knew of Terman's statistical inadequacy. Plausibly, Stoddard may have turned the discussion to technical issues to trap his adversary
in a web of data that only the two of them would have recognized for what it
was: the authority of Stoddard's wit over Terman's wrath.

"Psychology War Rages: Theory of Increasing Child Intelligence Scored
at Conference" was the headline in the next day's *Los Angeles Times*. The *Oakland Tribune* told of Terman's "sharp language," and similar posts, many from
the Associated Press Wire Service, spread word of the battle nationwide.
An editorial in the *Daily Iowan*, the University of Iowa's award-winning student newspaper—during the 1920s George Gallup had been its editor-in-
chief—immediately struck back at Terman, reminding him that the Iowans
had published skeptical reports of their own work, that they had only published their conclusions when their "new truths could be believed. Dr. Terman certainly knows . . . that Iowa research has met every challenge placed
before it . . . that Dr. Stoddard has gone to every meeting in recent years
equipped for battle."[45] On July 11, Stanford's student newspaper, *The Stanford Daily*, sandwiched a one-paragraph article about the meeting between
two movie reviews. The paper described a heated debate in which Terman declared that his studies revealed that changes in environment did not
change IQs.[46]

If Terman and McNemar thought that withholding McNemar's critique of
the Iowa work from the *Yearbook* would keep Stoddard from pursuing the

opportunity to debate McNemar at the NSSE meeting, they had the wrong George Stoddard. In fact, Terman's July attacks only intensified Stoddard's resolve to use the February meeting to bring his case and McNemar's critical paper to the attention of the full NSSE membership. On July 12, Stoddard wrote to Terman, reminding him that "the decision not to offer the McNemar manuscript was your own" and urging him to reverse course and allow the paper to appear in the *Yearbook*.[47] Terman's dodgy reply omitted any reference to his own role, and in what may have been but a charade of agreement, he wrote, "I personally feel . . . that it ought to appear in the *Yearbook*."[48] Perhaps disingenuously, Terman wrote that because McNemar could not be budged, he had "decided to let the matter drop."[49] It is also worth considering that Terman's reluctance to pressure McNemar might not have been a result of McNemar's stubborn insistence, but rather related to the power balance between the two. That Terman relied on McNemar to interpret statistical material for him was no secret, certainly not to Stoddard. It may also explain why the Iowans' chief accuser, an iconic figure in mental test psychology, published no technical analyses of the Iowa research. Thus, the decision to place the paper in a large-circulation journal might well have been McNemar's and one that Terman was in no position to challenge.

Later that summer, Beth Wellman and her Iowa station colleague, Kurt Lewin, a founder of the field of social psychology, traveled to San Francisco to attend a meeting of the American Psychological Association. Lewin, a much admired and highly gregarious figure, in 1933 had fled Nazi Germany and briefly held a position under Terman at Stanford. When Terman could not get funding to keep him, Lewin accepted an offer from Stoddard and moved to the Iowa station. (Soon he would move again, to head a research institute at MIT.) Lewin well knew of McNemar's writings against the Iowans, but hoping that Wellman and McNemar might establish a less contentious relationship, Lewin arranged a dinner where they would be his guests. In his autobiography, McNemar recalled that for most of the evening, Wellman maintained her composure, but finally, in exasperation, she turned to McNemar and told him, "Dr. McNemar, you should realize that Lewis Terman has poisoned your mind."[50]

In a score of letters, that fall Terman and Goodenough consulted about papers for the *Yearbook* and gossiped about the Iowans. On September 26, Goodenough reported that in October she would give a talk at Columbia University about the Iowans' incompetence—an opportunity that Terman had arranged—in which she planned to "point out their shortcomings without too much attempt at politeness."[51] "Don't mince words," Terman replied, "You know I was none too polite in my address July 7. . . . Polite methods simply don't accomplish the job."[52] Goodenough also told Terman that her colleague John Anderson would present a paper at the NSSE meeting that might anger Stoddard and suggested, should that occur, "[Anderson] will . . . take Master George's pants down and smack his bottom with a large Swedish hand."[53] Then, in November, she criticized the public's acceptance of Iowa's theories, because "teachers, social workers, and others . . . are less well qualified to judge the caliber of the evidence." Those who accepted Iowa's work, she said, were as "credulous as those who fled from Orson Welles' Martians."[54] Welles had recently directed a CBS radio drama, *The War of the Worlds*, so convincing it caused some listeners to believe that Martian space ships had landed in rural New Jersey.

No further combat erupted that fall and in December Wellman wrote to her friend, William Line, a psychologist at the University of Toronto: "There will appear shortly . . . a long criticism prepared by Quinn McNemar at the instigation of Dr. Terman . . . with a reply prepared by Dr. Skeels, Dr. Skodak, and myself. . . . The whole controversy has been brought to a head by the preparation of the 1940 *Yearbook*."[55] As the February meeting approached, McNemar's absent paper would become even more significant.

On the chilly morning of December 31, 1939, in Columbus, Ohio, Marie Skodak walked across the campus of her undergraduate alma mater, Ohio State, to attend the psychology session of the annual meeting of the American Association for the Advancement of Science. A decade earlier she had covered her college expenses by serving meals to the faculty of OSU's psychology department. When she learned that the AAAS would hold their annual meeting on campus, for old times' sake Skodak wanted to attend. That day marked just two years since Beth Wellman and Harold Skeels had first presented their discoveries at an annual AAAS meeting.

While it had not been their intention, since then Iowa's reports about nature and nurture had raised the temperature of the dispute to boiling, and the Iowans had been met with a backlash from other psychologists about their findings. At every professional meeting—the American Psychological Association, the Society for Research in Child Development, other AAAS meetings—mainstream psychologists would attack the Iowa discoveries and assert heredity's role in fixed intelligence. Although Skodak had published her dissertation in 1939, she had largely been spared the notoriety of her station colleagues. Unable to find an academic position, she now worked in a child guidance clinic in Flint, Michigan.

Only a few days earlier, Stoddard and Wellman had addressed this same meeting, and Skodak knew that many of the speakers, as well as those in the audience, would be critics of the Iowans. Attending only to observe the debate, the little-known Skodak was the sole Iowa psychologist in the hall. Relieved when no one in the crowd appeared to notice her, she quickly made her way to the auditorium's back row, where she listened to noted psychologists deliver censorious accusations against Iowa's discoveries. A 1967 report of the meeting chronicles that one of those speakers, Florence Goodenough, said, "The [Iowa] facts couldn't be true, because they violated what all psychologists knew to be true—intelligence cannot be changed."[56]

Neither Skodak's work, nor any of the Iowans' discoveries, directly connected the use of IQ tests to the nation's eugenically driven biases against immigrants. Nevertheless, from her own experience, she recognized that discrimination against orphanage children and against immigrants had striking similarities: both assumed that an individual's intellectual and social status had been inherited and could not change. As a child of immigrants, when Skodak had been assigned to sit with less proficient children, she understood that her teacher presumed her to be less intelligent. She told a later interviewer that in her community, immigrants were referred to as "nitwits."[57] Yet she recognized that her family models and experiences were a source of her self-confidence. During the 1917–1918 influenza epidemic, for example, along with her father, who spoke six languages and had been an intelligence officer in the Austro-Hungarian Army, Skodak had helped translate for local doctors. She was 7 years old.

Thus, when the AAAS moderator asked for audience questions and comments, the bias expressed that morning propelled Skodak to her feet:

> *I could take it no longer. I rose . . . with all my youth and all my inexperience for that kind of debate among important professionals. [I] held forth . . . about [the Iowa studies] and why [they] had happened, and why we were convinced that certain kinds of retardation were preventable. . . . I [told] of people . . . from peasant backgrounds in Central Europe who had children who were now professionals [and, she emphasized,] this was not unusual. . . . To this day, some people still remember me for that speech.*[58]

Chapter Nine

"EVEN IF IT DIDN'T WORK, IT WAS A GOOD IDEA!"

With the NSSE's February 1940 meeting only one week away, Barbara Burks, Lewis Terman's student and the lone psychologist at the Carnegie Institution in Washington, DC, read Quinn McNemar's paper with misgivings. Although firmly in the hereditarian camp, Burks had a fine grasp of statistics and was careful to consider research from a perspective of fairness. She told her mentor, "I do have a feeling shared by a good many others that his work contains certain biases that weaken its effect. Couldn't you have this out with Quinn so that his unique qualifications for . . . a high-class critical job can function most advantageously?"[1] Terman sent a snappish reply; she may have already irritated him by introducing her own article for the *Yearbook* with a reference to Lawrence K. Frank, a Rockefeller Foundation social scientist supportive of the Iowans' ideas. Terman vented his annoyance by forwarding her letter to McNemar with a sarcastic comment. In his reply he told Burks that although he would have preferred that McNemar eliminate some of his rough language, "the truth is at least 95% toward Quinn's side."[2]

When it opened in 1928, St. Louis's Jefferson Hotel regularly welcomed to its elegant Gold Room the city's bluebloods who dined and danced, enjoyed Dixieland jazz straight up from New Orleans, and sometimes viewed Hollywood's newest film sensation, the "talkies." But the Gold Room also hosted professional meetings, and in 1940 it was the site of the NSSE's *Yearbook* gathering about nature and nurture, a meeting many believed might bring a historic showdown between psychology's mainstream and Iowa's visionaries. Concerned that Midwest winter weather might trigger an episode of tuberculosis, Lewis Terman would not be among them.

That evening, NSSE members climbed the hotel's grand marble stairway to its glittering ballroom, perhaps the Midwest's most elegant. Against this dazzling setting, the mood of NSSE attendees "with blood in their eyes" gave dark warning as George Stoddard approached the podium to gavel the membership to order.[3] Expecting fresh attacks from Terman allies Goodenough, Simpson, and McNemar, Stoddard held high the two orange-jacketed volumes of the *Yearbook* and seized the advantage by opening the meeting with unexpected advice:

> May heaven reward the scholar who starts at page one and reads
> through to the bitter end. . . . For busier and less conscientious
> persons I have invented a little formula—a cure for compla-
> cency. . . . If you lean strongly toward environmentalism, read
> Terman, Goodenough and Hollingworth; if strongly toward
> hereditarianism read Stoddard and Wellman. They will all be
> good for what ails you. If you are neutral, or just bored, read
> Jones, Freeman and Carmichael.[4]

Stoddard then acknowledged what the attendees already guessed: "Only a confirmed Pollyanna would say that we have performed our task in a spirit of loving kindness."[5] Alluding to his struggle to have McNemar's paper included, Stoddard told the membership that when his committee began to gather research for the *Yearbook*, agreement on its contents seemed possible, but, he said, "now your committee can only reflect, like the disillusioned proponents of the league of Nations: 'even if it didn't work, it was a good idea!' Underscoring the absence of McNemar's paper, Stoddard said, "What is deposited in the yearbook is a pale residue."[6]

Time magazine's reporter noted that Stoddard's audience "looked at each other [and] wondered when the fireworks would start,"[7] but true to NSSE's tradition of courteous discussion, Stoddard managed to keep the peace. Perhaps Stoddard's equanimity also reflected that the station's views had lately won adherents. George Speer, a former skeptic whose own study had confirmed Skodak's, was in the hall. Stoddard also knew that Paul Witty, of Northwestern University, had prepared a full-throated endorsement that would quote John Rockwell, Minnesota's commissioner of education: "An atomistic, predetermined, rigidly stable intelligence may fit the current theories of psychology. It is out of place in the rest of the biological world."[8]

Stoddard might have been encouraged, too, because Albert Wiggam's article in support of the Iowa studies was about to be published in the nation's most popular women's magazine, the Ladies Home Journal. If a forthright discussion with the Iowans had shifted the views of an extreme eugenicist and Terman ally, others might be ripe for convincing. While Stoddard's wish for a direct debate at the meeting had been obstructed, it's plausible that he believed that the Iowans' arguments—they would each present papers—would win attention.

Environmental and hereditarian views received balanced hearings at the meeting. A notable contribution, a review of nearly one hundred studies from both sides of the argument, came from Berkeley psychologist Jane Loevinger. In "Intelligence as Related to Socio-Economic Factors," Loevinger included noteworthy data from Otto Kleinberg, of Columbia University, that the verbal test scores of African American students from the South who had migrated to New York increased with the length of their New York residence. Loevinger also included papers from hereditarians Lewis Terman and Robert Yerkes and from authors whose findings she found inconclusive. In the end, Loevinger could not judge any reports convincing. Instead, she observed that research in the field had expanded, but because many contributions failed to define terms such as "social-economic," and "intelligence," she judged that in most of the studies "conclusion is one word too often profaned."[9]

Supportive of the environmental argument was Newell C. Kephart, of the Wayne County Training School in Northville, Michigan, who showed that increased mental stimulation raised the IQ scores of a startling 50 percent of "mentally deficient boys." And a report from Martin L. Reymert and Ralph T. Hinton Jr., of Mooseheart, a residential facility west of Chicago, found that children made IQ test score gains when they had been moved from "a relatively inferior to a relatively superior environment . . . before they reach the age of 6." After that, IQ scores tended to remain constant.[10]

Supporting the heredity argument was a study by Grace E. Bird, of the Rhode Island College of Education, who found that nursery school children's intelligence showed a negligible effect from a superior school environment.[11] A comprehensive multi-year study of young children by Nancy Bayley, of the Institute of Child Welfare at the University of California at Berkeley, that considered socioeconomic factors showed that changes in constancy of intelligence were "most likely to be found in the natural processes of development in the organism."[12] And Gertrude Hildreth, of Columbia University, found no evidence that adopted children placed into superior homes and who attended an excellent school gained in intelligence to the level of the family's own children.[13]

In closing the meeting, Stoddard exposed an issue seldom mentioned in the debate, but which, he suggested, explained eugenicists' alarm about discoveries from the Iowans and other environmentalists: disbelief that intelligence actually could be increased when what was required to maintain a eugenically healthy society was sterilization. Stoddard pointed out that from 1909 to 1939, California, home to many leading eugenicists, was responsible for 43 percent of the nation's sterilizations of insane and low-intelligence citizens.[14]

For contrast, Stoddard highlighted the *Yearbook's* report from Robert Rusk, director of the Scottish Council for Research in Education. Rusk's study of the intelligence test scores of a random sample of Scottish children showed an even more unmistakable benefit of good environment than had the Iowans.[15] Rusk studied every Scottish child born on February 1, May 1, August 1, and November 1 of 1926. He found that the mean IQ of those children born in cities was 100.9, for those born in industrial areas it was 99.2, and for those born in rural areas it was 100.9. Stoddard wrote that Rusk did not find "the deficiency of ability of rural children . . . so frequently reported for American children."[16] Rusk reported, "Perhaps nowhere has scholastic opportunity been more evenly equated than in Scotland; 99.7 percent of Scottish teachers are fully trained."[17]

Stoddard also quoted C. H. Waddington, a geneticist and eugenicist at the University of Edinburgh, who wrote, "A much greater improvement in intelligence could be produced by measures of social amelioration than by any eugenic steps."[18] Stoddard concluded the meeting by affirming "of the demonstrable impact of different environments upon the plastic, maturing organism which is the child there can be no longer any doubt."[19] But according to Lewis Terman, the environmentalist research published in the Yearbook was "strikingly like . . . E.S.P."[20]

———

While Stoddard stood up for the Iowans' groundbreaking work, he knew his defense had been hobbled by an inability to rebut the severe critique that McNemar and Terman had withheld. He knew, too, that in the following weeks, as psychologists gained access to McNemar's paper, they would find it had borrowed Terman's combative style, promising to "demolish," "destroy," and "explode" Iowa's argument. But Stoddard's controlled demeanor cracked only once in St. Louis—when he addressed Terman's stratagem that had kept the paper out of the Yearbook. "The largest single body of criticism directed, as you may surmise, against the rather massive Iowa materials, was never available for the Yearbook itself."[21] McNemar, Stoddard explained, had chosen to publish his paper elsewhere. Stoddard labeled the paper's rhetoric "the tactics of a criminal lawyer" adding, "In such a melee truth is not so much crushed as smeared."[22] Finally, George Stoddard had lost his cool.

As the content of McNemar's paper, published in February, filtered through the profession, the months that followed the meeting confirmed Stoddard's fears. Although filled with careless or deliberate omissions and distortions, as well as criticism of the Iowans' statistics, some of it unreasonable or so unnecessarily complex that it eluded many readers, the paper accomplished what McNemar and Terman had sought: the shadow it cast on the Iowans' competence intensified doubts about their results.

McNemar's review began by maligning the Iowans because, following their initial publication in scholarly journals, their discoveries often appeared in the popular press, a criticism Terman had also made in his July 7 attack at Stanford. "The new gospel," McNemar wrote, "is being carried beyond . . . journals."[23] This summoned the age-old academic prejudice against any work that achieved popular acceptance—the perception that it must be slick or specious. As an example, McNemar cited a Wellman article that had appeared in the *New York Times*. He did not seem to know that the Iowa station's charter required that it inform the public of its discoveries. According to Stoddard, every article that appeared in nonacademic publications was submitted at the magazine or newspaper's request or came from local or national media coverage.[24] Moreover, sixty letters between Wiggam and Terman written from 1925 to 1953 reveal that Terman regularly supported Wiggam's popular-press articles, even providing him with suggested text.[25]

McNemar then tore apart the results of Wellman's 1932 preschool study, Skeels and Wellman's 1938 Davenport preschool study, Skodak's 1938 and 1939 adoption studies, along with the Iowans' other investigations that demonstrated the effects of environment. For reasons that are not clear, McNemar did not attack, or even mention, Skeels and Dye's 1939 study of Davenport's orphans at Woodward and Glenwood.

In his critique of Davenport's preschool investigation, McNemar claimed that Iowa's statistical analyses of children's intelligence were inaccurate because over three years "only a few" of the original children remained in the experimental and control groups due to the adoptions of the others. In fact, eleven of the original twenty-one experimental children left the study because they were adopted. Each time this occurred, another child, similar in age, sex, and IQ, had been substituted. McNemar criticized the inclusion of substituted children, writing that this made it difficult to control variables such as numbers of days of residence and school attendance.

Because the preschool study occurred in a real-world setting, from its outset the psychologists knew that they might lose subjects to adoption. They noted that it would have been unethical to deny a child the opportunity to be raised in a family. The same problem of attrition by adoption occurred in every orphanage study of that time.[26] In Skeels's study, children whose socialization and intelligence improved as a result of preschool experience became those more likely to be adopted. A perfectly executed study would have denied the opportunity for adoption for the sake of statistical scrupulosity. McNemar, however, turned the substitution of children into a cudgel to damage the Iowans' scholarly reputations.

McNemar next faulted the Iowans for their failure to emphasize the factor of rapport, that is, the IQ test examiner's ability to establish a setting of trust and comfort that enables children to perform at their best. Yet, McNemar supported this claim with an erroneous reference, suggesting that the children's negative experiences with their cottage matrons led them to mistrust all adults. As Wellman noted, establishing testing rapport with these needy subjects was close to effortless.[27]

McNemar then threatened to "explode" what the Iowans identified as a "leveling effect,"[28] when long institutional residence with limited human contact and almost no cognitive stimulation appeared to lower children's intelligence.[29] Specifically, they found that after three years, control group children who began with IQ test scores in the range of 65 to 105 ended with scores between 70 and 79. Control group children who initially had IQs of 103, 98, and 73 ended with IQs of 60, 61, and 62 and had to be transferred to an institution for persons with low intelligence. Overall, the preschool children with the longest residence lost a mean of 4.5 points, while control children with the longest residence lost 28.5 points.[30] Because McNemar rejected the notion that IQ could change, he attributed these shifts to the surfacing of a child's heredity and claimed that the Iowans' findings resulted from their improper substitution of children.[31]

In their rebuttal, published in the same journal edition as McNemar's attack, the Iowans' reanalyzed their data, including only the original children. Their results were nearly identical.[32] Further, McNemar inaccurately reported the amount of time the preschool children spent away from orphanage care as "five or six hours daily," or 37 to 44 percent of their waking hours. In fact, the children attended preschool for about 8 hours a day, five days per week, or 60 percent of their waking hours each week. McNemar also criticized Marie

Skodak's study of 154 mostly illegitimate children of prostitutes who were adopted before the age of 6 months and after two years had intelligence in the superior range. To support his claims, McNemar asserted that the birth mothers' and fathers' educational levels were what they had claimed, in the tenth-grade range, which accounted for the children's superior intelligence. However, as any educational statistician of that period would have known, and as Skodak's paper pointed out, at the time a policy known as "non-failing" (actually, automatic promotion) was well established in the United States, and Iowa routinely promoted students based on chronological age.[33]

McNemar also incorrectly reported the intelligence of the study's birth fathers, asserting that their occupational levels, at the time a proxy for male intelligence, were higher than Skodak claimed. In a response, Skodak showed that if the known birth fathers were employed at all, and many had never held a job, those who worked fell into the lowest occupational levels.[34] McNemar's assumptions about the children's fathers relied on a cultural surmise made by hereditarians, the "smart John" effect. Although that term is a modernism probably not then in use, it suggests that any prostitute's child with good intelligence—many of Skodak's subjects were such children—reflected the intelligence of the prostitute's patron. Providing no evidence, McNemar asserted that 23 percent of the fathers in Skodak's study were such patrons.[35] In a rebuttal, Skodak wrote, "The pregnancy may have followed an assault by a stranger, may have been a chance pick-up . . . or the mother may be unable or unwilling to give information identifying him."[36]

In an outright error, McNemar reported the average IQ for 2-year-old children in Skodak's study as 108. It was 114. When he challenged the validity of intelligence tests given to 1-year-old children, Skodak recomputed her calculations without those tests. She got the same result. Further, McNemar charged that Skodak had not considered selective placement as a factor in the children's high IQs. However, from pages 63 to 141 of her paper, she discussed selective placement fifteen times.

In their rebuttal, the Iowans also noted that McNemar had not read, or had ignored, the key chapter in Skodak's report "that showed marked gains in IQ following residence in average and above-average adoptive homes."[37]

Importantly, only those of McNemar's readers who closely studied the Iowans' rebuttals would have been aware of his inaccuracies.

Another major salvo directed at the Iowa discoveries came from Florence Goodenough. Like McNemar, she chose to publish her paper in another journal, one available in January, weeks before the NSSE meeting. In it she listed nine investigations on the subject of nursery school education and intelligence outcomes, only one of which, she claimed, demonstrated a positive effect.[38] Stoddard responded, "Since this is the kind of simple, straightforward statement that is likely to be cited in the years to come, it may be helpful to spend a few minutes in its analysis."[39] He showed that results from seven of the ten preschool studies that Goodenough cited demonstrated gains from 1.8 to 6.6 IQ points. The highest gains came from the University of Iowa's Laboratory Preschool.

Both McNemar and Goodenough challenged Skodak's test results in children under 2 years of age. To answer them, Skodak removed from her data all IQ tests on children who were younger than 2 years. Her results held up. Because the evaluation of very young children was based on the attainment of motor skills rather than verbal responses, any test instrument designed to assess their intelligence naturally aroused skepticism. However, the Iowans, and literally all other 1930s psychologists who evaluated very young children's intelligence, relied on such tests, notably the Kuhlman-Binet. In 1928, Goodenough herself had published a monograph recommending procedures for that test's administration.

Hoping to win support, the Iowa group revised their data according to methods McNemar suggested. In nearly every case, their original findings prevailed. Still not satisfied, McNemar accused them of making deceptive statements. In one example, he challenged their account that "more than one-third of the long-residence control children had final IQs within these limits [50s and 60s], while only one preschool child had a final IQ below 70."[40] McNemar said, "An exact statement would read: Initially four and finally eight of 22 control children were below 70; initially three, and finally one, of the 21 preschool children fell below 70."[41] Both statements were equally true accounts, despite McNemar's needless complexity and invidious implication.

McNemar's slanted language, careless use of material, feigned or true ignorance of known information, unsupported assertions, outright errors, along with his assumption of statistical superiority, all were known to the Iowans from their spring 1939 reading of his paper. That they could not—head to head—refute such faults before their colleagues undoubtedly drove Stoddard's introductory comment that the *Yearbook* was only a "pale" remnant of what it might have been.

———

Three Iowa papers answered McNemar's attack: Stoddard had arranged for the first, a rebuttal by Wellman, Skeels, and Skodak, published in the same journal issue as McNemar's critical paper;[42] and a second, this from Stoddard, was published soon after the St. Louis meeting, in April 1940.[43] Then, at a June 1940 meeting of her psychology honor society, Wellman presented a third.[44] Taken together these counterarguments identified McNemar's inaccuracies and included statistical revisions of the Iowa work according to McNemar's suggestions, almost none of which altered their studies' findings. Anyone wanting to understand both sides would have had no difficulty locating this information. But in the end, McNemar's implication of the Iowans' statistical incompetence aroused damning suspicion of their results, especially among readers who were already skeptical, and therefore Iowa's rebuttals made almost no impression. McNemar's paper, a proxy for the views of Lewis Terman and others, eclipsed the Iowans' evidence and became decisive.

Although Lewis Terman had not attended the St. Louis meeting, colleagues reported to him about how attendees regarded the Iowans and their supporters. Florence Goodenough remarked that Iowa supporter Paul Witty "had made very much an ass of himself."[45] Her comment was sharp but not specific. Witty had in fact spoken about research that showed African Americans were being disadvantaged in education because of assumptions that their intelligence was low. He also provided evidence that gifted African American children were denied enriched experiences that would allow them to fully develop their abilities.[46] Moreover, Witty fiercely indicted the use of intelligence tests, which he said favored those with a "fortunate social heritage," leading educators to assume that the less fortunate lacked potential.[47] The use of the tests, Witty asserted, contradicted the founding ideas of democracy.

With some pleasure, in a letter to Terman, Goodenough reported that Iowa's ideas may have generated opposition within their own university. She related her "amusing experience" when the chair of the University of Iowa's social work department introduced her to a colleague as "the person who had made Iowa infamous." The social work head assured Goodenough that "our department is on the same side of the fence that you are" and told her "no other departments at Iowa . . . agreed with Stoddard's and Wellman's claims." The social work chair also reported "there was a great deal of feeling . . . that the Research Station had done a good deal to discredit the University."[48]

A second report to Terman came from Benjamin Simpson, who wrote that because Stoddard did not back down when attacked, he was an effective spokesperson—so effective that an Ohio State colleague told Simpson, "George Stoddard is a dangerous man." Simpson added that Stoddard "is out to win popular support . . . [and] a force to be reckoned with." Yet the hot-tempered Simpson noticed that attendees maintained control of their responses and he admitted that he had been chastised because "his writings had been too emotional."[49] What neither Goodenough nor Simpson said, but what might have been evident to both, was that by the meeting's end there was no clear victor in the contest between the environmentalist and hereditarian views of development.

———

Only two months after the St. Louis meeting, in April 1940, California educators and Stanford faculty, along with the university's president, Ray Lyman Wilbur, came together in Cubberly Auditorium for a second Terman-Stoddard debate. For the evening's topic, the NSSE's latest *Yearbook*, Terman arranged to speak for an hour and gave Stoddard 10 minutes. A panel discussion by others would follow. Although the moderator later reported that Stoddard had the audience cheering, Stoddard's memory of that evening was the wound Terman inflicted on him. "Terman," he remembered, "pronounced 'Skeels' and 'Skodak' explosively, lip curled, as if these two young

Iowa researchers were a species of insect that had crept under his collar."[50] Stoddard said that he began to think that Terman's invitation had been a setup to inflict more abuse, that "the performance was rigged . . . I had traveled 2000 miles for my bit part." The moderator, Stoddard wrote, had confessed to a colleague that he "held Stoddard down while Terman beat him."[51] The two antagonists did not meet again.

Only limited analysis exists of Terman's bellicose attacks on Stoddard and his other critics. In one, his biographer, Henry L. Minton, has suggested that certain weaknesses in Terman's own work may have contributed. Minton wrote, for example, that especially when he was younger, but even into the 1940s, Terman "tended to interpret the data to fit his preconceived notions [and] drew causal conclusions from correlational findings." Such fundamental research errors would naturally have drawn peer disapproval to someone, Minton observed, who had an "intolerance of accepting personal criticism." Minton concluded that Terman's battles with his critics "seemed driven more by a need to prove himself than to settle a scientific issue."[52]

In another view, historian Hamilton Cravens suggested that Terman's rage was defensive of his, and most psychologists', social status; that for them, how child development was studied represented

> part of the tacit social and cultural understandings that knit
> together the social order, and as such . . . had explosive impli-
> cations for the distribution of status, power, wealth, and jus-
> tice in society. If the Iowans and their allies were . . . right . . .
> then the social network of groups and their relative positions . . .
> could be regarded as cruel, arbitrary, and oppressive.[53]

Cravens speculated that Terman understood "only too well the implications of the Iowa work," and suggested that the Iowans provoked his fury because they challenged assumptions of inherited privilege, that they "crossed some line . . . [and] betrayed their science, their profession, and their social class."[54]

Unbeknownst to Stoddard, in the spring of 1940 he faced further under-mining unfolding in the corridors of the Carnegie Institution in Washington. From the station's research, Stoddard appreciated the importance of early development and had hoped to promote a program of national preschools, something that other nations had already established. In over fifteen articles, he had reported on the economics of bringing his idea to scale: teacher salaries and teacher training; potential benefits for children's health; positive effects on intelligence; the relation of early education to democratic principles. Alert to opportunities to capture public attention, he even gave advice about how to educate the world-famous Dionne quintuplets, in Ontario, the first quintuplets known to have survived infancy. In 1937, when the quints were 3 years old, Stoddard asked: "Are children today paying the price for the prolonged controversy on heredity versus environment? This 'case for the quints,' gives encouragement to continue the quest for the optimum environment."[55]

Stoddard's advocacy had brought him national attention, and he served on a New Deal emergency committee for the Works Progress Administration that established nursery schools for children from 2 to 6 years old—a total of 3,000 schools in thirty-one states. The program hired thousands of unemployed teachers and supported children's well-being with nutritious meals—essential during the Great Depression and Dust Bowl—and also guaranteed adequate health care.[56] Finding widespread support, Stoddard had proposed to Henry A. Wallace, a longtime Iowa friend who was now Franklin Delano Roosevelt's secretary of agriculture, that the program might be expanded to serve the entire nation. Wallace agreed.

But just at the time of the post-NSSE downdraft, in May of 1940, Terman's student Barbara Burks, at the Carnegie Institution, learned of Wallace's interest. She told Terman that along with two colleagues, eugenicists Robert Cook and Harold Jones, she thought the plan absurd, and the three hoped to make "at least a dent on Secretary Wallace."[57] To that end, Terman provided copies of his July 7, 1939, Stanford attack on the Iowa work, which Burks circulated at Carnegie.[58] The next week she wrote again, now to say that although Iowa's media publicity had influenced Wallace and "the Iowa ideology had filtered down to everyone in the Department . . . including the most far-flung field workers," Burks and her colleagues had convinced Wallace that the Iowa ideas were mistaken. Wallace, she said, was no longer ready to "buy IQ's . . . to manufacture them by given dosages of nursery school, [or] moron nursemaids."[59]

Later she told Terman that Wallace would certainly have accepted "the Iowa stuff in toto" had Cook, now her fiancé, not intervened and that "it is a safe . . . bet that Iowa-ism would have assumed the proportions of a national movement."[60] It may never be known whether the chilly reception of Iowa's ideas after the St. Louis meeting influenced Wallace, but in the end, a Lewis Terman confederate subverted George Stoddard's program for the kind of preschool experience that most industrialized nations now consider essential in children's development.

It is reasonable to wonder how the dispute between the Iowans and McNemar might have unfolded had today's academic peer review requirements then been in place. Peer review, the process by which scientific claims are vetted, requires that prior to journal publication an article's methods and findings are reviewed by scholars in the same field. While at times these reviews can be partisan, even brutal, in the main they bring more eyes to new material and allow for shared judgments. One can imagine, for example, that a peer reviewer might have flagged McNemar's unsupported errors and assumptions. Likewise, the Iowans might have been asked to rework some of their data using different statistical methods. But until the post–World War II era, peer review was scattershot, with few established procedures,[61] and played no role in the publication process of the Iowans' work, nor in that of their critics, nor in much of psychology's academic publishing.

Although following the *Yearbook* meeting the Iowans received little support from their profession, they might not have gauged how gravely McNemar's and Goodenough's critiques had damaged their studies' credibility. But the only social science historian to thoroughly study the Iowa station, Hamilton Cravens, concluded that the doubt that McNemar cast on the station's methodology weighed heavily. Citing 1970s interviews by Yale child psychiatrist Milton J. E. Senn, Cravens wrote that many individuals remembered the 1940 controversy "and without exception reported that it was the statistical criticisms that dissuaded them from looking more closely."[62]

However, research suggests that like Lewis Terman, many 1930s psychologists lacked expertise in areas that relied on statistical measurement. For example, NSSE's secretary, psychologist Guy M. Whipple, who had a PhD from Cornell and was director of the Bureau of Tests and Measurements at

the University of Michigan, warned 1940 *Yearbook* readers that he had struggled with the statistical material in many of the publication's reports.[63] Moreover, Diane Paul, a modern-day social scientist who has studied the history
of genetics as related to the heritability of intelligence, reported that authors
who are "expected to write on a topic where they lack confidence but which
they know is a source of controversy . . . [may] turn to . . . sources thought to
be good authorities." Paul suggested that this results in the republication of
material that "appears plausible because it confirms deeply rooted assumptions about the influence of genes on intellectual performance."[64] Paul's 1980s
insight may explain why many psychologists of the Iowans' time relied on
McNemar's analysis rather than their own analyses of the Iowa studies' sug-
gestive research.

Were the Iowa station researchers surprised at McNemar's critique?
According to Marie Skodak, they were not as resentful as they might have
been: "Their feeling was, well, this is what you would expect." But she also
reported that the criticisms "hurt Wellman and Skeels very much."[65] One
of Skeels's subjects, Louis Branca, who as an adult discussed the attacks
with Skeels, said, "I can't begin to express how wounded he was."[66] Yet for
Skeels's experimental group children, the Iowa station's research brought
striking opportunities: eleven of those children now lived with adoptive
families.

———

In the summer of 1939, one of those children, Wendell Hoffman, said good-
bye to the Glenwood women who had mothered and supported him and
arrived in St. Paul, Minnesota, as the adopted son of Louis and Genevieve
Branca. The Brancas had no idea that their 5-year-old, whom they renamed
after his adoptive father, had already lived two identities: as a normal 1-year-
old, then as a borderline deficient 2-year-old with a 75 IQ. Now, as Louis
Carroll Branca, his IQ was 86, in the low average range, a positive outcome
Skeels had hoped his subjects would experience. In the fall Louis's parents
enrolled him in a parochial school's kindergarten and arranged for a tutor to
help him achieve academic levels comparable to most children his age. A year
later, when Skeels retested his intelligence, Louis's IQ had risen to 92; in the

four years after he left the Davenport Home, he had gained 17 IQ test score points, more than one standard deviation.[67]

Following his painful Chicago appearance, Skeels's 1942 follow-up of Louis and the other Woodward and Glenwood children was the only study he conducted. Here he reported that after his experiment, the test scores of nearly every experimental group member had continued to advance, with the greatest gain, 16 points, in a child adopted into a highly stimulative home. The single child who lost IQ points had been placed in a home with parents who, Skeels reported, seemed "far below the average for the group."[68] But in the contrast group, Skeels found that low IQ test scores persisted and suggested this was because "the psychological recipe [for intellectual stimulation] was . . . inadequate as to kinds of ingredients, amounts, and relative proportions."[69] Yet, Skeels also found that if placed in enriched environments, some contrast group children made progress. For example, one child transferred to Glenwood as a permanent resident gained 24 IQ test points, although that did not bring him to a normal IQ. The most significant finding from his 1942 report, Skeels explained, was "the marked relationship between rate of mental growth and the nature of the environmental impact."[70]

———

Following this report, Skeels—who since his college days had been in the military reserves—was called to serve in World War II as a captain in the army air force. He soon was promoted to major, and when the Blitz ended he was transferred to a desk job in London. Stoddard, Wellman, and Skodak had all received harsh criticism from Terman and his adherents, but the attacks on Skeels had been some of the most brutal. Skodak knew that his suffering had lingered and thought he might have been grateful to leave the Iowa station in order to serve in the war.[71] However, Skeels may have had yet another reason for feeling relief when he departed for service overseas, something Marie Skodak intimated in her recollections: a fear that his sexuality would become a subject for further ad hominem abuse.

For nearly a decade Skodak and Skeels had worked closely together, and a powerful bond had grown up between them based on their shared unease about the Davenport Home's management and their empathy for its children. With such a relationship it would be natural to wonder whether the connection between two young, single professionals sharing their work day after day might not have become something more intimate. But Skeels always maintained a core of reserve that Skodak could not breach. Many years later, after his death Skodak spoke of his intense privacy. She told historian of child development Milton J. E. Senn that although Skeels cared very much about little children, he was "not a man cut out for marriage,"[72] words that at the time conveyed more innuendo than information. The evidence is scant and circumstantial, but if Skeels were gay, in 1930s Iowa—as in most of the world—it would have been far safer for him to remain closeted. Still, the two researchers would remain friends for life, even after their careers took them far apart. And decades later, their work with the children of Davenport would bring them together again.

While we have only indirect evidence that Skeels might have been gay, it's plausible he may have been alarmed by concurrent events: at the same time Skeels was being savaged by Terman, another Iowa professor was under scorching censure from his own department chair, who "tried mightily to have him fired, in part on explicit moral grounds."[73] That professor was Grant Wood, at the time a celebrated artist and creator of the iconic painting "American Gothic." While his department chair, Lester Longman, cast his criticism as a disagreement about artistic vision and creative direction, recent scholarship has determined that what provoked his attack was Wood's semi-open homosexuality.[74] For Wood, or anyone so attacked, exposure would have meant ruinous public shaming or worse: given Iowa's 1929 sinister sodomy laws designed to punish "moral degeneracy" and "sexual perversion," sterilization and incarceration might soon have followed.[75]

Further linking Skeels and Wood, both had close connections to George Stoddard, a champion of each in the face of controversy. From 1934, when Wood joined the University of Iowa faculty, he and Stoddard shared a friendship, at first based on Stoddard's role as the dean of the university's graduate school. "From the beginning," Wood wrote to Stoddard, "we saw eye to eye on the art school situation. We spoke the same language."[76] In 1936, Wood had lectured on the role of art in children's lives at the Iowa station's annual child development conference. When Longman's attacks unfolded, Stoddard became Wood's confidant and acted as his intercessor with the university's new president, Virgil M. Hancher, suggesting to Hancher that the attack on Wood was "a hatchet job." Stoddard advised the president that "Mr. Wood is the particular glory of Iowa's contribution to art . . . when the University is known at all it is known for just a few . . . and Grant Wood is at the top."[77] Whether the two discussed the motive for Longman's attack is not revealed in their letters. However, with Stoddard's intervention, in August 1941, the university transferred Wood from Longman's department to the School of Fine Arts and promoted him to full professor.

While Wood's and Skeels's circumstances were far from identical, it seems credible that the attack on Wood suggested to Skeels that he would be wise to avoid public conflict, especially with Terman. Perhaps heightening Skeels's concern would have been his knowledge that in addition to an emphasis on mental tests about intelligence, Terman's scholarship also included studies of masculinity, femininity, and homosexuality. During the mid-1930s, Terman wrote many scholarly papers and a 600-page book in these areas, and to assess those traits he created his "M-F" test. One section of the test rated how homosexuals differed from the larger male population.[78] He devoted a book chapter to "A Tentative Scale for the Measurement of Sexual Inversion in Males."[79]

In 1935, Wood, who had not been known to have had a relationship with a woman, married suddenly, but by the summer of 1939, he claimed that marital discord had led to financial woes and he actively sought a divorce. In 1934, Skeels had briefly married, but his divorce almost two years later was not contentious. He did not marry again. In retrospect, like Wood's, Skeels's marriage may have been a masquerade undertaken to camouflage his sexuality.

Skeels's practice of keeping mum about his private life is further revealed in a detailed letter Skodak wrote soon after his death to one of his only known relatives. "Despite his talkativeness about his research," Skodak told Skeels's cousin, "he was not communicative about his life, his family, his friends . . . in many ways [he was] a solitary and lonely fellow."[80] Skeels's extreme reticence may have reflected a fear of exposure; it is also possible that to shield him, and so protect the integrity of his discoveries, Stoddard had encouraged Skeels to keep his head down. For Skeels, that would have been welcome advice.

————

During the late 1930s, when the nature versus nurture dispute had become the most important topic in psychology and when the young Skodak had challenged important mainstream psychologists at a professional meeting, another early career psychologist, Lois Barclay Murphy, had helped found a laboratory nursery school at Sarah Lawrence College, in Bronxville, New York. From her own experience testing intelligence in young children, Murphy knew that the Iowa reports had to be correct, but alert to the possible career risks of speaking out, Murphy chose not to provoke Iowa's attackers. However, after a forty-year silence during which she had become a leading scholar of early development, in 1980 Murphy delivered the Molony Memorial Lecture at the City College of New York. In it she explained that because 1930s psychologists looked only at group norms and disregarded case studies, they did not find evidence of individuals' intelligence changes:

> The stable IQ fitted in with the wishes of psychologists who in the first quarter of the century felt insecure and timid because psychology was a new science and psychologists wanted it to be respected, like physics. . . . It was important for them to think in terms of . . . high correlations and predictability . . . unpre-dictability would have made people very nervous.[81]

Murphy's insights about the mental test psychologists of Lewis Terman's era may explain the profession's insistence that intelligence was inherited. She went on to confess:

> I feel guilty because in the 1930s I didn't think anyone would pay attention, but I was finding parallel results with children who came to school with low IQs. One child's IQ went from 89 to 136. I knew that Skeels and Skodak were sound, but with the whole establishment against us I didn't think there was any

point in trying to convince people. I didn't have a statistical
study as a weapon.[82]

How many researchers may have avoided the potential career costs of supporting the Iowa station's discoveries is unknown, but as Marie Skodak observed of Terman, "There was no way of saying him nay."[83] George Stoddard, reflecting later about psychology's resistance to Iowa's ideas, recognized that "all of us 'environmentalists' were confronting a state of mind," but also, he said, "an entrenched position, at times . . . a lucrative business."[84] Stoddard and his colleagues had found that despite the benefits of Iowa's discoveries for future Davenport children and institutionalized children throughout the nation, Terman's commanding influence meant that his storm of attacks probably could not be turned back.

Chapter Ten

A CHILL IN THE AIR

With the nation's attention drawn to Europe's conflict with Germany and America debating entry into that war, during the spring and summer of 1940, the Iowa psychologists failed even to return psychology's quarrel to its previous stalemate. At the station the calendar of speaking engagements and research related to the Iowa studies was close to empty; no peers outside of Iowa initiated studies to follow up on environment's role. It also became clear, despite a suggestion Stoddard had made at the St. Louis meeting that educators might curtail their use of IQ tests, and despite forebodings from Terman's test publisher that orders for tests might decline, almost all the nation's schools continued to purchase and administer the tests. By November Goodenough cheerlessly complained to Terman of her obligation to visit the University of Chicago "for one more discussion about the sins of our neighbors at Iowa." It felt, she said, "like kicking a dead horse."[1]

By 1941, existential threats from Nazi Germany and Japanese aggression eclipsed research in child development and in most nonessential academic areas, and after the December attack on Pearl Harbor, nothing but the war mattered. From Flint, where Marie Skodak was now the director of a child guidance clinic, came her observation about that time: "You gave up careers, you gave up plans, gave up your personal life, because this was crucial."[2] Skeels had left Iowa for his war assignment, and Beth Wellman had been diagnosed with breast cancer. As was common medical practice in that era, she underwent significant surgery. Dauntless, she continued to teach and train graduate students, but her research slowed and she next published in the late 1940s. She died of her illness in 1952.

George Stoddard, to whom the Iowa station represented everything he valued, now wondered if perhaps it was time to leave. First in his family to graduate from college, he had thrilled to the university's and the station's congenial faculty and intense intellectual life. Along with his lively household— there were four, soon to be five children—at his summer home on an Iowa lake, Stoddard gathered friends like Henry Wallace, Grant Wood, "who dropped by in his famous overalls,"[3] and Robert Frost, who during several summers taught at Iowa. On cooler evenings Frost sat in the glow of the family's stone fireplace reciting his poems to the Stoddards' enthralled guests. "It was the full force of Iowa" Stoddard recalled, "a magnet, that kept me there."[4]

For the gregarious, charismatic Iowan there had been tantalizing offers to join other faculties. In 1935, Teachers College at Columbia University tempted him with a significant salary increase and the promise of potential colleagues the likes of John Dewey and Edward L. Thorndike, as well as New York's sophisticated cultural scene. But that offer arrived as the station's work on intelligence had begun to suggest startling outcomes. In 1939, Stoddard's Iowa mentor, G. M. Ruch, now at the University of California at Berkeley, tried to lure him west. Again, Stoddard's commitment to discoveries that had become even more thrilling, along with his NSSE leadership position, kept him planted.[5]

Stoddard may have resisted moving, too, because his role as a trailblazer and nurturer of daring young psychologists supplied much of what his intellectual navigation system demanded: original thinking, a chance to innovate, and a route for his passion to uncover new knowledge. He explained his outsized intellectual drive as an unexpected gain from his partial deafness, a factor that, he said, made him attentive to "his constant inner life." He recognized that such persistent self-reflection might suggest that he was

deafer than I am . . . and can become a source of unintentional
rudeness. . . . On the other hand . . . the hardest stance for me
is to remain cool to what I regard as original and exciting. . . .
My most intense pleasure is to be in touch with a warm creative
person who represents what human nature is or could be.[6]

But when the 1940 flood of contempt washed over Iowa's research landscape, Stoddard's perspective shifted. In an ordinary time, this effect might
have been a setback, but not lethal. Now world events put research on hold,
and with the station's agenda suspended, he recognized that the vibrant
milieu he helped create might not return soon, or ever. As he watched the
University of Iowa's student body melt away into the armed services and most
research come to a near standstill, Stoddard began to search for a new position. His older children were approaching college age, which made the financial rewards of an administrative appointment even more tempting. In neither
of his two autobiographical reports, nor in a detailed 1971 interview with
Milton J. E. Senn, did Stoddard indict the failure of Iowa's work to gain acceptance as decisive, but he must have wondered what role in research leadership
he could envision for himself if he remained in place.

In 1938, Stoddard had given a speech in New York State on "Child
Development: A New Approach to Education." In a region with almost no
child development research programs, his talk about the interdependence
of democracy and education was considered bold—even, some said, tilted
toward socialism and communism.[7] Nevertheless, in 1942, Stoddard accepted
the position of president of the State University of New York and, concurrently, as New York's commissioner of education.

After Stoddard announced he would leave Iowa, close to 2,000 congratu-
latory letters from every part of the nation poured in—although none came
from mental test psychologists. In that prodigious response, the Iowa station's leader must have found testimony that in the wider world of American
thought his ideas had more impact than he had realized.

One letter came from Luther H. Gulik, President Franklin Roosevelt's
National Resources Planning Board chair. Weary from war concerns, Gulik

told Stoddard that his appointment was "the best news for the schools of the whole country that we have had. . . . Everyone [sic] in a while when one is pretty discouraged a thing like this happens and faith is restored."[8] Edmond E. Day, president of Cornell University, told Stoddard he would be filling one of the most important educational posts in the nation. And Wiley B. Rutledge— who in less than a year would sit on the United States Supreme Court— called Stoddard "the last bulwark of liberal thinking" at the university.[9]

A message of particularly wistful admiration came from an Iowa citizen, Ethel Collester, who wrote: "It is becoming too common . . . this lifting of our fine men from Iowa into further fields . . . Iowa has lost so many. I take advantage of my nothingness to say that I could have given up three or four others before I could . . . let you go. You so tenaciously stood by the things you believed in."[10] From this perspective Stoddard's battle with the nation's mental test psychologists might have begun to seem less material.

Along with his administrative talent, Stoddard brought to New York State his social justice commitment, during his inauguration warning of the hypocrisy of "school trustees [who drive] up in handsome cars on million-dollar roads, in order to cast a vote to lower the meager salary of the teacher."[11] Never forgetting that public higher education had made his own career possible, he helped enlarge New York's university system, expanding its two-year campuses to bring higher education to students in rural areas.

While leading the way in these and other initiatives, in 1943 Stoddard also published his exhaustive consideration of children's cognitive development, *The Meaning of Intelligence*, in which he analyzed past and recent research about the interaction of innate ability and environment. With little focus on Iowa's attackers, Stoddard gave special emphasis to the Iowa findings, offering views that since the 1930s had won him much scorn. Stoddard also demonstrated the linkage between the attacks against the Iowans and eugenics' "contempt for mass inferiority."[12] He reported that a leading eugenics group, the Human Betterment Foundation, in Pasadena, California, extolled America's record of sterilizations—by 1939 a total of 30,690.[13] How many of those victims, Stoddard had to wonder, had been raised in inadequate environments? The reading public paid attention, and the book went to ten printings; Stoddard earned royalties that in current dollars totaled about $400,000.

By 1945, Stoddard's New York success encouraged the University of Illinois to name him its president. At a farewell dinner, Governor Thomas E. Dewey toasted, "My only regret is that . . . we have lost the warmth of his personality and the clarity of his thinking."[14]

Before moving to Illinois, in 1946 Stoddard briefly headed a committee of the United Nations Educational, Scientific, and Cultural Organization (UNESCO) that advised Japan concerning its establishment of postwar school programs and where he reported directly to General Douglas MacArthur. Among the committee's recommendations was that Japan's schools consider teaching history and geography as objective subjects, rather than departure points for "militaristic indoctrination."[15] As he completed his assignment, Japan's emperor, Hirohito, asked Stoddard to help him locate an American tutor for his son, 12-year-old Crown Prince Akihito. Contrary to custom, the emperor said he would prefer the tutor be female. From the hundreds of American teachers who applied, Stoddard recommended Elizabeth Grey Vining, whose personal warmth and obvious love of children told him she had to be the choice. Vining, a childless widow of 40, considered this her opportunity "to serve the cause of peace."[16] The emperor agreed. In April 2019, after thirty years as Japan's 125th emperor, Akihito abdicated the throne to his oldest son.

———

Several months after Stoddard became president of the University of Illinois, he drove down to Iowa to give a talk to his former university colleagues. A member of that audience nostalgically told the student newspaper that Stoddard "diffused exciting ideas that make everyone around him feel things happening."[17] The talents Stoddard brought with him wherever he landed would not change, but at Illinois, they would not always find appreciation. The writing may have been on the wall when, just as he began his new assignment, a national panel ranked the standing of the boards of trustees of America's state universities: Illinois came in at number 47.[18]

However, Stoddard's first efforts, directed at the 12,000 GI Bill freshmen entering the university after the war, were expensive but successful. And when, to great acclaim, he brought major artistic figures such as Igor

Stravinsky to campus, he appeared to have the support of the university's board of trustees. Perhaps overconfident, Stoddard seemed not to notice quiet manipulations of McCarthy-era trustees who had turned on him because of his spending, his "socialist tendencies"—such as his continuing service on a UNESCO committee—and his support for faculty who refused to sign McCarthy-era loyalty oaths. He also became entangled in a conflict with a board member he had appointed who sought to promote Krebiozen, a questionable cure for cancer based on mineral oil and other organic solvents. When the American Medical Association declared the cure worthless, Stoddard withdrew the university from further Krebiozen research and refused to keep quiet about it: as at Iowa, he defended empirical evidence against pseudoscience. Within days the board engineered a no confidence vote and Stoddard immediately resigned.

Although Stoddard had the support of Illinois governor Adlai Stevenson, much of the faculty, the American Civil Liberties Union, and a major Illinois newspaper that claimed that "from the day he took over as president" statehouse politicians seeking to use the university for political advantage had been stalking him,[19] none of it mattered. Declaring that Stoddard had been "hot-tempered, sometimes high-handed," *Time* magazine headlined the board's action "The Final Arrow."[20] After his firing, he and his family moved to Princeton, a university town where one of his sons was attending graduate school and where he thought he would feel at home. During his yearlong stay, the university offered him a position, which he refused. He needed time to recover and decide how to proceed.

With Stoddard's 1942 departure from the station, the University of Iowa faced the task of filling the position of station director at a time when most qualified administrators were in the military or had jobs they would not leave. Yet the choice of Robert R. Sears—a candidate with no research background or training in child psychology, early development, mental testing, or child institutionalization, and who had never held an academic leadership role—seemed baffling. But in Sears's mostly Ivy League curriculum vitae, the university found one matchless credential: for a significant part of his life, Sears had been closely connected to Lewis Terman.

Sears's father and Terman had been colleagues and friends, and as a first-grade student in Palo Alto, Sears qualified as one of approximately 1,500 highly intelligent young subjects for Terman's groundbreaking work, *Genetic Studies of Genius*. (On Stanford's campus those children became known as "Termites.") Terman hoped his research about gifted children would counter the stereotypical view that they were bookish, socially inept young eccentrics. As an undergraduate at Stanford, Sears had studied psychology under Terman, but found his lectures unstimulating. However, with Terman's encouragement he went on to earn a PhD in psychology at Yale, and before relocating to Iowa, he taught at the University of Illinois and then at Yale. In both appointments his research focused almost solely on aggression and frustration in adults.

When World War II began, Sears sought a war-related position in Washington, DC, but was unable to find an assignment. However, when offered the directorship of the Iowa station, what he called his most interesting option, he accepted. In an extensive 1968 interview, Sears did not address why someone who lacked a research history related to child development might have been offered that role. But he recognized that leadership of the Iowa station gave him a new academic credential—it made him a "developmental psychologist by fiat" rather than by training.

It is likely that the university knew exactly the type of scholar it sought to replace Stoddard—a figure who, by returning the station to a more orthodox research program, would restore academic credibility some feared had been lost. Sears did not describe how Iowa's offer came about, but early in September of 1942, he and his family moved from New Haven to Iowa City, where Sears became the Iowa Child Welfare Research Station's third director. Nearly thirty years later, Sears remembered, "I really was a coast-type culture person, and moving to a rather prominent position in a Midwestern community proved . . . a shock."[21]

Sears encountered an even greater shock when he recognized that his Iowa colleagues, all child development specialists, "simply didn't include the kind of people" that were at Yale. Other handicaps also contributed to his poor fit, first among them his age—while he was the station's leader, he was the youngest member of its faculty. Just as important, Sears had no administrative experience. His "slightly stormy" debut made him uncomfortable, and he admitted later that he had suffered extreme anxiety for which he sought psychotherapy. Within a month of his arrival, he wrote to Stoddard, "I swear I have never worked harder in my life."[22] Although the two regularly exchanged collegial letters, each suggesting to the other that their families should visit, Sears only once mentioned his rocky transition.

As he began his duties, Sears became the lone student in an ad hoc intensive tutorial to qualify him for a job he already had. He plowed through child development readings, which he discussed with Beth Wellman and other station members, and found himself "struck . . . with astonishment to discover that here were some extremely able people."[23] He said that academics like Wellman were unknown to him, and he found it "interesting" that she and others had a remarkably different view of child development and behavior than most. Because many of the station's psychologists, medical personnel, and other experts had left to become war specialists, Sears's on-the-job training came from a much-reduced staff. He noted:

> Psychologists moved off into research on gunnery. . . . Someone editing the Journal of Child Development did so from a military post in Europe. There was very little to do because there was very little research being done. . . . It was a very dim period for child development because there was nobody left to keep the shop running.[24]

But bringing fresh eyes to what had been, for him, an unknown area granted Sears freedom to articulate the complex demands of child development research, demands the Iowans implicitly understood but had not formally described. "Every child is a multidisciplinary object," Sears observed, and the study of the child's complexity required the contributions of separate disciplines of psychiatry, pediatrics, education, social work, and clinical psychology—"all have to deal with a child [who is] contained within one skin."[25]

Without referencing the Iowans' studies or McNemar's flawed critique, Sears had identified an aspect that may have made those studies less satisfactory: they attempted to trace multiple developmental processes from a single perspective—the development of intelligence—when, Sears predicted, "the best research is going . . . to be done by people thoroughly grounded in one discipline, [who] understand the others . . . enough to talk the language of their colleagues."[26] Although unmentioned, embedded in Sears's analysis was the Iowans' core concept—that development emerged in a dynamic environmental framework—and he paid no attention to eugenic beliefs about inherited ability.

Central to Sears's intensive study had to have been Lawrence K. Frank's seminal 1943 forecast of what lay ahead for the field of child development research, *Research in Child Psychology: History and Prospect*.[27] Frank had graduated from Columbia University as an economist, then worked with Beardsley Ruml at the Rockefeller Foundation. He later directed its Laura Spelman Memorial in child development, eventually directing all Rockefeller Foundation child development programs. In that role, Frank became a familiar presence at the Iowa station and one of the nation's most respected theorists in child development. In 1947 he won the prestigious Lasker Award in mental health.

Intolerant of any aspect of hereditarianism, in the harshest terms Frank condemned what he viewed as the tyranny of intelligence tests:

> *The assumption that a child of given chronological age has had the same opportunity as his contemporaries to develop his capacities . . . is becoming increasingly dubious. Moreover, the designation of these unhappy children as congenitally handicapped or defective and their assignment to the categories of the hopelessly retarded begins to appear as a cruelly unfair and socially intolerable practice for which no amount of quantitative and seemingly scientific sanction can be offered as justification.*[28]

In the same article, Frank held that the recent formation of the Society for Research in Child Development, now one of the field's most highly regarded organizations, was a signal to researchers that the field must collaborate with many disciplines to understand child growth, behavior, and personality.

Clearly, Sears's thinking borrowed from Frank's, yet with Skodak and Skeels gone and Wellman ill, during his tenure the station launched no initiatives about environmental influences on the development of institutionalized children, initiatives that might have safeguarded those who, at that very moment, lived in the Davenport Home. During that period, too, Sears allowed the productive alliance of the Davenport Home, the Iowa station, and the Iowa Board of Control to lapse to its pre-1934 status.

―――――

For several summers during the 1940s, Marie Skodak had returned to Iowa to follow up on her studies of children adopted into middle-class homes, investigations of how those children's superior intelligence held up as they got older. On those visits, Skodak worked at the Iowa station under Sears's leadership but recognized that she had reentered a changed world—one altered not only by a world war. The station's work had shifted radically and now included no research into the development of institutionalized children, nor effects related to adoption, and little in the area of preschool attendance. Speaking of her 1946 visit, Skodak said: "[Sears] was not just a newcomer. . . . I found the whole atmosphere . . . so different that I said I would never go back. . . . The idea of doing something in the real world was not part of the thinking."[29] At the Davenport Home, and at the station, it seemed that the Iowa group's vision and investigations had disappeared and left no trace.

It is likely that Sears arrived at the Iowa station certain that he would alter its research agenda, and when he shifted its studies from the effects of environment to areas of personality and social adjustment, he accomplished that goal. For example, in 1946 Sears published a paper, "Sex Differences in the Projective Doll Play of Preschool Children," and in 1947 another, titled "Influence of Methodological Factors on Doll Play Performance." As with much of Sears's Iowa research, these topics bore no relation to Davenport's children, who lacked dolls or other toys or even opportunities for ordinary play. When only two papers in this period, each by Beth Wellman, continued the station's research path, America's psychologists may have interpreted Sears's neglect as further confirmation that the Iowans' mission had lacked value.

Yet after the war, Sears would warmly welcome Skeels's return to the station and support the continuation of his research. One could imagine, then, that earlier in his tenure, Sears's inexperience may have presented a barrier to his appreciation of the Iowa scholars' novel insights.

Less than a year after Sears's arrival at the station, Harold Skeels wrote in 1943 from the Office of the Commanding General of the Army Air Forces Gulf Coast Training Center to say that he looked forward to returning to "roll up my sleeves and have a part in the challenging program."[30] Over the next two years, the men exchanged friendly letters, Sears signing one "with enthusiasm for seeing you again."[31] Just before Skeels was demobilized, on December 1, 1945, he wrote, "I am looking forward with a great deal of plea- sure to . . . the opportunity of working with you."[32] By the time of his official discharge, he had already submitted a proposal to Sears that spelled out his next project, a study of the mental development of children in adoptive homes who were now approaching adolescence.

It is even plausible that the inexperienced Sears had been anticipating Skeels's return as a means to restore the Iowa station's mission. He held noth- ing back when he approached the George Davis Bivin Foundation for funding to allow Skeels to travel throughout Iowa and beyond to test the intelligence of several hundred children. In a detailed three-page letter to the founda- tion's president, R. H. Singleton, Sears explained that Skeels's earlier reports on this cohort were "responsible for extensive changes in adoptive proce- dure in a number of states." His new study would follow up on the children's mental development, including an investigation of their schooling. He added that there was "resistance [to his findings] in some states because the data have not been carried through to the final conclusion."[33] He defined the study as one "of very extreme importance," adding that Skeels's early reports had been essential to modifying foster care placements in Iowa and had "saved a very large number of children in the state."[34] Skeels had already met with the foundation's administrators, who seemed receptive to his research, and now they had Sears's letter, which assured them of the station's full support. Sears's request to the Bivin Foundation to fund Skeels's investigation suggested that after three years as director he had now embraced its historic child development focus.

At his return, in December 1945, Skeels resumed testing Davenport inmates' intelligence, supervising adoptions at the Davenport Home, and transferring youngsters with low intelligence to other institutions. But Skeels had come back unprepared for a new reality: during his absence, staff changes at Davenport had resulted in even greater deprivation for its residents, creating even worse conditions. Discouraged, by early February Skeels asked Sears to make inquiries for him at the Veterans Administration, where he could work as a psychologist. Then, in mid-March, word came from the Bivin Foundation about funding for Skeels's next project. The foundation's president wrote, "We feel unable to respond favorably." It was a one-sentence letter.[35]

Skeels's close-up exposure to Iowa's failure to nurture its residents, a failure he had observed for over a decade, now seemed unendurable, perhaps even caused him to feel that he, too, had become an agent of harm. His research had made all too plain that Davenport's environment erased the futures of many of its residents, condemning them to adult lives in institutions when changes in their environments would have saved them.

After months of indecision, in August Skeels wrote an explosive letter that spelled out to the Iowa Board of Control how Davenport's poor management and neglect affected its inmates. In his three-year absence, Skeels said, the state had crowded Davenport's staff with incompetents hired because of political patronage. Needed rehabilitation services for 4,000 older children in the state's institutions, he wrote, would require radical staff increases. Skeels criticized the hiring of untrained matrons who worked "fourteen-hour days with two days off per month for a paltry salary of seventy dollars per month" and added, "High caliber teachers seldom accept a position or stay long on a salary of one hundred dollars per month."[36] Skeels attacked the appointment of institutional superintendents who lacked any training and stressed that the Board of Control, supposedly in charge, had been denied any authority. He also emphasized that unqualified state agents charged with helping children make life plans were hired because of their political connections.

He reported that when older Davenport children left the orphanage, many turned to crime and were sent to the state's homes for delinquents.

Life at Davenport, Skeels said, stole the intelligence of some of the children who lived there. "Of twenty-two older feebleminded children recently transferred from the Iowa Soldiers' Orphans' Home to the Glenwood State School for Feebleminded," Skeels wrote, "nine, or forty percent, were of normal or low average intelligence" when they entered Davenport four or five years earlier. Skeels observed that the low salaries for psychologists at Iowa's other institutions meant that more than half of the positions remained unfilled. He declared his "moral obligation to the unfortunate wards of the state to register this protest."[37] And with his unprecedented letter, Skeels resigned his position as Iowa's director of psychological services.

Perhaps in a signal to the state, the Board of Control released Skeels's letter to the Des Moines Register, which, under the front-page banner headline "Expert Says Institution Children Hurt by Politics,"[38] quoted much of Skeels's commentary. But when Harold Skeels turned away, he left Davenport's children marooned. Following his resignation, and grateful for the station's past promotion of his work, Skeels told Sears that the station's "moral support . . . [had] affected child welfare policies throughout the country" and that he "deeply regretted" that he would not be working with Sears.[39]

Within two weeks the Veterans Administration offered Skeels his choice of posts in Denver or San Francisco, and he accepted Denver's offer. But by December, Skeels told Sears of his misgivings. He confessed that he missed the station "gang" and "even the program in the Iowa institutions which seemed so futile."[40] He wished Sears had talked him out of accepting his new position. In responding, Sears told him, "We certainly miss you and don't know when in the world we are ever going to find a man to replace you. All my efforts have met with utter blanks."[41] Perhaps the most likely candidate to replace Skeels would have been Marie Skodak, but there is no evidence Sears considered offering her the position. None of Skodak's later interviews or memoirs discuss this, but it is possible that Skodak had not kept her disapproval of Sears's station leadership to herself. It is also plausible that Sears would have agreed with a University of Michigan academic who had refused to consider Skodak for a position because "unfortunately" she was a woman.

By March, Iowa's Board of Control had proposed reforms of Iowa's institutions based on increased state appropriations and closer work with the Iowa station. Board discussions with Sears that included Skeels's possible return found some board members cool to that idea, but as one acknowledged, "Well, it was all true."[42] In the end, Skeels remained at the Denver office of the Veterans Administration as chief clinical psychologist. In 1949, he moved to San Francisco as consulting clinical psychologist with the US Public Health Service, an arm of the National Institute of Mental Health (NIMH). In 1951, NIMH promoted him to scientist director and chief of Special Program Development of the Community Services, in Bethesda, Maryland.

In 1949, Sears resigned his Iowa position, saying he had "become a little tired of the Middle Western atmosphere . . . and very tired of the administrative responsibility."[43] As he left, however, he accepted the presidency of the American Psychological Association. In his next appointment, at Harvard's Graduate School of Education, Sears made use of the good fortune of his Iowa experience. He had gained some mastery in a new field and also inherited the Iowa station's organizational model in which specialists cross-referenced their expertise to serve a single goal. He said that seemed "the best device I've seen yet for creating a genuinely stimulating environment for the study of child development,"[44] although he did not credit Stoddard's leadership for its evolution and application. After Sears left the station, Beth Wellman briefly served as station director, and in 1952, her former student, Boyd McCandless, became the station's leader. Also in 1952, Sears left Cambridge to return to Stanford to lead the psychology department previously headed by Lewis Terman.

In 1940, Marie Skodak became assistant director of the Flint, Michigan Child Guidance Clinic, a social service agency that provided therapy for children suffering psychological adjustment problems. With her male colleagues serving in World War II, in 1942 she became the agency's director, the only woman in the United States to hold such a position.[45] When the war ended and the men returned, Skodak left to open her own practice, becoming one of only two psychologists practicing privately in Michigan. Also during the 1940s, Skodak became a part-time lecturer at the University of Michigan, where she trained social workers.

Skodak's 1930s Iowa sojourn had delayed her plan to become a school psychologist, but in 1949 the Dearborn public schools hired her in that position. Once the turf of Henry Ford and other Detroit-area industrialists, by the time Skodak arrived, Dearborn had a professional class and also a diverse immigrant population. In her public school work, Skodak supported the roles of social workers and teachers in understanding the needs of all students, especially those with disabilities.[46]

From 1943 to 1950, Skodak published four investigations that followed up on her earlier Iowa work, two of them with Skeels. In these she confirmed the persistence of intelligence gains in children she had previously studied, who at 2 years of age had a mean IQ score of 116. In the later work she found that at age 4, the mean IQ was 112, and at age 7, it was 113. To Skodak, these longitudinal results confirmed that an innate aristocracy of intelligence simply did not exist. On one of Skodak's Iowa research visits, she learned that priceless records belonging to her and to Skeels were "destroyed in a 'housecleaning operation' during or shortly after Dr. Sears' administration."[47] Although she had rushed to save what she could, irreplaceable historic research files and notes were gone, including Skeels's 1938 8mm home movies of Glenwood children who recovered their intelligence, and of the women who cared for them. Skeels's discovery of the discarding of his research materials only seemed to revive his feelings of disgrace.[48]

———

In 1942, Lewis Terman retired as head of Stanford's psychology department. In three decades he had grown a little-known department at a young university—Stanford had been founded in 1885—to a position of national and professional recognition. During that period five psychologists from the department, including Terman, were elected as presidents of the American Psychological Association. Those psychologists were also elected to the National Academy of Sciences, one-third of the psychologists elected during that period.

Shortly after he retired, Terman suffered extensive burns from a fire when he fell asleep while smoking in bed. (In a time before the dangers of smoking were known, Terman had been a heavy smoker.) His recovery, including many skin grafts, extended over three years. From that point he limited his research to follow-up reports related to his longitudinal study of genius, such as his 1947 "Factors in the Adult Achievement of Gifted Men" and "Psychological Approaches to the Biography of Genius." Because Terman believed that very intelligent people produced their best work in their 20s, he also devoted himself to promoting early identification of gifted children and encouraged their acceleration in school.

In 1949, psychologist Nicholas Pastore, of Teachers College at Columbia University, published *The Nature-Nurture Controversy*, a collection of essays analyzing the work of twenty-four social scientists who had "expressed themselves on nature-nurture issues and controversial social and political questions."[49] Eleven of these were psychologists. Based on the analyses of others, Pastore classified each as a hereditarian or environmentalist, and to accurately represent their views, he also studied the writings of the scientists themselves. Pastore showed that in nearly all cases, those who held conservative social ideologies supported the hereditarian position, while those favoring ideas considered progressive leaned toward the environmentalist view. Learning that Pastore would describe him as a conservative, Terman wrote the author to dispute that characterization.

In a detailed letter that Pastore's book quoted at length, Terman described his consistently progressive voting record, emphasizing, "I hate every form of national totalitarianism. . . . Our failure to insure [the Bill of Rights] to minority groups I consider a national disgrace."[50] Pastore noted that in Terman's 1930 autobiography, he had written "the major differences in the intelligence test scores of certain races, Negroes and Whites, will never be fully accounted for on the environmentalist hypothesis."[51] However, to Pastore, Terman also wrote, "I am now inclined to think that [the differences] may be less than I formerly believed them to be."[52] This private comment was as close as the typically unrestrained Terman came to amending the record of his hereditarian views.

In 1956, while at work on the fifth volume of *Genetic Studies of Genius*, Terman died. He was 79 years old. In his 1957 remembrance of Lewis Terman, Robert Sears wrote:

> *In a science that seems . . . to orient itself too often toward the care and understanding of the weak and inept, Terman turned*

*resolutely toward the positive side of man's existence. As a stu-
dent of the intellect, his interest in feeblemindedness was per-
functory, his zeal for the study of genius, burning.*[53]

Another recollection came from Stanford psychologist Ernest Hilgard, who had twice moderated as Terman and Stoddard did battle. In it, Hilgard reported that in Terman's personal copy of his autobiography, next to his comments that racial differences drove intelligence levels, he had written two notations. The first, from 1951, said, "I am less sure of this now." And in 1953, "Still less sure."[54]

PART III

Revival

Chapter Eleven

REVERSAL OF FORTUNE

O n April 7, 1945, the *Baltimore Sun*'s World War II correspondent, Lee McCardell, arrived at Ohrdruf, a small subcamp of Buchenwald and the first concentration camp liberated from Nazi control. McCardell wrote:

> *Good God! . . . in a wooden shed, piled up like so much cord-wood, were the naked bodies. . . . You had heard of such things in Nazi Germany. You had heard creditable witnesses describe just such scenes. But now that you were actually confronted with the horror . . . you almost doubted your own eyes.*[1]

As Lieutenant General George Patton's 4th Armored Division fast approached, panicked guards murdered the camp's nearly 2,000 mostly Jewish prisoners, although a few escaped into the surrounding forest, only emerging when the Americans arrived. McCardell had heard about the camps but had dismissed them as "just another atrocity story, probably true."[2] A few days later, America's best-known radio journalist, Edward R. Murrow, reported from Buchenwald:

Dead men are plentiful in war, but the living dead, more than
20,000 of them in one camp. . . . In another part of the camp
they showed me children, hundreds of them. . . . One rolled
up his sleeve, showed me his number. . . . I could see their ribs
through their thin shirts. . . . The children clung to my hands
and stared.[3]

From 1933, when Adolf Hitler was elected Germany's chancellor, until the nation's defeat in 1945, the American public had nearly daily access to newspaper and radio reports documenting Nazi efforts to eradicate degenerates from German society.[4] News of Nazi race laws, the forced removal of Jews and other minorities to ghettos, then to concentration camps to be tortured and murdered, all of this information was widely available. Although concerned organizations attempted to aid those trying to escape, for many reasons, including America's eugenically based immigration laws, their efforts were almost entirely unsuccessful.

But according to Daniel Kevles, after World War II knowledge of Nazi war crimes radically altered the nation's thinking: "The revelations of the Holocaust had all but buried the eugenic ideal. . . . Eugenics . . . became virtually a dirty word in the United States."[5] Historian Allan Chase also reported that "the word 'eugenics' was . . . no longer even whispered on America's campuses, in America's laboratories."[6] But how would this retreat from eugenics influence the postwar priorities of mental test psychologists, the powerful group that had invoked eugenic explanations for human development longer and more vigorously than almost any other? Would it undermine psychology's confidence that heredity alone decided human traits?

Perhaps due to public distaste, postwar those psychologists retreated from the measurement of children's intelligence, which had dominated their studies of child development, and took up research about adults, especially, as the war ended, related to millions of returning GIs. According to Marie Skodak, postwar research emphasized "clinical and adult needs . . . [and] adoption studies were totally abandoned."[7] A similar report came from Harold Anderson, a Michigan State University scholar who during the 1930s had studied children's learning and motivation at the Iowa station. Anderson told a historian of child development that following World War II, "as a culture we [were] not interested in children." Organizations in which child development had once been paramount, such as the National Research Council, the Social Science Research Council, and the Society for Research in Child Development, now treated it with indifference. "Anybody," Anderson said, "could have done more to support child development research."[8] The field of psychology that only recently had been a battleground for hereditarian versus environmental dominance became quiet as an empty library.

A review of four research journals that had previously published studies related to the influence of environment in the development of children's intelligence suggests that between 1940 and 1960, the majority of reports about child development focused on personality types and social behaviors, as well as teaching and learning. Research into child development emphasized nutrition and children's physical characteristics, including their health and growth. Some investigations examined academic programs and teacher training. During these decades, for example, the *Journal of Experimental Education* published 105 articles in the areas of teaching methods, teacher personality, and teacher-student relationships, but just 4 studies that related to environmental stimulation and intelligence. Similarly, during this period the *Journal of Child Development* published 497 papers, of which only 7 examined environment and intelligence. In the *American Journal of Mental Deficiency*, only 10 of 1,115 articles addressed this area. In the *Journal of Genetic Psychology*, 5 of 791 articles examined environmental stimulation and intelligence in children. Of a total of 26 articles, 6 were from Iowa station psychologists.

Psychology's postwar turn from the study of child development had many causes, among them the loss to research of Stoddard, Skeels, and Skodak and, due to her illness, of Wellman. But a further explanation may be found in a 1956 essay from Iowa station leaders Boyd R. McCandless and Charles C. Spiker. In "Experimental Research in Child Psychology," they addressed the postwar absence of new research and theoretical models and a preoccupation, instead, "with the application of available knowledge."[9] They attributed this decline to a profession that had failed to train students in statistical techniques, research methods, and the construction of theory. Additionally, they suggested that psychologists were now perceived as clinicians expected to teach and apply their training to practical concerns rather than theoretical constructs.[10] The failures McCandless and Spiker described were less present at the Iowa station, and with its fiftieth anniversary in 1967, the station (now renamed the Institute for Child Behavior and Development) published an index of its over 2,000 scholarly publications in child development. This is especially remarkable because during the station's first two decades, there were never more than six faculty on its staff, and later, never more than a dozen.[11]

———

A lthough Iowa's 1930s work did not immediately revise psychology's epistemology, its influence surfaced in a daring study from émigré physician and psychoanalyst René A. Spitz. Born and educated in Vienna, later a professor in Paris, in 1939 Spitz, who was Jewish, escaped the Nazis when he came to the United States. Settling in New York, he practiced and taught psychoanalysis, and to better understand his patients' adult lives, he began to study early development. Working in an unidentified Western Hemisphere location, Spitz confirmed the Iowans' discoveries. In 1945, he published "Hospitalism: An Inquiry into the Genesis of Psychiatric Conditions in Early Childhood," in which he cited each of the Iowa psychologists—the most significant notice they had received from an investigator outside their circle.[12] Then and today considered a work of great insight, Spitz's paper reported on the development of institutionalized children under 1 year of age. He found that, as BD and CD, many grew asocial, became feebleminded, and showed profound developmental declines. Much subsequent literature about the deterioration suffered by institutionalized children confirmed Spitz's observation of a condition first defined in 1897 as "hospitalism."[13]

Accompanying his report was a quotation from a 1760 Spanish bishop translated here: "In the children's home, many die of sadness."[14] The infants' deterioration, Spitz suggested, resulted from extreme neglect. Spitz studied two groups of children from similar social backgrounds. One group lived in a nursery located in a penal institution, where their pregnant, incarcerated mothers had given birth and remained. The other group lived in a foundling home. Although each institution provided excellent nutritional and medical care, aspects of the children's environments differed considerably. For example, the nursery children had many more toys, purchased or made for them by their mothers. Also, from their cribs they had views of the outdoors, and each day their mothers cared for and played with them.

Like the children in Davenport's nursery, infants in the foundling home lay in cribs wrapped with protective sheeting that created an environment of nearly total seclusion and that Spitz likened to "solitary confinement."[15] Also like the Davenport children, overburdened staff provided little attention or stimulation. Spitz found that the foundling children had poor motor development, failed to gain weight, and suffered from poor health. Some died. Although Iowa's studies included almost no references to the deaths of Davenport children, Marie Skodak reported that they occurred.[16] At the end of one year, the mean developmental score of children cared for by their mothers remained in the average range, but the foundling children became retarded. In 1952, Spitz circulated his films of young institutionalized children who appeared to have significant cognitive deficits. After child development professionals viewed these amateur movies, they successfully lobbied to outlaw nearly all orphanages in the United States.[17]

Spitz was not alone in his concern about institutional effects on children, and in 1949 additional research appeared from Harry Bakwin, a pediatrician at Bellevue Hospital in New York. Bakwin reported that the illnesses and deaths of infants in hospitals and institutions were not the result of poor nutrition, as had been thought, but of neglect. With exquisite empathy, Bakwin understood that the isolation and loneliness experienced by babies could prove deadly. At Bellevue he replaced a sign that hung outside the hospital's nursery that said "Wash your hands twice before entering this ward" with one that said "Do not enter this nursery without picking up a baby."[18]

In descriptions remarkably similar to Skeels's discussion of CD and BD, Bakwin reported that young children in hospital wards "failed to gain weight, and show listlessness, emaciation and pallor, relative immobility, quietness, unresponsiveness to stimuli like a smile . . . and [have the] appearance of unhappiness."[19] These conditions, he said, improved within about six months after the infants were placed in homes. While Bakwin did not reference the Iowa discoveries, that time interval closely paralleled the period BD and CD had spent with the Woodward women when changes in their development became obvious.

In 1952, John Bowlby, a pediatrician and psychologist and the director for child guidance at London's Tavistock Clinic, published *Maternal Care and Mental Health,* a comprehensive report for the World Health Organization and the United Nations, which confirmed what Spitz and Bakwin had found:

> *When deprived of maternal care the child's development is almost always retarded . . . and that symptoms of physical and mental illness may appear. . . . This is a somber conclusion which may now be regarded as established. . . . [The evidence] leaves no room for doubt that the development of the institution infant deviates from the norm at a very early age.*[20]

Bowlby did not reference the Iowa studies, but he cited the important work of William Goldfarb, a psychologist with the Foster Home Bureau of the New York Association for Jewish Children. Goldfarb found that by age 3, children who lived in an institution had a mean IQ score of 68, while those who had been adopted had a mean IQ score of 96, a differential similar to what Skeels had reported in his experimental and contrast groups in 1939. Both psychologists had used the Stanford-Binet IQ test.[21] Like the Iowans, Goldfarb found that the "most significant group for psychological consideration is the infant."[22] His research notwithstanding, a critic told him, "The supposed love of the foster mother for the foster child, is frequently fiction."[23] Further, his employer added a disclaimer to the published version of Goldfarb's paper, which said, "Judgments . . . do not necessarily reflect the views of the N. Y. Association for Jewish Children."[24] Spitz, Bakwin, Bowlby, and Goldfarb might have expected their work to move psychologists and the public closer to the environmental view. However, unlike the exhilarating 1938–1939 period when word of Iowa's discoveries led to intense media coverage, postwar newspaper and magazine journalists paid little attention to these ideas.

Yet, the research may have persuaded Wayne Dennis, a psychologist at Brooklyn College, to reconsider his 1941 study in which he had found that children's maturation developed "without encouragement or instruction, without reward or example," that what children learned from adults was "relatively unimportant."[25] Like much research, Dennis's ideas were a work in progress, and in the 1950s, along with Pergrouhi Najarian, of the American University in Beirut, Dennis studied children cared for in a Beirut foundling home that they called the Crèche. In 1957, the two psychologists published "Infant Development under Environmental Handicap." The authors warned, however, that readers might find their results confusing because of "the many divergent opinions concerning the effect of early environment."[26] Although they did not reference Skeels's studies, the Crèche and the Davenport Home had significant similarities: both suffered from inadequate funds, limited staff, and brusque caretakers and provided almost no opportunities for children's learning. Infants at each institution were fed with bottles propped beside their mouths, and their visual stimulation was restricted by sheets that wrapped the sides of their cribs.

Dennis and Najarian compared 12-month-old infants at the Crèche with infants of the same age from impoverished families who received regular health care at American University's Beirut Hospital.[27] Until they were 2 months, both groups had similar development. But after one year, the mean IQ test score of the Crèche children had declined from 100 to 63. The mean test score of the hospital infants had not declined.[28] Yet when the Crèche children were retested at age 5, the psychologists found they "approximated the performance of children in normal environments."[29] This may reflect that after the Crèche children reached 1 year, each matron cared for a group of ten children and so provided greater attention and stimulation than was possible at Davenport, where from ages 2 to 6, one matron cared for about 35 children. The authors concluded that the "doctrine of the permanency of early environmental effects" could not be correct.[30] Dennis's use of the phrase "doctrine of permanency" is unusual: at that time, little about environment's role in development had been formalized as a "doctrine."

Then, in 1958, Samuel A. Kirk, head of the Institute for Research on Exceptional Children at the University of Illinois and a harsh critic of the Iowa studies, published an investigation that confirmed Iowa's work. Kirk's turnaround came after he reviewed Iowa's studies referenced in the 1946 work of a young psychologist, Bernadine Schmidt. Schmidt had investigated a group of 322 adolescents who were from economically impoverished backgrounds and had IQ test scores below 70. When those students entered high school, half were placed in highly individualized classes where every effort was made to improve their functioning. If they required glasses or hearing aids, they received them; if they had difficulty reading or writing exams, including IQ tests, readers or writers were provided, accommodations that are routine today. After five years, the mean IQ test score gain for those in the individualized program was 25.2 points, nearly identical to the gains for Skeels's Woodward and Glenwood children. But Schmidt found that students who had remained in a regular program lost a mean of 4 IQ points, and all continued to have low IQs.[31]

Kirk's criticism of Schmidt's research methods virtually ended her career. But for reasons that are not clear, in the 1950s Kirk reconsidered the Iowa studies and in his own investigation examined ideas similar to the Iowans'. Kirk reported on 81 retarded children whose IQ test scores ranged from 45 to 80 and who did or did not attend preschool. Half the children lived in the community and half in institutions. He found that compared with the control group, 70 percent of the preschool children showed significantly accelerated intellectual and social growth, which they retained during a one-year follow-up.[32] Ten percent of Kirk's references were from the Iowa group. Of special importance, in his conclusion Kirk quoted George Stoddard: "To regard all changes in mental status as an artifact [of heredity] is to shut one's eyes to the most significant and dramatic phenomenon in human growth."[33] Later, Skeels said that Kirk's recognition of the Iowa studies encouraged others in the field to "sit up and take notice."[34] In the 1960s, Kirk became widely known for strategies that helped students with learning differences and as the popularizer of the term *learning disabilities*. Today he is regarded as 'the Father of Special Education."[35]

Yet despite these few but persuasive studies, by 1960 the tide still had not turned, and Iowa's discoveries were rarely cited. An important factor in that neglect was hidden in plain sight: the Iowa Child Welfare Research Station had lost its essential core, the ensemble of researchers focused on studies of

environment's effect on intelligence. For a decade their research had been just
about the only light in that room, and when it was extinguished, few mental
test psychologists or psychologists in related fields attempted to replicate or
extend Iowa's contributions.

———

B y 1960, Harold Skeels, who for many years had been chief of Special
Program Development in NIMH's Community Research and Services,
was the sole Iowa group psychologist with access to research facilities, yet he
made no effort to rekindle interest in child study investigations. It is unclear
what stopped him. Was it that the field had taken other directions? Or that
Skeels wished to avoid further belittling of his work and of himself? Did
he want to keep knowledge of his past humiliation from contaminating his
NIMH status?

"Skeels was his own person" was the way Simon Auster explained it.
During the early 1960s, Skeels and Auster, an NIMH child psychiatrist
whom Skeels supervised, met twice weekly. The two shared a deep concern
about children's well-being, and Auster's easygoing nature might have led to
exchanges about their lives and professional experiences. But Auster reported
that in years of discussions, the two talked only about Auster's projects, and
Skeels never spoke of his past work or of any aspect of his life outside the
office. As Auster described, "Harold was a very private individual, very circumspect. There was no lack of warmth, but he didn't in any way pick up on
the personal."[36] During the time the two worked together, Auster remained
unaware that Skeels had made important discoveries, and Auster's NIMH colleagues never mentioned them.[37]

One of the few people with whom Skeels discussed the Iowa work, Marie
Skodak, visited Washington now and then to attend professional meetings.
On those occasions, the friends of nearly thirty years would recall their Iowa
adventures and struggles, and they were often in touch by letter and telephone. Skodak and Skeels were closer to one another than to any of their
past Iowa associates. Knowing him so well, Skodak said she viewed his life as
"lonely and restricted," but respected his reticence.[38]

———

One January morning in 1961, when Robert J. Havighurst, of the University of Chicago, arrived at NIMH to attend a professional meeting, he noticed that Skeels's office was right down the hall. Remembering Skeels's pioneering Woodward and Glenwood research, it suddenly occurred to him that the children who had lived with low-intellect women would now be in their late 20s. Havighurst, who had a special interest in longitudinal studies, wondered if their changed intelligence had persisted? What were their educational, social, and economic outcomes? Their adult status, he believed, might reveal much about their environments. And if they had children of their own, what was *their* intelligence? Havighurst and Skeels had never met, but he knocked, walked in, and introduced himself.

Born in 1900, Havighurst was a polymath who trained in chemistry at Ohio State, then in physics at Harvard. Since the 1930s, he had been at the University of Chicago, where he focused on experimental education. He had not taken a side during the Iowans' 1940 battle and might have been one of the few attending his NIMH meeting who would have given Skeels's discoveries much thought. But with some intensity that morning Havighurst suggested that Skeels undertake a study to learn the fates of his original twenty-five Davenport subjects. He told him this was "urgent."[39] The Iowa psychologist was taken aback by Havighurst's emphasis, and although Skeels politely heard him out, he opposed the idea.

Yet Skeels could not let go of Havighurst's argument about the importance of his research and sought advice from one of the few at NIMH who knew of his discoveries, Thomas Gladwin. An anthropologist and researcher of mental development, Gladwin had recently coauthored *Mental Subnormality*, an influential summary of current knowledge in the area. Gladwin, who had hoped Skeels would write a book about his discoveries, agreed with Havighurst about the follow-up's importance. To support the projected study, he sent a memorandum to NIMH administrators about its potential significance.

Gladwin explained that his conversations with Skeels about child development were "wiser [and] more mature than [those] he had with many alleged experts." He said it would be "tragic" if Skeels did not share his ideas beyond the few he had spoken to at NIMH. The prospect of a longitudinal follow-up, Gladwin wrote, thrilled everyone who heard of it. Moreover, Gladwin unconditionally endorsed Iowa's 1939 conclusions. He reframed the station's maligned statistical methods as an "extremely conservative approach [that] permitted [the work] to survive a succession of violent attacks."[40] Moreover, Gladwin asserted that decades ahead of their time, Skeels and Skodak were "in a unique position as elder statesmen. . . . The time [is] now or never to communicate the wisdom of Skodak and Skeels to a large audience and . . . change the direction of child development . . . to a degree I believe will be large and lasting."[41] After decades of neglect, Skeels now had what every pioneering researcher hopes for: recognition of their work's importance from an erudite leader in their own field.

Skeels would, of course, have known of René Spitz's 1945 study of institutionalized infants and of the few after Spitz whose findings also supported environment, although he also would have recognized that postwar research had not softened psychology's hereditarian bias. Yet, Havighurst's and Gladwin's passionate encouragement signaled possible revisions in psychology, perhaps happening in slow motion, but happening nonetheless.

At about this time, other evidence emerged for such a possibility. In 1958, Joseph McVicker Hunt, a psychologist previously at Brown University and now at the University of Illinois, was someone who had known little about child development but recently had begun to consider its importance. Hunt's earlier research in abnormal and psychoanalytic psychology had led to his acclaimed 1944 work *Personality and the Behavioral Disorders*. It was at an impasse in writing about intelligence and motivation in adults—his ideas would not jell was how he put it—that he recognized his ignorance in the area of early intelligence and began a review of Iowa's research and that of others. Later he said that this reconsideration forced "a dramatic change" in his thinking.[42]

Hunt never did anything by halves, and by 1961 he had published a landmark work, *Intelligence and Experience*, considered "one of the most important contributions of twentieth century psychology."[43] Although new to the early development field, Hunt's reputation as a scholar, along with the book's novel insights, brought him wide recognition. The work, he said, "got me tagged as an environmentalist," an identification he rejected because he defined himself

as an "interactionist," like the Iowans, someone who recognized that heredity and environment acted together.[44] (The Iowans did not use this term to
describe their perspective, nor did others at that time. Today, it is most often
found in the scholarly work of sociologists.) Hunt knew of the 1930s hereditarian versus environmentalist struggle, but had done no work in that field
and played no role in those events. However, his new work addressed the current status of hereditarian thought, ideas he wrote that might be "weakening
[but were] still widely accepted."[45] Importantly, his 1961 monograph reshaped
his career, turning Hunt into a leader in early childhood education. While
Hunt acknowledged the methodological limitations of the Iowa studies, he
emphasized their provocative evidence for the relation between stimulation
and intelligence.

At about this time, President John F. Kennedy read of Hunt's work, which
triggered his campaign trail memory of impoverished West Virginia children
who lacked decent schooling, housing, nutrition, and health care. Kennedy
told a Hunt associate: "If there's this much plasticity in early development and
if there are these differences in classes, then the ethic of equal opportunity
applies not only to the adult and the school age child, but it applies to the child
before he goes to school."[46] Kennedy's initiatives for government programs in
early education aligned with Hunt's thinking, but were cut short by his death
in 1963. Soon, President Lyndon Johnson's Great Society programs took up
Kennedy's efforts.[47] Johnson called attention to the developmental effects of
growing up in poverty that "contributed to the scientific justification for the
Head Start program," a federally funded early learning program for children
up to the age of 5. During Johnson's administration, Hunt chaired a presidential advisory committee on preschool education related to Head Start.[48]

In his monograph *Intelligence and Experience,* Hunt addressed the decades-
long rejection of the Iowa station's discoveries and suggested that the profession's response had impeded psychology's progress. He pointed, especially, to
Florence Goodenough's oft-cited ridicule of Iowa's investigations. Such hereditarian dominance, Hunt said, meant "most investigators withdrew from the
field."[49] After decades of neglect, Hunt's attention and prestige provided support for the Iowa view from a scholar willing to take psychology to task for
its earlier contempt.

In a 1962 address at Columbia University's Arden House, Hunt told an audience of educators, child specialists, social workers, and psychologists of Iowa's discoveries that early stimulation preserved and raised institutionalized children's intelligence, that development *required* stimulation. Scathingly, he described what had kept the work in the shadows, but assured his audience that this was a new day:

> Their work was picked to pieces by critics and lost much of the suggestive value it was justified in having. Many of you will recall the ridicule that was heaped upon the "wandering I. Q." [in 1939, by Benjamin Simpson] and the way . . . Florence Goodenough derided . . . the idea of "feeble-minded" infants being brought . . . to normal mentality by moron nursemaids. . . . The fact that just such a use of preschool experience is now being seriously planned by sensible people with widespread approval means that something has changed.[50]

Moreover, based on Iowa's discoveries, Hunt became a champion for an even more penetrating anti-racist, anti-classist vision: "So long as these fictions of fixed intelligence and predetermined development prevailed, the observed characteristics of races, classes, and individuals were considered . . . inevitable."[51] Finally, through Hunt's advocacy, the Iowa psychologists had been transformed from outcasts in their own profession to inspired theorists who were ahead of their time.

Early 1960s reports from the American Psychological Association endorse Hunt's claim that psychology had begun to accept the evidence that heredity worked together with environment. A 2004 APA review of that period cited Hunt's 1964 declaration that "any laws concerning the rate of intellectual growth must take into account the . . . environmental encounters which constitute the conditions of that growth."[52] The APA also recognized the role of Martin Deutsch, whose 1960s work, supported by the Ford Foundation, examined the causes of learning difficulties among children from lower social economic status homes in the African American community.[53] Deutsch understood that the children he studied suffered from "a poverty of experience . . . some had never even seen themselves in a mirror."[54] He became one of the most important contributors to Head Start's theoretical framework. Considered, too, was the work of pediatrician Julius Richmond, who, at the start of his career in the 1930s, recognized that young children who lived in poverty suffered developmental declines. In the 1940s, Richmond lost a battle—he described himself as "bloodied"—in which he sought to introduce a child development curriculum at the University of Illinois's medical school.[55] In the 1960s, Richmond became a leader in Head Start's development. Later he served as the nation's Surgeon General.

In his 1961 book, and now in his 1962 Arden House talk, Hunt told of Canadian neuroscientist Donald O. Hebb's discoveries that the brain changes itself when it interacts with experience. In the 1920s and 1930s, Bird Baldwin and George Stoddard had speculated that this was how development worked, but they lacked proof—Hebb had not yet begun to publish. Hunt now called attention to Hebb's 1940s discoveries.[56] A Canadian who had studied at McGill University, Hebb earned a Harvard PhD, then worked in brain science at the Montreal Neurological Institute, Queens College, in Ontario, and the Yerkes Laboratory, in Orange Park, Florida. While at Yerkes, he wrote his 1949 monograph, *The Organization of Intelligence*, long recognized as a trailblazing work that married neuroscience and psychology. Soon after the book's publication, Hebb returned to McGill, where he remained.

Hebb pursued the radical idea that in a dynamic process stimulative experience changed the developing brain and therefore changed intelligence. Neither Skeels nor Skodak, both still active in the 1960s, reference Hebb's studies, but to Hunt it seemed clear that understanding Hebb was essential to understanding the transformations of the Davenport children. In 1949 Hebb wrote: "There is in fact an overwhelming body of evidence to show that experience is essential to development. . . . Why then should we object to the idea that enriching an inadequate environment will raise the IQ, as Stoddard and Wellman and others have urged?"[57] Where the Iowans had failed to convince, Hebb met with great success. His work challenged eugenic dogma and offered an evidence-based scientific explanation of the neuroscience of cognitive development. His conclusions were inescapable, and eventually, they were decisive.[58]

Hebb suggested that when neural cells worked together—he called them "cell assemblies"—they stimulated one another. "The general idea," Hebb explained, "is an old one, that any two cells or systems of cells that are repeatedly active at the same time will tend to become 'associated,' that activity in one promotes activity in the other."[59] To study whether experience altered these neural networks, Hebb housed half of a rat litter in standard laboratory cages and set the other rats free in his home, where they explored, searched for food, and received affection from Hebb's two young daughters. The girls provided "enthusiastic" attention, Hebb wrote, because, after all, the rats had become the family pets.[60]

Hebb found that the explorer rats scored higher on maze tests of rat intelligence than the caged rats, and, surprisingly, during the last ten days of their adventure their intelligence accelerated still further. Hebb explained that just as with humans, as they became smarter, they became "better able to profit from new experiences." Hebb showed that stimulation drove brain development and explained how "cognition, emotion, thought, and consciousness" worked.[61] His impact on the understanding of the development of intelligence has been likened to Charles Darwin's contribution to the understanding of evolution.[62]

During this period, original contributions about environment also came from another scholar, Urie Bronfenbrenner, of Cornell University. Born in Russia in 1917, when Bronfenbrenner was 6 years old his family emigrated to the United States. Once arrived, they lived on the grounds of Letchworth Village, a New York State institution for developmentally disabled children and adults, where his physician father was employed. Occasionally, Dr. Bronfenbrenner treated institutional patients whose intelligence appeared normal, but he noticed that the longer they lived as inmates, the more their behaviors resembled those of the impaired residents.

When Dr. Bronfenbrenner arranged for one of those possibly normal patients to work in the family's home, he found that "gradually she resumed a 'normal' life." Without his intervention, it seemed likely that the young woman would have spent many years, perhaps her entire life, in an institution. Observing these events, the young Bronfenbrenner became impressed with the power of others' expectations to influence an individual's behaviors.[63]

"I offer a new theoretical perspective for research in human development," Bronfenbrenner wrote in 1979, "the evolving interaction of the developing person and the environment."[64] When he was at Harvard, one of Bronfenbrenner's professors, Walter Fenno Dearborn, advised, "If you want to understand something, try to change it."[65] Even if Harold Skeels never heard those words, he had lived them.

———

Havighurst and Gladwin's persuasion achieved what they hoped, and Skeels agreed to investigate the adult outcomes of the Woodward and Glenwood children he had studied decades earlier. He also arranged NIMH approval for Marie Skodak's follow-up of her earlier research of Davenport children adopted when they were under 6 months and a small group who had been adopted when they were between 2 and 5 years. During the 1940s, when they were adolescents still living with their families, Skodak had done some follow-up investigations of their progress. By 1961, most of the research subjects of both psychologists were in their late 20s.

Keenly interested in the relationships between adoptive parents and their children, they would first interview the parents and request permission to talk with their now-adult children. Their investigation would continue for about two years and include nearly 250 interviews; they would conduct IQ tests on the children of those subjects but not on the subjects themselves—a choice their planning notes left unexplained. Hoping to prevent the parents or their adult children from "rehearsing" for these meetings, the psychologists would arrive in each home unannounced. Including travel, the study would cost $50,000 to $75,000—today, about $400,000 to $600,000.[66] NIMH agreed to fund the work.

Although the follow-up occurred before privacy laws protected the rights of research subjects, the Iowans anticipated that some of the subjects or their parents might not wish to be interviewed. They assured authorities of their "careful, tactful, and diplomatic handling of the children, and of any contacts . . . necessary to locate a family."[67] There is no record that this informal pledge had been requested, but in the early 1960s there were no standards for ethical research that involved human subjects. (To ensure that no harm would come to human research subjects, since 1983, institutional review boards have overseen such investigations.)

As their research got underway, Skodak and Skeels refitted their cars as mobile offices, stocking them with decades of Davenport's medical and IQ test reports, files filled with family names and addresses, and years of progress notes and referrals. They also brought along state and local maps, local residential telephone directories, specialized business directories, and, to locate information that might not be found anywhere else, Polk's directories to American cities. And those were only their print resources. In small towns they copied residents' telephone numbers from what often were the only telephone directories—lists thumbtacked to the walls of local filling stations—or made notes of conversations with chatty neighbors or telephone operators. Skeels tracked down one family by asking a woman mailing a letter at a small-town Iowa post office if she knew them. He located another whose last address was now in the path of a six-lane freeway. With some luck, Skeels found every subject and family from his 1939 study, and Skodak located every subject and family from the 1949 final adoption study. They became so adept at searching for people that they advised the public to put away the illusion that someone could seem to vanish and leave no trail.[68]

In their searches, the psychologists identified themselves to neighbors or shopkeepers as old Iowa friends trying to reconnect. In a sense that was true, as over years of visiting children's homes to test their intelligence, they had established comfortable relationships with the children and their parents. Because of the difficulty finding accurate addresses, they rejected searching for subjects and families by mail, but they also made that choice because they believed that only through direct contact would they hear the parents' and subjects' true responses to their adoption experience.

From the beginning, the two psychologists were alert to how a subject's early history and later environment might have influenced their adult outcomes. During the 1940s, Skodak had done four follow-up investigations of the adopted children she had studied and found that her subjects' IQs, most of them in the superior range, had remained stable. This suggested that as adults those subjects' IQs would probably continue to be stable. But Skeels's subjects had lived at Davenport for one to two years, where their IQ test scores had declined, but then risen when they experienced intensive stimulation from the women at Woodward or Glenwood. As Skeels had found in 1942, after their adoptions, the scores of all but one subject increased still further.

Now he considered whether those subjects' early IQ instabilities—the fact that led to his study in the first place—might have resurfaced in their adulthoods. Although Skeels would not test the IQs of his adult subjects, he planned to make rough calculations based on how they managed their jobs, homes, and children. He also feared that their intelligence might have declined to the point that they would have been returned to an institution. If he found that the adult IQs of his experimental group subjects had fallen back to lower levels, would that mean that the hereditarian dictum "blood will tell" was accurate?[69] Or could some other factor have caused the decline? He also wondered whether the contrast group subjects, each of whom had early IQ test score declines, had remained at low levels into their adult lives. Here is some of what Skeels discovered.

Skeels made one of his first visits to the adoptive parents of CD. In 1934, CD had been placed at the Woodward Home, where her IQ test score climbed from 46, at the imbecile level, to 95, comfortably in the normal range. But about the time that CD was adopted in 1936, Skeels had completed a study indicating that children's IQ test scores tracked with the professional status of their adoptive fathers: the higher the father's professional level, the higher the child's IQ test score.[70] In 1942, when Skeels had tested CD for his follow-up, he found her IQ score had declined to 90, still in the average range, but lower than it had been. This concerned him because he thought that her adoptive home might not have been sufficiently stimulative and that her IQ test score might have fallen still more.

Knocking at the door of what had been her parents' home, CD's aunt greeted Skeels and told him that during CD's adolescence, both of CD's parents had died. He discovered that because of a chronic illness, CD had dropped out of school after ninth grade. Following an early marriage, CD, her husband, and their two young children had moved to the far west, but CD's aunt did not have their address.

Eventually, Skeels located the family in a "tar paper shingle" rental home in an impoverished neighborhood. Now 29, CD told him that her husband had steady landscaping work and the family's finances were stable. Skeels felt reassured when he saw that her children and her home were well taken care of. But as CD walked Skeels back to his car, with some emotion she asked if he could help her find her birth parents. Realizing she believed that her birth mother had abandoned her, he provided some resources. He told her that when mothers gave up their babies, "it did not mean they didn't love them, but that the mother thought adoptive parents could do better by her child than she could." Now aware of her struggles, Skeels's asked himself,

> had I really done [CD] a favor by getting her out of the Wood-
> ward State Hospital. However, I guess, everything considered,
> it is a rather commendable record. She is still living with her
> husband, they are eating and have two nice [children], and at
> least at no time has she been returned to a state institution.[71]

Because CD seemed well able to manage her home and children, Skeels felt reassured that her intelligence had probably not fallen further. But he also noted: "It seems probable that this will be the lowest level of the 13 [subjects]." When Skeels tested the IQs of CD's children, her 8-year-old, who had been premature, had a lower test score than her older son, but both were within the normal range.

A few months later, Skeels interviewed the adoptive mother of BD, the other Davenport toddler placed at Woodward, whose IQ during the earlier study had climbed from 35 to 93. Her 58-point gain was the largest made by any subject in his experiment. By his 1942 follow-up, her IQ had risen to 96. With obvious affection, BD's mother told Skeels that in high school BD had academic difficulties, earning mostly Cs, but had graduated and held low-paying jobs in the community. BD's adoptive mother had also grown up in an orphanage, the Home for the Friendless, one of many such institutions then located in eastern and midwestern states. "If I was thirty years younger," she told Skeels, "I would adopt another child. My love for BD is a different kind of love."

When Skeels located BD, now 29, she and her family were living in a small midwestern town where her husband worked for the railroad. They were a close-knit, financially secure household in which both parents also felt close to their own families. Skeels tested the intelligence of two of BD's children and found that one had an average IQ and the other's was above average. He noted that BD's intelligence seemed to have remained stable. "The marvel in all this" he wrote, "is that she is not in an institution and able to assume her role in life."[72] Although BD had information about her birth family, she expressed no interest in contacting them. However, Skeels noted,

> *BD inquired with much feeling about CD. . . . While at Woodward State Hospital they lived on the same wards and later were transferred back to Davenport together. In the interview with CD she also inquired about BD. This close relationship has never been forgotten by either of them. BD remarked that it might be possible for her to meet CD on the street . . . and not know.*[73]

Following his interviews, Skeels provided each young woman with the identity and location of the other. He did not report that he knew of any subsequent contact between them.

Skeels next visited the adoptive parents of experimental group case 7, whose intelligence, when she entered Davenport at 9 months, was in the same range as the infant CD's had been. Born prematurely, she spent two months in an incubator, and when she arrived at Glenwood at 17 months, she was extremely frail. At Glenwood she made spectacular gains and was adopted. By the time of Skeels's 1942 follow-up, her IQ score was 109. Her adoptive parents, both of whom graduated from college, reported that "they only wished they had adopted two."[74]

Case 7's parents would have helped her find her birth parents, but her adoptive mother told Skeels, "They had not kept her and that was enough for her." She had outstanding musical talent and a successful high school career. Although accepted for stewardess training by an airline, she instead married an airline flight engineer. The couple moved west, where her husband worked for a specialist aviation group. When Skeels located case 7, she was 27, and as Skeels described, "a charming young woman . . . cheerful and attractive . . .

who appears a comfortable sort of mother."[75] He suspected her marriage was a happy one. When Skeels tested the IQs of her four children, he found they ranged from 107 to 114.[76]

The parents of case 4 were one of four families who, out of privacy concerns, did not wish Skeels to contact their child.[77] They said they would have adopted another child, but the state agent refused because "the mother was too wrapt [sic] up in the adopted daughter." Case 4 had arrived at Davenport as a sickly 3-month infant, and after a year, when her IQ test score was 73, Skeels transferred her to Glenwood. Eight months later her IQ score had risen to 100, and she was adopted. In Skeels's 1942 follow-up, she had an IQ of 116, in the superior range. Her parents told him she had graduated from high school, had earned an RN degree, and worked as a nursing supervisor.[78]

Experimental case 9, the youngest of six siblings, fared the least well of the children in her family. A normal infant, she had been inadvertently poisoned by her incompetent, alcoholic parents and also diagnosed with syphilis. Although her disease had been cured, at Glenwood she never achieved normal intelligence and therefore was unadoptable. When the study ended, she had an IQ test result of 80 and was returned to Davenport, where her intelligence declined and severe visual problems were first diagnosed. By age 10 she had an IQ test score of 60 and, nearly blind in one eye, she reentered Glenwood as a permanent inmate.

At Glenwood, case 9 received training in childcare and housekeeping and as a teenager left the institution to live with an older sister, although she continued in state supervision. She hired a lawyer to challenge that status and eventually was permitted to live on her own. When Skeels interviewed the older sister, she told him that she had suffered more from her mother's neglect than her younger sibling and wondered why *she* had remained intact. "Was there someone in the family" he asked, "with whom you had a close, emotional relationship?" "Oh yes," the sister told him, "I was much closer to my grandmother than my own mother."[79] Her grandmother's attention, Skeels suggested, might have made the difference. Case 9 had been removed from the home at 3 months, before her grandmother's care could have influenced her development.[80]

Now 27, case 9 had not seen Skeels since she was 9 years old, but when she heard his voice in the hallway of the home in which she was the house-keeper, she ran to greet him. She was now working for a widower and a "kind of mother" to his two children, and Skeels realized that she had more maturity than most former institutional inmates. She lived with the family, participated in social and religious programs, and did day work for other neighborhood families. She made a point to tell Skeels that Glenwood sterilized young women, often against their will, and that her sister had intervened to prevent that from happening to her.[81]

When admitted to Davenport, case 10 had been a normal 8-month-old baby. By age 2 his IQ score was 72 and Skeels transferred him to Glenwood. There, his IQ was unstable—when the study ended it was 79—in the low-average range, and he was returned to Davenport. After five months in Davenport's new preschool this boy's IQ score rose to 96 and he was adopted. When Skeels interviewed his adoptive parents, they told of their family's satisfying life with their child in the small Iowa town where he graduated from high school. He enrolled in a business college, received a real estate license, and earned the equivalent today of about $60,000.[82] Later, Skeels interviewed the son, who said he wondered about his birth parents, but worried that if he tried to locate them he would hurt his adoptive parents' feelings. Skeels tested case 10's four children and found that their IQ scores ranged from well within the normal range to above average.[83]

Case 11, 27-year-old Louis Branca, once Wendell Hoffman, had been a normal 1-year-old whose intelligence declined at Davenport. (Because Branca shared his story with the author, much detail about his life is available.) When he was a little over 2, Skeels transferred him to Glenwood. In 1962, Branca filled Skeels in about the twenty-two years since his adoption by a St. Paul couple, Genevieve Carroll Branca and Louis P. Branca.[84]

With his adoption, Branca's longing to be part of a family had been fulfilled. His adoptive mother—whom he described as a "society woman"—had grown up in a Davenport family that traced their forebears to the Mayflower. Genevieve Branca had cofounded the St. Paul Women's Club, and Louis reported that from time to time "groups of overdressed women" met for tea in the Brancas' living room to plan community events. Yet, almost from the beginning, Louis believed he disappointed his mother "because I was not growing up to be the kind of boy she wanted: I was exactly the opposite of high society." Although Louis and his mother were not close, Louis's father, a chiropractor whose parents immigrated to the United States from Milan, was a loving, accepting parent.

Yet, grandparents on both sides of Branca's adoptive family treated him coldly, something he attributed to their unspoken worries about his background. "You know, what kind of blood did I come from?" Branca wanted to know that, too, and from his Iowa records he had learned that when his birth mother entered the maternity ward, she appeared confused and gave authorities several last names. Whenever he met someone with one of those names—Foster or Hoffman or others—he would wonder if that person might be a relative. As an adult, Branca searched unsuccessfully for clues to his father's identity and eventually questioned whether his birth mother even knew who his father had been.[85]

Branca's Glenwood preschool experiences were poor preparation for the educational program at St. Mark's, a Catholic school that served advantaged upper-middle-class students, and in kindergarten he felt "shell-shocked" and like "the weird kid." Sensitive to his needs, his teacher, "a wonderful nun," taught him basic information that his peers had already learned. "She saved my life," he remembered. Throughout elementary school the Brancas, who had no books in their home and never took Louis to a library, provided tutors to support his learning. He recognized that his institutional history had resulted in academic gaps, "but as I got older," he recalled, "I got better and better and better and by the time I was in eighth grade I was competitive . . . I was almost like a normal St. Mark's kid."[86]

As at Glenwood, at St. Mark's Branca formed rich friendships, now with classmates who had known one another most of their lives. Much later those school friends would connect him with his first wife, and after a divorce, with his second. While at Davenport and Glenwood, Branca had been one of the children who soothed themselves by rocking back and forth, but as he got older and felt more confident, he found he rocked less.

In 1949, Branca began high school at St. Thomas Academy in St. Paul, where he did well academically and enjoyed a typical high schooler's life of academics, sports (including football), and social events. But toward the end of his high school years, his mother, aged 56, died suddenly, which destabilized him for a while. When Branca graduated in 1954, he entered the same chiropractic program his father had attended, but concerned that his degree would not win his peers' respect, he decided to attend college. With the Korean War recently ended, he enlisted in the army in order to have GI Bill benefits. During his service he worked as a long-distance radio operator on Cold War defense ships located off Greenland and Labrador and also earned his pilot's license.

Returning home in 1956, Branca discovered that his father's health had deteriorated, and Louis Sr. soon died of brain cancer. Again an orphan, he always felt guilty that he had left his father alone. At the time he met with Skeels in 1962, Branca had completed his undergraduate degree in psychology at the University of Minnesota, was attending graduate school, and had recently married. His wife, who also had an undergraduate degree, worked in marketing. Skeels discovered that Branca had read some of the literature about the effects of institutional life on children's development and expressed some anxiety about adjustment problems in those who had experienced early institutionalization.[87]

———

When Skeels interviewed the eleven contrast group subjects (one had died of Gaucher's disease), most of whom had been normally intelligent when they entered Davenport, he found distinctly different outcomes. Contrast group case 15 seemed a normal infant when she arrived at Davenport only days after her birth. At 1 year, her IQ test score was 92. But by age 3, her score had fallen to 54 and Skeels transferred her to Glenwood for permanent custodial care, where she was later sterilized. Glenwood trained her in housekeeping, and as an older teenager she was discharged to live with a couple who considered her one of the family. They helped her enter a protected work setting, and she became self-supporting as a dishwasher at a nearby restaurant. Her IQ remained in the range of 54, and she did not learn to read or write. Skeels spoke with her when she was 28 years old and found her more competent than he expected. When he accompanied her to pay a bill, he noticed that she seemed quite poised.[88]

Contrast case 17 arrived at Davenport's nursery after a forceps delivery. According to his early record, he made a good recovery, but in 1966 Skeels discovered that during his birth the boy had suffered a brain hemorrhage, which might have led to his retardation. At age 1 his development seemed in the normal range, but by age 3 his IQ test score was 58, where it remained. When the boy was 4, Skeels transferred him to the Woodward School as a permanent inmate, where visual problems, not corrected by glasses, were discovered. As a teenager, case 17 had a verbal intelligence score of 46, but his score on a test that measured performance was 76—an indication of nonverbal ability important for activities at work and in daily living. When he was 21, another test of nonverbal intelligence, the Ravens Progressive Matrices, placed him in the low average range of 82. Because case 17 worked productively without supervision, when he was 26 Woodward discharged him. At the small restaurant where he cooked and washed dishes, his employer said she "had never seen anyone come into a place and win the hearts of all those who work with them so much." Skeels interviewed him at his rooming house, where the young man told him that after several years of employment he had saved $2,600, today about $22,000. According to Skeels, his functional level and achievement ranked well above most of the contrast children.[89]

As a baby, contrast case 20's very low intelligence parents had given him to a Syrian peddler and his wife, who applied to Iowa for permission to adopt him. The state refused and placed him in Davenport. When he was an adolescent, he ran away but was returned to Davenport by the police. At that time he was identified as mentally ill and committed to an Iowa asylum for the insane. When Skeels visited, case 20 was 31 years old and diagnosed as schizophrenic. Although he executed a daily work assignment in the institution's laundry, his responses to real-world situations indicated limited contact with reality. When Skeels asked him how old he was, he gave an age ten years younger. Asked if he were married, he said he was and gave his mother's name as his wife's. In Harold Skeels's view, contrast group case 20 was

> *an illustration of the devastating effects of institutionalization throughout most of his life. From the day of his birth he has never had a chance. It is interesting to speculate as to what would*

have happened had he been permitted to stay with the Syrian
peddler and his wife who loved him dearly and would probably
have given him the advantages of a home and parental love.[90]

Skeels's reflection about case 20's mental health suggests that the boy's severe emotional deprivation may have contributed to the development of his schizophrenia. Although many years have passed, the causes of schizophrenia are still not well defined, but today it is thought that the illness is a result of genetic and environmental factors as well as possible imbalances in brain chemistry.

Because the developmental path of contrast case 19 differed significantly from that of other contrast group subjects, Skeels viewed him as "the ultimate surprise."[91] Skeels said that this boy's outcome was so different, he shouldn't be considered a member of that group.[92] Surrendered to Davenport by his mother when he was 9 days old, at about age 1 case 19 had normal intelligence. As a child he lost some hearing due to bouts of otitis media. Each year his test scores declined, and when he was 4 his IQ score was 67. At age 8 he was only minimally hard of hearing, but Skeels transferred him to a school for the deaf. There he received a good education and had much attention from a dormitory matron who each weekend brought him home to her family. At the school his IQ tests rose into the normal range, and when he was a teenager the school trained him as a linotype operator. Although he was accepted at a college for the deaf, after one semester he was asked to leave because he wasn't sufficiently hard of hearing.[93]

Over the course of this boy's education, his intelligence test results tracked closely with the levels of his environmental stimulation, a factor that, Skeels believed, made case 19 the most consequential for psychology of any in his study. When Skeels met with him in 1962, case 19 was an accomplished linotype operator and active in his state's deaf association. He had married a college-educated hearing woman, and their four children had normal hearing. Two of the children had intelligence in the average range, and the other two were in the superior range. As a young man, case 19 located his birth mother, who was thrilled that her son had found her. They established a close relationship.[94]

In her 1960s follow-ups, Marie Skodak located one hundred Davenport children who had been placed into middle-class homes before the age of 6 months and a few placed at ages 2 to 5 years. She interviewed those subjects' parents and the subjects themselves. For reasons she did not describe, Skodak did not fully analyze and write up her follow-up results. In 1996, in her last memoir, she wrote, "The boxes of data, the sheets of incomplete evaluations, continue to induce guilt and determination to get at the unfinished business."[95] It might not be surprising that Skodak, overcommitted in her work, delayed writing up her data. During the years when she had searched for her adult subjects, she also served as the director of psychological services for the Dearborn, Michigan, public schools (a 150-mile round-trip commute from her home), served as a consulting psychologist in Flint, Michigan, led several professional organizations, and was soon to be married. It may also be relevant that after she earned her PhD, she worked almost exclusively in public school and clinical environments, settings in which academic research could not have been her first priority.

However, in those one hundred sets of parents and subjects, Skodak remarked that she found "tremendous cooperation from everyone." She had previously done some follow-ups in the 1940s, so those later visits felt like "old friends getting together." She summarized the 1960s meetings positively; they usually lasted a few hours and showed that the children exceeded not only the educational attainments of their birth parents, but to her surprise, also had surpassed their adoptive parents as well.[96]

Skodak suggested that her subjects' accomplishments represented outcomes from good schooling, but also a generational shift in priorities. Many of them had earned graduate degrees, and at least twenty were in some kind of social service; especially interesting was that four of the subjects had entered the field of psychology. She attributed their career choices in part to her 1940s follow-up testing, which perhaps made them more familiar with psychology. Skodak found it especially thought-provoking that most in the group were less motivated by money than by careers in which their work improved the well-being of others—and they were quite successful in these altruistic fields.[97]

Unlike Skeels, whose reports tended to be somewhat formulaic, Skodak had a gift for entering the emotional lives of her subjects. In one rich case study, she reports on a boy of about 11 who had taken her out to the barn to show off his calf, and asked if she knew about him. She reminded him that she'd known him for a long time. But, he told her, that wasn't what he was asking.

"Do you know that I am adopted?"

"I know that," she told him.

"Well, don't tell my parents that you know," he said. She promised, but he continued, "They don't think I know, but I know."

Later, she asked the parents if they had told their son that he was adopted.

"Nobody knows," they answered.

She told them that in any community there may always be someone who guesses the truth, or that their son may even suspect, and suggested that it might be a good idea to tell him. That was all she felt she could say at the time.[98]

When Skodak next visited the family during her 1960s follow-up, they described their son as "rebellious." When he was in high school, he had been picked up by the police for some joyriding and car thefts. Angry, the family failed to hire a lawyer to defend him, and he was sent to a boys' training school. When Skodak interviewed his high school counselor, she learned that the school felt sympathetically toward the boy because his parents' excessive strictness had led them to want authorities to penalize him. From the parents' report about his behavior after his release Skodak understood that the boy now had become alienated from his family, and during her visit she observed that he did not feel welcome in his own home.[99] He was not involved with the law again. Skodak speculated that his adoptive parents attributed his teenage lawbreaking and defiance to his "bad blood."

———

At the end of January 1965, Harold Skeels received a letter from John Bowlby, who wrote to thank Skeels for sending mimeographed material about his recent study and to say that he had read Skeels's just published "preliminary" results. Bowlby added, "The results are really of the very greatest value. . . . The enquiry has proved immensely worthwhile and brought your early researches to a triumphant conclusion."[100] Bowlby was referring to Skeels's first journal article about his follow-up, "Some Preliminary Findings of Three Followup Studies on the Effects of Adoption on Children from Institutions," published in the US Department of Health journal *Children Today*.

Then, early in April 1965, British pediatrician Margaret Lowenfeld received a packet of research articles from her friend and Skeels's colleague, Simon Auster. The journal reprints had arrived just in time for her presentation to a government committee on adoption. Thanking Auster, she wrote, "That was a massive piece of cooperation!" But she added:

> There is a puzzle that must be cleared up, the latest date of these publications is December 1948. We are now in April, 1965, 17 years later. I have not heard before of Skeels and the Iowa City Research, nor does this fundamentally radical work seem to have affected any of the current thinking on child development, IQ . . . etc. WHY? . . . It may be that this is an example of a situation I have suffered all my working life: . . . that the conclusions . . . are too upsetting to be accepted . . . "better treat them as if they didn't exist."[101]

If anyone who studied young children should have known Harold Skeels's name it was Lowenfeld—a guiding light in child therapy, the originator of play therapy techniques used worldwide to treat troubled children, someone honored in the British Museum of Science's Group Collection. Now she peppered Auster with questions: "Is Skeels still working? How was this work . . . received when it appeared? Has any parallel work been carried out? What do your geneticists and top psychologists working on brain function think of it?"[102]

Auster, who for some years had worked with Skeels, could not answer Lowenfeld's questions because only when searching for material about adoption to send to his friend had he discovered Skeels's Iowa work. "Your delight on reading the material I sent you," he told her, "did not exceed mine."[103] To answer Lowenfeld and satisfy his own curiosity, Auster reached Skeels, recently retired from NIMH, in his new home in Southern California. No longer reticent, Skeels laid bare history about his work that until then he had shared with almost no one. He related to Auster his "serendipitous discovery" and told him of psychology's refusal to recognize that IQs might change, but that Iowa had revised its adoption process so that children were placed at earlier ages.

But Skeels had little information for Lowenfeld about geneticists and psychologists working on brain function and intelligence because in the United States that was not happening, and he appeared not to know about the work of Donald Hebb, the Canadian neuroscientist who had shown that the brain changes with experience. Remarkably, in the 1963 edition of the standard experimental psychology textbook by Robert S. Woodworth, of Columbia, and Harold Schlosberg, of Brown, "environment" has one index notation and "intelligence" none at all. Although the book mentions Hebb, it does not include his work that showed the relation between experience and brain development.[104] According to a 1968 review essay from psychiatrist Allan Marans and social worker Dale Meers, "the application of research to child-care programs in the United States falls far short of work elsewhere."[105]

Skeels told Auster that after a long drought, his studies were now admired. He described his recent dinner at the Rockville, Maryland, home of President John F. Kennedy's sister Eunice Kennedy Shriver and her husband, administrative powerhouse Sargent Shriver, where he had been invited to discuss his discoveries. At the time, Shriver simultaneously served as head of the late president's Peace Corps, President Johnson's War on Poverty, the Head Start project, and in Johnson's Office of Economic Opportunity. That summer of 1965, a Head Start pilot program was about to enroll half a million children. At the dinner, too, was Stafford L. Warren, President Johnson's special assistant for mental retardation.

Shriver let Skeels know he had learned that early education increased IQs, and said, "Being of an era when we thought you were born with an IQ just as you are born with blue eyes, that fact really . . . stuck in my head."[106] For Skeels, dinner in the midst of the Shrivers' warm family signaled recognition of his life's work from some of the nation's most powerful officials. And of course, Harold Skeels could not have missed how far his ideas had come in the twenty-five years since Barbara Burks and other Carnegie Institution eugenicists had quashed George Stoddard's blueprint for a national pre-school program.

————

On a snowy January morning in 1966, as Marie Skodak worked at home in Flint, she received a long-distance call from a complete stranger. At a time when psychologists and biologists rarely talked to one another about their work, there was no reason Alfred Mirsky's name would have been familiar, no way she would have known that he was a biologist at the Rockefeller Institute, now Rockefeller University, in New York City. From his book-lined office overlooking Rockefeller's manicured Upper East Side campus, Mirsky sounded almost casual. He told Skodak he "had just run across" Skeels's "marvelous" 1939 orphans study and Skodak's adoption studies. When her caller identified himself as a "cell-biologist interested in the behavior of gene particles in different environments," she immediately understood that this might be important. In a letter that day to Skeels and Gladwin, she said that Mirsky "went on at enthusiastic length . . . about how tremendous and significant" he found Iowa's studies and how they related to his own scientific investigations.[107] She told them that in *Who's Who*, she had found inches about Mirsky's credentials: "Harvard '26 . . . membership in all kinds of distinguished societies . . . chief interest in cell proteins."[108] She suggested that Skeels send Mirsky additional papers.

That day Skodak mailed Mirsky a rough draft of Skeels's 1966 follow-up report—the paper he would present at a May meeting and later publish in a prestigious psychology journal. Her enclosed letter told him, "I was much intrigued by the suggestion . . . that genes would respond differentially depending on the nature of the stimuli . . . the responsibility of schools and social institutions . . . under these circumstances becomes enormously more significant."[109]

But the Rockefeller scientist had been cagy with Skodak. His interest in the Iowa work was neither recent nor casual. Alfred Mirsky had followed Iowa's studies since the 1950s when his nephew, Lewis Lipsitt, then a PhD candidate in psychology at the University of Iowa and today an emeritus professor at Brown, first brought word of them. From that point, Mirsky frequently discussed Iowa's findings with one of his graduate students, Eric H. Davidson, later the CalTech biologist who unraveled the role of genomic regulation in development and in 2011 won the International Prize in Biology. According to Davidson, Lipsitt, and Bruce McEwen, another of Mirsky's students, what propelled Mirsky's interest in Iowa's discoveries was his long-standing abhorrence toward the racial, social, and cultural biases promoted by eugenics. Unknown to one another until 1966, Alfred Mirsky and the Iowans had long been allies.[110]

In the March 1964 issue of *Scientific American*, Mirsky had published a highly critical review of renowned British biologist Julian Huxley's book in support of eugenics, *Essays of a Humanist*. In that review Mirsky challenged Huxley's hereditarian statement that "it is now well established that the human I.Q . . . is largely a measure of genetic endowment."[111] Mirsky countered, plausibly referencing the Iowa studies: "It is now well known that not only 'genetic endowment' but also environment affects a person's I.Q. and that it is exceedingly difficult to evaluate the relative importance of these two variables."[112]

In a letter to Skeels, Mirsky explained why "a cell biologist should be so much interested in all this." He wrote:

> In my laboratory we investigate the activities of the chromosomes in the cell nucleus. We find that . . . genes become active or inactive depending on influences reaching them from the cytoplasm and from the surrounding environment. The conception of the genome handed down by classical genetics is rigid and biologically unsound. Perhaps . . . you can see that a sound cell biology goes along beautifully with the kind of psychology you did so much to develop.[113]

Skeels replied that while geneticists and biologists appreciated his work, psychologists "continued to be of the old school of intelligence being fixed at birth." He told of psychologists' disdain for Iowa's claims, but at the same time confessed his own difficulty, even after his follow-up discoveries, in "coming to accept our findings."[114]

According to Nobel laureate neuroscientist Eric Kandel and his colleague Larry Squire, it was not until the "latter part of the twentieth century when the study of the brain moved from a peripheral position within both the biological and psychological sciences to become an interdisciplinary field called neuroscience." Beginning in the 1960s, Kandel wrote, the work of neurophysiologists eventually reversed psychology's long-standing perception that the "neural approach to mental processes" was "too reductive."[115] Thus, it appears that Skodak and Skeels were among the first psychologists to receive an authoritative neuroscience hypothesis, simplified as it was, about how environment gets under the skin to influence development. As the Iowans now understood, Alfred Mirsky had perhaps explained the mystery of the changes in the Davenport children's intelligence. What Mirsky's work predicted, his student Bruce McEwen, along with other scientists, transformed into elegant explanations of complex phenomena that govern the interaction of environment and heredity to shape development. When he died in 1974, Alfred Mirsky was at work on a book for the general public about the interaction of environment and genetics, called *Genetics and Human Behavior*.

Chapter Twelve

THE COUNTER-ARGUMENT

In 1966, scholars from the American Association for Mental Deficiency (AAMD) gathered in Chicago's Hotel Sherman—notorious for its 1920s mobster gatherings—to signal acceptance of the work of one of their own. On May 12, they welcomed Harold Skeels back into their fold. Skeels had not publicly presented any research since 1939, when members of this same professional association, meeting in this same city and at this same hotel, had crushed him with their ridicule.

For nearly three decades Skeels had ruminated about whether he had deceived himself. Perhaps his study made too much of small changes in development, so fleeting others never bothered to mention them. Or perhaps the intelligence changes he reported resulted from incorrect statistical analysis or errors in the IQ tests themselves. Well aware of her friend's uncertainties, Skodak shared these herself, even suspecting that Skeels had encouraged her 1938–1939 adoption studies as possible confirmation of his own work.[1]

Now, with NIMH support, Skeels had found evidence in his subjects' life paths that demonstrated his studies' import. An experimental group of thirteen once low-intelligence children had maintained their intelligence gains, unmistakable in their academic success and well-functioning lives. And with

grief he had found that his contrast group subjects had paid a steep price—
the loss of what might have been intellectually normal adulthoods—for the
Davenport Home's institutional indifference. Spectacular and terrible, Skeels
wanted his findings to have psychology's full attention.

Yet following his travels, Skeels, now in his mid-60s, found himself
plagued with health difficulties. In 1964, when Skodak had arrived in Washington for a conference Skeels had organized, she found him confused. She
and an NIMH colleague hospitalized him and she took over the meeting. In
the following months, Skeels was in and out of hospitals for evaluation, and
when Skodak spoke with him on the phone, his speech sounded "disconnected, and sometimes slurred" and she created excuses to visit Washington
to check on him. An eventual diagnosis said that he had suffered a series of
small strokes.

In 1965 Skeels admitted that his full-time job was now too demanding and took an early retirement, relocating to Balboa Island, California,
a seaside community south of Los Angeles where he had friends. While he
seemed to function day-to-day, his condition left him too distracted to write
up the longitudinal findings to be presented in Chicago and he called upon
Skodak, the only other psychologist who understood the arc of his work, for
assistance. Together they penned the talk he planned to deliver at the American Association for Mental Deficiency meeting, and Skodak also wrote
Skeels's paper about his study, which had been accepted in the *Monographs
of the Society for Research in Child Development.* Although both psychologists'
names appeared on the unpublished talk, Skeels did not credit Skodak as the
second author of his paper. Possibly this reflected an editorial decision at the
journal. Possibly, too, Skeels did not wish to call his editor's attention to Skodak's role. However, in the paper's acknowledgments he expressed "deepest
gratitude" for Skodak's "meticulous care and complete editorial revision" of
his text.[2]

———

Presenting his work for the first time in twenty-seven years, Skeels knew
that some at the Chicago meeting would be unfamiliar with what had
come before, and he briefly reviewed the results of his 1939 study: an experi-

mental group of thirteen once low-intellect children who lived with affectionate women labeled "morons" had become normal, and a contrast group of eleven once normal children who continued to live at Davenport and in other institutional settings had suffered significant intelligence declines. But the heart of Skeels's talk compared the groups' outcomes in education, marriage and family patterns, earnings, physical and mental health, and current institutionalization status, which in every area revealed the groups' stark disparities.

The experimental group's median educational level was twelfth grade; in the contrast group it was third grade. Eleven of the experimental group subjects had married and had twenty-eight children among them. Their children's mean intelligence test score was 104, and their individual scores ranged from 86 to 125. Two of the contrast group subjects had married and had a total of five children, four of whom were children of the one subject who had experienced increased environmental stimulation and who achieved greater educational, relationship, employment, and financial success than any other contrast subject. Those four children had normal intelligence, but the one child of a contrast group parent who had low intelligence, a child Skeels believed had been abused, had below-normal intelligence. No experimental subject was divorced, and one contrast group member was divorced. Skeels reported that all of the experimental group adults were employed or married to someone who was. Seven contrast subjects were independent and minimally employed, and four lived in institutions. No experimental group members were mentally ill, but one member of the contrast group was institutionalized because of mental illness. No experimental group member had died, but one contrast group member had died during adolescence of a genetic condition, Gaucher's disease.

There were significant differences in the costs to the state of Iowa for the two groups. Thirteen experimental group members lived in institutions for a total of 72.3 years, at a cost of about $31,000 (today about $251,000). Twelve contrast group members spent a total of 273 years in institutions, at a cost of about $139,000 (today about $1,122,000). In 1963 the experimental group's median income was $5,220 (in current dollars, about $42,000). The median income for the contrast group was $1,200 (today about $9,700).[3] The contrast

group's outlier subject, case 19, had yearly earnings greater than the earnings of the rest of the group combined.[4] Clearly, the state of Iowa would have
benefited financially from improved conditions at Davenport, both in savings
from long-term institutionalization and from added tax revenue generated by
employed citizens.

Published weeks later, Skeels's paper described that while most adopted
experimental group subjects lived in their own homes and had positive relations with their adoptive families (or if not adopted, with community members), contrast group members, with the exception of case 19, tended to live
isolated lives. Those who were not in institutions lived as boarders and had no
family contact. He reported that on the 1960 US census socioeconomic status
rating scale of 1–100, the experimental group ranked 52.2 and the contrast
group ranked 14.4.[5]

His study, Skeels said, suggested that enough is known to counter the
crushing effects of deprivation, lack of money, and ignorance of children's
need for affection and educational stimulation.[6] He showed that those in one
group might have had completely different lives if they had changed places,
early, with the other. And Skeels told an interviewer of his hope that the
grievous lives of those in the contrast group might serve as a warning so that
"their lives will not have been in vain."[7]

Skeels's Chicago account and the research monograph that followed
would radically reshape psychology's perception of the Iowa station's discoveries. But reported in just a few small-town newspapers, the results would
only become widely known to the public in August of 1967 in a feature article
published in *Redbook*, a popular women's magazine. "The Case of the Wandering IQs," Bernard Asbell's detailed account of Skeels's work, told of Davenport's neglect, the children's startling progress, and the adult outcomes that,
at long last, had begun to convince Skeels himself.

Asbell, who taught writing at Yale and served as president of the American Society of Journalists and Authors, wrote that Skeels credited the work
of Samuel A. Kirk and Martin Deutsch, 1960s scholars whose investigations
confirmed Iowa's discoveries. Asbell's article captured psychology's understanding of how the effects of environment contributed to Head Start, the
national program that provides stimulating preschool experience to economi-

cally deprived populations. With some journalistic overstatement, Asbell wrote that "almost overnight the 'wandering IQ' . . . became a subject of high fashion in educational and psychological research,"[8] but despite his remarkable discoveries, Asbell pointed out, almost no one knew Harold Skeels's name.

Asbell's article handed Skeels an opportunity that many academics hope for: to have their academic research translated for public understanding. Quoting Skeels, the article said that while his study was small—it was based on only twenty-five children—it had wide-ranging importance because

> there are hundreds of thousands of babies born into deprivation. . . . If we can bring them the Head Start kind of experience early . . . and make sure it sticks, we'll find that most of these children can become successful.[9]

"The tide of history," Skodak said of Skeels's work, "had reversed."[10] From that point, whenever Marie Skodak spoke of Skeels, she told of psychology's acceptance of Skeels's discoveries as a success beyond all expectations. His work made the case, she said, for eliminating institutional care and improving opportunities for all disadvantaged children.

The year 1966 became a milestone in Marie Skodak's personal life as well when she married former Iowa station member and her longtime professional colleague Orlo Crissey. Her new husband, an originator of the field of industrial psychology, had helped identify those skills and personal characteristics that made for employee success in their work assignments. Eventually, he became a leader in several industrial psychology associations and led the American Psychological Association's division in this new area. Skodak and Crissey's family had been friends since they met at the Iowa station, and she and Crissey had later worked together at the Flint Child Guidance Clinic. It was Skodak's first marriage. Crissey, who had been widowed, was the father of three adult children. Eventually, there would be nineteen grandchildren and great-grandchildren and even one great-great-grandchild. In 1969 Skodak Crissey retired from the Dearborn schools, and she and her husband traveled extensively.

With the recognition of Skeels's work, Skodak found that her friend's mood shifted, and he recaptured some of the good feeling of his Iowa years. In 1967, the American Psychological Association selected Skeels as the first recipient of its G. Stanley Hall Award in Developmental Psychology. As president of Clark University, Hall had founded the American Psychological Association and became mentor to Lewis Terman. The irony of receiving an honor bearing Hall's name could not have escaped Skeels's notice.

The APA's selection of Urie Bronfenbrenner to present the award further confirmed Skeels's recognition. In the 1950s, Bronfenbrenner's ideas had accelerated psychology's understanding of environment's impact on early development. It was little surprise when his citation lauded not only Skeels's discoveries, but his character. Bronfenbrenner contrasted Harold Skeels with those

> clever enough not to see things that would clash too sharply with the current scientific fashions. . . . But there are a few who, in place of being clever, are simply clear—. . . clear in stating the most defensible interpretation of the findings without fear or favor or the prevailing scientific climate. Harold M. Skeels is such a man. In an era when the constancy of the IQ was a sacred cow, he . . . had the vision . . . to exploit an experiment of nature—Skeels . . . demonstrated the power of the environment both to cripple and to foster the child's intellectual development. For asserting such heresy, Skeels was mercilessly attacked by the psychological establishment . . . but he stood his ground.[11]

Further recognition arrived the following year when, at its presidential banquet held at Boston's Sheraton Hotel, the AAMD honored "the once ostracized" Skeels for "pioneering work" that demonstrated the effect of "love and attention" on children's development.[12]

What Skeels and Skodak viewed as their greatest distinction arrived in 1968, when the Joseph P. Kennedy Jr. Foundation, which honored the Kennedy son who died fighting in World War II, selected Skeels and Skodak as two recipients of the foundation's International Award for Research in the Field of Mental Retardation. "Words fail me," Skeels said upon acceptance, "and I feel very thankful and humble for the scientific opportunities which have fallen [to] my lot, and for this honor."[13] Unlike his previous awards, the Kennedy accolade came from a world beyond academic psychology, recognition that the Iowan's revelations about development had reached the audience of those concerned with disabilities. Foundation director Eunice Kennedy Shriver told Skeels: "Your extraordinary work over many years has more than qualified you to join this small but distinguished group of Kennedy Laureates. We hope this award will be a further inspiration for you and for many others."[14]

Shriver's dedication to the intellectually challenged emerged from her experience with her sister Rosemary Kennedy, who as a young child was diagnosed as retarded and in her 20s suffered a brain surgery error that confined her to an institution for the rest of her life. For Shriver, Skeels's and others' discoveries may have been bittersweet when they suggested that her sister's outcome might have been avoided "if we had known then what we know today—that 75 to 85% of the retarded are capable of becoming useful citizens."[15] In a magazine article, she voiced relief: "We are just coming out of the dark ages in our handling of this serious national problem."[16]

On April 29, 1968, Skeels, Skodak, and Louis Branca, who would present the award, gathered in Chicago with foundation president Edward M. Kennedy, the Shrivers, Kennedy family members Robert and his wife Ethel, and the family's grande dame, Rose Kennedy, along with Muriel Humphrey, the wife of Vice President Hubert Humphrey, for a dinner followed by a concert and awards program.[17] With Gregory Peck as the master of ceremonies, the evening featured a concert by the Chicago Symphony conducted by maestro Seiji Ozawa, performances by Metropolitan Opera diva Grace Bumbry, and celebrated folk singers Peter, Paul and Mary. In presenting the award to Skeels and Skodak, Branca told the audience that they changed his life: "I sat in a corner, rocking, until these two took action. . . . I am here tonight because they gave me love, and understanding."[18] As the audience rose to give Branca a standing ovation, Edward M. Kennedy handed him a Steuben cut crystal award engraved with a seraph, a baby in its arms, which Branca presented to Skodak and Skeels. Each psychologist also received a financial award of $20,000 (today about $145,000).

The following day, Branca, along with Shriver, Skeels, and Skodak, flew to New York for an interview with Barbara Walters on NBC's *Today Show*. After he returned home, Branca received a letter from Skodak telling him that her friends and colleagues spoke admiringly about "that wonderful young man" whom they had watched on TV. Branca had so impressed the Kennedy family that they offered him a position working for them, which he declined, explaining that he wanted to complete graduate school. In a 2012 interview, Branca expressed concern that amidst the many powerful Kennedy figures, it would have been difficult for him to establish his own path. He added, too, that once people know that a person previously had low intelligence, they might not be able to perceive them as intellectually capable. "It takes grit," he said, "to ignore what other people say about you."[19]

Branca never regretted his decision and established a successful career as an associate in the Dean of Students Office at the University of Minnesota, the university at which Florence Goodenough once conducted her research. From time to time he made presentations to Minnesota's faculty about Skeels's and Skodak's discoveries and about his own history. After one such talk, a member of the university's psychology department who knew of Goodenough's 1930s attacks on the Iowa group assured him, "We don't think that way anymore."[20]

With Skeels's health limiting his travel, during the next years Skodak became the spokesperson for Iowa's discoveries. In February 1967, at a New York City presentation before the American Educational Research Association, she defined the five environmental factors that had enabled thirteen cognitively challenged Davenport orphans, as well as several hundred Davenport adoptees, to thrive, but alerted her audience that her findings, essential for normal early development, applied to children "without clear organic pathology."[21] During the 1960s, studies about methods to support development in children who had such pathology were rare. Today, it is well established that the conditions Skodak defined for the nurture of young children are essential to the healthy development of every child.

Skodak argued, first, that "early delays in mental development . . . can

be altered by establishing a close affectional tie with a mothering individual."
Next, she told of the significance of "a high level of cognitive stimulation,"
specifically, "exposure to an excess of language." Skodak also noted that the
best outcomes for adopted Davenport children developed "in an atmosphere
of encouragement and approval." These interventions, she said, are effective
when the emotional and intellectual environments remain stable and are
accompanied by consistent nurturing and stimulation that persists over time.
Finally, Skodak emphasized that while very early stimulation is highly important, an exact time frame had not yet been defined.

Concluding her talk, Skodak linked the Iowa discoveries to present
thinking: "Thirty years ago, [the Iowa work] provoked studies to disprove
such fantastic [IQ] changes. Today . . . it is hoped [they] will provoke studies
that describe those elements of experience which are significant for optimum
intellectual growth and its maintenance into productive adulthood."[22]

In September 1968, Skodak journeyed to Montpellier, in the south of
France, for the first World Congress of the International Association for the
Scientific Study of Intellectual and Developmental Disabilities. Affiliated with
the World Health Organization, IASSIDD is the only international association that promotes research and policy about health, family life, behavior, and
mental health related to intellectual disability. Addressing researchers who
may have known little about the Iowa studies, Skodak emphasized that "the
influence of environment . . . covers the range from profound mental defect,
to intellectual giftedness. [These] factors are within the control of man . . .
and inferences can be drawn for remediation and prevention."[23]

But after her return, Skodak was alarmed by a phone call with Skeels in
which she found his thinking quite disconnected. Because several of those
close to her, including her mother, were ill—during 1969 she lost twelve relations and friends—she and Skeels did not speak as frequently as had been their
custom. However, in one phone call, thinking that a trip might buoy Skeels's
mood, she encouraged him to travel abroad. On March 14, 1970, in a routine
letter discussing candidates for professional awards, he responded: "That sort
of trip leaves me cold," he explained, because "friends and colleagues travel-
ling outside of the United States . . . have returned to their home base in a
rough box." Skeels then added a jokey postscript: "P.S. Of course, since you

and your husband are so much younger than Jerry and myself—you can travel around the world—if you insist."[24] His mention of "Jerry," which suggests a male companion with whom he could not travel as freely as Skodak and her husband, underscores his trust in her friendship and assumes her knowledge of that relationship.

This was Skeels's last letter to his research partner and lifelong friend. He passed away while he slept, on Saturday, March 28, 1970, of a massive heart attack and stroke. "He went as he wished," Skodak wrote to Skeels's cousin, "quickly, painlessly, without bothering anyone."[25] Only weeks earlier Harold Skeels had mailed the Kennedy award to Louis Branca. Branca died on August 30, 2015, and the award remains with Branca's widow, the novelist Cass Dalglish.

It fell to Marie Skodak to inform those who knew Skeels of his death. In a letter to the Kennedy Foundation, she related that Skeels had seen his work as a means to

> *alleviate the consequences of social and familial disadvantage. The rejection and the acrimonious attacks on both his integrity and the concepts of the studies wounded him in a way from which he never fully recovered. He was fortunate to live long enough to see his theories vindicated and carried forward.*[26]

And to Eunice Kennedy Shriver, Skodak expressed what Shriver's interest meant to "a lonely man who had seen his life work denigrated for years." She reminded Shriver of Skeels's dinner with her family, and wrote: "He saw [that dinner] as sign of the turning point in social awareness of the significance of his earlier work. He was ever grateful for your interest and zeal on behalf of the handicapped and underprivileged."[27]

For information about Skeels's death, one of his cousins had been in touch with Skodak. In a detailed response, she described Skeels's medical condition and also that Skeels's life seemed

> *solitary and lonely . . . with little commitment of himself to the relationships which bring both joy and sorrow. . . . . Perhaps I*

have written in more detail than you wanted, but Harold has
always been a rather special person to me, and if you loved him
you might want to know.[28]

———

Skeels's death left unanswered the question of how to interpret his near total silence about his work and his life, from his Iowa departure in 1946 to the period before his 1966 follow-up study. Skeels's reticence is made starker by Skodak's comments that during their Iowa days her friend had been "congenial and social,"[29] "the master tactician"[30] who had confidently worked with academics, institutional administrators, and political appointees to enable Iowa's research. While based in London with the Army Air Force, Skeels spoke so freely about the babies and children for whom he arranged adoptions that his war buddies bestowed on him the nickname Storky.

But the abrupt turndown Skeels received after the war from the Bivin Foundation when he had applied for funds for additional research may have signaled that his profession continued to view him as a failed researcher. To avoid further humiliation, he may have distanced himself from interactions with colleagues and, as Skodak and Simon Auster observed, remained private about his past work and his friendships.

In another interpretation of Skeels's retreat, one Skodak implied, he may have been fearful of being revealed as a homosexual. Grant Wood's biographer, Tripp Evans, points out that archival or concrete evidence from Skeels's time that would provide confirmation of sexual orientation rarely exists because, on exposure, gay men and women faced toxic stigmatization, as the attacks on Wood at Skeels's own university clearly showed.[31]

In their onslaught against the Iowa group, Terman and his followers were equal-opportunity aggressors, and all of the Iowans received rough treatment. While Stoddard, Wellman, and Skodak answered those attacks, Skeels, whom commentators acknowledge received the harshest treatment, withdrew from the stage. Skodak's discreet comments, previously detailed, indicate that she suspected his situation and understood his self-imposed silence. Skeels's casual reference to "Jerry" in his last letter suggests she may have been privy to a personal life he shared with no one else. Further, in retirement, Skeels had chosen to live in Balboa, a California coastal town about 8 miles north of Laguna Beach. From the 1930s to about 2000, Laguna, along with Province-town in Massachusetts, the Florida Keys, New York City's Christopher Street, and other enclaves, was a gathering place friendly to homosexuals. In 1982, Laguna elected America's first openly gay mayor.[32]

Moreover, Skeels's post-Iowa career coincided with a wider cultural con-text, revealed in the American Psychiatric Association's 1952 decision to label homosexuality a mental illness.[33] From that perspective, no one who was gay was safe. In 1954, Alan Turing, the closeted British war hero who helped defeat Nazi Germany when he cracked its secret Enigma codes, was caught in a homosexual act and offered chemical castration in lieu of prison, but soon took his own life.

Although by the early 1960s two of Skeels's attackers, Lewis Terman and Florence Goodenough, had died, fear of being revealed may have caused Skeels to refrain from discussing his work with Auster and, as Gladwin implied, with others. This may also explain Skeels's initial reluctance to move ahead when Havighurst suggested a follow-up study. To call attention to himself by aggressively challenging his profession's orthodoxy or by engaging in research related to studies that had previously brought disgrace might have put both him and the work at risk. Thus, Skeels's eventual commitment to a follow-up may represent more than his hope for answers about his subjects or a drive to discover new knowledge. It may have gone unrecognized as a remarkable act of courage.

———

In 1972, with Skeels and Wellman deceased and Stoddard retired as chan-cellor of New York University, Marie Skodak remained the only Iowa group member still active in psychology. As the keeper of that flame, she was not surprised when a letter arrived from French experimental psychologist Michel Schiff. Schiff had begun to study the influence of environment on the intelligence of adopted children, although with a different research design from the Iowans': using France's detailed records about its schoolchildren, Schiff would compare intelligence test scores in pairs of siblings in which one child had been adopted by a high-status family and another continued to live with their low-status birth parents.

In his review of the adoption literature, Schiff wrote that he "could not find any postwar adoption studies in the US besides those of the Iowa School" and wondered if that could be correct.[34] Schiff also explained that the work of other specialists in human behavior and genetics—two of the field's leaders, Sir Cyril Burt and Arthur Jensen—did not stand up to analysis, but that she and Skeels had "been right, or at least . . . reversed the burden of proof."[35] In 1976, Burt's studies purporting to show that 53 pairs of identical twins separated at birth and raised apart had identical intelligence, studies eugenicists regularly cited as hard evidence in support of their beliefs, were revealed as entirely fraudulent.[36] In 1985, Stephen Jay Gould would label Burt's studies "perhaps the most spectacular case of . . . scientific fraud in our century."[37]

In her reply, Skodak told Schiff of several recent small studies and of what she learned from her 1966 longitudinal investigation—though, she confessed, the data had not yet been analyzed. She invited Schiff, soon arriving in the United States to prepare for his investigations, to visit her in Michigan to discuss his work and review her extensive library of past and recent adoption studies. The two met during the summer of 1972.

Schiff's study grew out of a resurgence of hereditarian thought as expressed in a 1969 article by Arthur R. Jensen, once a student of British eugenicist Hans Eysenck. Jensen's article suggested that the "educational lag of disadvantaged children" was explained by their heredity.[38] Schiff designed his research specifically to test Jensen's assertion.[39] In the late 1960s, Jensen, a controversial psychologist at the University of California, Berkeley, had become a figure in the resurgence of American hereditarian thought. A historic 1969 issue of the *Harvard Educational Review* brought together an important article by Jensen with responses from other scholars. Here Jensen argued that "compensatory education"—Head Start and similar programs— "has been tried and it apparently has failed" and that "the traditional forms of instruction have actually worked quite well for the majority of children."[40] Jensen argued that intelligence constancy, not systemic bias and socioeconomic factors, accounted for the failure of remedial programs to influence children's intelligence.

One response to Jensen came from developmental psychologist Jerome Kagan, of Harvard University. Kagan pointed out that a study of identical twins reared in different environments found mean differences in IQ of 14 points and that 25 percent of the subjects differed by 16 points, "larger than the average difference between black and white populations." Kagan added, "The value of Head Start . . . has not yet been adequately assessed."[41]

The Harvard editors also presented Joseph McVicker Hunt's review of current neuroscience literature, including Donald O. Hebb's discovery of the mechanisms that govern how experience alters brain development. Hunt wrote, "Increases in the development of brain structures following enrichments of early experience are hardly consonant with [Jensen's] position."[42] Hunt also described the effects of environment on the two groups reported in Skeels's 1966 follow-up and argued that the "vast majority" of intelligence test results report on subjects who live in stable environments and produce stable intelligence test scores. Reliance on measures of consistent environment, not "intelligence constancy," had led psychology to conclude that IQ test scores do not change.[43]

In the same issue William F. Brazziel, a psychologist from Virginia's Norfolk State College who, since 1968, had followed Jensen's writing, presented a Southerners' perspective when he homed in on a dispute about Virginia's local school integration then playing out in federal district court. In a letter to the *Review*, he quoted Virginia's legal argument that since "white teachers could not understand the Nigra mind," those students should attend schools where "teachers who understood them could work with them." Brazziel wrote that the defense "quoted heavily from the theories of white intellectual supremacy as expounded by Arthur Jensen."[44]

In the introduction to his paper, published in 1978, Schiff referenced Jensen and also Harvard psychologist Richard J. Herrnstein (in 1994, with Charles Murray, Hernstein would coauthor *The Bell Curve*), who had written, "The class structure of modern society is essentially a function of the innately differing intellectual and other qualities of the people making up these classes."[45] In a paper that echoed Marie Skodak's adoption studies, Schiff examined intelligence test results in two groups: a group of thirty-two working-class children adopted at about 4 months and placed with parents who had high socioprofessional status and a group of thirty-two of those children's siblings, close in age to the adopted children, who continued to live with their birth families. He found the test scores of the adopted children "almost embarrassingly close to those expected solely on the basis of the social class of their adoptive parents" and the test scores of their nonadopted siblings close to those found in children of unskilled workers.[46] In a 1982 follow-up, Schiff confirmed these results. As had Skodak, Schiff found that environment significantly influenced children's IQ test outcomes. In words comparable to Skeels's, Schiff wrote, "If French children of lower-class parents were reared under exactly the same conditions as the adopted children of our study, they would obtain IQ scores . . . close to those presently observed for upper-middle-class children."[47]

———

After being fired in 1953 from the University of Illinois and then a year spent living in Princeton to consider his future, George Stoddard had returned to New York as a member of New York University's administration and by 1960 had been named the university's chancellor. Along with those duties, Stoddard served on the founding committee for UNESCO and aided Japan, Korea, and Iran as they restructured their educational systems. He also participated in New York's creative life as a board member at Lincoln Center for the Performing Arts. During this period, Stoddard wrote several books, among them an autobiography, *The Pursuit of Education*, published in 1981. In August of 1981, he was selected by the American Psychological Association to receive the G. Stanley Hall Award in Developmental Psychology, the same honor Harold Skeels had received in 1967.

In presenting the award, Marie Skodak recognized Stoddard for transforming the Iowa station from its modest goals of examining the lives of rural children to one of the nation's leading centers for studying a novel idea, that early experience influences intellectual development. Stoddard, she said, had the wisdom to appreciate the long-range implications of the station's research and to take on the cascade of disapproval set loose against the station's research by orthodox psychology's belief in pseudoscience. Emphasizing Stoddard's integrity, Skodak noted that with his confidence in the improvability of man Stoddard became an exemplar for his profession.[48] A few months later, on December 28, 1981, Stoddard died at 84 years of age.

———

Marie Skodak's Iowa experience turned her into a scholar and—even with her good-humored, pragmatic temperament—something of a rebel. Mentored by Skeels, she accomplished benchmark investigations into the development of infants and young children, reported on the outcomes of hundreds of adopted children, and with NIMH support embarked on her 1962 follow-up research about the adult status and cognitive outcomes of one hundred children, most of whom who were adopted early. Her discoveries shifted ideas about what normal development requires and led to further investigations, including Michel Schiff's. Had female scholars of her day had greater access to academic opportunities, she might well have established a research career. But "in at least four different occasions," she discovered, "the fact that I was a woman resulted in an appointment going to a man."[49] In one such occurrence, at the University of Michigan, where she worked as a part-time lecturer, she applied for a faculty appointment, knowing her request was hopeless—the one female on the faculty was the head of women's physical education.

Yet like the young Ohio State student who, in the days of the Depression, had to decide whether to leave college to aid her family or invent a way forward, Skodak pushed ahead. Working in Michigan's public schools, where she served with superintendents, principals, and agency heads, she routinely found herself the sole woman and the committee's leader. Often she was the only person in the room, or the school, or the school district's administration, with a PhD, which granted her access to ever greater responsibilities.

Known as a "red tape cutter," Skodak used her school psychologist credentials and leadership expertise at the local level to set up programs that supported intellectually challenged students and their families, to create university internships for graduate students, and to establish and lead in-service training and counselor and school psychologist training, replicated in other school districts. She led at the state level as president of the Michigan Psychological Association and served on the national level as a member of the

American Board of Professional Psychology and as president of American Psychological Association committees in the areas of retardation and school services. She served as president of two APA divisions, Consulting and Mental Retardation. When gender blocked her academic ambitions, she created missions that made her talents count.

Yet toward the end of her life, Skodak acknowledged obliquely, and with forgiveness, slights she sustained, perhaps including Harold Skeels's failure to credit her as second author on his culminating 1966 paper, which she had written:

> *My professional life . . . has been . . . mostly among men. It was men who were my peers. There . . . have always been barriers to advancement . . . sometimes because you are a woman, or have a foreign name, or different philosophy of life. . . . What is remembered are the successes, the challenges that have been met. The inevitable disappointments, small heartaches, fade like old photographs, and that is probably the way it should be.*[50]

Reflecting about her career decisions, Skodak wrote that if she had a chance to go back to 1930, she would choose the same professional path. But if she were making the choice in the 1990s, she would study the neuropsychological bases of behavior and how they mediated environment's influence.[51] And Skodak left unfinished business. Her research data from the 1960s, which demonstrated that modified environments led to changed development, as well as investigations she completed in Michigan's public schools, never received the formal processing required for academic contributions. She called this her "major disappointment": "Planned, executed, the data analyzed . . . they sit neatly boxed, waiting for the final writeup. There is decreasing hope that I will get to them in the years that remain."[52]

―――

In the 1930s, the Iowa station's visionary, George Stoddard, had forecast that the mechanisms that changed the Davenport orphans would one day be explained by neuroscience. For that belief, he and his colleagues, Beth

Wellman, Harold Skeels, and Marie Skodak, suffered unrelenting attack, yet insisted their discoveries represented new knowledge. On December 5, 2000, during a period when decisive neuroscience findings about early brain development had begun to emerge, the last of the Iowa gang, Marie Skodak, died at age 90. Those findings would offer profound insights into what shapes the minds of young children—concrete evidence, down to the cellular level, of what the Iowans had grasped decades before: the minds of children are handmade.[53]

Epilogue

THE MIRACLE OF SCIENCE

After a 1-hour trial, at exactly 4 p.m. on the freezing afternoon of December 25, 1989, Romanian soldiers executed the nation's megalomaniacal Communist leader, Nicolae Ceauşescu, and his wife, Elena, by firing squad. Ceauşescu had ruled for twenty-four years; when he died, more than 170,000 Romanian orphans, about 7.5 percent of the nation, were living in abusive state-run institutions.

Convinced that the human capital of a huge workforce would bring prosperity and international authority to one of Europe's poorest countries, Ceauşescu had launched a radical plan to increase Romania's birth rate: he outlawed contraception and abortion and reduced the legal age of marriage to 15. Girls and women who became pregnant were tracked to ensure that they did not abort their fetuses, but during his reign over 10,000 died in illegal abortions. Ceauşescu further ordered families with fewer than five children to pay a "celibacy tax."[1] When poverty-stricken Romanians could not support their politically mandated children, they turned them over to the state to raise in its overcrowded, understaffed, ill-funded government institutions.

Three decades and over 5,000 miles separate 1930s Depression-era Iowa from Communist Romania. Yet in each, children in state-run orphanages suffered callous neglect that severely impaired their development. As in

Iowa, in Romania a scientific study and intervention aided the recoveries of some, adding significantly to our understanding of child development. The two landmark studies differ in period, scale, and complexity—yet history seemed to repeat itself in their strikingly similar findings. Using scientific tools never dreamed of by the Iowa psychologists, sophisticated neuroscience investigations of the Romanian children's brain functions found that environmentally determined factors impacted the children's emotional responsiveness, relationships, and intelligence. This suggests that similar effects may have changed the Davenport orphans.

During Ceaușescu's rule, his regime succeeded in significantly raising Romania's birth rate. But in a nation that sold most of its food products as exports and attempted to pay off its massive foreign debt by imposing harsh austerity measures, his policies only worsened conditions. Romanians had their food rationed and their electricity turned off at night, and in winter they lived and worked in barely heated buildings.[2] Neither adoption nor foster care had become established in Romania, and each year thousands of infants were abandoned to state institutions by parents unable to provide for them. One observer reported that in Romania, child abandonment became "implicitly endorsed."[3]

Staffed by poorly trained, overburdened, and often indifferent workers, Romania's orphanage management bore no relation to any accepted child-care standards. The tens of thousands whom Ceaușescu boasted would lift the nation to international greatness instead suffered damaged health and impaired motor, social, and cognitive development due to poor nutrition and criminal neglect. The children lacked any environmental stimulation: like the Davenport orphans, they had no possessions or playthings, rarely left their institutional wards, and had almost no responsive interactions with adults. Due to unsanitary conditions 63 percent of Romania's institutionalized children suffered from HIV/AIDS as well as hepatitis B.[4] In some of the worst institutions, child mortality was 25 to 50 percent per year.[5]

Almost immediately after Ceaușescu's death, the world's media flooded the nation. They found scandalous conditions in state-run institutions for "normal" children and far worse in asylums for disabled children called "irrecoverables." In 1990, ABC television's *20/20* documented "naked underfed children sitting ankle deep in their own urine; scabrous children herded like pigs to 'bathe' in filthy troughs of black water; infants starving to death because of treatable conditions such as cerebral palsy."[6] A reporter for the *Los Angeles Times* described babies "in long rows of cribs [where] the caretaker walks down one aisle and sticks bottles in the babies' mouths, and then walks up another aisle and removes bottles."[7] The *New York Times* told of babies and toddlers who remained in cribs all day without any attention, soothing themselves by rocking.[8]

Because they destroyed their clothes, many residents who lived in unheated institutions for the disabled were kept naked.[9] A visiting French doctor labeled conditions for these "irrecoverables" as "something between Auschwitz and Kampuchea" and reported: "Children are handcuffed to beds so tightly that the cuffs eat into their wrists. . . . Those too small or unable to feed themselves often waste away because their nursing bottles propped on piles of rags, slip away and there is no one to right them."[10] Nonfiction author Melissa Fay Greene reported in *The Atlantic* that in these institutions, Romania applied the Soviet Union's science of "defectology," classifying even children with cleft palates or crossed eyes as "unsalvageable."[11]

Exposing Romania's orphanages to the world inspired a rush to the nation from potential adoptive parents. In 1992, 7,328 Romanian children were adopted by Americans, Canadians, and Europeans—2,450 by Americans alone.[12] Needless to say, many of these children arrived in poor health, and that year the health and development of sixty-five Romanian orphans newly adopted into American families was assessed by Dana E. Johnson, a University of Minnesota pediatrician with expertise in the evaluation of international adoptees. Johnson and his team found that only ten of the children were physically healthy and developmentally normal, and eight of those were under 5 months and had very short orphanage stays.

Most of the children had been identified as HIV-free before parents agreed to take them, but other diseases were common: more than half had evidence of past or present hepatitis B infection; twenty-two had intestinal parasites; and twenty-nine had evidence of two or more pathogens. Johnson also found that the children suffered from small stature and low weight as well as small head circumference. He classified 85 percent as having serious medical developmental or behavioral disorders. Neurological issues from nutritional and emotional deprivation had led to severe developmental delays that required professional attention. "The adverse effects of the orphanage on normal development," Johnson wrote, "may explain why twenty percent or more of the Romanian children had been misdiagnosed as being mentally deficient."[13]

In 1986, Johnson had founded the Adoption Medicine Clinic at the University of Minnesota and better than others understood that most of the Romanian children faced immediate and long-term developmental challenges. He shared his experience with a colleague, another scientist deeply committed to the study of the developmental effects of deprivation, cognitive psychologist and neuroscientist Charles A. Nelson, then at the University of Minnesota, now at Harvard. Johnson also connected Nelson with Romania's newly appointed first-ever minister of child protection, Cristian Tabacaru, a post-Ceaușescu government official who believed that foster families would provide better environments for children than institutions. Tabacaru aimed to shut the institutions down, but he needed scientific evidence to convince government skeptics.

"In countries like Romania," Nelson said, "institutionalizing children was part of the culture. In a Communist system, officials and many citizens thought the state could do a better job of raising children than families."[14] Romanian officials expressed concern that in foster homes children would be treated harshly and would be vulnerable to pedophilia and organ trafficking. They also doubted that untrained foster parents had the expertise to handle the developmental problems of formerly institutionalized children.[15]

When a 1997 White House conference on young children's development and learning increased public interest about early brain development, the John D. and Catherine T. MacArthur Foundation became curious. This led to conversations with Nelson and colleagues Nathan A. Fox, a University of Maryland psychologist, and Charles H. Zeanah, a psychiatrist at Tulane University, all of whom had concerns about the harm to Romanian children that Johnson had reported. Zeanah had found similar severe effects in some neglected American children, so starved for adult attention they approached and befriended random strangers.[16] (Skeels and Skodak had reported similar behaviors in Davenport residents.) The next year the MacArthur Foundation launched its Network on Early Experience and Brain Development, with Nelson as director.

To translate their concern into action, Nelson and his colleagues established the Bucharest Early Intervention Project (BEIP), a study conceived as both a scientific and humanitarian undertaking. Sponsored by MacArthur, the BEIP would ask two essential questions: what are the effects of institutionalization on brain development, and would living with families reverse those effects? Utilizing the method of a randomized controlled trial, the investigation would test three hypotheses:

Compared with children who lived in institutions, children who lived with families would have better developmental outcomes.

The longer children lived in institutions, the more their development became compromised.

The age of placement into foster care could be more important than the length of time spent in foster care.[17]

At the time of the study, fostering children was not an accepted method of childcare in Romania, and Bucharest, a city of 2 million, had only one approved foster family. This meant the BEIP would have to establish its own foster care program. With Tabacaru's help, the scientists received government permission to establish Romania's first such network. Eventually, Tabacaru established a Romanian foster care system that relegated institutionalizations to a last resort.[18]

Because American foster care is temporary, the establishment of foster care in Romania meant creating an entirely different system than the one the researchers were accustomed to. In the United States, children remain with their foster families for eighteen months, although there can be frequent placement changes. At the end of that time, children either return to their parents or are released to agencies for adoption. In the BEIP model, foster care would continue indefinitely, and no child who had been fostered would ever be returned to an institution. Social workers helped the Romanian foster parents establish warm relationships and provided psychological as well as material support. Foster parents were encouraged to "care about . . . the children as if they were their own."[19] Several of the fostered children were later adopted by their foster families.

An essential feature of the study would be comparisons of the brain development of the children who experienced foster care with those who remained in institutional care, a contrast not previously studied. To accomplish this, the investigators assembled a well-equipped laboratory in Bucharest. With the use of electroencephalogram (EEG) and event-related potential (ERP) technology, scientists planned to study electrical patterns in the children's brains to assess neurological, cognitive, and behavioral development. Eventually, researchers also employed magnetic resonance imaging (MRI) to analyze brain differences between the groups.

Another feature of the BEIP research protocol also set it apart from previous studies. It would be the first comparison of adopted and institutionalized children in which subjects would be randomly selected. Children would be assigned by chance to live either in a home with a nurturing foster family or to remain in an institution. That the study's design left children in facilities known to be neglectful and even abusive raised sharp ethical questions. There were two principal reasons why BEIP scientists nonetheless went forward. First, they believed that strict randomization could dispel the suspicion raised by every previous adoption study that results favoring adoption had been contaminated by selective placement bias. Critics might ask whether children had been chosen for adoption because they had qualities that made them more desirable—perhaps they appeared healthier or more attractive, livelier or more intelligent.[20] If so, adoptees' superior outcomes might indicate some genetic advantage rather than their adoptive parents' nurturing. In Romania and many other nations, suspicion regarding selective placement bias was supported by another cultural assumption: that children in institutions were somehow defective.[21] After all, why else would they be there? A truly random selection of children would refute such suspicions.

Second, the investigators hoped to combat Romania's entrenched policies of child institutionalization. If the BEIP's methods demonstrated that family environments achieved significantly better outcomes, the government might be persuaded to direct orphans toward foster care and adoption rather than into the state's inadequate facilities. In the words of BEIP scientist Charles

Zeanah, a randomized study might "benefit the larger society rather than each individual participant."[22]

When early results indicating the benefits of foster care were provided to Bucharest officials, they began to remove children from institutions. By the end of the study, only 13.6 percent of the BEIP's institutional group children remained. The others had been adopted, transferred to newly established government foster care, or returned to their parents. Ultimately, the BEIP resulted in better conditions for a large majority of the children in both the experimental and control groups.

After assessments ruled out children who had obvious medical problems, 136 institutionalized babies and toddlers from 6 to 31 months, who lived in six different Bucharest institutions, were selected for the study. Half the children were assigned to remain in their institutions and the other half were transferred to homes where foster parents awaited them, for many the first such caring encounters of their lives. A third group of children who had never been institutionalized was selected for comparison.[23]

The BEIP's longitudinal study began in the fall of 2000 and ended in 2005, although the participants are being followed even today. The results were remarkable, though not surprising in light of what Skodak, Skeels, and their colleagues had found long before. The three groups showed distinct differences in development, intelligence, and attachment to caregivers. At 42 months, the children were evaluated using the Bayley Scales of Infant Development II (BSID II), an assessment analogous to an IQ test. The BEIP scientists found that the mean developmental quotient (DQ) for the institutionalized group was 77.1; for the foster care group, it was 85.7; and for children who had never been institutionalized, it was 103.4 (average scores ranged from 90 to 110). A year later, when the children were 54 months, the researchers assessed them using the standardized Weschler Preschool and Primary Scale of Intelligence (WPPSI). They found that the institutional group's mean IQ was 73.3; the mean score for the foster care group was 81.0; and the mean for those never institutionalized was 109.3.[24]

The researchers discovered that the age the children entered foster care dramatically influenced their development. Just as Marie Skodak had found in Davenport's orphans, without exception the BEIP results showed that the earlier the children had been placed, the higher their scores. Those fostered before 18 months had a mean DQ test score of 94.4 and a mean IQ score of 84.8. Those who entered after 30 months had a mean DQ score of 79.7 and a mean IQ score of 71.5. The evidence was clear: earlier intervention was not just a little better; it significantly enhanced outcomes.[25]

The test results yielded yet another striking difference in children's age-related scores. Children who entered foster care at younger ages, when they were between 19 and 24 months, had a mean developmental quotient of 89.0, but those who entered between 24 and 30 months had a mean DQ score of 80.1. The better performance of the earlier entrants suggests the effect of "sensitive periods" in early development—periods when evolution structured the brain to respond to certain types of experience.[26]

Whether caregivers' competence would influence the children's out-comes had not initially been included in the study, but it became a variable to be investigated. This one factor, BEIP researcher Anna Smyke found, made "significant contributions to children's competence, over and above any other factors."[27]

The BEIP studies officially ended when all of the children had reached 54 months. However, with Romania's cooperation and MacArthur funding, Nelson and his colleagues extended their study. Over eight years, Nelson and his group found that children who remained in institutional care suffered progressive IQ declines. These results echo Harold Skeels's and Eva Fillmore's 1937 report of the IQ scores of siblings surrendered to Davenport by Iowa families. They found that older children's IQ scores were consistently lower than their younger siblings', probably because of longer exposure to adverse home environments.[28] In addition, in his 1939 report about the Woodward and Glenwood children, Skeels found radical declines in once normal children the longer they lived in Davenport, many to the level then called "retarded." Skeels's investigations may be the earliest longitudinal reports of such declines in institutionalized children's IQ scores.[29]

Finally, the BEIP scientists asked a question no other researchers had examined: did institutional and foster care environments literally "get under the skin" and change the children's brains? To find out, the children's brain activity was measured using noninvasive EEG readings of three types of brain wave oscillations, called alpha, beta, and theta. Roughly, alpha activity responds to attention, beta to complex cognition, and theta, a slower rate, marks the performance of automatic tasks.[30] When tested before the study, the institutionalized children had greater low-frequency theta activity—"as if" Nelson said, "someone had turned down the dimmer switch on the higher frequency . . . [alpha and beta] activity." By the time the children were age 8, the brain activity levels in those moved to foster care before age 2 was identical to that of children who had never been institutionalized. The study noted that this "catch up . . . required years of exposure to foster care to emerge."[31]

When the children reached age 9, the investigators used MRI scans to study randomly selected subjects from each group. They found that the head circumferences of the institutionalized children were smaller than those in the other two groups, and the MRIs helped explain why. Brain activity takes place within both gray matter—neurons—and white matter—the waxy myelin that coats neurons, allowing quicker connections between areas of the brain. On their MRI scans, children who had been institutionalized showed less gray matter *and* less white matter: starved of stimulation and affective encounters, their young brains had developed both fewer neurons and fewer connections between them.[32] Neuroscience explorations at this level were unavailable when the Iowa group was issuing its reports on the malleability of children's IQs. In Iowa, intellectually challenged children recovered intelligence when cared for by institutionalized women who made them the centers of their lives. The Romanian orphans recovered when nurtured by caring foster parents who provided stimulation, support, and emotional warmth. Clearly, the message that gets under the skin to change young brains goes through the heart. But how, physiologically, does a reciprocal caring relationship give rise to dramatic brain transformations?

Nelson and his colleagues' theories about early brain development drew on neuroscience research from the 1980s, an era when brain studies of early development began to accelerate. Scientists found that infant brains are hardwired to respond to certain stimuli: for example, babies learn the sound of their mothers' or caretakers' voices and respond when they hear them; infants perceive patterned light and respond by looking more closely; they learn that crying usually brings food that eases discomfort. Thus, the infant—once thought incapable of meaningful behavior—actively *learns* to utilize ordinary experience to ensure it is cared for.

As early as 1962, Yale pediatricians Sally Provance and Rose C. Lipton had studied the behavior of institutionalized infants who did not receive responsive care. They found that by age 3 months, the infants had "tenuous emotional ties" and failed "to establish a personal attachment" to their caregivers. By 7 months, they did not "seek out the adult either for pleasure or when in distress."[33] Their findings (which came from observing infants in an existing situation, not a controlled study) were echoed by BEIP psychologist Nathan A. Fox, who reported the eerie silence of a Romanian orphanage ward in which the babies, in their way "scholars" capable of assessing the response potential of their caregivers, had learned it would be pointless to seek their comfort.[34]

With their universal language of babbling, cooing, crying, and reaching their arms and legs into the air, infants "invite" their caregivers into a conversation and "expect" a response. Infants' inborn developmental program drives that behavior—it helps the baby stay alive—but it achieves far more. This reciprocal communication between child and caregiver, defined by Harvard's Center on the Developing Child as "serve and return," is recognized today by neuroscientists as critical for healthy brain development.[35] Serve and return interactions open a conversation that literally builds strong connections between brain areas. In the BEIP, the MRIs of Romanian orphans suggested that being deprived of serve and return relationships might impede the growth of brain cells and neural tissue. When the Iowa psychologists told of the absence of interactions between the Davenport children and their caretakers, they were describing just such deprivation.

———

Even when caregivers are accessible and well-intentioned, other adverse conditions can harm children's brain development; for example, poverty, violence, emotional neglect, or abuse each have the potential to increase stress. Like adults, babies and children will never be totally free of all stressors. But in a safe environment, most recover quickly from their alarm at a clap of thunder or the stick of a needle, and as safety returns, they may gain resilience from the experience. However, longer-term adversity, repeated exposure to violence, or the harsh, neglectful environments familiar to the orphans of Iowa and Romania can result in persistent stress that travels a more ominous course.

A convergence of science findings indicates that such "toxic stress" may harm the developing brain's sensitive architecture, especially when a caring figure is not available to help the young child manage difficult experiences.[36] In chronically high-stress situations, the child's heart continues to beat faster, blood pressure remains elevated, and stress hormones remain in the circulatory system. Bruce McEwen, of Rockefeller University, a pioneer in the study of the effects of stress on the brain, wrote, "The brain is the central organ of stress because it perceives what is threatening and determines a . . . response that may include fighting, fleeing, vigilance, and anxiety."[37] So it is not surprising that research shows disturbing events may impair not only a young child's brain development but also their physical and mental health, an effect that may last even into adulthood.[38]

In the 1960s, in his lab next door to his Rockefeller mentor, Alfred Mirsky, McEwen discovered the mechanisms for how stress influences the brain. It had been Mirsky who, in 1965, suggested to Skeels and Skodak how environment might have changed the brains of the Davenport children. McEwen, who died in 2020, had remembered Mirsky discussing Skeels's research and was among the first to show that prolonged stress may impair three critical brain areas: the center for memory, called the hippocampus; the amygdala, which is sensitive to early life stress and regulates mood and anxiety; and the prefrontal cortex, associated with executive function, judgment, and reactivity to social threat. McEwen noted that in a test of cognitive attention, a part of the prefrontal cortex associated with stress showed elevated blood pressure. McEwen and colleague Andrea Danese reported that stress creates "structural and functional abnormalities" in the prefrontal area that especially affect maltreated children and adults and may be related to hyperactivity, substance abuse, and conduct problems, among others.[39]

Poverty, and the environmental ills that may accompany it, is one of the most pervasive sources of children's stress. New York University cognitive psychologist Clancy Blair and developmental psychologist Cybele Raver found that poverty's adversities affect brain development even in infancy. In a 2016 longitudinal study of newborn infants to age 4, they reported that children in low-income environments had smaller gray matter brain volumes—half a standard deviation smaller—than children who had not lived in poverty.[40] Another major study compared children raised in poverty (family incomes were under $5,000 per year) with ones in well-off families (with incomes of $100,000–$150,000 per year). The authors found "atypical gray matter development associated with lower social economic status, limited environmental stimulation, and inadequate nutrition of the kind considered critical for learning."[41] And a study in Chicago found that children who had direct exposure to gun violence suffered immediate declines in their vocabulary and reading scores; some recovered from single episodes, but those exposed to repeated gun violence showed longer-term effects.[42]

The interaction of childhood adversity with later illness and impaired cognition first came to light with the 1998 publication of investigations of physicians Vincent Felitti, of the Kaiser Permanente health maintenance organization in San Diego, and Robert F. Anda, of the Center for Disease Control in Atlanta. After following over 17,000 mostly white, mostly middle-class subjects for seventeen years, they found a direct relationship between childhood abuse and adult disease,[43] including, in 2006, neurological impairment.[44] To learn about their subjects' backgrounds, they developed the Adverse Childhood Experience (ACE) questionnaire—an easy-to-apply tool now used worldwide to assess a patient's health vulnerabilities related to early adversity. They showed that adults who had endured significant stress as children had measurably higher rates of mental and physical illness and higher long-term risks than those who had not. As Paul Tough, a journalist and author whose life's work focuses on children's and teenagers' educational experience, has noted, "Children don't experience parental divorce or mental illness or neglect on a specific day; they experience them every day. What the ACE study was really tracing . . . was the influence of adverse environments."[45]

———

In 2015, child psychiatrist Joan Luby, founder and director of the Early Emotional Development Program at Washington University's School of Medicine, in St. Louis, argued that a "healthy human brain represents the foundation of civilization." She reported that 22 percent of American children live in poverty and that "enhancing the early nurturing environment is a public health issue—critical for child development and cost-effective for society."[46]

In 2013, Nobel laureate James Heckman, a University of Chicago economist and leader in policy studies of the economic and human costs of poverty, spelled out that "the accident of birth . . . [is] a principal source of inequality in America today."[47] For Heckman, adult success rests on a foundation of "neural pathways . . . for cognitive, linguistic, social, and emotional competencies . . . all shaped powerfully by the experiences of the developing child. . . . Disadvantage arises more from a lack of cognitive and noncognitive stimulation . . . than simply from the lack of financial resources."[48]

Heckman examined two interventions that radically changed the trajectories of children who lived in disadvantaged environments. From 1962 to 1967, the Perry Preschool Program studied 58 low-income African American children in Ypsilanti, Michigan, randomized into experimental and control groups. The experimental children attended preschool in the morning, and each week a teacher visited the children's homes. Focusing on noncognitive traits such as planning and social skill development, the program raised achievement test scores, because, Heckman observed, when children received such support they were eager to learn. After forty years, the Perry children had significantly higher high school graduation rates and higher salaries, and they owned more homes; they also had fewer arrests, and fewer received welfare. Heckman calculated the rate of return on the cost of the preschool program at 15 to 17 percent, from higher tax revenue, lower criminal justice expenses, and lower remedial education costs.[49]

Heckman's second report examined North Carolina's Abecedarian Project. For five years beginning in 1972, Abecedarian investigated 111 mostly African American children, half from families that lived below the poverty line.[50] When it began, the program's psychologist, Frances Campbell, was a skeptic who believed in nature over nurture. Incredulous that the researchers thought it would be possible to stimulate the cognition of young babies, she asked, "What in the world are you going to teach a baby that little?"[51] From 8 weeks to age 5, the children participated for 10 hours per day, five days a week, in a year-round intervention and have been followed for thirty-five years. During the program, teachers met with parents to suggest supplemental activities, helped them locate employment, and provided other support.

The children gained 1.8 years in reading skills and 1.3 years in math. Their IQ scores rose 14 points.[52] By age 30 they were four times more likely than those in the control group to graduate from college, 81 percent less likely be on public assistance, and 42 percent more likely to be employed over the previous two years.[53] A skeptic no more, Campbell went on to direct Abecedarian research at the University of North Carolina. Along with Heckman, in 2014 she reported that as adults the research subjects had no risk factors for metabolic diseases, heart disease, stroke, and diabetes, while 25 percent of the control group showed those risks.[54]

In the 1980s, a third high-quality early intervention program, the Chicago Child Parent Centers (CPC), began and continues today. Like its two predecessors, CPC is a dual-generation program for low-income families. However, the program takes a long view, to have its subjects earn higher education degrees, which research calls "the most important . . . outcome of early childhood intervention."[55] CPC studied 1,539 subjects, a far larger cohort than in previous studies. It showed higher third-grade literacy and reduced special education assignments. CPC is nested into the Chicago public schools, and children remain in the program from age 3 until they are about 9 years old. Participants have been studied into their 40s. At a time when college graduation has become essential to climbing the career ladder and when CPC finds "barriers . . . make [that] more difficult for poor and minority youth," CPC raised "rates of earned degrees by nearly 50%,"[56] a success that spills into every aspect of the individual's future, changes outcomes for family members, and benefits society.

The largest and most widely studied preschool intervention program in the United States, Project Head Start, the program Harold Skeels had discussed with the Shrivers, began in 1965 as part of President Lyndon Johnson's Great Society initiative. Its initial goal—six weeks of summer school to provide skills that would equalize children's later school performance compared with children from more advantaged environments—today seems naive. Head Start soon expanded to a half-day, school-year-long intervention now established in every state and territory. Along with its ancillary program, Early Head Start for children from 8 weeks to 2 years, Head Start serves 38 percent of eligible children—a total of nearly 1 million—including about 50,000 who are homeless and nearly 150,000 who are disabled. About 50 percent of Head Start programs now operate on a full-day, school-year schedule. The program targets school readiness; provides medical and social services, including those for mental health; supplies parents with access to education and job training; and gives children one hot meal per day.[57]

The value of Head Start has been debated for decades. In 2010, a nationwide, randomly controlled trial found that Head Start's success appeared limited, with "few sustained benefits" except for improved parent-child relationships through first grade.[58] Subsequent evaluations, however, disagree. For example, a 2016 report from the Brookings Institution, a nonprofit public policy research group, showed that "Head Start increased the probability that participants graduate from high school, attend college and receive a post-secondary degree, license, or certification."[59] Brookings found that Head Start significantly increased two qualities important to life success: self-esteem and self-control. In 2013, two Wharton School economists analyzed data collected but not included in Head Start's own 2010 report that showed Head Start parents became far more involved in their children's learning. They hypothesized that when parents saw their children's increased interest in school, they became more committed to their education.[60] Moreover, in 2018, Elise Chor, of Northwestern University's Institute for Policy Research, discovered that the one-quarter of children whose own mothers had participated in Head Start performed sharply better than Head Start's full 2010 sample. Through third grade they gained half a standard deviation in literacy and had higher mathematics skills, suggesting that their mothers' Head Start experience resulted in increased investment in their children's success.[61]

With investigations demonstrating that Head Start may significantly increase children's social and cognitive skills, how can we understand reports that find that some cognitive skills gained in the program may not last? One interpretation may be that children who receive Head Start's enriched curriculum and responsive attention lose ground when they move to under-resourced "struggling" schools. In those circumstances, education journalist

Lillian Mongeau wrote in *The Atlantic*, "none of the biggest benefits are likely to accrue. Preschool is not an inoculation against the next 12 years of a kid's life."[62]

———

I f the researchers of the 1930s Iowa Child Welfare Research Station could visit Harvard University's Center on the Developing Child, they would see that for all the attacks they endured during their careers, their work has been fully absorbed into the mainstream understanding of early development. One of the most advanced and dynamic institutions of its kind, the center utilizes today's neuroscience scholarship in the design of policy initiatives in the United States and other nations and also provides information resources that help caregivers understand the needs of children's developing brains.

The center's founder and director, developmental pediatrician Jack P. Shonkoff, articulates the science of early development to colleagues and national and international leaders, legislators, policy experts, and even members of the US House of Representatives. No matter his audience, Shonkoff's rallying points are clear:

> *Virtually every aspect of early human development, from the brain's evolving circuitry to the child's capacity for empathy, is affected by the environments and experiences that are encountered in a cumulative fashion, beginning early in the prenatal period and extending through the early childhood years.*[63]

———

A grainy image of Davenport's orphans, taken in 1901 when the Iowa Soldier's Orphans' Home had been operating for thirty-five years, conveys a sense of all-is-wellness. Posed by the photographer in front of the Davenport Home's well-kept administration building are a few hundred boys and girls grouped by age—the girls wear matched wide-collared calico dresses and light-colored high button shoes, the boys sport knickers, shirts and ties, high button shoes, and visored caps, some rakishly tilted. The photograph appears in a slim pamphlet authored by Davenport's superintendent to show off the orphanage and its residents and detail its acceptance procedures. Included are views of the Davenport Home's 57-acre property, "the most beautiful in the vicinity,"[64] its working farm's planted fields and livestock, and the institution's two-story school finished with an elaborate cupola. Other views show eighteen children's "cottages," once wooden barracks but rebuilt in brick, each housing about twenty-four children and fronting on acres of playing fields equipped with swings and other apparatus.

The superintendent tells of children who arrive from families "of broken-down old soldiers, or from the unfortunate but worthy poor . . . [others] from homes of crime; some come in a most wretched condition."[65] With about 400 residents (by the mid-1930s there would be close to 800), he indicates "almost parental affection . . . between the cottage matron and her little group [where] cheerfulness and contentment reign in these happy cottage homes" and where the children benefit from some luxuries of the time, "pure water . . . steam heat, and electricity." Sympathetically, he refers to Davenport's "bright, promising children who . . . if brought under the right influences . . . become good and useful citizens."[66]

Even if the pamphlet's rosy account of institutional contentment were only moderately accurate, it was far from the Davenport Home that Harold Skeels and Marie Skodak found in the 1930s—an institution transformed by that era's adversity into a place of neglect and indifference. But no one could have predicted that those conditions might cause some children to lose intelligence.

The arc of discovery about the effects of environment that began in Iowa did far more than transform the lives of Davenport's orphans. It helped to launch a new field that seeks to protect children's intellectual and social development. The Iowans became some of the first to explain why childhood interventions matter, very much. Their work, validated in Head Start, in the Perry and Abecedarian experiments, and in CPC and others, was shown in fresh detail by the BEIP's foster care and today inspires countless programs worldwide. Each finding builds on the one before, and together they suggest that even after the stress of adversity, children can recover when caring interventions buffer them from toxic stress, provide stimulation and responsive care, and deliver good education. As Charles Nelson and his colleagues affirm, neuroscience's expanding knowledge about how to counter the effects of disadvantage brings a special promise: translated into public policy it can relieve the "many ills that have challenged societies for millennia."[67] When that promise comes alive in children's experience, they can thrive.

ACKNOWLEDGMENTS

*O*rphans of Davenport benefited from comprehensive scholarship about the Iowa station from Hamilton Cravens, who addressed the station's challenge to eugenics as a clash of opposing views of social enlightenment and who spoke with me at length about his findings. Also, Lewis Terman's biographer Henry Minton deepened my understanding of Terman's commitment to eugenics and generously replied to my queries concerning Terman's motivations and shortcomings. Psychologist Bernadine Barr's perceptive investigations of institutional life were essential, as were her reviews of my drafts and her consistent support for this project. And most crucial were the recollections of Marie Skodak Crissey, who recognized the importance of the Iowans' discoveries and in the decades after the station's work had ended became its unofficial historian. Fundamental to the narrative were the unpublished papers, drafts, letters, memos, and reports she saved.

Special thanks to art historian Tripp Evans, who provided important background, as well as to historian of eugenics Jonathan Spiro, whose research addressed the interconnections among eugenicists. Historian John Burnham shared his insights about pre–World War II psychology, and psychologist Leon Kamin talked with me at length about eugenics' influence upon the events I discuss. Biologist Caleb Finch kindly provided information about Alfred Mirsky. Social psychologist Arlene Vadum read and unstintingly critiqued the narrative and helped me clarify historical issues, all with great good cheer. And from his long career in experimental psychology and association with some of the narrative's figures, Lewis Lipsitt's contribution and friendship were invaluable.

Neuroscientists Bruce McEwen, of Rockefeller University, and Charles Nelson, of Harvard, read drafts, talked with me about their studies, and provided essential feedback. In addition, Jack Shonkoff, Director of Harvard's Center on the Developing Child, whose work introduced me to the scientific and policy issues related to early development, provided important insights. From Harvard's Kurt Fischer and Terrance Tivnan, I gained extensive knowledge of psychology's history that significantly expanded my thinking.

In researching the lives of Davenport's orphans, I was fortunate to have been in touch with a subject from Harold Skeels's 1939 and 1966 studies, Louis Branca. Lou's accounts of his lived institutional experience and its influence upon his early and adult life provided vivid context. My debt to him, and to his wife, Cass Dalglish, can never be repaid. My conversations with Harold Skeels's mentee, Simon Auster, granted me access to their exchanges. Also, Milton J. E. Senn's interviews with figures from the child study movement were indispensable.

Dedicated archivists provided immeasurable assistance, especially University Archivist David McCartney, at the University of Iowa Special Collections, whose knowledge, expertise, discoveries, and generosity greatly benefited the narrative. Mary Bennett, Special Collections Coordinator at the State Historical Society of Iowa, supplied important documents and shared her knowledge of the university's history. From my first reading of Marie Skodak Crissey's papers, David Baker, now Emeritus, and Senior Archivist Lizette Royer Barton, at the Cummings Center for the History of Psychology, always provided unstinting aid. Tim Noakes, Library Specialist at Stanford University's Special Collections, went above and beyond, as did staff at the many archives I consulted, including at the National Library of Medicine, the Joseph P. Kennedy Jr. Foundation, the University of Illinois libraries' Special Collections, the Rockefeller University Archives, and the University of Minnesota Special Collections.

In countless ways this project benefited from the tireless assistance of University of Iowa's Olsen Graduate Research Fellow, Richard Dana, whose wide-ranging knowledge and research expertise constantly amazed. Also, University of Iowa library science student, Anna Tonsfeldt, unearthed unexpected documents, and Hang Nguyen, reference librarian at the State Historical Society of Iowa, helped locate important photographs.

Bringing the narrative to public attention became possible because my extraordinary agent, Ayesha Pande, took a chance on me. From our first meeting she grasped the significance of the Davenport orphans' story and scaffolded its journey to publication. Also, Peter Ginna asked important questions and provided critiques that always enhanced my thinking. At Liveright, editors Katie Adams, Gina Iaquinta, and Dan Gerstle believed in the work and brought to it their outstanding skills and judgment. Especially important was Janet Greenblatt's editorial discernment. And for the opportunity to realize this project, I am especially grateful to Liveright's editor in chief, Bob Weil.

The long arm of the universe granted me support from loving friends and family. Mary Kiesling, at Harvard, first affirmed that the Iowa story should be told and provided steadfast encouragement. Also, Maya Chaudhari, Louise and Doug Colligan, Kaila and Arthur Eisenkraft, Carol Fishman, Maggy Gorrill, Priscilla Macmillan, Ellen Rafel-Frankel, Diane Ranes, Isabel Sklar, Alexandra Sacks, Jill Sacks, Phyllis Sonnenschein, Stella Um and Colin Teichholtz, and Christine Wasserstein provided tangible and spiritual sustenance along with critical judgments. Of exceptional importance were Sheridan Gould and Gerry Lewis, whose active support exceeded anything I could have imagined. Marjorie Brent, Katie Liberman and Ezra Cohen, and especially my son, Daniel Berkman, and daughter-in-law, Elyse Berkman, inspired me with their confidence, humor, insight, and love. And my lifelong friend Eric Davidson's belief in this project, and in me, made the rest possible.

NOTES

The primary sources for *The Orphans of Davenport* are records, letters, memorandums, and reports, held in twelve archives. The Cummings Center for the History of Psychology at the University of Akron holds Marie Skodak Crissey's papers, and because Harold Skeels entrusted his papers to her, most of those are included there. Crissey saved everything, and her archive provides a comprehensive record of the Iowa station's work and much about Skodak's colleagues. The University of Iowa Special Collections in Iowa City holds papers from Beth Wellman and also some from George Stoddard and Harold Skeels. Of particular note is the transcript of discussions between the Iowans and Albert E. Wiggam— reading it is close to being there. In this archive, too, are documents related to the three institutions in which Davenport orphans lived, as well as additional material related to the Iowa Child Welfare Research Station. The State of Iowa Historical Society holds a treasury of important material, especially an extensive autobiographical report from Cora Bussey Hillis. Invaluable and unique are Iowa records and newspaper articles privately held by Louis C. Branca's widow, Cass Dalglish. Essential are Lewis M. Terman's letters held in Stanford University's Special Collections. These cover several decades of correspondence with publishers, colleagues, fellow eugenicists, and with Wiggam. George Stoddard's papers, held at the University of Illinois, contain drafts, reports, and a collection of letters. In the National Library of Medicine Archives at the National Institutes of Health are the indispensable transcripts of Milton J. E. Senn's interviews. Senn's appreciation for the significance of the 1930s–1950s child study movement has not been adequately recognized. Also important are Alfred E. Mirsky's papers from Rockefeller University's archive and documents from the Joseph P. Kennedy Jr. Foundation. Valuable, too, were the Florence Goodenough papers held in the University of Minnesota's Special Collections.

Abbreviations

AEM   Alfred E. Mirsky Papers, Archives of Rockefeller University

CBH   Cora Bussey Hillis Papers, State of Iowa Historical Society, Des Moines

CGI   Child Guidance Interviews, National Library of Medicine Archives, Bethesda, MD

FLG   Florence L. Goodenough Papers, Special Collections, University of Minnesota

GDS   George D. Stoddard Papers, Special Collections, University of Illinois Libraries

JPK   Joseph P. Kennedy Jr. Archive, Kennedy Library, Columbia Point, Boston, MA

LCB   Louis C. Branca Papers, privately held

LMT   Lewis M. Terman Papers, Special Collections, Stanford University Libraries

MJES   Milton J. E. Senn Oral History Collection, National Library of Medicine Archives, Bethesda, MD

MSC   Marie Skodak Crissey Papers, Cummings Center for the History of Psychology, University of Akron, OH

SIHS   State of Iowa Historical Society Collections

UISC   University of Iowa Special Collections

Prologue

1. Mae Habenicht, 1935, State of Iowa Official Summary on Case of Infant Wendell Hoffman. Iowa Child Welfare Bureau State Board of Control. LCB.

2. Amy Vogel, "Regulating Degeneracy: Eugenic Sterilization in Iowa, 1911–1977," *Annals of Iowa* 52, no. 2 (1995): 129.

3. Lewis M. Terman, *The Measurement of Intelligence: An Explanation of and a Complete Guide for the Use of the Stanford Revision and Extension of the Binet-Simon Intelligence Scale* (Boston: Houghton Mifflin, 1916), 324–30.

4. Lewis M. Terman, "The Mental Test as a Psychological Method," *Psychological Review* 31, no. 2 (1924): 106.

5. Vogel, "Regulating Degeneracy," 119, 123; Lutz Kaelber, "Eugenics: Compulsory Sterilization in 50 American States," accessed December 12, 2011, http://www.uvm.edu/~lkaelber/eugenics/.

6. Vogel, "Regulating Degeneracy," 123.

7. Louis C. Branca, interview by Marilyn Brookwood, September 10–11, 2012.

8. Anna Gaul, "The Day the Civil War Orphans Arrived in the Quad-Cities," *Quad-City Times*, November 16, 2015, accessed April 9, 2019, https://qctimes.com/news/local/the-day-the-civil-war-orphans-arrived-in-the-quad/article_e4d2ae88-3df7-58ff-8a39-1f812f4ef70d.html.

9. M. T. Gass, The Iowa Soldiers' Orphans' Home, Iowa Board of Control, 1901.

10. Gass, Iowa Soldiers' Orphans' Home.

11. Gass, Iowa Soldiers' Orphans' Home.

12. Case 11, Harold M. Skeels, Experimental Group Records, MSC.

13. Harold M. Skeels and Harold B. Dye, "A Study of the Effects of Differential Stimulation on Mentally Retarded Children," paper presented at the Annual Meeting of the American

Association of Mental Deficiency, Chicago, May 3–6, 1939. *Journal of Psycho-Asthenics* 44, no.1 (1939): 114–36.

14. Hamilton Cravens, *Before Head Start: the Iowa Station & America's Children* (Chapel Hill: University of North Carolina Press. 1994), 156.

15. Cravens, *Before Head Start*, 156.

16. Charles B. Davenport, *Eugenics: The Science of Human Improvement by Better Breeding* (New York: Holt, 1910), 15.

17. Florence L. Goodenough, "Racial Differences in the Intelligence of School Children," *Journal of Experimental Education* 9, no. 3 (1926): 388–97.

18. Bird T. Baldwin, Eva A. Fillmore, and Lora Hadley, *Farm Children: An Investigation of Rural Child Life in Selected Areas of Iowa* (New York: Appleton, 1930), 163.

19. Benjamin R. Simpson, "The Wandering IQ: Is It Time for It to Settle Down?" *Journal of Psychology* 7, no. 2 (January 1939): 351–67.

20. Florence L. Goodenough to Leta S. Hollingworth, April 5, 1939, FLG.

21. Benjamin R. Simpson, "You Can't Train the Intellect before It Arrives," *Scientific Monthly* 43, no. 4 (1936): 346.

Chapter One: How It All Began

1. Marie Skodak Crissey, interview by Milton J. E. Senn, November 29, 1978, unnumbered transcript, MJES.

2. Marie Skodak Crissey, interview by Barbara Kalbfell, November 5, 1979, CGI.

3. Tom Morain, "The Great Depression Begins (1920s)," Iowa Pathways, Iowa Public Television, July 17, 2017, accessed November 17, 2017, http://www.iptv.org/iowapathways/mypath/great-depression-begins-1920s.

4. William H. Thompson, *Transportation in Iowa: A Historical Summary* (Ames: Iowa Department of Transportation, 1989), 167–202.

5. Marie Skodak Crissey, "Marie Skodak Crissey," in *A History of Developmental Psychology in Autobiography*, ed. Dennis Thompson and John D. Hogan (Boulder: Westview Press, 1996), 46–70.

6. Skodak Crissey, "Marie Skodak Crissey," in *History*, 51.

7. Skodak Crissey, in *History*, 51.

8. Skodak Crissey, in *History*, 51.

9. Skodak Crissey, in *History*, 51.

10. Skodak Crissey, in *History*, 51.

11. Skodak Crissey, in *History*, 50.

12. Marie Skodak Crissey, "Marie Skodak Crissey," in *Models of Achievement: Reflections of Eminent Women in Psychology*, ed. Agnes N. O'Connell and Nancy F. Russo (New York: Columbia University Press, 1988), 72.

13. Daniel J. Kevles, *In the Name of Eugenics: Genetics and the Uses of Human Heredity* (Cambridge, MA: Harvard University Press, 1995), 80.

14. Skodak Crissey, "Marie Skodak Crissey," in *History*, 51.

15. Skodak Crissey, in *History*, 52.

16. Skodak Crissey, in *History*, 52.

17. Skodak Crissey, in *History*, 52.

18. Skodak Crissey, "Marie Skodak Crissey," in *Models*, 73.

19. Leila Zenderland, *Measuring Minds: Henry Herbert Goddard and the Origins of American Intelligence Testing* (New York: Cambridge University Press, 2001), 92–93.

20. Marie Skodak Crissey, interview by Henry Minton, January 15, 1982, 26, MSC.

21. Alfred Binet, *Les Idées Modernes Sur Les Enfants* (Paris: Flammarion, 1909), 346.

22. Zenderland, *Measuring Minds*, 95.

23. Alfred Binet and Theodore Simon, *The Development of Intelligence in Children* (Nashville, TN: Williams Printing, 1980), 40.

24. Binet and Simon, *Development of Intelligence*, 40.

25. Frank S. Freeman, *Theory and Practice of Psychological Testing* (New York: Holt, 1955), 104.

26. Binet and Simon, *Development of Intelligence*, 59.

27. Binet and Simon, *Development of Intelligence*, 59, 62.

28. Binet and Simon, *Development of Intelligence*, 50.

29. Zenderland, *Measuring Minds*, 95.

30. Henry H. Goddard, *The Kallikak Family: A Study in the Heredity of Feeblemindedness* (New York: Macmillan, 1912), 42–61.

31. Sarah F. Rose, *No Right to Be Idle* (Chapel Hill: University of North Carolina Press, 2017), 82–83.

32. Rose, *No Right to Be Idle*, 10.

33. Ward W. Millias, "Charles Bernstein, 1872–1942," *American Journal of Mental Deficiency* 47, no. 1 (1942): 17.

34. Michael A. Bernstein, 2009, "Dr. Charles Bernstein," Find a Grave website, accessed June 17, 2017. www.findagrave.com/cgi-bin/fg.cgi?page=gr&GRid=34459219.

35. Skodak Crissey, "Marie Skodak Crissey," in *History*, 68.

36. Zenderland, *Measuring Minds*, 102–103.

37. Harold Skeels, R. Updegraff, B. L. Wellman, and H. M. Williams, "A Study of Environmental Stimulation: An Orphanage Preschool Project," *University of Iowa Studies in Child Welfare* 15, no. 4 (1938): 10–13.

38. William H. Thompson, "The 1930s—Depression and Its Aftermath," in *Transportation in Iowa: A Historical Summary* (Ames: Iowa Department of Transportation, 1989), 183.

39. "Agricultural Reports Forecast Crop Failure Over Most of United States, Grain Shortage Possible," *Ames Daily Tribune*, June 26, 1933.

40. Tim Egan, *The Worst Hard Time* (Boston: Houghton Mifflin, 2006), 117.

41. Skodak Crissey, "Marie Skodak Crissey," in *History*, 56.

42. Skodak Crissey, "Marie Skodak Crissey," in *Models*, 74.

43. Skodak Crissey, in *Models*, 74.

44. Skodak Crissey, in *History*, 57.

45. Louis C. Branca, interview by Marilyn Brookwood, June 4, 2015.

46. Marie Skodak Crissey, interview by Henry L. Minton, January 15, 1982, 5.

47. Skodak Crissey, "Marie Skodak Crissey," in *History*, 57.

Chapter Two: Starting Over

1. Marie Skodak Crissey, interview by Senn, 1978, 18–19, MJES.

2. Lauren G. Wispe and James H. Ritter, "Where America's Recognized Psychologists Received Their Doctorates," *American Psychologist* 19, no. 7 (1964): 634–44.

3. Cora B. Hillis, "How the Iowa Child Welfare Research Station Came into Being" (unpublished, 1919), 2, CBH.

4. Alice B. Smuts, *Science in the Service of Children 1893–1935* (New Haven: Yale University Press, 2006), 130–31.

5. Hillis, "Iowa Child Welfare Research Station," 3.

6. Hillis, "Iowa Child Welfare Research Station," 7.

7. Hillis, "Iowa Child Welfare Research Station," 17.

8. Carl Seashore to Cora Bussey Hillis, in *Pioneering in Child Welfare: A History of the Child Welfare Research Station, 1917–1933*, ed. Dorothy Bradbury (Iowa City: University of Iowa, 1933), 17.

9. Ginalie Swaim, "Cora Bussey Hillis: Woman of Vision," *Iowa Heritage Illustrated* 85, no. 2 (2004): 124.

10. Quoted in Hillis, "Iowa Child Welfare Research Station," 22.

11. Cravens, *Before Head Start*, 28.

12. Baldwin, Fillmore, and Hadley, *Farm Children*, 27–48, 64, 122.

13. Cravens, *Before Head Start*, 102–105.

14. Baldwin, Fillmore, and Hadley, *Farm Children*, 163.

15. Thomas H. Morgan, "Human Inheritance," *The American Naturalist* 58. no. 658 (September-October 1924): 406–9.

16. Bird T. Baldwin, "Heredity and Environment—or Capacity and Training?" *Journal of Educational Psychology* 19, no. 6 (1928): 405.

17. George D. Stoddard, "George Stoddard, An Autobiography," in *Leaders in American Education*, ed. Robert J. Havighurst (Chicago: University of Chicago Press, 1971), 321.

18. Stoddard, in Havighurst, *Leaders*, 322.

19. Raymond E. Fancher, *The Intelligence Men, Makers of the I.Q. Controversy* (New York: W. W. Norton, 1985), 58.

20. George D. Stoddard, *The Pursuit of Education: An Autobiography* (New York: Vantage Press, 1981), 38.

21. Terman, *Measurement of Intelligence*, 79.

22. Stoddard, *Pursuit of Education*, 329.

23. Skodak Crissey, interview by Senn, 1978, 16–17, MJES.

24. James Fox, "Dean Stoddard Defends Work of Iowans at Columbus Meeting of AAAS," *The Daily Iowan*, December 29, 1939.

25. Beth L. Wellman, "Some New Basis for Interpretation of the IQ," *Pedagogical Seminary and Journal of Genetic Psychology* 41, no. 1 (1932): 119.

26. Beth L. Wellman, "The Effects of Preschool Attendance upon the IQ," *Journal of Experimental Education* 1, no. 2 (1932): 69.

27. Barbara S. Burks, "The Relative Influence of Nature and Nurture upon Mental Development: A Comparative Study of Foster Parent-Foster Child Resemblance and True Parent-True Child Resemblance," in *National Society for the Study of Education Yearbook* (Bloomington, IL: Public School Publishing, 1928), 309.

28. Marie Skodak Crissey, "Beth Lucy Wellman," in *Women in Psychology: A Bio-Bibliographic Sourcebook*, ed. Agnes N. O'Connell and Nancy Felipe Russo (New York, Greenwood Press, 1990), 355.

29. Skodak Crissey, "Beth Lucy Wellman," 354.

30. Marie Skodak Crissey, "Harold Manville Skeels," *American Journal of Mental Deficiency* 75, no. 1 (1970): 1.

31. Skodak Crissey, interview by Senn, 1978, 3, MJES.

32. Marie Skodak Crissey, interview by Henry L. Minton, January 15, 1982, MSC.

33. Skodak Crissey, "Marie Skodak Crissey," in *Models*, 10.

34. George D. Stoddard, Informal Discussion III, in "Issues Emerging from the Discussion of Intelligence in the Yearbook," in *The Thirty-Ninth Yearbook of the National Society for the Study of Education*, ed. Guy Montrose Whipple, *Addresses and Discussions: "Intelligence: Its Nature and Nurture"* (Salem, MA: Newcomb and Gauss, 1940) 41.

35. David Seim, *Rockefeller Philanthropy and Modern Social Science* (London: Pickering and Chatto, 2013), 107.

36. Cravens, *Before Head Start*, 61–63.

37. George D. Stoddard, interview by Milton J. E. Senn, February 4, 1971, 24–25, interview 69.

38. Harold M. Skeels and Eva A. Fillmore, "The Mental Development of Children from Underprivileged Homes," *Journal of Genetic Psychology* 50, no. 2 (1937): 427.

39. Skodak Crissey, interview by Duane Fischer, December 16, 1969, 14, MSC.

40. Skodak Crissey, "Marie Skodak Crissey," in *History*, 60–61.

41. Marie Skodak Crissey, "How It All Began: Festschrift for George Stoddard, 1968" (unpublished manuscript, ca. 1968), 7–8, MSC.

42. "Orphan Internments, 1866–1959," Oakdale Memorial Gardens, Davenport, IA (unpublished).

Chapter Three: Transparent Waifs, Pitiful Creatures

1. David Pfeiffer, "Bridging the Mississippi: The Railroads and Steamboats Clash at the Rock Island Bridge," *Prologue*, Summer 2004, 40–47.

2. US census. http://www.webcitation.org/6YSasqtfX?url=http://www.census.gov/prod/www/decennial.html.

3. Harold Skeels, "Adult Status of Children with Contrasting Early life Experiences: A Follow-Up Study," *Monographs of the Society for Research in Child Development* 15, no. 3 (1966): 3.

4. Bernadine Barr, "Educating Orphans and Educating Psychologists: The Iowa Soldiers' Orphans' Home 1900–1945" (unpublished manuscript, 2003), 1.

5. Barr, "Educating Orphans," 27, quoted from Annie Wittenmyer Oral History Project, Davenport Public Library.

6. Barr, "Educating Orphans," 35.

7. H. A. Mitchell, "Thirty-Fifth Biennial Report of the Superintendent and Fifteenth Biennial Report of the Placement Department of the Iowa Soldiers' Orphans' Home," 1935, Archives Davenport Public Library, Davenport, IA.

8. R. L Woolbert, "Proposed Remedies for Crime in Iowa," Iowa State Planning Board, 1935, 4–5.

9. Harold M. Skeels and Marie Skodak, "Adult Status of Individuals Who Experienced Early Intervention" (1966), draft of talk presented at the 1966 meeting of the Society for the Study of Mental Deficiency, 2, MSC.

10. Skodak Crissey, "How It All Began," 5, MSC.

11. Louis C. Branca, interview Marilyn Brookwood, June 4, 2015.

12. Harold M. Skeels, "Records of Experimental and Contrast Group Cases, 1933–1966," unpublished, MSC.

13. Skodak Crissey, 1968, "How It All Began," 5. MSC.

14. Barr, "Educating Orphans," 31.

15. Skodak Crissey, interview by Senn, 25–27.

16. Skodak Crissey, "How It All Began," 8, MSC.

17. Marie Skodak Crissey and Harold Skeels, "A Final Follow-Up Study of One Hundred Adopted Children," *Journal of Genetic Psychology* 75, no. 1 (1949): 86–87.

18. Boyd R. McCandless, interview by Milton J. E. Senn, March 17, 1971, interview 47, MJES.

19. Harold M. Skeels, "Mental Development of Children in Foster Homes," *Journal of Genetic Psychology* 49 (1936): 92.

20. Skodak, "Adult Status," draft, 10, MSC.

21. Barr, "Educating Orphans," 35.

22. Skodak Crissey, interview by Fischer, 7, MSC.

23. Skodak, interview by Senn, 10, MJES.

24. Skodak Crissey, "Harold Manville Skeels," 1–2.

25. Marie Skodak, interview by Henry L. Minton, January 15, 1982, 6, MSC.

26. Paul D. Chapman, *Schools as Sorters: Lewis M. Terman, Applied Psychology, and the American Intelligence Testing Movement, 1890–1930* (New York: New York University Press, 1988), 84.

27. H. A. Mitchell, *Thirty-Fifth Biennial Report of the Superintendent of the Iowa Soldiers' Orphans' Home* (Eldora, IA: Board of Control of State Institutions, 1934), 7.

28. Arnold Gesell, "Infant Behavior Research," *Biological Medicine* 7 (May 1935): 453–55.

29. Skodak, "Marie Skodak Crissey," in *History*, 60.

30. Skodak, 1978, interview by Senn, 12–13, MJES.

31. Skodak Crissey, "How it All Began," 9–10, MSC.

32. Skeels, Records, Case 5, MSC.

33. Neil, J. Van Steenberg, "An Independent Evaluation of the Skodak Data on Foster Children," cited in George D. Stoddard, *The Meaning of Intelligence* (New York: Macmillan, 1943), 361–63.

34. Vogel, "Regulating Degeneracy," 131, 137.

35. Vogel, "Regulating Degeneracy," 132.

36. Lutz Kaelber, "Eugenics: Compulsory Sterilization in 50 American States." http://www.uvm.edu/~lkaelber/eugenics/.

37. Vogel, "Regulating Degeneracy," 138.

38. Skodak, interview by Senn, 1978, 20, MJES.

39. Wayne Dennis and Pergrouhi Najarian, "Infant Development under Environmental Handicap," *Psychological Monographs* 71 (1957): 2–3; Samuel Frant and Harold Abramson, "Diarrhea of the Newborn," *Journal of Pediatrics* 11, no. 6 (1937): 780.

40. Henry D. Chapin, 1915, "Are Institutions for Infants Necessary?" *Journal of the American Medical Association* 64, no. 1 (January 1915): 2–3.

41. Tobias Grossman and Mark H. Johnson, "The Development of the Social Brain in Human Infancy," *European Journal of Neuroscience* 25, no. 4 (2007): 909–14.

42. "Serve & Return Interaction Shapes Brain Circuitry," National Scientific Council on the

Developing Child, Center on the Developing Child, Harvard University, 2019, https://www.youtube.com/watch?v=m_5u8-QSh6A.

43. Charles A. Nelson III, Nathan A. Fox, and Charles H. Zeanah, *Romania's Abandoned Children: Deprivation, Brain Development, and the Struggle for Recovery* (Cambridge, MA: Harvard University Press, 2014), 213.

44. Skeels and Skodak, "Adult Status of Individuals," draft, 3, MSC.

45. Sally Provance and Rose Lipton, *Infants in Institutions* (New York: International Universities Press, 1962), 128.

46. Van Steenberg, "An Independent Evaluation," 361–3.

47. Skeels, Records, Case 8.

48. Skeels, Records, Case 8.

49. Skeels, "Adult Status of Children," 4.

50. Skeels, "Adult Status of Children," 3.

51. Skeels and Skodak, "Adult Status of Individuals," draft, 3, MSC.

52. Skeels et al., "A Study of Environmental Stimulation," 11.

53. Skodak, "Adult Status," draft, 9, MSC.

54. Skeels, Records, Case 8.

55. Skeels and Dye, "Study of the Effects of Differential Stimulation," 116.

56. Skeels and Skodak, "Adult Status of Individuals," draft, 4. MSC.

57. Skeels, "Adult Status of Children," 5.

58. "Weather Proves Iowa's Best 1934 News Story," *Los Angeles Times*, December 23, 1934.

59. "Iowa's Best 1934 News Story."

60. Skeels and Skodak, "Adult Status of Individuals," draft, 4, MSC.

61. Bernard Asbell, "The Case of the Wandering IQs: How an Accidental Discovery about Two Feeble-Minded Children Triggered a 30-Year Search—and Shattered All Assumptions Psychologists Had Made about a Baby's Intelligence," *Redbook*, 33.

62. Skodak, "Adult Status," draft, 3.

63. Skodak and Skeels, "A Final Follow-Up Study," 86.

64. Skeels and Skodak, "Adult Status of Individuals," draft, 4, MSC.

65. Skeels and Skodak, "Adult Status of Individuals," draft, 4, MSC.

66. Elmer G. Powers, *The Farm Diary of Elmer G. Powers, 1931–1936,* ed. H. Roger Grant and L. Edward Purcell (Ames: Iowa State University Press, 1976), 86.

Chapter Four: From a Dog You Do Not Get a Cat

1. Lewis M. Terman, "Trails to Psychology," in *A History of Psychology in Autobiography*, ed. Carl Q. Murchison (Washington, DC: American Psychological Association, 1930), 297.

2. Terman, "Trails to Psychology," 310.

3. Terman, "Trails to Psychology," 312.

4. Terman, "Trails to Psychology," 316.

5. Terman, "Trails to Psychology," 311.

6. Bernadine Barr, "Thinking Psychology, Discovering Normalcy: Lewis Terman and the Stanford-Binet Test of Intelligence," paper presented at the Annual Meeting of Cheiron, the International Society of Behavioral and Social Sciences, University of Oregon, Eugene, OR, June 27, 2002, 11.

7. Raymond E. Fancher, *The Intelligence Men: Makers of the IQ Controversy* (New York: W. W. Norton, 1985), 139.

8. John Carson, *The Measure of Merit: Talents, Intelligence, and Inequality in the French and American Republics, 1750–1940* (Princeton, NJ: Princeton University Press, 2007), 5.

9. Lewis M. Terman, "A Report of the Buffalo Conference on the Binet-Simon Tests of Intelligence," *Pedagogical Seminary and Journal of Genetic Psychology* 20, no. 4 (1913): 554.

10. Theta Wolf, *Alfred Binet* (Chicago: University of Chicago Press, 1973), 203.

11. Stephen J. Gould, *The Mismeasure of Man* (New York: W. W. Norton, 1996), 27.

12. Terman, *Measurement of Intelligence*, 20.

13. Steve McNutt, "A Dangerous Man: Lewis Terman and George Stoddard, Their Debate on Intelligence Testing, and the Legacy of the Iowa Child Welfare Research Station," *Annals of Iowa* 72, no.1 (2013): 10.

14. Wolf, *Alfred Binet*, 203.

15. Terman, *Measurement of Intelligence*, 92–93.

16. Lewis M. Terman, "A New Approach to the Study of Genius," *Psychological Review* 29, no. 4 (1922): 318.

17. Lewis M. Terman, "Intelligence in a Changing Universe," *School and Society* 29, no. 1330 (1940): 470.

18. Gould, *Mismeasure of Man*, 224.

19. Gould, *Mismeasure of Man*, 231.

20. Allan Chase, *The Legacy of Malthus: The Social Costs of the New Scientific Racism* (New York: Knopf, 1976), 246.

21. Daniel Kevles, *In the Name of Eugenics: Genetics and the Uses of Human Heredity* (Cambridge, MA: Harvard University Press, 1995), 82–83.

22. Digital Public Libraries of America, accessed October 1, 2017, https://dp.la/exhibitions/history-us-public-libraries/segregated-libraries.

23. Alexander Clark and the First Successful School Desegregation Case in the United States. Iowa Pathways, Iowa PBS, accessed November 9, 2020, http://www.iowapbs.org/iowapathways/artifact/alexander-clark-and-first-successful-desegregation-case-united-states.

24. Franz Samelson, "Putting Psychology on the Map: Ideology and Intelligence Testing," in *Psychology in Social Context*, ed. Allan R. Buss (New York: Irvington, 1979), 106.

25. Samelson, "Putting Psychology on the Map," 106.

26. Leon J. Kamin, *The Science and Politics of IQ* (Potomac, MD: Lawrence Erlbaum, 1974), 18.

27. Kevles, *In the Name of Eugenics*, 81.

28. Kevles, *In the Name of Eugenics*, 104.

29. Fancher, *Intelligence Men*, 139–141.

30. Lewis M. Terman, "The Mental Test as a Psychological Method," *Psychological Review* 31, no. 2 (1924): 106.

31. Henry L. Minton, "Lewis M. Terman and the 'World' of Test Publishing," paper presented at the annual meeting of the American Psychological Association, Los Angeles, 1985, 2, MSC.

32. Edwin G. Boring, *Lewis Madison Terman, 1877–1956: A Biographical Memoir* (Washington, DC: National Academy of Sciences, 1959), 104.

33. Wispe and Ritter, "America's Recognized Psychologists," 640–64.

34. Jennifer R. Crosby and Albert H. Hastdorf, "Lewis Terman: Scientist of Mental Measurement and Product of His Time," in *Portraits of Pioneers in Psychology*, ed. Michael Wertheimer and Gregory A. Kimble (London: Psychology Press, 2000), 142.

35. Theresa Richardson and Ewin V. Johanningmeier, "Intelligence Testing: The Legitimation of a Meritocratic Educational Science," *International Journal of Educational Research* 27, no. 8 (1998): 707.

36. "German Jewish Refugees," United States Holocaust Museum, accessed August 11, 2017, https://encyclopedia.ushmm.org/content/en/article/german-jewish-refugees-1933-1939.

37. Marie Skodak Crissey, interview by Milton J. E. Senn, MJES.

38. Geoffrey Searle, *Eugenics and Politics in Britain, 1900–1914* (Leyden, Netherlands: Noordhoff Publishers, 1976), 20.

39. Francis Galton, "Hereditary Talent and Character," *Macmillan's Magazine*, May 1, 1865, 326.

40. Fancher, *Intelligence Men*, 36.

41. Francis Galton, "Eugenics: Its Definition, Scope and Aims," *Nature* 70 (May 26, 1904): 82.

42. Francis Galton, *Hereditary Genius: An Inquiry into Its Laws and Consequences* (London: Macmillan, 1869): 1.

43. Francis Galton, "Hereditary Improvement," *Frasier's Magazine* 7, no. 37 (1873): 116.

44. Galton, "Eugenics: Its Definition," 82.

45. Galton, Quoted in Caleb W. Saleeby, *Parenthood and Race Culture: An Outline of Eugenics* (London: Cassell, 1909), 303.

46. Ruth C. Engs, *The Eugenics Movement: An Encyclopedia* (Westport, CT: Greenwood Press, 2005), 161, 182.

47. Leslie C. Dunn and Theodosius Dobzhansky, *Heredity, Race and Society* (New York: Mentor Books, 1952), 44.

48. Mario Livio, *Brilliant Blunders from Darwin to Einstein: Colossal Mistakes by Great Scientists That Changed Our Understanding of Life and the Universe* (New York: Simon and Schuster, 2013), 57.

49. Charles Rosenberg, "Charles Davenport and the Beginning of Human Genetics," *Bulletin of the History of Medicine* 35 (1961): 268.

50. Daniel Kevles, "Eugenics in the United States and Britain, 1890 to 1930," *Humanities Working Paper* 19 (1979): 2, accessed January 18, 2018, https://authors.library.caltech.edu/14563/1/HumsWP-0019.pdf.

51. Quoted in Stanley P. Davies, "Social Control of the Feebleminded: A Study of Social Programs and Attitudes in Relation to the Problems of Mental Deficiency" (PhD diss., Columbia University, 1923), 39–40.

52. Daniel Ritschel, "Demography and Degeneration: Eugenics and the Declining Birthrate in Twentieth Century Britain," *History of Education Quarterly* 3, no. 4 (1991): 543.

53. Samuel J. Holmes, *The Trend of the Race: A Study of Present Tendencies in the Biological Development of Civilized Mankind* (New York: Harcourt Brace, 1921), 139–40.

54. Saleeby, *Parenthood and Race Culture*, viii.

55. Kevles, *In the Name of Eugenics*, 61–62.

56. Lewis M. Terman, "Were We Born That Way?" *World's Work* 44 (1922): 658.

57. Ben Harris, "Arnold Gesell's Progressive Vision: Child Hygiene, Socialism and Eugenics," *History of Psychology* 14, no. 3 (2011): 313.

58. Arnold Gesell, "Village of a Thousand Souls," *The American Magazine* 77, no. 4 (1913): 12.

59. Gesell, *Village*, 12–13.
60. Gesell, *Village*, 15.
61. Harris, "Arnold Gesell's Progressive Vision," 321.
62. Harold J. Laski, "The Scope of Eugenics," *Westminster Review* 174, July (1910) 30.
63. Galton, "Eugenics, Its Definition," 1.
64. Harris, "Arnold Gesell's Progressive Vision," 321–22.
65. Jonathan P. Spiro, *Defending the Master Race: Conservation, Eugenics and the Legacy of Madison Grant* (Burlington: University of Vermont Press, 2009), 395–96.
66. Charles Davenport, *Eugenics: The Science of Human Improvement by Better Breeding* (Rahway, NJ: Quinn & Boden, 2010), title page.
67. Herbert Spenser Jennings, quoted in Bentley Glass and Curt Stern, "Geneticists Embattled: Their Stand against Rampant Eugenics and Racism in America During the 1920s and 1930s," *Proceedings of the American Philosophical Society* 130, no. 1 (1986): 144.
68. Carleton E. MacDowell, "Charles Benedict Davenport, 1866–1944," *Bios* 17 (1): 14.
69. Garland E. Allen, "The Eugenics Record Office at Cold Spring Harbor, 1910–1940: An Essay in Institutional History," *Osiris* 2 (1986): 230.
70. Davenport, *Eugenics*, 80.
71. Davenport, *Eugenics*, 263.
72. Allen, "Eugenics Record Office," 239.
73. Allen, "Eugenics Record Office," 239, 243.
74. Allen, "Eugenics Record Office," 245.
75. Allen, "Eugenics Record Office," 236.
76. "Eugenical Ideas in Tennessee," "Quality, Not Quantity of Population," "Prenuptial Examinations in Belgium, Luxemburg, Germany." *Eugenical News* 12, no. 8 (1927): 104–124.
77. Allen, "Eugenics Record Office," 227.
78. Adam Cohen, *Imbeciles: The Supreme Court, American Eugenics, and the Sterilization of Carrie Buck* (New York: Penguin Press, 2016), 122.
79. Rachel Gur-Arie, "Harry Hamilton Laughlin (1889–1943)," Arizona State University, School of Life Sciences, Center for Biology and Society, Embryo Project Encyclopedia (2014), accessed January 26, 2018, https://embryo.asu.edu/pages/harry-hamilton-laughlin-1880-1943.
80. Kevles, *In the Name of Eugenics*, 103.
81. Cohen, *Imbeciles*, 61.
82. Albert Wiggam, *The New Decalogue of Science* (New York: Blue Ribbon Books, 1922), 127.
83. "Thinks Intelligence of Race is Decreasing," *New York Times*, December 25, 1922, 2.
84. Kevles, *In the Name of Eugenics*, 199.
85. Spiro, *Defending the Master Race*, 140.
86. Spiro, *Defending the Master Race*, 148.
87. Mark H. Haller, *Eugenics: Hereditarian Attitudes in American Thought* (New Brunswick, NJ: Rutgers University Press, 1963), 73.
88. Madison Grant, *The Passing of the Great Race: Or The Racial Basis of European History* (New York: Charles Scribner's Sons, 1922), passim. From 1916 to 1922, Scribner's published four editions of Grant's book, each slightly different from the others.
89. Grant, *Passing of the Great Race*, 153.
90. Grant, *Passing of the Great Race*, 16.

91. Grant, *Passing of the Great Race*, 319.

92. Stefan Kühl, *The Nazi Connection: Eugenics, American Racism, and German National Socialism* (New York: Oxford University Press, 1994), 83.

93. Paul J. Wendling, *Nazi Medicine and the Nuremberg Trials: From Medical Warcrimes to Informed Consent* (London: Palgrave Macmillan, 2004), 229.

94. Spiro, *Defending the Master Race*, 195.

95. Edith R. Spaulding and William Healy, "Inheritance as a Factor in Criminality: A Study of a Thousand Cases of Young Repeated Offenders," paper presented at the Physical Basis of Crime Symposium, Annual Meeting of the American Academy of Medicine, Minneapolis, 1914, 857.

96. Walter Lippmann, "The Abuse of the Tests," *The New Republic* 32, no. 415 (1922): 9.

97. Clarence Darrow, "The Eugenics Cult," *American Mercury* 8, no. 30 (1926): 129–130.

98. R. C. Punnett, quoted in Daniel Okrent, *The Guarded Gate: Bigotry, Eugenics, and the Law That Kept Two Generations of Jews, Italians, and Other European Immigrants Out of America* (New York: Scribner's, 2019), 125.

99. Garland E. Allen, *Thomas Hunt Morgan: The Man and His Science* (Princeton, NJ: Princeton University Press, 1978), 142.

100. Garland E. Allen, "Is a New Eugenics Afoot?" *Science* 264 (2001): 61.

101. Kevles, *In the Name of Eugenics*, 122.

102. Allen, "Eugenics Record Office," 250.

103. Chase, *The Legacy of Malthus*, xxiv.

104. Allen, "Is a New Eugenics Afoot?" 61.

105. T. M. Sonneborn, *Herbert Spencer Jennings (1868–1947): A Biographical Memoir* (Washington, DC: National Academy of Sciences, 1975), 188.

106. Herbert S. Jennings, "Heredity and Environment," *The Scientific Monthly* 19, no. 3 (1924): 226.

107. Jennings, "Heredity and Environment," 225–31.

108. Harry Bruinius, *Better for All the World* (New York: Knopf, 2006), 51.

109. Deposition of Harry Laughlin, National Archives identifier 45637229, 470; National Archive DocsTeach, accessed March 21, 2019, https://www.docsteach.org/documents/document/deposition-of-harry-laughlin-eugenics-buck-v-bell? tmpl=component&print=1&ml=1&iframe=1.

110. Cohen, *Imbeciles*, 270.

111. Edwin Black, *War Against the Weak: Eugenics and America's Campaign to Create a Master Race* (New York: Four Walls Eight Windows, 2003).

112. Thomas C. Williams, "Crimes of Being," *New York Times Magazine*, January 29, 2017, 35.

113. Kühl, *Nazi Connection*, 25.

114. Kühl, *Nazi Connection*, 88–89.

115. Philip R. Reilly, *Surgical Solution: A History of Involuntary Sterilization in the United States* (Baltimore: Johns Hopkins University Press, 1991), 69.

116. Black, *War against the Weak*, 386.

117. Iowa Planning Commission, White House Conference on Child Health and Protection, Proceedings, Des Moines, IA, 1932, 397, GDS.

118. Kuhl, *Nazi Connection*, 58.

119. Kuhl, *Nazi Connection*, 43.

120. Black, *War against the Weak*, 390.
121. Black, *War against the Weak*, 392.
122. Allen, "Eugenics Record Office," 252.
123. Bentley Glass, "Geneticists Embattled: Their Stand against Rampant Eugenics and Racism in America During the 1920s and 1930s," *Proceedings of the American Philosophical Society* 130, no. 1 (1986): 152.
124. Eric Kandel and Larry Squire, "Neuroscience: Breaking Down Scientific Barriers to the Study of Brain and Mind," *Science* 290, no. 5494 (2000): 1113, 1117.
125. Henry L. Minton, email to Marilyn Brookwood, December 15, 2010.
126. Minton 2010 email to Brookwood.

Chapter Five: A Clinical Surprise

1. Skeels, "Children in Foster Homes," 92.
2. Skodak and Skeels, "A Final Follow-Up Study," 94.
3. Skodak Crissey, "Marie Skodak Crissey," in *Models*, 77; Skodak and Skeels, "A Final Follow-Up Study," 89; Skodak, "Adult Status," draft, 10.
4. Skodak Crissey, in Fischer, 8, MSC.
5. Claudia Goldin and Lawrence F. Katz, "Human Capital and Social Capital: The Rise of Secondary Schooling in America, 1910–1940," *Journal of Interdisciplinary History* 29, no. 4 (1999): 703.
6. For employment classifications the psychologists relied on the US census scale of occupations I to VII. Occupations in the highest category, I, were classified as "professionals"; those in the lowest, VII, were day laborers.
7. Skeels, "Children in Foster Homes," 93–97.
8. The mothers for whom there were IQ test records gave birth in the indigent care ward of University Hospital. No other mothers were asked to take IQ tests.
9. Skeels and Skodak, "Adult Status of Individuals," draft, 2, MSC.
10. Skodak, "Adult Status," draft, 10.
11. Skodak Crissey, interview by Senn,
12. Skodak Crissey, interview by Barbara Kalbfell, October 31, 1979 CGI.
13. Albert Wiggam, "Are Dummies Born or Made?" *Ladies Home Journal*, March 1940, 37, 123–24.
14. Skodak Crissey, "How It All Began," 11.
15. Skodak Crissey, "How It All Began," 11.
16. Skeels, "Children in Foster Homes," 105.
17. Beth Wellman, "The Fickle IQ," *Sigma Xi Quarterly* 28, no. 2 (1940): 60.
18. Harold Skeels, George Stoddard, Beth Wellman, interview by Albert E. Wiggam, April 21, 1939, 3. Faculty and Staff Vertical Files, University of Iowa Libraries.
19. Skodak Crissey, interview by Fischer, December, 10, 1969, MSC.
20. M. N. Voldeng, Tenth Biennial Report of the Superintendent, Hospital for Epileptics and School for Feebleminded at Woodward, IA, 1934, 4.
21. Joseph F. Wall and the Federal Writers' Project, *Iowa, A Guide to The Hawkeye State* (New York: Viking, 1938), 510.
22. Skodak, "Adult Status," draft, 4.
23. Asbell, "Case of the Wandering IQs," 33.

24. Skeels and Skodak, "Adult Status of Individuals," draft, 4–5, MSC.

25. Skeels and Skodak, "Adult Status of Individuals," draft, 4–5, MSC.

26. Frederick Kuhlman, *A Handbook of Mental Tests: A Further Revision and Extension of the Binet-Simon Scale* (Baltimore: Warwick & York, 1922), 89–91.

27. Skeels, "Adult Status of Children," 6.

28. Asbell, "Case of the Wandering IQs,"32.

29. Asbell, "Case of the Wandering IQs," 33.

30. George D. Stoddard, "Intellectual Development of the Child: An Answer to the Critics of the Iowa Studies," *School and Society* 51, 1322 (1940): 532.

31. Arthur R. Vinsel, "He Gave the Retarded Hope: Newport Man Reflects on Effects of Research," *Daily Pilot*, August 31, 1968, 3.

32. Asbell, "Case of the Wandering IQs,"33.

33. Asbell, "Case of the Wandering IQs," 123.

34. Asbell, "Case of the Wandering IQs," 33.

35. William T. Greenough, James E. Black, and Christopher S. Wallace, "Experience and Brain Development," *Research in Child Development* 58, no. 3 (1987): 539.

36. Marie Skodak Crissey, "Environmental Factors in Intelligence," paper delivered at the Annual Meeting of the American Educational Research Association, New York, February 16, 1967, 9.

37. Harold M. Skeels and Harold B. Dye, "Study of the Effects of Differential Stimulation," 117.

38. Skeels and Skodak, "Adult Status of Individuals," draft, 4, MSC.

39. Skodak, "Adult Status," draft, 6.

40. Skodak, "Adult Status," draft, 6.

41. Vinsel, "He Gave the Retarded Hope," 2.

42. Vinsel, "He Gave the Retarded Hope," 2.

Chapter Six: A Revelation and a Mystery

1. Lamar Smith, "In Our Care": The Glenwood State Hospital and School, WOI TV Ames, IA., 1952, http://www.asylumprojects.org/index.php/Glenwood_State_School https://www.youtube.com/watch?time_continue=1743&v=RfVN-e0vgFk.

2. *Southwest Iowa Guide Book: Geology—History—Points of Interest*, ed. L. S. Hill, Federal Writer's Project, ca. 1937, 162.

3. Wall, *The Hawkeye State*, 534.

4. Skeels and Dye, "Study of the Effects of Differential Stimulation," 134.

5. Wayne Dennis, "Causes of Retardation among Institutionalized Children: Iran," *Journal of Genetic Psychology* 96 (1960): 59.

6. Baldwin, "Heredity and Environment—or Capacity and Training?" 405.

7. Hunt, *Intelligence and Experience*, 19.

8. Lippmann, "Abuse of the Tests."

9. Lewis M. Terman, "The Great Conspiracy or The Impulse Imperious of Intelligence Testers, Psychoanalyzed and Exposed by Mr. Lippmann," *The New Republic*, December 27, 1922, 119.

10. Lewis M. Terman and Dorothy Wagner, "The Intelligence Quotients of 68 Children in a California Orphanage," *Journal of Delinquency* 3 (1918): 120.

11. Bernadine Barr, "Spare Children, 1900–1945: Inmates of Orphanages as Subjects of

Research in Medicine and in the Social Sciences in America" (PhD diss., Stanford University, 1992), 187.

12. Terman and Wagner, "Intelligence Quotients of 68 Children," 121.

13. Edward L. Thorndike, "Measurement in Education," in *The Twenty-First Yearbook of the National Society for the Study of Education: Intelligence Tests and Their Use*, ed. Guy M. Whipple (Bloomington, IL: Public School Publishing, 1921), 9.

14. Stephen S. Colvin, "Principles Underlying the Construction and Use of Intelligence Tests," in *The Twenty-First Yearbook of the National Society for the Study of Education*, 11, 18.

15. Marion R. Trabue, "The Use of Intelligence Tests in Junior High Schools," in *The Twenty-First Yearbook of the National Society for the Study of Education*, 177.

16. William C. Bagley, "Educational Determinism; or Democracy and the I.Q.," *School and Society* 15, no. 380 (1922): 380, 376.

17. Terman, *Measurement of Intelligence*, 91–92.

18. Terman, *Measurement of Intelligence*, 60–61.

19. Lewis M. Terman, "The Psychological Determinist; or Democracy and the I.Q.," *Journal of Educational Research* 6, no.1 (1922): 58.

20. William C. Bagley, "Professor Terman's Determinism: A Rejoinder," *Journal of Educational Research* 6, no. 5 (1922): 385.

21. Helen T. Woolley, "Educational Research and Statistics: The Validity of Standards of Mental Measurement in Young Childhood," *School and Society* 21, no. 538 (1925): 478–79.

22. Lewis M. Terman to Guy M. Whipple, December 3, 1927.

23. William C. Bagley to Lewis M. Terman, December 17, 1927.

24. Spiro, *Defending the Master Race*, 179.

25. Carl C. Brigham, *A Study of American Intelligence* (Princeton, NJ: Princeton University Press, 1923), xiii.

26. Franz Samelson, "World War I Intelligence Testing and the Development of Psychology," *Journal of the History of the Behavioral Sciences* 13 (1977): 278.

27. Brigham, *Study of American Intelligence*, 146.

28. Brigham, *Study of American Intelligence*, 159.

29. Brigham, *Study of American Intelligence*, 95, 100.

30. Carl C. Brigham to Lewis M. Terman, December 27, 1927.

31. Brigham to Davenport, December 8, 1929.

32. Carl C. Brigham, "Intelligence Tests of Immigrant Groups," *Psychological Review* 37, no. 2 (1930): 165.

33. Nicholas Lemann, *The Big Test: The Secret History of the American Meritocracy* (New York: Farrar, Straus and Giroux, 2000), 29.

34. Garland Allen, "The Role of Experts in Scientific Controversy," in *Scientific Controversies: Case Studies in the Resolution and Closure of Disputes in Science and Technology*, ed. Hugo T. Englehardt and Arthur L. Caplan (New York: Cambridge University Press, 1987), 197.

35. Raymond Pearl, "The Biology of Superiority," *American Mercury* 12, no. 47 (1927): 260.

36. Brigham to Terman, December 27, 1927.

37. Truman Kelley, *Interpretation of Educational Measurement* (Yonkers, NY: World Book, 1927), 124.

38. Brigham, "Intelligence Tests of Immigrant Groups," 164–5.

39. Brigham, cited in Lemann, *The Big Test*, 34.

40. Lemann, *The Big Test*, 32.

41. Barbara Burks, "A Summary of Literature on the Determiners of the Intelligence Quotient and the Educational Quotient," in *The Twenty-Seventh Yearbook of the National Society for the Study of Education: Nature and Nurture*, Part II, ed. Guy M Whipple (Bloomington, IL: Public School Publishing, 1928), 280.

42. Helen E. Barrett and Helen L. Koch, "The Effects of Nursery-School Training upon the Mental-Test Performance of a Group of Orphanage Children," *The Pedagogical Seminary and Journal of Genetic Psychology* 37 (1930): 119.

43. Mandel Sherman and Cora B. Key, "The Intelligence of Isolated Mountain Children," *Child Development* 3, no. 4 (1932): 279.

44. Sherman and Key, "Intelligence of Isolated Mountain Children," 289.

45. Frank N. Freeman, "The Concept of Intelligence as a Fixed or Unmodifiable Feature of the Personality." Fourth Conference on Research in Child Development, National Research Council Committee on Child Development, 1933, Appendix H, 2.

46. Skodak Crissey, "Beth Lucy Wellman," 353.

47. Asbell, "Case of the Wandering IQs," 122.

48. Skodak, "Adult Status," draft, 6.

49. Skeels, "Records of Experimental Group."

50. Skeels, "Records of Experimental Group."

51. Skeels, "Records of Experimental Group."

52. Skeels, "Records of Experimental Group."

53. Skeels, "Records of Experimental Group."

54. Louis C. Branca, interview by Marilyn Brookwood, September 12, 2012.

55. Skeels Records, 1939–1966, Case 11.

56. Louis C. Branca, telephone call with author, June 4, 2015.

57. Samuel Z. Orgel and Jacob Tuckman, "Nicknames of Institutional Children," *American Journal of Orthopsychiatry* 5, no. 3 (1935): 276–285.

58. Robert Wallace, "A Lifetime Thrown Away by a Mistake 59 Years Ago," *Life*, March 24, 1958, 121.

59. Wallace, "A Lifetime Thrown Away," 121.

60. Branca, interview by Marilyn Brookwood, June 5, 2015.

61. Branca, interview by Marilyn Brookwood, June 5, 2015.

62. Branca, email to Marilyn Brookwood, February 25, 2014.

63. Branca, interview by Marilyn Brookwood, June 12, 2012.

64. Skeels, Records, 1933–1966, Case 15.

65. Skeels, Records, 1933–1966, Case 17.

66. Skeels, Records, 1933–1966, Case 20.

67. Skeels, Records, 1933–1936, Case 20.

68. Skeels, Records, 1933–1966, Case 20.

69. Branca, interview by Marilyn Brookwood.

70. Asbell, "Case of the Wandering IQs," 117.

71. Marie Skodak Crissey, interview by Fischer, 14.

72. Skeels's Records, 1933–1966, Case 19.

73. Skeels and Dye, "Study of the Effects of Differential Stimulation," 129.

Chapter Seven: Orphan Studies Out in Public

1. Wellman, "Fickle IQ," 52.
2. Wellman, "The Effect of Pre-School Attendance," 48–69; Beth Wellman, "Some New Bases for Interpretation of the IQ," *Pedagogical Seminary and Journal of Genetic Psychology* 41, no. 1 (1932): 116–126.
3. Skeels et al., "Study of Environmental Stimulation," 20.
4. Skeels et al., "Study of Environmental Stimulation," 10–11.
5. Skeels et al., "Study of Environmental Stimulation," 21.
6. Skeels and Skodak, "Adult Status of Individuals," draft, 9.
7. Skeels et al., "Study of Environmental Stimulation," 4.
8. Wellman, "Fickle IQ," 54.
9. Skeels et al., "Study of Environmental Stimulation,"13–21.
10. Skeels et al., "Study of Environmental Stimulation," 13–14.
11. Barr, "Educating Orphans and Educating Psychologists," 35.
12. Quoted in Skeels et. al., "Study of Environmental Stimulation," 25.
13. Quoted in Skeels et. al., "Study of Environmental Stimulation," 26.
14. Skeels et al., "Study of Environmental Stimulation," 23–24.
15. Skeels et al., "Study of Environmental Stimulation," 23–24.
16. Skeels et al., "Study of Environmental Stimulation," 23–24.
17. Skeels et al., "Study of Environmental Stimulation," 23.
18. Skeels et al., "Study of Environmental Stimulation," 34–35.
19. Skeels et al., "Study of Environmental Stimulation," 4.
20. Skeels et al., "Study of Environmental Stimulation," 13.
21. Wellman, "Fickle IQ," 54.
22. Skeels et al., "Study of Environmental Stimulation," 44–46.
23. Skeels et al., "Study of Environmental Stimulation," 44.
24. Skeels et al. "Study of Environmental Stimulation," 118.
25. Wellman, "Fickle IQ," 55.
26. Wellman, "Fickle IQ," 60.
27. Marie Skodak Crissey, interview by Barbara Kalbfell, October 31, 1979, CGI.
28. Marie Skodak Crissey, "The Mental Development of Children Whose True Mothers Are Feebleminded," *Child Development* 9, no. 3 (1938): 303–304.
29. Skodak Crissey, "Mental Development of Children," 305–307.
30. Marie Skodak, "Children in Foster Homes: A Study of Mental Development," *University of Iowa Studies in Child Welfare* 16, no. 1 (1939): 37–126.
31. Skodak, "Children in Foster Homes," 42.
32. Skodak, "Children in Foster Homes," 45.
33. George S. Speer, "Intelligence of Foster Children," *Pedagogical Seminary and Journal of Genetic Psychology* 47, no. 1 (1940): 51–53.
34. George D. Stoddard, *The Meaning of Intelligence* (New York: Macmillan, 1943), 361–3.
35. Stoddard, *Meaning of Intelligence*, 363.
36. Beth L. Wellman, "Growth of Intelligence under Differing School Environments," *Journal of Experimental Education* 6, no. 2 (1934): 80–81.
37. Skeels, "Children in Foster Homes," 91.

38. Harold M. Skeels, "A Cooperative Orphanage Research," *Journal of Experimental Education* 30, no. 6 (1937): 444.
39. Skeels, "Children in Foster Homes," 106.
40. Harold M. Skeels and Eva A. Fillmore, "The Mental Development of Children from Underprivileged Homes," *Journal of Genetic Psychology* 50, no. 2 (1937): 438.
41. Thomas R. Henry, "Report on Test Variation Blasts Old Theories on I.Q." *Washington Star,* Washington, DC, December 30, 1937, A-2.
42. Henry, "Report on Test Variation," A-2.
43. Thomas R. Henry, "The Wandering IQ," *National Rehabilitation News,* June 1, 1938, 13–14.
44. Henry, "Report on Test Variation," A-2.
45. Henry, "Report on Test Variation," A-2.
46. Beth L. Wellman, "Mental Growth from Preschool to College," *Journal of Experimental Education* 6, no. 2 (1937): 138.
47. Dorothy A. Pownall, "The Dull Child Made Bright by a New Environment," *New York Herald Tribune,* April 10, 1938, 16.
48. Associated Press, June 29, 1938.
49. *Time,* July 11, 1938.
50. *New York Times,* September 11, 1938, 51.
51. *Time,* November 7, 1938.
52. *Time,* November 7, 1938.
53. Albert E. Wiggam, *The Fruit of the Family Tree* (Indianapolis: Bobbs-Merrill, 1924), frontmatter.
54. Wiggam, *Fruit of the Family Tree,* 346.
55. Wiggam, *Fruit of the Family Tree,* 4.
56. Albert E. Wiggam to Lewis M. Terman, June 29, 1939, LMT.
57. Harold M. Skeels, interview by Albert E. Wiggam, April 21, 1939, 1.
58. Skeels, interview by Wiggam, April 21, 1939, 3.
59. Beth L. Wellman, interview by Albert E. Wiggam, April 21, 1939, 7.
60. Wellman, interview by Wiggam, April 21, 1939, 9.
61. Wellman, interview by Wiggam, April 21, 1939, 10.
62. George D. Stoddard, interview by Albert E. Wiggam, April 21, 1939, 17.
63. Kandel and Squire, "Breaking Down Scientific Barriers," 1113–20.
64. Kandel and Squire, "Breaking Down Scientific Barriers," 1113–20.
65. Wiggam to Terman, June 29, 1939, LMT.
66. Lewis M. Terman to Albert E. Wiggam, July 10, 1939, LNT.
67. Wiggam, "Are Dummies Born or Made?" 124.
68. Albert E. Wiggam, *Let's Explore Your Mind* (New York: Penguin Pocket Books, 1949), 235.
69. Frederick Osborn, "To What Extent Is a Science of Man Possible?" *Scientific Monthly* 49, no. 5 (1939): 453.
70. Osborn, "Science of Man," 455.

Chapter Eight: The Way the Land Lies

1. Simpson, "Wandering IQ, 358, 365–366.
2. Simpson, "Wandering IQ," 351.
3. Simpson, "Wandering IQ," 362.

4. Simpson, "Wandering IQ," 366.
5. Terman to Simpson, March 16, 1939, LMT.
6. Terman to Simpson, April 7, 1939, LMT.
7. Simpson to Terman, May 29, 1939, LMT.
8. May V. Seagoe, *Terman and the Gifted* (Los Angeles: William Kaufmann, 1975), 47.
9. Terman to Cattell, November 29, 1944, LMT.
10. Goodenough to Hollingworth, April 4, 1939, FLG.
11. Skeels and Dye, "Study of the Effects of Differential Stimulation," 115.
12. Skodak, "Adult Status," draft, 2, MSC.
13. Skodak Crissey, "Harold Manville Skeels," 1.
14. Skeels and Dye, "Study of the Effects of Differential Stimulation," 114.
15. Alfred Binet, *Les Idèes Mordernes sur Les Enfants* (Paris: Flammarion, 1911), 346. Quoted in George D. Stoddard, "The I.Q.: Its Ups and Downs," *Educational Record Supplement* 12 (1939): 54.
16. Frederick Weizmann, "From the 'Village of a Thousand Souls' to 'Race Crossing in Jamaica': Arnold Gesell, Eugenics and Child Development," *Journal of the History of the Behavioral Sciences* 46, no. 3 (2010): 268.
17. Skeels and Dye, "Study of the Effects of Differential Stimulation," 133.
18. Asbell, "Case of the Wandering IQs," 114.
19. Personal communication, Hamilton Cravens to author, January 8, 2011.
20. Skodak Crissey, "Harold Manville Skeels," 2.
21. Hunt, *Intelligence and Experience*, 19.
22. Vinsel, "He Gave the Retarded Hope," 2.
23. "Put among Morons, Dull Babies Improve," *New York Times*, May 7, 1939, 6.
24. "Confirming a Belief," editorial, *Atlanta Constitution*, May 19, 1939, 10.
25. "Feeble-Minded Love," *Time*, May 15, 1939, 42.
26. "Feeble-Minded Love," *Time*, May 15, 1939, 42.
27. Kühl, *Nazi Connection*, 43.
28. Terman to Gozney, January 13, 1939, LMT.
29. "Psychology War Rages," *Los Angeles Times*, July 8, 1939, 8.
30. Beth Wellman and George Stoddard, "The IQ: A Problem in Social Construction," *The Social Frontier* 5, no. 42 (1939): 152.
31. Skodak, "Adult Status," draft, 13, MSC.
32. Marie Skodak Crissey, interview by Milton J. E. Senn, 20, MJES.
33. Thomas Gladwin, "Statement by Dr. Thomas Gladwin, June 14, 1961" (unpublished), 1, MSC.
34. Stoddard, *Pursuit of Education*, 46.
35. Franz Boas, "Evidence on the Nature of Intelligence Furnished by Anthropology and Ethnology," in *The Thirty-Ninth Yearbook of the National Society for the Study of Education*, ed. Guy Montrose Whipple, *Addresses and Discussions: "Intelligence: Its Nature and Nurture"* (Salem, MA: Newcomb and Gauss, 1940), 11.
36. Frederick Osborn, "Implications of the Yearbook for Eugenics," in *The Thirty-Ninth Yearbook of the National Society for the Study of Education*, ed. Guy Montrose Whipple, *Addresses and Discussions: "Intelligence: Its Nature and Nurture"* (Salem, MA: Newcomb and Gauss, 1940), 57.
37. E. W. Burgess, "The Social Implications of Nature-Nurture Studies," in *The Thirty-Ninth*

Yearbook of the National Society for the Study of Education, ed. Guy Montrose Whipple, *Addresses and Discussions: "Intelligence: Its Nature and Nurture"* (Salem, MA: Newcomb and Gauss, 1940), 80.

38. Terman to Simpson, June 7, 1939, LMT.
39. Stoddard to Whipple, July 18, 1939, 2, UISC.
40. *Oakland Tribune*, July 5, 1939, 2.
41. James Fox and Bill Bartley, "Good Morning," *Daily Iowan*, February 21, 1940, 1.
42. "Psychology War Rages," *Los Angeles Times*, 6.
43. "Psychology War Rages," *Los Angeles Times*, 6.
44. "Psychology War Rages," *Los Angeles Times*, 6.
45. "Intelligence—Its Nature AND NURTURE," *Daily Iowan*, July 8, 1939, 2.
46. Dwight Mitchell, "Educators Debate Freedom, Heredity, Cinema at Session," *Stanford Daily*, July 11, 1939.
47. Stoddard to Terman, July 12, 1939, UISC.
48. Terman to Stoddard, July 13, 1939, UISC.
49. Terman to Stoddard, July 13, 1939, UISC.
50. Quinn McNemar, "Quinn McNemar," in *A History of Psychology in Autobiography*, ed. Gardner Lindzey (San Francisco: W. H. Freeman, 1980), 320.
51. Goodenough to Terman, September 26, 1939, LMT.
52. Terman to Goodenough, October 3, 1939, LMT.
53. Goodenough to Terman, December 31, 1939, LMT.
54. Florence Goodenough, "Look to the Evidence! A Critique of Recent Experiments on Raising the I.Q." *Educational Method* 19, no 2 (1939): 74.
55. Wellman to Line, December 18, 1939, UISC.
56. Asbell, "Case of the Wandering IQs," 114.
57. Marie Skodak Crissey, interview by Barbara Kalbfell, October 31, 1979, CGI.
58. Asbell, "Case of the Wandering IQs," 114.

Chapter Nine: "Even If It Didn't Work, It Was a Good Idea!"

1. Barbara Burks to Lewis M. Terman, February 14, 1940, LMT.
2. Terman to Burks, February 19, 1940, LMT.
3. "Education: Nature V. Nurture," *Time*, March 11, 1940.
4. George D. Stoddard, "Introducing the Yearbook on 'Intelligence: Its Nature and Nurture,'" in *The Thirty-Ninth Yearbook of the National Society for the Study of Education*, ed. Guy M. Whipple, *Addresses and Discussions: "Intelligence: Its Nature and Nurture"* (Salem, MA: Newcomb and Gauss, 1940), 3.
5. Stoddard, "Introducing the Yearbook," 3
6. Stoddard, "Introducing the Yearbook," 3.
7. *Time*, March 11, 1940.
8. Paul A. Witty, "Evidence Regarding the Nature of Intelligence from the Study of Superior Deviates," in *The Thirty-Ninth Yearbook, Intelligence of the National Society for the Study of Education*, ed. Guy M. Whipple, *Addresses and Discussions: "Intelligence: Its Nature and Nurture"* (Salem, MA: Newcomb and Gauss, 1940), 30.
9. Jane Loevinger, "Intelligence Related to Socio-Economic Factors," in *The Thirty-Ninth Year-*

book of the National Society for the Study of Education, *Intelligence: Its Nature and Nurture*, ed. Guy M. Whipple, Part I (Bloomington, IL: Public School Publishing, 1940), chapter 5, 204.

10. Martin L. Reymert and Ralph T. Hinton, "The Effect of a Change to a Relatively Superior Environment upon the IQs of One Hundred Children," in *The Thirty-Ninth Yearbook of the National Society for the Study of Education, Intelligence: Its Nature and Nurture*, ed. Guy M. Whipple, Part II (Bloomington, IL: Public School Publishing, 1940), chapter 17.

11. Grace E. Bird, "The Effect of Nursery School Attendance upon the Mental Growth of Children," in *The Thirty-Ninth Yearbook of the National Society for the Study of Education, Intelligence: Its Nature and Nurture*, ed. Guy M. Whipple, Part II (Bloomington, IL: Public School Publishing, 1940), chapter 4.

12. Nancy Bayley, "Mental Growth in Young Children," in *The Thirty-Ninth Yearbook of the National Society for the Study of Education, Intelligence: Its Nature and Nurture*, ed. Guy M. Whipple, Part II (Bloomington, IL: Public School Publishing, 1940), chapter 3.

13. Gertrude Hildreth, "Adopted Children in a Private School," in *The Thirty-Ninth Yearbook of the National Society for the Study of Education, Intelligence: Its Nature and Nurture*, ed. Guy M. Whipple, Part II (Bloomington, IL: Public School Publishing, 1940), chapter 10.

14. Stoddard, "Introducing the Yearbook," 49.

15. Stoddard, "Introducing the Yearbook," 51–52.

16. Stoddard, "Introducing the Yearbook," 51–52.

17. Robert R. Rusk, "The Intelligence of Scottish Children," in *The Thirty-Ninth Yearbook of the National Society for the Study of Education, Intelligence: Its Nature and Nurture*, ed. Guy M. Whipple, Part II (Bloomington, IL: Public School Publishing, 1940), chapter 18.

18. Conrad H. Waddington, *Introduction to Modern Genetics* (New York: Macmillan, 1939), 357–58.

19. Stoddard, "Introducing the Yearbook," 55.

20. Lewis M. Terman, "Personal Reactions of the Committee," in *The Thirty-Ninth Yearbook of the National Society for the Study of Education, Intelligence: Its Nature and Nurture*, ed. Guy M. Whipple, Part I (Bloomington, IL: Public School Publishing, 1940), 460.

21. Stoddard, "Introducing the Yearbook," 4.

22. Stoddard, "Introducing the Yearbook," 4.

23. Quinn McNemar, "A Critical Examination of the University of Iowa Studies of Environmental Influences upon the IQ," *Psychological Bulletin* 37, no. 2 (1940): 64.

24. George D. Stoddard et al. Reply to McNemar, 1939 (unpublished notes), MSC.

25. Lewis M. Terman and Albert E. Wiggam, Correspondence, 1925–1953, LMT.

26. Bernadine Barr, "Spare Children," 230.

27. Beth L. Wellman, Harold M. Skeels, and Marie Skodak, "Review of McNemar's Critical Examination of Iowa Studies," *Psychological Bulletin* 37, no. 2 (1940), 96.

28. McNemar, "Environmental Influences upon the IQ," 70.

29. Harold Skeels et al., "Study of Environmental Stimulation," 55.

30. Harold Skeels et al., "Study of Environmental Stimulation," 44.

31. McNemar, "Environmental Influences upon the IQ," 70.

32. Wellman et. al, "Review of McNemar's Critical Examination," 97.

33. Brueckner, L. J., "The Cumulative Effects of a Policy of Non-Failing," *Journal of Educational Research* 29, no. 4 (1934): 289.

34. Wellman et al., "Review of McNemar's Critical Examination," 101.
35. McNemar, "Environmental Influences upon the IQ," 75.
36. Marie Skodak, "Comments on a Reply to Quinn McNemar: A Critical Examination of Iowa Studies of Environmental Influences upon the IQ" (unpublished, 1940), 6, MSC.
37. Wellman et al, "Review of McNemar's Critical Examination," 106.
38. Florence L. Goodenough, "Can We Influence Mental Growth: A Critique of Recent Experiments," *The Educational Record Supplement* 21, no. 13 (1940): 135.
39. George D. Stoddard, "Intellectual Development of the Child: An Answer to the Critics of the Iowa Studies," *School and Society* 51, no. 1322 (1940): 529–30.
40. Wellman et al., "Review of McNemar's Critical Examination," 98.
41. Quinn McNemar, "More on the Iowa IQ Studies," *Journal of Psychology: Interdisciplinary and Applied* 10 (1940): 239.
42. Wellman et al., "Review of McNemar's Critical Examination."
43. Stoddard. "Intellectual Development of the Child," 530–36.
44. Wellman, "Fickle IQ." 51-60.
45. Florence L. Goodenough to Lewis M. Terman, March 11, 1940, LMT.
46. Paul A. Witty, "Research Upon The American Negro," in *The Thirty-Ninth Yearbook of the National Society for the Study of Education, Intelligence: Its Nature and Nurture*, ed. Guy Montrose Whipple, Part I (Bloomington, IL: Public School Publishing, 1940): 267.
47. Witty, "Study of Superior Deviates," 30.
48. Goodenough to Terman, March 11, 1940, LMT.
49. Benjamin R. Simpson to Lewis M. Terman, March 9, 1940.
50. Stoddard, *Pursuit of Education*, 59.
51. Stoddard, *Pursuit of Education*, 59.
52. Henry L. Minton, *Lewis M. Terman, Pioneer in Psychological Testing* (New York: New York University Press, 1988), 266–67.
53. Cravens, *Before Head Start*, 212–13.
54. Cravens, *Before Head Start*, 213.
55. George D. Stoddard, "What Every Teacher Should Know—About the Dionne Quintuplets," *Childhood Education* 14, no 9 (1937): 399–402.
56. Sheldon H. White and Stephen L. Buka, "Early Education: Programs, Traditions, and Policies," *Review of Research in Education* 14, no. 13 (1987): 63.
57. Barbara Burks to Lewis M. Terman, May 20, 1940, LMT.
58. Steve McNutt, "A Dangerous Man," 25.
59. Burks to Terman, May 29, 1940, LMT.
60. Burks to Terman, October 16, 1942, LMT.
61. John Burnham, "The Evolution of Editorial Peer Review," *Journal of the American Medical Association* 263, no. 10 (1990): 1328.
62. Cravens, *Before Head Start*, 307.
63. Guy M. Whipple, ed., *The Thirty-Ninth Yearbook of the National Society for the Study of Education, Nature and Nurture* (Bloomington, IL: Public School Publishing, 1940), xviii.
64. Diane Paul, "Textbook Treatments of the Genetics of Intelligence," *Quarterly Review of Biology* 60 (September 3, 1985): 324.
65. Marie Skodak Crissey, interview by Henry L. Minton, January 15, 1982, 13–14.
66. Louis C. Branca interview by Marilyn Brookwood, September 10, 2012.

67. Harold M. Skeels, "A Study of the Effects of Differential Stimulation on Mentally Retarded Children: A Follow-Up Report." *American Journal of Mental Deficiency* 46, no. 3 (1940): 342.
68. Skeels, "Effects of Differential Stimulation: A Follow-Up Report," 346.
69. Skeels, "Effects of Differential Stimulation: A Follow-Up Report," 348.
70. Skeels, "Effects of Differential Stimulation: A Follow-Up Report."
71. Skodak Crissey, interview by Senn, 20, MJES.
72. Skodak Crissey, interview by Senn, 25, MJES.
73. Peter Schjedahl, "Return of the Native," *The New Yorker*, March 12, 2018, 80–81.
74. Joni Kinsey, "Cultivating Iowa: An Introduction to Grant Wood," in *Grant Wood's Studio: Birthplace of American Gothic*, ed. Jane C. Milosch (Munich: Prestel, 2005), 29.
75. George Painter, "Sodomy Laws: The Sensibilities of Our Forefathers: The History of Sodomy Laws in the United States," accessed May 19, 2018, https://www.glapn.org/sodomylaws/sensibilities/iowa.htm.
76. Grant Wood to George D. Stoddard, March 29, 1940, UISP.
77. George D. Stoddard to Virgil M. Hancher, April 14, 1941, UISP.
78. Lewis M. Terman and Catherine C. Miles, *Sex and Personality: Studies in Masculinity and Femininity* (New York: McGraw-Hill, 1936), 259–260.
79. Terman and Miles, *Sex and Personality*, 284–320.
80. Marie Skodak Crissey to Harold M. Skeels's unnamed cousin, ca. April 1970, MSC.
81. Lois Barklay Murphy, "On Coping and Change," Catherine Molony Memorial Lecture, 1980, 6.
82. Murphy, "On Coping and Change," 8.
83. Marie Skodak Crissey, interview by Kalbfell, CGI.
84. Stoddard, *Pursuit of Education*, 63.

Chapter Ten: A Chill in the Air

1. Florence L. Goodenough to Lewis M. Terman, November 19, 1940, LMT.
2. Skodak Crissey, interview by Minton, 14, MSC.
3. Stoddard, *Pursuit of Education*, 49.
4. Stoddard, *Pursuit of Education*, 49.
5. Stoddard, *Pursuit of Education*, 49.
6. Stoddard, "An Autobiography," in *Leaders*, 331.
7. Stoddard, *Pursuit of Education*, 67.
8. Luther H. Gulick to George D. Stoddard, November 1, 1941, GDS.
9. Wiley B. Rutledge to George D. Stoddard, September 22, 1941, GDS.
10. Esther Collester to George D. Stoddard, June 17, 1942, GDS.
11. Stoddard, *Pursuit of Education*, 71.
12. Stoddard, *Meaning of Intelligence*, 321.
13. Stoddard, *Meaning of Intelligence*, 461.
14. Stoddard, *Pursuit of Education*, 75.
15. Stoddard, *Pursuit of Education*, 92.
16. Stoddard, *Pursuit of Education*, 98.
17. John McDonough, "Stoddard Back in Old Haunts," *Daily Iowan*, October 5, 1947.
18. Stoddard, *Pursuit of Education*, 110.
19. *Chicago Sun Times*, July 23, 1953, quoted in Stoddard, *Pursuit of Education*, 136.

20. "The Final Arrow," *Time*, August 3, 1953, 41.
21. Robert R. Sears, interview by Milton J. E. Senn, October 3, 1968, interview 64, 4, MJES.
22. Robert R. Sears to George D. Stoddard, October 8, 1942, UISP.
23. Sears interview by Senn, 5, MJES.
24. Sears interview by Senn, 12–13, MJES.
25. Sears interview, by Senn, 15, MJES.
26. Sears interview, by Senn, 15, MJES.
27. Lawrence K. Frank, "Research in Child Psychology: History and Prospect," in *Child Behavior and Development*, ed. Robert G. Barker, Jacob S. Kounin, and Herbert F. Wright (New York: McGraw Hill, 1943), 1–16.
28. Frank, "Research in Child Psychology," 7.
29. Marie Skoda Crissey, interview by Henry L. Minton, January 15, 1982, 19, MSC.
30. Harold M. Skeels to Robert R. Sears, May 2, 1943, UISP.
31. Sears to Skeels, November 14, 1945, UISP.
32. Skeels to Sears, November 7, 1945, UISP.
33. Robert R. Sears to R. H. Singleton, December 19, 1945, 2, UISP.
34. Sears to Singleton, December 19, 1945. UISP.
35. George Davis Bivin to Robert R. Sears, March 14, 1946, UISP.
36. Harold M. Skeels to P. F. Hopkins, August 10, 1946, 1, UISP.
37. Skeels to Hopkins, August 10, 1946, 3, UISP.
38. George Mills, *Des Moines Register*, August 13, 1946, 1.
39. Skeels to Sears, August 12, 1946, UISP.
40. Skeels to Sears, December 22, 1946, UISP.
41. Sears to Skeels, January 10, 1947, UISP.
42. Sears to Skeels, March 22, 1947, UISP.
43. Sears Interview by Senn, 9, MJES.
44. Sears Interview by Senn, 18, MJES.
45. Skodak Crissey, "Marie Skodak Crissey," in *Models*, 79.
46. Skodak Crissey, "Marie Skodak Crissey," in *History*, 6.
47. Marie Skodak Crissey to Earl M. Rogers, December 21, 1982, MSC.
48. Asbell, "Case of the Wandering IQs," 115.
49. Nicholas Pastore, *The Nature-Nurture Controversy* (New York: Kings Crown Press, Columbia University, 1949), 16.
50. Lewis M. Terman, quoted in Pastore, *Nature-Nurture Controversy*, 95.
51. Terman, "Trails to Psychology," 329.
52. Terman, in Pastore, *Nature-Nurture Controversy*, 88.
53. Robert M. Sears, "Lewis M. Terman, Pioneer in Mental Measurement," *Science* 125 (1957): 978.
54. Earnest R. Hilgard, "Lewis Madison Terman: 1877–1956," *American Journal of Psychology* 70, no. 3 (1957): 478.

Chapter Eleven: Reversal of Fortune

1. Lee McCardell, "McCardell Visits Scene of Nazi Mass Murder," *Baltimore Sun*, April 7, 1945.
2. McCardell, "Nazi Mass Murder."
3. Edward R. Murrow, *In Search of Light: The Broadcasts of Edward R. Murrow*, ed. Edward Bliss Jr. (New York: Avon Books, 1967), 108, 110.

4. Deborah E. Lipstadt, *Beyond Belief: The American Press and The Coming of the Holocaust 1933– 1935* (New York: The Free Press, 1986), 135–239.

5. Kevles, *In the Name of Eugenics*, 251.

6. Chase, *Legacy of Malthus*, 364.

7. Skodak Crissey, "How It All Began" 17, MSC.

8. Harold Anderson interview by Milton J. E. Senn, December 8, 1970, interview 2, transcript, 37, 40, MJES.

9. Boyd R. McCandless and Charles C. Spiker, "Experimental Research in Child Psychology," *Child Development* 27, no. 1 (1956): 77–78.

10. McCandless and Spiker, "Experimental Research," 78.

11. Institute of Child Behavior and Development, *Fifty Years of Research, 1917–1967* (Iowa City: University of Iowa, 1967), iii.

12. René Spitz, "Hospitalism: An Inquiry into the Genesis of Psychiatric Conditions in Early Childhood," in *The Psychoanalytic Study of the Child*, Vol. I, ed. Anna Freud, Willie Hoffer, and Edward Glover (London: International University Press, Imago Publishing, 1945), 73.

13. Floyd M. Crandall, "Hospitalism," *Archives of Pediatrics* 14, no. 6 (1897): 448–54, accessed November 13, 2019, http://www.neonatology.org/classics/crandall.html.

14. Spitz, "Hospitalism: An Inquiry," 53.

15. Spitz, "Hospitalism: An Inquiry," 67.

16. Skodak, "Adult Status," draft, 6, MSC.

17. Joseph McVicker Hunt, interview by Milton J. E. Senn, June 9, 1974, interview 30A, transcript, MJES.

18. Harry Bakwin, quoted in Robert Karen, *Becoming Attached: First Relationships and How They Shape Our Capacity to Love* (New York: Oxford University Press, 1998), 20.

19. Harry Bakwin, "Psychologic Aspects of Pediatrics: Emotional Deprivation in Infants," *Journal of Pediatrics* 35, no. 4 (1949): 512.

20. John Bowlby, *Maternal Care and Mental Health: A Report Prepared on Behalf of the World Health Organization as a Contribution to the United Nations Programme for the Welfare of Homeless Children*, Geneva, 15.

21. Bowlby, *Maternal Care and Mental Health*, 19.

22. William Goldfarb, "Infant Rearing and Problem Behavior," *American Journal of Orthopsychiatry* 13 (1943): 249.

23. Goldfarb, "Infant Rearing," 249.

24. Goldfarb, "Infant Rearing," 249.

25. Wayne Dennis, "Infant Development under Conditions of Restricted Practice and Minimal Social Stimulation," *Genetic Psychology Monographs* 23 (1941): 187.

26. Dennis and Najarian, "Environmental Handicap," 6.

27. Dennis and Najarian, "Environmental Handicap," 1–4.

28. Dennis and Najarian, "Environmental Handicap," 12.

29. Dennis and Najarian, "Environmental Handicap," 11.

30. Dennis and Najarian, "Environmental Handicap," 12.

31. Bernadine Schmidt, "Changes in Personal, Social, and Intellectual Behavior of Children Originally Classified as Feebleminded," *Psychological Monographs* 60, no. 5 (1946): 1–144.

32. Samuel A. Kirk, *Early Education of the Mentally Retarded: An Experimental Study* (Urbana IL: University of Illinois Press, 1958), 205.

33. Stoddard, *Meaning of Intelligence*, 281.
34. Asbell, "Case of the Wandering IQs," 116.
35. Robert M. Thomas, "Samuel A. Kirk, 92, Pioneer of Special Education Field," *New York Times*, January 16, 1964.
36. Simon Auster, interview by Marilyn Brookwood, May 1, 2014.
37. Simon Auster, interview by Marilyn Brookwood, May 24, 2012.
38. Marie Skodak Crissey to Harold M. Skeels's unnamed cousin, ca. April 1970.
39. Asbell, "Case of the Wandering IQs," 116.
40. Thomas Gladwin, "Statement By Dr. Thomas Gladwin," June 14, 1961, 1–2, MSC.
41. Gladwin, "Statement," 1–2.
42. Joseph McVicker Hunt, "A Professional Odyssey," in *The Psychologists*, ed. T. S. Krawiec (New York: Oxford University Press, 1974), 181.
43. Wade E. Pickren, "Joseph McVicker Hunt, Golden Age Psychologist," in *Portraits of Pioneers in Developmental Psychology*, ed. Wade E. Pickren, Donald A. Dewsbury, and Michael Wertheimer (New York: Psychology Press, 2012), 197.
44. Hunt, "A Professional Odyssey," 185.
45. Hunt, *Intelligence and Experience*, 19.
46. Hunt, interview by Senn, 45, MJES.
47. Maris Vinovskis, *The Birth of Head Start: Preschool Education in the Kennedy and Johnson Administrations* (Chicago: University of Chicago Press, 2005), 73–74.
48. Vinovskis, *Birth of Head Start*, 11; Edward Zigler and Sally Styfco, *The Hidden History of Head Start* (New York: Oxford University Press, 2010),: 16.
49. Hunt, *Intelligence and Experience*, 28.
50. Joseph McVicker Hunt, "The Psychological Basis for Using Pre-School Enrichment as Antidote for Cultural Deprivation," *Merrill-Palmer Quarterly of Behavior and Development* 10 (1964): 209. (Paper delivered at Arden House in 1962.)
51. Joseph McVicker Hunt, "Environmental Programming to Foster Competence and Prevent Mental Retardation in Infancy," in *Environments as Therapy for Brain Dysfunction*, ed. Roger N. Walsh and William T. Greenough (New York: Plenum Press, 1976), 210.
52. Hunt, "Psychological Basis," 212.
53. Martin Deutsch, "Facilitating Development in the Pre-School Child: Social and Psychological Perspectives," *Merrill Palmer Quarterly of Behavior and Development* 10, no. 3 (1964): 252.
54. Anahad O'Connor, "Dr. Martin Deutsch, an Innovator in Education, Dies at 76," *New York Times*, July 5, 2002.
55. Julius Richmond, interview by Milton J. E. Senn, July 12, 1958, interview 58, 15, MJES.
56. Hunt, *Intelligence and Experience*, 83–87.
57. Donald O. Hebb, *The Organization of Behavior: A Neuropsychological Theory* (New York: Wiley, 1949), 295.
58. Richard E. Brown, "The Life and Work of Donald Olding Hebb, Canada's Greatest Psychologist," *Proceedings of the Nova Scotian Institute of Science* 44 (2007): 12.
59. Hebb, *Organization of Behavior*, 70.
60. Hebb, *Organization of Behavior*, 298.
61. Brown, "Life and Work of Donald Olding Hebb," 2.
62. Brown, "Life and Work of Donald Olding Hebb," 13.

63. Edward Zigler and Susan Muenchow, *Head Start: The Inside Story of America's Most Successful Educational Experiment* (New York: Basic Books, 1992), 16.

64. Uri Bronfenbrenner, *The Ecology of Human Development: Experiments by Nature and Design* (Cambridge, MA: Harvard University Press), 3.

65. Bronfenbrenner, *Ecology of Human Development*, 37.

66. Harold Skeels and Marie Skodak, "Techniques for a High-Yield Follow-Up Study in the Field," *Public Health Reports* 80, no. 3 (1965): 249–57.

67. Skeels and Skodak, "Techniques for a High-Yield Follow-Up," 252.

68. Skeels and Skodak, "Adult Status of Individuals," draft, 9, MSC.

69. Skodak, "Adult Status," draft, 13.

70. Harold M. Skeels, "The Relation of the Foster Home Environment to the Mental Development of Children Placed in Infancy," *Child Development* 7, no. 1 (1936): 4–5.

71. Skeels Records, 1933–1966, Case 5.

72. Skeels, Case 8.

73. Skeels, Case 8.

74. Skeels, Case 7.

75. Skeels, Case 7.

76. Skeels, "Adult Status of Children," 42.

77. Skeels and Skodak, "Adult Status of Individuals," draft, 9.

78. Skeels, Case 4.

79. Skeels, Case 9.

80. Skeels, Case 9.

81. Skeels, Case 9.

82. Skeels, Case 10.

83. Skeels, Case 10.

84. Because Louis Branca had publicly told his story of institutionalization and recovery, the author was able to interview him. The information about his life after Glenwood comes from those interviews and from Harold Skeels's records, in which he is case 11.

85. Skeels, Case 11.

86. Skeels, Case 11.

87. Skeels, Case 11.

88. Skeels, Case 15.

89. Skeels, Case 17.

90. Skeels, Case 20.

91. Asbell, "Case of the Wandering IQs," 117.

92. Skeels and Skodak, "Adult Status of Individuals," 10.

93. Skodak Crissey, interview by Fischer, 14.

94. Skeels, Case 19.

95. Marie Skodak Crissey, "Marie Skodak Crissey," in *History*, 67.

96. Skodak Crissey, interview by Senn, 50.

97. Skodak Crissey, interview by Senn, 51.

98. Skodak Crissey, interview by Senn, 51.

99. Skodak Crissey, interview by Senn, 51.

100. John Bowlby to Harold M. Skeels, January 28, 1965, MSC.

101. Margaret Lowenfeld to Simon Auster, April 5, 1965, MSC.

102. Lowenfeld to Auster, April 5, 1965.

103. Simon Auster to Margaret Lowenfeld, April 20, 1965.

104. Robert S. Woodworth and Harold Schlosberg, *Experimental Psychology* (New York: Holt Rinehart and Winston, 1963), 910–48.

105. Allen E. Marans and Dale R. Meers, "Group Care of Infants in Other Countries," in *Early Child Care: The New Perspectives*, ed. Caroline Al Chandler, Reginald S. Lourie, and Anne DeHuff Peters (New York: Atherton Press, 1968), 274.

106. Edward Zigler and Sally J. Styfco, *The Hidden History of Head Start* (New York: Oxford University Press, 2010), 7.

107. Marie Skodak to Harold M. Skeels and Thomas Gladwin, January 14, 1966, MSC.

108. Skodak to Skeels and Gladwin, January 14, 1966, MSC.

109. Marie Skodak to Alfred E. Mirsky, January 14, 1966, MSC.

110. Eric H. Davidson, in conversation with Marilyn Brookwood, Pasadena, March 24, 2008; Bruce McEwen, interview by Marilyn Brookwood, January 25, 2012.

111. Alfred E. Mirsky, "Genetics and Human Affairs," *Scientific American* 211, no. 4 (1964): 137.

112. Mirsky, "Genetics and Human Affairs," 137.

113. Alfred E. Mirsky to Harold M. Skeels, January 18, 1966, MSC.

114. Skeels to Mirsky, January 22, 1966, MSC.

115. Kandel and Squire, "Breaking Down Scientific Barriers," 1113.

Chapter Twelve: The Counter-Argument

1. Marie Skodak, "Adult Status," draft, 13.

2. Skeels, "Adult Status of Children," iii.

3. Skeels, "Adult Status of Children," 12.

4. Skeels, "Adult Status of Children," 37.

5. Skeels, "Adult Status of Children," 37.

6. Skeels and Skodak, "Adult Status of Individuals,"draft, 14.

7. Skeels and Skodak, "Adult Status of Individuals," draft, 15.

8. Asbell, "Case of the Wandering IQs," 15.

9. Asbell, "Case of the Wandering IQs," 18.

10. Skodak Crissey, "Harold Manville Skeels," 3.

11. Urie Bronfenbrenner, First American Psychological Association Division 7 Award to Harold M. Skeels, 1967, 1–2, MSC.

12. Personal communication, Maggie Nygren, November 14, 2018.

13. Harold M. Skeels to Eunice Kennedy Shriver, March 6, 1968, MSC.

14. Eunice Kennedy Shriver to Harold M. Skeels, April 29, 1968.

15. Eunice Kennedy Shriver, "Hope for Retarded Children," *Saturday Evening Post*, September 22, 1962.

16. Shriver, "Hope for Retarded Children."

17. *Minneapolis Star*, April 30, 1968.

18. *Minneapolis Star*, April 30, 1968.

19. Louis C. Branca, interview by Marilyn Brookwood, September 12, 2012.

20. Branca, interview by Brookwood, September 12, 2012.

21. Skodak, "Environmental Factors in Intelligence."

22. Skodak, "Environmental Factors in Intelligence."
23. Marie Skodak Crissey, "Adult Status of Individuals Who Experienced Early Intervention," talk presented at the First Congress of the International Association for the Scientific Study of Mental Deficiency, Montpellier, France, September 12–20, 1967, 7.
24. Harold M. Skeels to Marie Skodak Crissey, March 14, 1970.
25. Marie Skodak Crissey to Harold M. Skeels's unnamed cousin, ca. April 1970, MSC.
26. Marie Skodak Crissey to Diann Sheahan, April 16, 1970, MSC.
27. Marie Skodak Crissey to Eunice Kennedy Shriver, April 16, 1970, MSC.
28. Skodak to Skeels's cousin ca. April 1970.
29. Skodak Crissey, interview by Fischer, MSC.
30. Skodak Crissey, "Harold Manville Skeels," 1.
31. Tripp Evans email to Marilyn Brookwood, May 22, 2018.
32. "A Gay Hayday," *Laguna Beach Magazine*, December 1, 2012.
33. LGBT Mental Health Syllabus, The History of Psychiatry and Homosexuality, Group for the Advancement of Psychiatry, 2012, https://www.aglp.org/gap/1_history/.
34. Michel Schiff to Marie Skodak, May 16, 1972, MSC.
35. Schiff to Skodak, May 16, 1972.
36. Oliver Gillie, "Did Sir Cyril Burt Fake His Research on Heritability of Intelligence? Part I," *Phi Delta Kappan* 58, no. 6 (1977): 469–71.
37. Stephen Jay Gould, *The Flamingo's Smile: Reflections in Natural History* (New York: W. W. Norton, 1985), 387.
38. Arthur R. Jensen, "How Much Can We Boost IQ and Scholastic Achievement?" in *Environment, Heredity and Intelligence*, compiled from the *Harvard Educational Review*, 1969, 1.
39. Michel Schiff, Michel Duyme, John Stewart, Stanislaw Tomkiewicz, and Josue Feingold, "Intellectual Status of Working-Class Children Adopted Early in Upper-Middle-Class Families," *Science* 200 (June 30, 1978): 1504.
40. Jensen, "How Much Can We Boost IQ," 2, 7.
41. Jerome Kagan, "Inadequate Evidence and Illogical Conclusions," in *Environment, Heredity and Intelligence*, compiled from the *Harvard Educational Review*, 1969, 127–128.
42. Joseph McVicker Hunt, "Has Compensatory Education Failed? Has It Been Attempted?" in *Environment, Heredity and Intelligence*, compiled from the *Harvard Educational Review*, 1969, 139.
43. Hunt, "Has Compensatory Education Failed?" 142.
44. William F. Brazziel, "A Letter from the South," in *Environment, Heredity and Intelligence*, compiled from the *Harvard Educational Review*, 1969, 200.
45. Richard J. Herrnstein, *IQ in the Meritocracy* (Boston: Little Brown, 1973), 214.
46. Schiff et. al, "Intellectual Status of Working-Class Children," 1504.
47. Michel Schiff, Michel Duyme, Annick Dumaret, and Stanislaw Tomkiewicz, "How Much Could We Boost Scholastic Achievement and IQ Scores? A Direct Answer from a French Adoption Study," *Cognition* 12 (1982): 186.
48. Marie Skodak Crissey, citation for George D. Stoddard, G. Stanley Hall Award, 1981, MSC.
49. Marie Skodak Crissey, "A Career Review," *Professional Psychology: Research and Practice* 23, no. 1 (1992): 12.
50. Skodak Crissey, "Marie Skodak Crissey," in *Models*, 87.
51. Skodak Crissey, "Marie Skodak Crissey," in *History*, 69.

52. Skodak Crissey, "A Career Review," 13.

53. Lorine Pruette, *G. Stanley Hall, a Biography of a Mind* (New York: Appleton, 1926), 217.

Epilogue: The Miracle of Science

1. Charles A. Nelson III, Nathan A. Fox, and Charles H. Zeanah Jr., "Anguish of the Abandoned Child," *Scientific American* 308, no. 4 (2013): 62.

2. Ralph Blumenthal, "Upheaval in the East: Obituary; The Ceaușescus: 24 Years of Fierce Repression, Isolation and Independence," *New York Times*, December 26, 1989, A18.

3. Charles A. Nelson III, Elizabeth A. Furtado, Nathan A. Fox, and Charles H. Zeanah Jr. , "The Deprived Human Brain: Developmental Deficits among Institutionalized Romanian Children—and Later Improvements—Strengthen the Case for Individualized Care," *American Scientist* 97 (May-June 2009): 222.

4. Bradley S. Hersh et. al., "Acquired Immunodeficiency Syndrome in Romania," *Lancet* 338, no. 8768 (1991): 645.

5. Mary Battiata, "Despite Aid, Romanian Children Face Bleak Lives," *Washington Post*, January 7, 1991.

6. Mary Battiata, " '20/20' Inside Romanian Orphanages," *Washington Post*, October 5, 1990.

7. Susan Christian, "The Waiting Game: Hundreds of Americans Anxious about Adopting Romanian Orphans," *Los Angeles Times*, August 16, 1990.

8. Sandra Blakeslee, "Timetable Key to Brain Growth," *New York Times*, August 29, 1995.

9. Battiata, "Inside Romanian Orphanages."

10. Battiata, "Inside Romanian Orphanages."

11. Melissa Fay Green, "30 Years Ago, Romania Deprived Thousands of Babies of Human Contact: Here's What's Become of Them," *The Atlantic*, July-August, 2020, https://www .theatlantic.com/magazine/archive/2020/07/can-an-unloved-child-learn-to-love/612253/.

12. "Statistics on Intercountry Adoptions," *Ours* 25 (1992): 8–9.

13. Dana E. Johnson, Laurie C. Miller, Sandra Iverson, William Thomas, Barbara Franchino, et al., "The Health of Children Adopted from Romania," *Journal of the American Medical Association* 268, no. 24 (1992): 3450.

14. Charles A. Nelson III, interview by Marilyn Brookwood, July 1, 2009.

15. Charles A. Nelson III, Nathan A. Fox, and Charles H. Zeanah, *Romania's Abandoned Children: Deprivation, Brain Development, and the Struggle for Recovery* (Cambridge, MA: Harvard University Press, 2014), 75.

16. Nelson, Fox, and Zeanah, *Romania's Abandoned Children*, 15.

17. Nelson, Fox, and Zeanah, *Romania's Abandoned Children*, 16.

18. Nelson, Fox, and Zeanah, *Romania's Abandoned Children*, 62.

19. Nelson, Fox, and Zeanah, *Romania's Abandoned Children*, 102.

20. Charles A. Nelson III, Charles H Zeanah, Nathan A. Fox, Peter J. Marshall, Anna T. Smyke, and Donald Guthrie, "Cognitive Recovery in Socially Deprived Young Children: The Bucharest Early Intervention Project," *Science* 318 (2007): 1938.

21. Nelson, Fox, and Zeanah, *Romania's Abandoned Children*, 57.

22. Charles H. Zeanah, Nathan A. Fox, and Charles A. Nelson III, "Case Study in Ethics of Research: The Bucharest Early Intervention Project," *Journal of Nervous Mental Disorders* 200, no. 3 (2012): 7.

23. Nelson et al., "Cognitive Recovery in Socially Deprived Young Children," 1938.

24. Nelson et al., "Cognitive Recovery in Socially Deprived Young Children," 1938–39.

25. Nelson et al., "Cognitive Recovery in Socially Deprived Young Children," 1938–39.

26. Nelson, Fox, and Zeanah, *Romania's Abandoned Children*, 160.

27. Anna Smyke, Sebastian F. Koga, Dana E. Johnson, Nathan A. Fox, Peter J. Marshall, et al., "The Caregiving Context in Institution-Reared and Family-Reared Infants and Toddlers in Romania," *Journal of Child Psychology and Psychiatry* 48, no.2 (2007): 215.

28. Skeels and Fillmore, "Children From Underprivileged Homes," 427–39.

29. Skeels, "Adult Status of Children," 36–37.

30. Nelson, Fox, and Zeanah, *Romania's Abandoned Children*, 191.

31. Nelson, Fox, and Zeanah, *Romania's Abandoned Children*, 190–192.

32. Nelson, Fox, and Zeanah, *Romania's Abandoned Children*, 208–209.

33. Sally Provence and Rose Lipton, *Infants in Institutions* (New York: International Universities Press, 1962), 175.

34. Kirsten Weir, "The Lasting Impact of Neglect: Psychologists Are Studying How Early Deprivation Harms Children—and How Best to Help Those Who Have Suffered from Neglect," *Monitor on Psychology* 45 (June 2014): 36.

35. "Serve & Return Interaction Shapes Brain Circuitry."

36. "Toxic Stress Derails Healthy Development," National Scientific Council on the Developing Child, Center on the Developing Child, Harvard University, 2011, https://www.youtube .com/watch?v=rVwFkcOZHJw.

37. Bruce S. McEwen, "Effects of Stress on the Developing Brain," *Cerebrum* (September-October 2011), accessed March 10, 2014, https://www.ncbi.nlm.nih.gov/pmc/articles/ PMC3574783/.

38. Robert E. Anda, Vincent J. Felitti, J. Douglas Bremner, John D. Walker, Charles Whitfield, et al., "The Enduring Effects of Abuse and Related Adverse Experiences in Childhood: A Convergence of Evidence from Neurobiology and Epidemiology," *European Archives of Psychiatry and Clinical Neuroscience* 256 (2006): 174–86.

39. Andrea Danese and Bruce S. McEwen, "Adverse Childhood Experiences, Allostasis, Allostatic Load, and Age-Related Disease," *Physiology and Behavior* 106 (2012): 35.

40. Clancy Blair and Cybele Raver, "Poverty, Stress, and Brain Development: New Directions for Prevention and Intervention," *Academic Pediatrics* 16, no. 35 (2016): S30.

41. Nicole L. Hair, Jamie L. Hanson, Barbara L. Wolfe, and Seth D. Pollak, "Association of Child Poverty, Brain Development, and Academic Achievement," *Journal of the American Medical Association Pediatrics* 169, no. 9 (2015): 852.

42. Patrick Sharkey, "The Acute Effects of Local Homicides on Children's Cognitive Performance," *Proceedings of the National Academy of Sciences USA* 107, no. 26 (2010): 11733–34.

43. Vincent J. Felitti, R. F. Anda, D. Nordenberg, D. F. Williamson, A. M. Spitz, et al., "Relationship of Childhood Abuse and Household Dysfunction to Many of the Leading Causes of Death in Adults: The Adverse Childhood Experiences (ACE) Study," *American Journal of Preventative Medicine* 14, no. 4 (1998): 245.

44. Anda et al., "Enduring Effects of Abuse," 175.

45. Paul Tough, *Helping Children Succeed: What Works and Why* (New York: Houghton Mifflin Harcourt, 2016), 21.

46. Joan Luby, "Poverty's Most Insidious Damage: The Developing Brain," *Journal of the American Medical Association Pediatrics* 169, no. 9 (2015): 811.

47. James J. Heckman, *Giving Kids a Fair Chance* (Cambridge, MA: MIT Press, 2013), 3.
48. James J. Heckman, "Skill Formation and the Economics of Investing in Disadvantaged Children," *Science* 312 (June 30, 2006): 1900.
49. Heckman, "Skill Formation," 1902.
50. Jeanne Morris Hines, "An Overview of Head Start Program Studies," *Journal of Instructional Pedagogies* 18 (2017): 5.
51. Madeline Ostrander, "How Preschool Can Make You Smarter and Healthier," NOVA, WGBH, April 9, 2015.
52. Hines, "Overview of Head Start," 5.
53. "The Carolina Abecedarian Project," Frank Porter Graham Child Development Institute, University of North Carolina at Chapel Hill, https://abc.fpg.unc.edu/.
54. Frances Campbell, Gabriella Conti, James J. Heckman, Seong Hyeok Moon, Rodrigo Pinto, et al., "Early Childhood Investments Substantially Boost Adult Health," *Science* 343 (2014): 1484.
55. Arthur J. Reynolds, Ou Suh-Ruu, and Judy A. Temple, "A Multicomponent, Preschool to Third Grade Preventive Intervention and Educational Attainment at 35 Years of Age," *Journal of the American Medical Association Pediatrics* 172, no. 3 (2018): 248.
56. Reynolds et al., "Multicomponent," 255.
57. Hines, "Overview of Head Start," 3.
58. Head Start Impact Study, US Department of Health and Human Services, Final Report, 2010, xxvi.
59. Diane W. Schanzenbach and Lauren Bauer, "The Long-Term Impact of the Head Start Program," The Hamilton Project, Brookings Institution, August 2016, 3.
60. Alexander M. Gelber and Adam Isen, "Children's Schooling and Parents' Investment in Children: Evidence from the Head Start Impact Study," *Journal of Public Economics* 101 (2013): 26.
61. Elyse Chor, "Multigenerational Head Start Participation: An Unexpected Marker of Progress," *Child Development* 89, no. 1 (2018): 264.
62. Lillian Mongeau, "Why Does America Invest So Little in Its Children?" *The Atlantic* (in Partnership with the Hechinger Report), July 12, 2016.
63. Jack P. Shonkoff and Diane Phillips, *From Neurons to Neighborhoods: The Science of Early Development* (Washington, DC: National Academy Press, 2000), 6.
64. Gass, Iowa Soldiers' Orphans' Home, 1–16.
65. Gass, Iowa Soldiers' Orphans' Home, 1–16.
66. Gass, Iowa Soldiers' Orphans' Home, 1–16.
67. Nelson et al., *Romania's Abandoned Children*, 1.

SELECTED BIBLIOGRAPHY

Allen, Garland E. "The Eugenics Record Office at Cold Spring Harbor, 1910–1940: An Essay in Institutional History." *Osiris* 2 (1986): 225–64. http://www.jstor.org/stable/301835.

Baldwin, Bird T., Eva A. Fillmore, and Lora Hadley. *Farm Children: An Investigation of Rural Child Life in Selected Areas of Iowa.* New York: Appleton, 1930. https://hdl.handle.net/2027/uc1.b3427602.

Binet, Alfred, and Theodore Simon. *The Development of Intelligence in Children (the Binet-Simon Scale).* Classics in Psychology. New York: Arno Press, 1916.

Boyce, Thomas W. "A Biology of Misfortune." Electronic Newsletter, Institute for Research on Poverty, University of Wisconsin, Madison. *Focus* 29, no. 1 (2012): 1–7.

Bronfenbrenner, Urie. *The Ecology of Human Development: Experiments by Nature and Design.* Cambridge, MA: Harvard University Press, 1979.

Carson, John. *The Measure of Merit: Talents, Intelligence, and Inequality in the French and American Republics, 1750–1940.* Princeton, NJ: Princeton University Press, 2007.

Chapman, Paul D. *Schools as Sorters: Lewis M. Terman, Applied Psychology, and the American Intelligence Testing Movement, 1890–1930.* New York: New York University Press, 1988.

Cohen, Adam. *Imbeciles: The Supreme Court, American Eugenics, and the Sterilization of Carrie Buck.* New York: Penguin Press, 2016.

Committee on Integrating the Science of Early Childhood. *From Neurons to Neighborhoods: The Science of Early Childhood Development.* Edited by Jack P. Shonkoff and Deborah A. Phillips. Washington DC: National Academy Press, 2000.

Cravens, Hamilton. *Before Head Start: The Iowa Station & America's Children.* Chapel Hill: University of North Carolina Press, 1993.

Crissey, Marie Skodak. "Marie Skodak Crissey." In *A History of Developmental Psychology in Autobiography,* edited by Dennis Thompson and John D. Hogan, 46–70. Boulder, CO: Westview Press, 1996.

Davenport, Charles B. *Eugenics: The Science of Human Improvement by Better Breeding.* Rahway, N.J.: Quinn & Boden Co. Press, 1910.

Davies, Stanley Powell. "Social Control of the Feebleminded." PhD diss., Columbia University, 1923.

Dennis, Wayne. *Children of the Crèche.* East Norwalk, CT: Appleton-Century-Crofts, 1973.

Deutsch, Martin, and associates. *The Disadvantaged Child: Studies of the Social Environment and the Learning Process.* New York: Basic Books, 1967.

Dworkin, Gerald, and Ned Joel Block, eds. *The IQ Controversy: Critical Readings.* New York: Pantheon Books, 1976.

Evans, B. Tripp. *Grant Wood: A Life.* New York: Alfred A. Knopf, 2010.

Egan, Tim. *The Worst Hard Time: The Untold Story of Those Who Survived the Great American Dust Bowl.* Boston: Houghton Mifflin, 2006.

Fancher, Raymond E. *The Intelligence Men: Makers of the I.Q. Controversy.* New York: W. W. Norton, 1985.

Fancher, Raymond E., and Alexandra Rutherford. *Pioneers of Psychology.* 4th ed. New York: W. W. Norton, 2012.

Frank, Lawrence. "Research in Child Psychology: History and Prospect." In *Child Behavior and Development: A Course of Representative Studies,* edited by Robert G. Barker, Jacob S. Kounin, and Herbert F. Wright, 1–16. New York: McGraw-Hill Books, 1943.

Glass, Bentley. "Geneticists Embattled: Their Stand against Rampant Eugenics and Racism in America During the 1920s and 1930s." *Proceedings of the American Philosophical Society* 130, no. 1 (1986): 130–54.

Goddard, Henry H. *The Kallikak Family: A Study in the Heredity of Feeblemindedness.* New York: Macmillan, 1912.

Gould, Stephen J. *The Mismeasure of Man.* New York: W. W. Norton, 1996.

Greenough, William T., James E. Black, and Christopher S. Wallace. "Experience and Brain Development." *Research in Child Development* 58, no. 3 (1987): 539–99. http://www.jstor.org/stable/1130197?seq=1#page_scan_tab_contents.

Grossman, Tobias, and Mark H. Johnson. "The Development of the Social Brain in Human Infancy." *European Journal of Neuroscience* 25, no. 4 (2007): 909–19. https://doi.org/doi:10.1111/j.1460–9568.2007.05379.x.

Haller, Mark H. *Eugenics: Hereditarian Attitudes in American Thought.* New Brunswick, NJ: Rutgers University Press, 1963.

Hebb, Donald O. *The Organization of Behavior: A Neuropsychological Theory.* Wiley Books in Clinical Psychology. New York: John Wiley & Sons, 1949.

Heckman, James J. "Skill Formation and the Economics of Investing in Disadvantaged Children." *Science* 312 (June 30, 2006): 1900–1902.

Hilgard, Earnest R. *Psychology in America.* New York: Harcourt Brace Jovanovich, 1987.

Hunt, J. McVicker. *Intelligence and Experience.* New York: Ronald Press, 1961.

Johnson, Dana E., Laurie C. Miller, Sandra Iverson, William Thomas, Barbara Franchino, Kathryn Doyle, Marybeth T. Kiernan, Michael K. Georgieff, and Margaret K. Hostetter. "The Health of Children Adopted from Romania." *Journal of the American Medical Association* 268, no. 24 (1992): 3446–51.

Kamin, Leon. *The Science and Politics of I.Q.* Potomac, MD: Lawrence Erlbaum, 1974.

Kevles, Daniel J. *In the Name of Eugenics: Genetics and the Uses of Human Heredity.* Cambridge, MA: Harvard University Press, 1995.

Kreuter, Gretchen. "The Vanishing Genius: Lewis Terman and the Stanford Study." *History of Education Quarterly* 2, no. 1 (1962): 6–18. http://www.jstor.org/stable/367332.

Kühl, Stefan. *The Nazi Connection: Eugenics, American Racism, and German National Socialism.* New York: Oxford University Press, 1994. http://hollis.harvard.edu/?itemid=%7Clibrary/m/aleph%7C003294020.

Lemann, Nicholas. *The Big Test: The Secret History of the American Meritocracy.* New York: Farrar, Straus and Giroux, 2000.

Leslie, Mitchell. "The Vexing Legacy of Lewis Terman." *Stanford Magazine*, July/August 2000. http://alumni.stanford.edu/get/page/magazine/article/?article_id=40678.

McEwen, Bruce S., and Peter J. Gianaros. "Central Role of the Brain in Stress and Adaptation: Links to Socioeconomic Status, Health and Disease." *Annals of the New York Academy of Sciences* 1186 (2010): 190–222.

McEwen, Craig A., and Bruce S. McEwen. "Social Structure, Adversity, Toxic Stress, and Intergenerational Poverty: An Early Childhood Model." *Annual Review of Sociology* 43 (2017): 445–72. https://doi.org/10.1146/annurev-soc-060116-053252.

McNutt, Steve. "'A Dangerous Man': Lewis Terman and George Stoddard, Their Debates on Intelligence Testing, and the Legacy of the Iowa Child Welfare Research Station." *Annals of Iowa* 72, no. 1 (2013): 1–30.

Minton, Henry L. *Lewis M. Terman: Pioneer in Psychological Testing*. American Social Experience Series. New York: New York University Press, 1988.

Morgan, Thomas Hunt. *The Scientific Basis of Evolution*. New York: W. W. Norton, 1932.

National Center for Children in Poverty. "Basic Facts about Low-Income Children," 2011. www.nccp.org/publications/pub_1074.html.

Nelson, Charles A. III. "Hazards to Early Development: The Biological Embedding of Early Life Adversity." *Neuron* 96, no. October 11, (2017): 262–66.

Nelson, Charles A. III, Nathan A. Fox, and Charles H. Zeanah. *Romania's Abandoned Children: Deprivation, Brain Development, and the Struggle for Recovery*. Cambridge, MA: Harvard University Press, 2014.

Pastore, Nicholas. *The Nature-Nurture Controversy*. New York: King's Crown Press, 1949.

Powers, Elmer G. *Years of Struggle: The Farm Diary of Elmer G. Powers, 1931–1936*. Edited by H. Roger Grant and L. Edward Purcell. Ames, IA: Iowa State University Press, 1976.

Reilly, Philip R. *Surgical Solution: A History of Involuntary Sterilization in the United States*. Baltimore: Johns Hopkins University Press, 1991.

Resource Library. Harvard University Center on the Developing Child. Accessed September 10, 2020. Comprehensive resources addressing early development/parent support for young children. https://developingchild.harvard.edu/resources/.

Rosenberg, Charles E. *No Other Gods: On Science and American Social Thought*. Baltimore: Johns Hopkins University Press, 1976.

Rutter, Michael, Edmund J. Sonuga-Barke, and Jennifer Castle. "Investigating the Impact of Early Institutional Deprivation on Development: Background and Research Strategy of the English and Romanian Adoptees (ERA) Study." *Monographs of the Society for Research in Child Development* 75, no. 1 (2010): 1–20.

Samelson, Franz. "Putting Psychology on the Map: Ideology and Intelligence Testing." In *Psychology in Social Context*, edited by Allan R. Buss, 103–41. New York: Irvington, 1979.

Schwieder, Dorothy. *Iowa: The Middle Land*. Ames, IA: Blackwell Publishing, 1996.

Seim, David L. *Rockefeller Philanthropy and Modern Social Science*. London: Pickering and Chatto, 2013.

Sherman, Mandel, and Thomas R. Henry. *Hollow Folk*. New York: Thomas Y. Crowell, 1933.

Skeels, Harold M. "Adult Status of Children with Contrasting Early Life Experiences: A Follow-Up Study." *Monographs of the Society for Research in Child Development* 31, no. 3 (1966): 1–65. http://www.jstor.org/stable/1165791.

Skeels, Harold M., and Harold B. Dye. "A Study of the Effects of Differential Stimulation on Mentally Retarded Children." *Journal of Psycho-Asthenics* 44, no. 1 (1939): 114–36.

Skodak, Marie. "Children in Foster homes: A Study of Mental Development." *University of Iowa Studies, Studies in Child Welfare* 16, no. 1 (1939): 1–141.

Spiro, Jonathan Peter. *Defending the Master Race: Conservation, Eugenics and the Legacy of Madison Grant.* Burlington:: University of Vermont Press, 2009.

Spitz, René. "Hospitalism: An Inquiry into the Genesis of Psychiatric Conditions in Early Childhood." In *The Psychoanalytic Study of the Child*, Vol. 1, edited by Anna Freud, Willie Hoffer, and Edward Glover, 53–74. London: International Universities Press, Imago Publishing, 1945.

Stoddard, George D. *The Meaning of Intelligence.* New York: Macmillan, 1943.

Stoddard, George D. *The Pursuit of Education: An Autobiography.* New York: Vantage Press, 1981.

Terman, Lewis M. *Genetic Studies of Genius.* Stanford, CA: Stanford University Press, 1959.

Terman, Lewis M. *The Measurement of Intelligence: An Explanation of and a Complete Guide for the Use of the Stanford Revision and Extension of the Binet-Simon Intelligence Scale.* Boston, MA: Houghton Mifflin, 1916.

Tough, Paul. *Helping Children Succeed: What Works and Why.* New York: Houghton Mifflin Harcourt, 2016.

Vogel, Amy. "Regulating Degeneracy: Eugenic Sterilization in Iowa, 1911–1977." *Annals of Iowa* 52, no. 2 (1995): 119–43. http://ir.uiowa.edu/annals-of-iowa/vol54/iss2/3.

Wall, Joseph Frasier, and The Federal Writers' Project. *Iowa, a Guide to the Hawkeye State.* American Guide Series. New York: The Viking Press, 1938.

Wellman, Beth L. "Some New Basis for Interpretation of the IQ." *The Pedagogical Seminary and Journal of Genetic Psychology* 41, no. 1 (1932): 116–26.

Wellman, Beth L., and George D. Stoddard. "The I.Q.: A Problem in Social Construction." *The Social Frontier* 5, no. 42 (1939): 151–52.

Zenderland, Leila. *Measuring Minds: Henry Herbert Goddard and the Origins of American Intelligence Testing.* Cambridge Studies in the History of Psychology. New York: Cambridge University Press, 1998.

Zigler, Edward, and Susan Muenchow. *Head Start: The Inside Story of America's Most Successful Educational Experiment.* New York: Basic Books, 1992.

INDEX